THE BUSINESS OF SHIPPING

THE BUSINESS OF SHIPPING

Sixth Edition

LANE C. KENDALL

and

JAMES J. BUCKLEY

CORNELL MARITIME PRESS
Centreville, Maryland

Library of Congress Cataloging-in-Publication Data

Kendall, Lane C.
    The business of shipping / Lane C. Kendall and James J. Buckley.—
6th ed.
       p.   cm.
    Includes bibliographical references and index.
    ISBN 0-87033-454-9
    1. Shipping.   I. Buckley, James J.   II. Title.
HE571.K4   1994
387.5′068—dc20   94-8041

"Them Damaged Cargo Blues" by James A. Quinby on page 226 is reprinted with permission from an article by Daniel A. Tadros in *Tulane Maritime Law Journal,* Vol. 17, No. 1 (Fall 1992), pp. 17–18, entitled "COGSA Section 4(5)'s 'Fair Opportunity' Requirement: U.S. Circuit Court Conflict and Lack of International Uniformity; Will the United States Supreme Court Ever Provide Guidance?"

Manufactured in the United States of America
First edition, 1973. Sixth edition, 1994

For my grandchildren
David, Sarah, Laura, and Gregory
in admiration and affection

Lane C. Kendall

For my parents
Joseph and Hannah Buckley
*in appreciation of their love
and for teaching me
the value of education and hard work,
all of which made the writing of this book possible*

James J. Buckley

Contents

Preface, ix

1   Liner Service and Tramp Shipping, 3

2   Tramp Shipping, 11

3   The Management of Tramp Shipping, 39

4   Chartering and Tramp Ship Operation, 57

5   Organization of a Liner-Service Company, 70

6   Terminal Management, 92

7   Terminal Operations, 110

8   The Stevedore Contract, 135

9   Procurement of Vessel Stores and Supplies, 146

10   Containerization: The Beginning, 171

11   The Ramifications of Containerization, 193

12   The Ocean Bill of Lading, 226

13   How Freight Rates Are Made, 241

14   The Traffic Study, 262

15   Steamship Conferences, 269

16   The Logic of Steamship Scheduling, 289

17   Scheduling and Bunkering, 301

18   Planning for a New Ship, 315

19   Passenger Cruises, 332

20   Industrial and Special Carriers, 358

21   Tanker Management, 374

22   The American Shipping Subsidy System, 397

23   The Business of Shipping, 417

Notes, 424

Glossary, 438

Index, 446

About the Authors, 455

Preface

This volume has been written to describe the business side of a commercial enterprise whose field is the entire civilized world. Historically, the theory and knowledge of shipping management, as distinguished from the practical skills of seamanship, have been transmitted from one generation to the next by word of mouth. Little has been put on paper, primarily because the finest exponents of the art of steamship management have been too busy with their day-to-day concerns. The "working level" personnel often are superbly competent, but rarely qualify as literary craftsmen.

It has been our aim, in preparing this analysis of the principles of the "business" of commercial shipping, to describe the workings of the various divisions of shipowning and operating organizations. The procedures followed in the different offices therefore have been described and explained. Wherever possible, we have set forth the underlying principles of management by which decisions are reached.

In the process of learning the principles and practices that are expounded in these pages, our respective careers have complemented each other, giving us diverse but related association with ships, seafarers, and office personnel. One of us enjoyed the experience of working in all aspects of the shoreside organization, while the other sailed in commercial ships in all licensed grades and also served ashore in a number of assignments. Both of us have been privileged to spend years in classrooms where we taught young men and women the principles we had learned from experience and from precept.

These years of association with the maritime community were filled with much toil and strain, but they also were crowded with pleasant contacts and exciting events. Both of us discovered that, as we increased our knowledge of the seemingly endless ramifications of the steamship business, our interest in each day's activities deepened and grew more rewarding. It is our hope that those who read this book will find in its pages the basis for understanding what was for us a worthwhile and joy-filled way of life.

This volume is the sixth edition; the first appeared in 1973. While a great deal of the material included in the fifth edition has been retained, new and up-to-date information has been added to reflect the many significant developments in the industry.

The names of those who have assisted us throughout the decades of our association with the steamship industry are far too numerous to list, even if all of them were known to us. Some who contributed greatly to our knowledge were nameless to us, but we have not forgotten their generosity in sharing their hard-earned knowledge and priceless wisdom. We acknowledge our debt to the guides and mentors who helped to shape our careers, and contributed to our growth by friendly and constructive criticism which saved us from many errors. To all these persons, we extend our heartfelt thanks.

Any errors, of course, are ours, and we assume full responsibility.

Lane C. Kendall
James J. Buckley

THE BUSINESS OF SHIPPING

CHAPTER ONE

Liner Service and Tramp Shipping

Merchant shipping, considered from the standpoint of service provided, may be divided into two major categories: *Liner Service* and *Tramp Shipping*. While there are some similarities, the differences in the theory and techniques of management of these two types of marine transportation are notable. The service rendered, the geographic area covered, the operating problems, the relationship between vessel owner and vessel user, and the actual employment of the ship, vary markedly between the two categories. It is important, therefore, to be aware of those areas where the management procedures are congruent; it is equally significant that the differences be comprehended.

Liner Service	*Tramp Shipping*
1. Sailings are regular and repeated from and to designated ports on a trade route, at intervals established in response to the quantity of cargo generated along that route. True liner service is distinguished by the repetition of voyages and the consistent advertising of such voyages. Once the service is established, the operator must conform, within narrow time limits, to the published schedule. Although the frequency of sailings is related directly to the amount of business available, it is general practice to dispatch at least one ship each month. Vessels engaged in liner service	1. Sailings under voyage charters are based on cargo commitments that vary with the vessel's employment, and are usually different for every voyage. There is no expected repetition of voyages as a normal part of tramp operation. Each trip is scheduled individually, subject to the requirements of the cargo to be carried and the particular route to be followed. In certain trades, such as oil and coal, owners often agree to make a number of repetitive voyages carrying the same commodity. These "consecutive voyages" are arranged expressly to fit the charterer's convenience,

may be owned or chartered; it is the regularity and repetitive nature of the operation, rather than proprietorship, which is crucial.

and do not establish a liner service.

Sailings under time charters may be for a single voyage between major geographic areas, or may be repetitive, transporting the same commodity such as coal or grain or lumber; or may take the form of a long trading voyage consisting of a series of legs on which different cargoes are lifted; or may be placed in the liner service operated by the charterer. The time-chartered vessel may be subchartered to other persons for voyages to be accomplished within the time limits imposed by the charter.

2. Liners are common (public) carriers, required by law to accept, without discrimination between offerors, any legal cargo which the ship is able to transport. Some liner operators stipulate the minimum quantity of cargo which must be presented by a single shipper; so long as the limitation is reasonable, this is permissible. In the break-bulk trades, cargo usually is varied, and is called either "general" or "package." In the container trades, the shipper fills and seals the container before it is delivered to the carrier. This sealed container is placed aboard the ship as a single unit. Small shipments are "consolidated" by the carrier or a third party, who loads

2. Tramps are contract (private) carriers, and normally carry full shiploads of a single commodity, usually in bulk. In most cases, there is only one shipper, but two or more shippers of the same kind of cargo may occasionally use a single ship.

A cargo liner built for the England-Argentina trade. With a speed of 14 knots, a deadweight of 9,640 tons, superior accommodation for crew, and rooms for twelve passengers, this ship was "revolutionary" when placed in service in 1948.

these "less than container lots" (LCL) into containers which are sealed by the party loading for the voyage, and opened by the carrier or a third party at the port of discharge, where the lots of cargo are distributed to the consignees.

3. Goods carried in liner-service ships usually are of higher value than the cargo hauled in tramps, and are charged higher freight rates. All shippers of a given item moving in a specified ship pay the same freight rate, which always includes handling (stevedoring) costs. In break-bulk operation, the variety of cargo and the number of shippers require procedures to assure that what is accepted for transportation is deliv-

3. Cargoes carried in tramps generally are those which can be transported in bulk (homogeneous cargoes) and have low intrinsic value. Typical cargoes are coal, grain, lumber, sugar, and phosphate rock. The cost of loading and unloading the ship in most cases is paid by the charterer, but this is subject to negotiation between shipowner and charterer. Freight rates (charter hire) for tramps reflect the fact

ered in like good order to the consignee at the port of discharge. Containers, except refrigerator units, do not require individual attention beyond being secured aboard ship. In both break-bulk and container services, cargo requiring special care (such as refrigerated meats and fruits) is accepted but is assessed a higher freight rate than less sensitive items.

that movements frequently are from a single port of loading to a single port of discharge, with minimum expense involved in the case of the cargo while it is in transit.

4. Freight rates in the liner services are stabilized by setting identical charges for all shippers of the same item aboard a certain ship. Rates may vary, however, from one sailing to another, but increases are announced in advance. Rates are compiled into detailed listings (freight tariffs) which are made available to shippers on demand.

On many trade routes, two or more carriers serving the same range of ports will form an association (known either as a "conference" or a "rate agreement") for the purpose of stabilizing rates and regulating competition between these carriers. The rates established by the association are binding uniformly on all the members, although independent action is permitted. In the United States, these agreements and rate structures are subject to review by the Federal Maritime Commission. Conforming to government

4. Freight rates (charter hire) for tramps fluctuate according to the supply of, and demand for, ships. The charterer's position is always strong, and the rates are low, when there are few cargoes and many ships are competing for the business. The shipowner's position is always strong, and rates are high, when there are plentiful cargoes and a scarcity of ships. In either case, competition between owners is always keen.

Hire for a vessel under voyage charter almost always is paid per ton of cargo loaded. For ships under time charter, the classic method was to pay the agreed sum per ship's deadweight ton per month. The pattern today is to pay an agreed sum per day for the duration of the charter.

Abrupt changes in the level of charter rates occur whenever there is an event of international significance, as, for instance, the outbreak of a war, a major crop regulation tends to restrict liner service operators from making sudden, sharp changes.

failure, or widespread strikes in a particular country.

Freight tariffs are not compiled by the owners of vessels engaged in tramping, and no associations exist to set rates and stabilize competition. Summaries showing the trends in charter hire are published frequently, and include specific quotations of the rates at which ships have been chartered.

5. A liner-service company issues a standard (or uniform) contract of carriage or bill of lading. Regardless of the size of the shipment, or the number of different commodities or items comprising a given lot of cargo, the provisions of the contract apply equally to all shippers who use any one vessel. These provisions are not subject to negotiation, but are unilaterally imposed by the carrier. Acceptance of the bill of lading is considered to be agreement to all terms and conditions set forth in the document.

5. The owner of a tramp ship must negotiate a separate contract (charter party) for every employment of its vessel. The terms of the charter party vary from ship to ship, depending upon the bargaining abilities of owner and charterer, and the general trend of the market. The terms of the agreement are applicable only to the ship named in the charter party. Although the basic charter parties are printed and follow a set form, they may be changed in any manner desired by the contracting parties. Since the changes apply to a particular ship for a designated voyage or a period of time, the alterations are not publicized widely.

6. Services—frequency of sailings and ports of call, as well as the capabilities of the ships themselves—are adjusted to meet the demands of shippers. Many liner operators arrange their schedules

6. Services, as well as rates, are determined by negotiations between shipowner and charterer, and reflect the specific requirements of the contracting parties. Regular and repeated voyages on

to meet their customers' minimum needs during the year, and then augment sailings when seasonal increases occur. Changes in liner service are often influenced as much by political and technological considerations as they are by economic factors. Drastic changes in established liner operations are infrequent; carriers' intentions, especially relating to withdrawals from the route, are publicized in advance. This is essential to the dependability of the liner trade.

the same route are not part of tramp operation, and therefore no conferences exist. Supervision in the public interest by a regulatory authority is unnecessary; the natural working of the laws of supply and demand assure adequate control.

7. Liner-service vessels often reflect in their design the special requirements encountered in their employment. Refrigerated fruit and meat carriers, roll-on/roll-off vessels, break-bulk general carriers, and container ships are operated on most sea routes, depending upon the demand for these specialized capabilities. Because very nearly identical items move in all the dry-cargo break-bulk liners on a given route, the capabilities of these ships are similar, regardless of ownership. Since 1945, break-bulk ships in liner service have grown in size and increased in speed; inevitably, the cost of their acquisition and operation has risen steeply.

 Container ships began transoceanic service in 1966, and today are found on all trade routes. They range in size from less than

7. Most general-purpose, dry-cargo tramp ships are intended for worldwide service, and are of moderate size and draft. Although used primarily to transport cargoes in bulk, many of these tramps have one or more 'tween decks and sufficient booms or cranes to permit them to carry assorted general cargo on a self-sustaining basis. Very large bulk carriers, designed to carry iron ore or coal, are now tramping on many trade routes. Compared to container ships, some of which are available for charter to liner-service companies, the conventional tramp is still simpler in design and much less expensive to build.

The break-bulk cargo liner *Fushimi Maru* was designed for efficient and economical handling of her cargoes. Photograph courtesy of NYK Lines.

one thousand 20-foot containers to over four thousand containers and are among the fastest ships in the world. Owing to their regular schedules and established berths in fixed ports, many liner service vessels are not self-sustaining.

8. Liner-service companies may have a large and somewhat complex organization in the shore establishment, especially in the home office. Normally, there are several divisions defined by function: traffic, operations, financial,

8. Tramp owners usually have small staffs in the home office, with little division of functions. No traffic department is needed; charters are negotiated by telephone, cable, or fax (facsimile transmission of documents).

and managerial, each with appropriate staff. Outport offices may duplicate this organization on a diminished scale. Liner-service operations entail personal contact with the shippers, maintenance of an active cargo-handling terminal, and processing of a great amount of detail work inherent in general cargo operations on a repetitive schedule.

Face-to-face contact with charterers is unusual. Because agents are employed to service the ships in ports of call and are paid on a fee basis for each task performed, there is no need for an operating department. Instead, the home office may send supervisory personnel to oversee the functions of the agents. Some owners contract with firms specializing in ship management to do everything except negotiate contracts. Stevedoring is very rarely a responsibility of the shipowner, and therefore no terminal department is included in the organization of the home office.

9. Procurement of cargo is the responsibility of the traffic department, which includes sales staff (solicitors) to call on regular as well as prospective shippers. Advertising is extensive and continuous, and major efforts are made to disseminate information concerning the capabilities of the line. Arrival and departure times of ships in many cases are widely publicized. Shippers are assisted in the development of markets for their goods as a means of increasing cargo offerings.

9. Procurement of cargo is handled through brokers who represent the tramp shipowner in negotiations with other brokers representing cargo interests. There is no advertising and no promotional activity. Ship movements normally appear only in the newspaper listing of vessels which have arrived or sailed.

10. Passengers are sometimes carried in cargo liners. By international agreement, the number is limited to twelve.

10. Passengers are not carried aboard tramp ships, and no provision for their accommodation is made in the vessels's design.

CHAPTER TWO

Tramp Shipping

During the half century which ended in 1914, most of the transoceanic cargoes of coal, ores, grain, and fertilizers were carried in comparatively small, general-purpose cargo ships. Moving as they did on routings which varied from voyage to voyage, hauling now one commodity and then another, entering and leaving port without fanfare or publicity, and often in need of paint, these vessels gained the appellation of "tramp steamers." To the extent that their wanderings and unkempt appearance paralleled those of that fraternity of homeless men known as "tramps," the sobriquet may have been appropriate. What was not apparent was the careful and constant concern exercised over the ships by their owners, contesting for the available business with each other and with the shippers of goods needing ocean transportation, and taking pride in their ability to deliver the goods in accordance with contracts drawn up with consummate skill and negotiated with great vigor.

The purpose of tramp ships may be stated quite simply: to provide the efficient, convenient, timely, and economical transportation required by the many kinds of goods needed for a complex, industrialized society. Converting this declaration of purpose into the reality of cross-ocean movement of millions of tons of commodities is a task requiring enormous skill and a multitude of resources. Underlying the dedicated effort of the people afloat and ashore who comprise the tramp shipping industry is the necessity to meet constantly changing demands, and therefore to find the ways and means of assuring the flexibility of ship operation which is one of the principal reasons for the existence of the tramp.

It is an acknowledged fact that the raw materials so essential to the life of industrialized nations rarely are located close to the places where they are needed. Chrome ore, for example, is a vital ingredient in high-grade steel, but it is found in large quantities only in areas far distant from iron-ore sources and processors. The availability of inexpensive and dependable transoceanic transportation is of crucial importance to both producing and consuming regions. More dramatic, perhaps, because of the greater volatility of demand, is the growth and distribution of grain. From the vast and fertile plains of the United States, Canada, Argentina, and Australia comes a never-ending stream of the golden staple. For generations, there has been a steady and predictable movement of grain from these four producing regions to England, northern Europe, and the Mediterranean nations. Irregularly, depending upon climatic and meteorological conditions beyond the control of man, there have been urgent appeals from India, China, the former Soviet Union, and those areas of Africa where drought and overgrazing have combined to bring on famine. Tramp ships fit into both delivery patterns, providing the means of transportation in the established trades and, whenever required, shifting to new routes to alleviate critical shortages wherever they may occur. Let a crop fail in Argentina, however, and the distribution of ships reflects immediately the reduction in the cargoes available for export. Should the unlikely combination of a crop failure in Argentina coincide with a sharply curtailed harvest in China, the rearrangement of tramp shipping routes to meet the new requirements for transportation would be on a worldwide basis.

This flexibility in adapting to unanticipated and major changes in patterns of shipping has made the tramping industry disproportionately significant in the economic life of the world. No other type of shipping service can claim to be so sensitive to demand. The very nature of tramp shipping is to seek cargoes where they may be found, rather than to operate on fixed routes with rigid schedules of departures and arrivals regardless of the quantity of goods which may be offered for carriage.

Another reason for the continued existence of tramp shipping is that it provides, at very low cost, the transportation required to add value to the basic products of agriculture (of which the numerous types of grain are predominant), forestry, mining, and manufactured raw materials such as cement, petroleum, steel, and fertilizers. The worldwide tonnage of these items moved in one year amounts to an estimated 2,361,000,000 metric tons.[1] This figure obviously has no reference to the cost of sea-carriage. So large a movement of low-value commodities, however, does depend upon the inexpensive transportation provided by the ships. The claim to low cost transportation is borne out by the fact that in 1991 a dry cargo bulk carrier of 65,000 deadweight tons incurred daily operating expenses, exclusive of capital costs, of about $4,600—equivalent to approximately seven cents per day per ton of cargo actually put aboard the ship.[2]

The huge tonnage of cargo lifted by dry bulk carriers represented just over half of the four billion tons of cargo handled worldwide by a fleet of

Tramp Shipping 13

A modern general-purpose tramp of 26,592 tons deadweight, the 15-knot *Mario G.L.* was built in 1974. Photograph by Jeff Blinn, courtesy of Moran Towing Co.

23,943 ships of over 1,000 gross registered tons in size.[3] Not many years ago, the popular ship for all commodities except iron ore was the vessel of 20,000 to 25,000 tons deadweight. The recent development of the so-called Handimax design—a dry bulk carrier of between 30,000 and 50,000 tons deadweight—has met with widespread approval. Ships of less than 50,000 tons deadweight in 1992 made up 47 percent of the dry bulk carrier fleet.[4]

Tramp ships, to repeat, contribute to the economic life of the world in an absolutely indispensable manner, and, as has been noted, do so at low cost. There are times when the freight rate, as compared to the value of the goods transported, is lower than the figure earlier cited, while occasionally and inevitably it is greater. Competition can explain these variations. When circumstances warrant, freight rates decline, as when there is a glut of wheat worldwide. The need for transportation is diminished, and the demand for ships is reduced correspondingly. As in any marketplace where the laws of supply and demand prevail, cutthroat competition among the suppliers commences in the attempt to find charters, and rates drop swiftly. Contrariwise, if there should be a major crop failure (as there was in the Soviet Union in 1974), enormous shipments of wheat from many producing areas will suddenly be required to replace that which could not be harvested. The demand for vessels exceeds the number available, and freight rates climb precipitately.

The example of the unexpected crop failure and the resultant effect upon the charter market focuses attention on one of the more interesting and significant aspects of the tramp shipping industry. Shipowners engaged in this trade constantly search for opportunities to capitalize upon situations similar to that described. When these enterprising individuals learn of such events, usually through their network of brokers, agents, and representatives worldwide, to say nothing of their own experience in gauging the market day by day, they react promptly and decisively. Orders are dispatched to vessels, not otherwise committed, to make their way to the critical area, and negotiations with potential charters are initiated. If the demand for transportation is very great, the owner of the ships which have the highest speed will stand to reap the highest rewards.

It is, however, a paradox of the tramping business that the very action of these audacious capitalists, who will risk a multithousand-mile voyage on the chance of winning a single lucrative cargo, is the guarantor that the high freight rates will be reduced substantially in a relatively short period. Only so long as there is a shortage of ships for the requirements of the moment will the rates be inflated; as the concentration of vessels in the exporting area increases, the scarcity is alleviated and freight rates plummet. All too often, instead of the gamble paying a premium to the speculator, it becomes necessary for the owner-speculator to accept substandard freight rates as a means of reducing the losses incident to working the ship to other ports where conditions seem more favorable.

Tramp shipping is not only extremely flexible in responding to the demands of commerce, but is also very sensitive to changes in the patterns of sea transportation. These characteristics may be explained in part by the fact that the world fleet of several thousand tramp vessels is owned by persons of at least a score of nationalities. Domiciled in many different parts of the world, these owners keep in touch with the demands of commerce through a complex and fascinating network of representatives which spreads to every geographic area. Included in the huge fleet are dozens of handsome, well maintained, expensive new ships which are large, fast, and very efficient. There also are many smaller, slower, less productive vessels significantly past their prime which remain active only so long as shortages of carriers make it possible for them to find employment.

Many ships of this fleet belong to individuals and to small corporations; a few larger entities will own sizeable fleets. In the period preceding the domination of liner routes by container ships, a number of steamship

Glenmoor, an economical, rugged, simple, general-purpose tramp ship built in 1954. Photograph courtesy of Moor Line.

companies included in their corporate structure a tramp operating division. One reason for this activity was to share in the potential profits from the business. Another was to use the tramps to explore trade routes with the idea of developing a liner service. If charters were to be had repeatedly between a range of ports in one region (for example, the United States north of Cape Hatteras but not east of New York, or the countries at the eastern end of the Mediterranean) carrying substantially the same cargoes trip after trip, the possibility of regular liner service could be probed with tramp ships participating in the business. Often the experiment proved that a liner service filled a need, and so was commercially justifiable. An additional, but considerably less compelling reason for owning tramps was to assure that vessels which became surplus to the liner service could be kept sailing, even when not returning a profit, at no greater cost than laying them up in idle status.

These reasons lost their force as the major liner services were converted from break-bulk to containerized operations. Whereas in the days of what is now described as "conventional break-bulk operation," the structural differences between liners and tramps were not so great as to make them incompatible, this no longer was true. Container ships had to be built specifically for that purpose, and could not be switched temporarily to any other type of transportation.

It is a fact of economic history that tramp shipping, as it is known today, did not come into being until the second half of the nineteenth century. By that time, steam had been harnessed to machines, and the Industrial Revolution was in full swing. The demand for raw materials to supply the machines had begun to be felt worldwide. Cotton and wool for the textile industry of England were brought from distant shores, and to those points were returned the manufactured goods of English mills and factories. During those same years of major change, steam power was adapted to ships. The insatiable requirement for coal to fire their relatively primitive, low-pressure boilers necessitated the establishment of refueling points which were not too far apart geographically, but which did have some commercial activity or promise of development. These coaling stations grew in number and, as trade routes expanded, were located farther and farther from England. A brisk export business in the high grade coal mined in Wales evolved rather quickly and made for a satisfactory balance in ship operation, especially when the coaling stations were comparatively close to those ports where return cargoes could be obtained. The sturdy but unglamourous tramps brought back to England whatever they could find, be it cotton or wool or grain or ore. Always assured of outbound cargoes of coal should there be no requirement for their services to haul loads of manufactured goods to the distant marketplaces, the tramps soon were the visible reminders of the vast reach of the British empire.

Admittedly, the steamships did cost more to operate than the wind-driven sailing ships, but their increased reliability and speed, and particularly the possibility of predicting within a few days the exact time of arrival of a cargo, erased that pecuniary disadvantage. Furthermore, the decreased time needed to accomplish a voyage, as compared to the sailing ship, meant that a single steamship could carry more tonnage during a year than could its more beautiful rival. If proof of the economy of the coal-fired steamer's great speed were needed, this was provided by performance. In a given period, the faster, engine-powered vessel could deliver more goods than the sailing ship, and so created greater carrying capacity without the need for building and operating more ships. Finally, the opening of the Suez Canal in 1869 sounded the death knell of the sailing ship, because only powered vessels could negotiate the Red Sea on any commercially acceptable schedule.

England was the great industrial center of the Western European area, and the combination of its need for raw materials, its exports of manufactured goods, and the constant flow of coal to outlying coaling stations resulted in the requirement for a large tramp fleet. Just as English capital had responded to the opportunities ashore which had been afforded by the Industrial Revolution, so English financiers in the last quarter of the nineteenth century saw the chance for rich profits in shipping. By 1900, half of the oceangoing steamship tonnage of the world was under British registry. While this numerical superiority gradually was lost as other national fleets were expanded, it remained true at least until 1920 that more ships flew the Union Jack—familiarly known in maritime circles as the "Red Duster"—than any other flag.

In 1900, the best and most modern tramp steamer, which was not necessarily the typical ship, had a cargo capacity of about 7,000 tons. When operated with a clean bottom and in fair weather (force 2 on the Beaufort scale of winds), she might achieve a speed of 10 knots. As described by the novelist William McFee, who served for years as an engineer in such a ship, the hull was 110.0 meters (370 feet) long, 14.4 meters (48 feet) in the beam, had no 'tween decks, and her full, rounded bow facilitated stowage of cargo at the expense of speed. There were three boilers which collectively burned 25 tons of Welsh coal each day as they supplied steam to the triple expansion engine of 1,800 indicated horsepower. One set of cargo booms was installed over each of the four or five hatches.

A ship of this type would find regular employment carrying coal outward from England, and would return in due course with a cargo of ore in bulk, of cotton in bales, or sugar in bags. A year's voyages would earn a profit of 12 percent for her owners, a figure supported by the fact that her acquisition cost was £42,000. This cost must be considered in the light of contemporary values. The full cargo of coal was worth about £2,000. Crew wages were comparably low: the master was paid £25 a month; the chief engineer earned £20, while the senior mate received £10. A junior engineer worked all month for £6.[5]

From 1900 to 1914, the size of general-purpose dry cargo ships was increased slightly to a maximum of 7,500 tons deadweight capacity. Greater engineering efficiency reduced the consumption of coal while improving the average speed of the tramp fleet to approximately 10 knots. Until the end of World War I, coal remained the predominant fuel. Between 1919 and 1939, these ships were enlarged to about 10,000 tons deadweight, and fuel oil for steamships came into more general use. During this same period, the diesel engine began to achieve popularity with shipowners.

The titanic ship construction program undertaken by the United States during World War II produced thousands of ships of a single standardized design. The Liberty ship was sold worldwide beginning in 1946, and quickly became the universal general-purpose tramp. Unlike the ear-

The "Fortune" class of 20,000-ton, 15.5-knot general-purpose carriers was built in Japan to replace World War II Liberty ships. Photograph courtesy of Ishikawajima Harima Heavy Industries.

lier ships of this class, the Liberty had a single 'tween deck, which enhanced her adaptability for both bulk and packaged cargoes.[6] Until they were twenty years old (1962 and thereafter), Liberties were used on every international trade route.

Not until about 1950 did dry cargo ship sizes begin to grow significantly. As the ravages of war were repaired, and European shipyards returned to full productivity, the requirements of seaborne commerce were met with new construction. New designs called for longer, wider, and deeper draft hulls with a deadweight tonnage of about 14,000 or 15,000 tons. In 1968, a British shipyard, Austin & Pickersgill, introduced its replacement for the aging Liberties. The "S. D. 14"—a title derived from the technical description of "Shelter Decker, 14,000 tons deadweight"—gained widespread acceptance, and a total of 211 ships of this design were built, making this the most successful series-produced ship in peacetime history. It is especially noteworthy that this was entirely a privately financed undertaking.[7]

The "S.D. 14" was designed in England, and was the most successful peacetime series-built ship in history. Over two hundred had been delivered by 1982. Photograph by Turner, courtesy of Austin & Pickersgill, Shipbuilders.

While the general-purpose tramp was growing in carrying capacity, the bulk carrier had been developed into a specialized vehicle for the transportation of coal, grains, and ores. Evolving from the distinctive iron ore carriers which had been in existence since early in the century, the new bulk carrier was intended to haul with equal efficiency and economy any one of these three commodities, all of which moved in enormous quantities. The first of these multipurpose bulkers could lift 40,000 tons, and demonstrated conclusively the economy of great scale. In 1993, there were 139 bulkers of 150,000 tons deadweight or larger.[8] The title of "world's largest bulk carrier" was claimed, on January 1, 1993, by the *Berge Stahl,* which had a deadweight of 364,767 tons.

Excellent reasons underlay this trend toward specialization. A vessel designed to transport a particular commodity would incorporate those features which made her ideal for that trade: overall size, draft, ratio of cargo stowage space to deadweight tonnage, dimensions of hatch openings, type of cargo-handling gear, speed, and economy of operation, to name some of the most important. For hauling the intended commodity, the specialized ship should be the most efficient and economical that can be built. So long as the trade in that commodity provides regular employment for the vessel, she will bring benefits to her owners because of her efficiency, and will gratify her charterers because of the lower freight rates and the faster delivery of cargoes she makes possible. The entire commercial community will gain because she permits the most efficacious use of capital.

Although restricted in their choice of cargoes, these specialized carriers often are operated as conventional tramp vessels—that is to say, they are offered for time or voyage charter on the world market, they seek out cargoes and carry them where it suits the convenience of the charterer to have them discharged, and they compete both among themselves and with the general-purpose tramps for what business there may be. Because of their great size, however, they are limited as to the ports they can enter, but in the normal course of business this restriction poses only a minor problem for them.

The emergence in recent years of these huge specialized carriers has intensified the traditional struggle for employment on the part of the conventional general-purpose tramp, but it has not eliminated that type of ship from the maritime scene. This ship, unlike its big competitor, is able to enter almost any port of commercial significance, and can be berthed at

With all hatches open, the 121,500-tons deadweight bulk carrier *Endeavor* (built 1975) awaits her cargo. Photograph courtesy of Overseas Shipholding Group.

existing port facilities. Furthermore, the smaller size of the general-purpose vessel, compared to the large specialized carrier, may serve the needs of a charterer very well.

A manufacturer of fertilizer, for example, normally processes 15,000 tons of phosphate rock each week, and has a stockpile maintained at a constant level of 50,000 tons. By chartering several 15,000-ton tramps to establish and maintain a schedule to deliver one shipload of phosphate rock approximately every seven to ten days, the manufacturer keeps current supplies at a satisfactory level, and has ample reserves even if the ships are delayed as much as three weeks. In effect, the ships have been integrated into the manufacturer's supply system at the cost of the slightly higher freight rate.

Shippers and receivers of goods who have the physical facilities to handle and to dispose of immense quantities of a particular cargo, and also possess the financial resources to handle transactions of great magnitude, demand that they be furnished carriers which will give them the economies of large scale. The big bulk carriers have been the logical response to these demands and, within the limitations on their employment imposed by their length and draft, provide the required transportation at the lowest possible cost.

This type of ship enjoys a well-earned and important place in ocean-borne commerce. It meets a defined need, and has demonstrated the soundness of the principle that the larger the vessel, the lower the unit cost of transportation. It must be noted, however, that only those organizations which are geared to handle, both physically and financially, enormous quantities of specific commodities are able to take the fullest advantage of the benefits accrued from chartering these big ships.

The modern general-purpose tramp is intended to serve, and does so very successfully, a number of different trades. In one year, for example, a fleet of four of these vessels lifted cargoes of pig iron, black iron, wheat middling pellets, scrap iron, logs, timber, tapioca, wood chips, poonac (co-conut oil cake), ilmenite sand, iron ore, grain coal, bauxite, and cement.[9] Designed to operate into and out of ports which have relatively shallow depth and only a minimum of port facilities (wharves, piers, and transit sheds with their supporting upland areas), these ships are equipped with sufficient booms, derricks, or cranes to make them "self-sustaining," i.e., capable of being loaded and discharged by the use of their own gear. The carrying capacity of the general purpose tramp and of its larger sister ships is established at least in part by the requirements of charterers for ships of a certain size for particular trades.

Top: A modern tramp with unusual gantry cranes, the *Bulk Eagle* is well-adapted to handle commodities like coal and iron ore. *Bottom:* Shipboard gantry cranes are paired to handle extra-long items. Photographs courtesy of Munck International.

An analysis of the employment of three types of bulk carriers illustrates this point. The study concerned a general service tramp of 25,000 tons deadweight (at summer load line) assigned to a voyage from a port on the United States Gulf coast to Japan; a ship of 65,000 tons deadweight (at summer load line) carrying coal from Hampton Roads, Virginia, to Japan; and a bulker of 120,000 tons deadweight (at summer load line) hauling iron ore from Tubarão, Brazil, to Rotterdam. Details of the operations are set forth as follows:

	25,000- ton carrier	65,000- ton carrier	120,000- ton carrier
Commodity	Grain	Coal	Iron ore
Loading port	U.S. Gulf	Hampton Roads	Tubarão
Discharge port	Japan	Japan	Rotterdam
Approximate voyage miles (includes ballast voyage from Europe to load port)	14,000	13,000	10,000
Days at sea, per voyage, @ 13 kts, plus one day Panama Canal passage	44	41	31
Days in port, per voyage	8	6	6
Voyages per 350-day year	6.7	7.4	9.5
Fuel oil consumed per voyage, metric tons	960	1,220	1,480
Diesel fuel consumed per voyage, metric tons	105	120	115 [10]

The same study included details of the annual cost of owning these ships:

	25,000- ton carrier	65,000- ton carrier	120,000- ton carrier
Manning	$611,000	$592,000	$633,000
Maintenance & repair	276,000	320,000	428,000
Stores & lubricating oils	189,000	272,000	317,000
Insurance	247,000	288,000	390,000
Administration	131,000	128,000	150,000
Total	$1,454,000	$1,601,000	$1,918,000
Daily cost, basis 350-day year	$4,155	$4,575	$5,480

Notes: Manning costs include pay, social and national insurance, pensions, crew travel expenses, and victualing.

Fuel is not included; it varies with the ship's employment, and would not be an owner's expense when the vessel is time-chartered.

The break-even cost per ton per day is: 25,000-ton ship—$0.1662; 65,000-ton ship—$0.07038; 120,000-ton ship—$0.04566.

To build a new ship in 1991, the owner would have paid $17,000,000 for the 25,000-ton ship; $31,700,000 for the 65,000-ton carrier; and $59,000,000 for the 120,000-ton bulker. The daily capital costs were correspondingly high: $6,000 for the small ship, $12,680 for the intermediate vessel, and $26,960 for the big bulker.[11]

Competition in the tramping trades is not solely between similar ships seeking the same cargo, but often is between owners whose similar ships have widely variant costs. The table below sets forth the difference which characterized identical 30,000 deadweight ton bulk carriers under different national registries:

	Registry "A"	Registry "B"	Registry "C"
Finance	$4,500,000	$1,595,000	$1,476,000
Crew	2,800,000	1,500,000	500,000
Fuel	1,200,000	1,200,000	1,200,000
Stores	300,000	130,000	110,000
Maintenance & repair	600,000	160,000	130,000
Insurance	380,000	210,000	120,000
Administration & overhead	240,000	70,000	35,000
Taxes & fees	1,264,000	609,000	10,000
Total	$11,374,000	$5,475,000	$3,581,000[12]

The controlling depth of water and the peculiarities of the channels in a port fix the limits of ship sizes which can be accommodated in a given harbor. If a ship drawing 10.5 meters (35 feet) of water, fully laden at summer load line, is offered for a trip to a harbor with a minimum depth of 9.6 meters (32 feet), there are two possibilities open to the potential charterer. One is to reject the offered ship because she is too large. The other is to accept the ship, load her only to the minimum depth, and make the best of the transaction. Circumstances prevailing in the freight market at the time when a decision must be reached will determine the alternative chosen.

Accommodations for personnel staffing tramp ships have been improved steadily through the years. At the turn of the century, most of the marine superintendents ashore as well as the licensed officers aboard the tramps had served apprenticeships in sailing vessels, and expected no more comforts in the steamers than they had found in the windjammers. Quarters were starkly utilitarian. Novelist William McFee, who was an engineer aboard British-flag tramps in pre-1914 days, described what he encountered: the small rooms allotted to licensed personnel were about as comfortable as cells in a penitentiary, with no electric lights, no heat, no running water, and no bathing facilities.[13] All this has changed, and progressive owners of modern ships provide excellent living arrangements for crew members. They give more attention to assuring that the food is ade-

Deck petty officer's quarters in a well-equipped British tramp. Photograph courtesy of Moor Line.

quate in quantity and properly prepared. It is unfortunately still true that unscrupulous operators exploit their crews, especially when the ships are old and only marginally profitable.

Harsh competition remains the predominant feature of tramp shipping. The law of supply and demand determines which ships earn a profit. If there are many cargoes and few bottoms, there is rivalry among shippers and the freight rates climb. When the opposite condition prevails, and too many ships are chasing too few cargoes, the shipowners fight among themselves to obtain what they can, often accepting business at suicidally low rates—which explains the old saying in the tramp trade that "one good year is balanced by seven bad ones."

Until 1966, when international transportation of cargoes loaded in containers began, tramps engaged in the foreign trade of the United States vied with the cargo liners for bulk cargoes such as grain, lumber, and some types of ore. The liners would seek "parcels" of 3,000 to 6,000 tons to fill otherwise unused space, and would quote freight rates which were barely adequate to cover the cost of stevedoring. This practice hurt the tramps because they had to accept these same low rates for full loads of 8,000 to 10,000 tons. The virtual disappearance of the break-bulk cargo liner on most of these trade routes in many instances has been accompanied by the entry of the specialized large bulkers, thus perpetuating and ac-centuating the competition with which the general-purpose tramp must deal.

Depreciation—the annual provision made by a prudent owner to write off the value of the units of its fleet—is based usually on a theoretical twenty-year life for a ship. In the tramp trade, however, earnings are not so consistent that it is feasible each year to put into the depreciation account even 5 percent of the purchase price, as good financial practice might sug-gest. Some owners strive to cut the book value of new ships by as much as they can afford in the first two or three years of ownership, and thereafter as earnings permit. The sooner a ship's value is written off, the more quickly the owner may compete for cargoes in the bad years. The purchase may have been amortized by the time the vessel is twenty years old, but replacement is not automatic. So long as cargoes can be found, it is likely that the old vessel will continue in service.

Competition for cargoes, slower speeds than those of the cargo liners, and nonrepetitive operations combine to restrict the tramp owner to a par-ticular segment of commercial activity. In practice, tramps carry, usually on a resupply and stockpile basis, materials such as cement, coal, grain, fertilizers, lumber, and ores of various kinds. The unit sales price of these commodities is small; the purchase price at the loading port is low, and the difference between purchase price and sales price does not permit very high freight rates. This becomes obvious when a given item from two widely separated regions is offered for sale in the same market. One source is within a day's travel of the market; the other is eight ship-days distant. The item is priced to compensate for costs at the nearby source. The far distant source must equal that price, or abandon the market. Despite pres-sure from the would-be seller on the shipowner, the freight rate cannot be reduced to a level which will permit the item from the far away source to compete in the market. It sometimes happens that the cost of transportation equals the value of the raw material, with predictable results as to market restrictions.

To succeed in the tramping enterprise requires that the operator know something about practically all the raw materials moving in the world's commerce. At the same time, this operator must be acquainted with the physical characteristics of, and the cargo-handling equipment available in, those places where these materials are loaded and discharged. Always, too, the tramp owner must be the optimistic speculator.

These venturesome shipowners must be supported by a system which maintains contact with potential charterers anywhere in the world. It would be prohibitively expensive, as well as administratively impractical, to attempt to maintain an office in every port, or to arrange for permanent representation in those cities. To meet the demand for some form of low cost, worldwide agency to provide commercial intelligence and advice when it is needed, the institution of the ship broker evolved through the decades. The members of this branch of the shipping fraternity are the specialists who find cargoes for ships and ships for cargoes.

The center of this fascinating activity is in London, and the headquarters are located in the Baltic Exchange, not far from the Thames river and famous Tower Bridge. Here at the "Baltic," brokers who have been elected individually to membership on the basis of their personal integrity, knowledge, and resourcefulness, meet to work out charters for their principals. One broker represents a shipowner and the other stands in the place of a shipper.

For example, suppose that Angus MacAndrew, of Glasgow, is seeking a load for his ship, the *Highlander,* now at anchor in Hampton Roads, Virginia. MacAndrew notifies John Lawson, his broker in London, who consults other brokers on the floor of the Baltic. In short order, he learns from Basil Smith that Li Wong in Shanghai needs a ship to carry grain to China from either an Atlantic or a Gulf Coast port of the United States. Following brief discussion between Lawson and Smith, an agreement as to price and terms is reached and, after approval from the principals, the contract is made. Before the sun sets in London, the *Highlander* has been notified of her next employment and is on her way to the loading port.

The advantage of the Baltic is that here are to be found daily the representatives of many owners of tramp ships as well as brokers whose principals are seeking tonnage for their goods. It is often more expeditious to obtain the information and then to negotiate the terms of a charter on the floor of the Baltic than to canvass brokers' offices by telephone, as is done in New York. The availability of vastly improved means of communication, however, has reduced the need to have face-to-face negotiation, and fewer brokers, compared to the period before 1970, appear daily on the floor of the Baltic Exchange.

Once a vessel has been offered on option to a potential charterer, that ship is unavailable to other bidders, no matter how attractive their offers may be. Until the option is exercised or expires, the broker is bound by the promise that the offeror will be protected. Only after negotiations have been completed and agreement reached is the formal contract drawn up.[14] To prevent confusion, especially when international telephone conversations are involved, it has become common practice to confirm all offers and counteroffers by cable or fax, but these written messages do not replace the spoken pledges made by the brokers.

Shipowners as well as charterers must be aware of what charter hire rates are being offered or accepted, in precisely the same way that traders in stocks and bonds must keep abreast of swings in the securities markets. Reports of vessel charters, or "fixtures," therefore are published in shipping journals in a technical language which conveys the essentials of the transactions in a minimum of words. The fixture of the *Highlander*, for example, would be publicized in a paragraph like this:

> U.S. Northern Range to coast of China. Motorship *Highlander*, British flag, 27,000 tons, five percent, heavy grain, $36.50; option two ports China $37.50; 60¢ extra for U. S. Gulf loading option; FIOT, three days load, SHEX, ten days discharge, SHinc, $10,000 demurrage, $5,000 dispatch; Feb. 1–12.

Interpreted for the layman, this reports that the motorship *Highlander*, British registry, has been chartered to carry about 27,000 tons of heavy grain, plus or minus 5 percent at the master's discretion, to obtain a seaworthy load and still store and fuel the ship adequately without losing too much revenue. The grain will be loaded in a port between Cape Hatteras, North Carolina, and Portland, Maine, and transported to the coast of China for $36.50 per ton loaded. If the charterer elects to discharge the cargo in two ports in China, the freight rate will be increased to $37.50 per ton. Should the ship proceed to a U.S. port on the Gulf of Mexico to take on her cargo, the charterer will pay an additional 60¢ per ton. FIOT (free in and out and trimmed) means that all expenses connected with loading, discharging, and trimming are for the account of the charterer. It is the charterer's responsibility to have the cargo ready to be loaded, and to make arrangements for its discharge. Three days, Sundays and holidays excluded (SHex) are allowed to load, and ten days, Sundays and holidays included (SHinc), to discharge. If either of these times is exceeded, the charterer will be assessed a charge (demurrage) of $10,000 per day; if the cargo-working time is less than that allowed, the shipowner will pay the charterer $5,000 (dispatch) per day. The *Highlander* must report no earlier than February 1 nor later than February 12.

In the instance described above, the *Highlander* has been obtained on a basis which suits the convenience of only one person, the shipper. It is much the same as hiring a truck to haul a load of goods, rather than sending the goods by rail. The truck will proceed to the pickup point set by the shipper, and will arrive at an hour arranged between trucker and shipper. It will be routed either as directed by the shipper or by the driver using the shortest route. If a train is used, the goods will move over the tracks on a fixed schedule, and will be picked up and delivered according to the rail-road's practice. The tramp is like the truck, whereas the seagoing counter-part to the train is the cargo liner, which sails between advertised ports on a relatively inflexible schedule to which the user must conform.

How does the shipper go about obtaining the exclusive use of a tramp vessel? What arrangements are made to safeguard the interests of the ship-owner? What guarantee does the shipper have that the vessel will perform as required? What sorts of agreements are made? The answers to these and related questions constitute the essence of the chartering business, and are based upon the maritime and commercial experience of thousands of peo-ple, both past and present.

The written agreement setting forth the terms and conditions under which the vessel owner makes a ship available to the shipper on an exclu-sive basis is a specialized form of contract known in maritime circles as a "charter party," a name derived from the Latin, *charta partita,* which means a paper divided so that each signatory may keep an identical copy.[15]

Charter parties are diversified into three principal categories: voyage, time, and bareboat.

The voyage charter is the most frequently employed because it places the lightest burden upon the charterer. In essence, it is a contract of af-freightment covering the movement of a particular cargo from one desig-nated area to another, at a stipulated rate of compensation (charter hire) for each ton of the goods actually transported. The shipowner is responsible for all details of vessel operation. The charterer, in addition to putting the cargo within reach of the loading gear (which may be the ship's equipment or dockside cranes or chutes for ores, coal, and grains) must arrange for the berthing places at ports of loading and discharge, and quite often also must contract with stevedores to handle the cargo. Payment for the ship's serv-ices must be made in accordance with the provisions of the charter party.

The time charter, while somewhat similar to the voyage charter in keeping the shipowner responsible for operation of the vessel, differs pri-marily in that the charterer obtains the use of the ship for a period of time to carry cargoes not barred by the contract anywhere within the geographical limitations set forth in the charter party. The charterer pays an agreed sum per deadweight ton per month, or a similarly agreed lump sum per day for the stipulated period. All expenses related to cargo, port fees, canal tolls, and fuel are for the account of the charterer. Crew hire, and costs of food, stores, and maintenance of the ship in good running order are paid by the owner.

Under the terms of the bareboat (or demise) charter, the owner transfers operational control of the ship to the charterer. The vessel must be seaworthy and fully equipped at the time she is delivered to the charterer, but the full burden and responsibility of operation are assumed by the charterer. Except for approving the nomination of master and chief engineer, the owner does not influence the selection of officers and crew. The charterer must purchase fuel, stores, and food, pay all maintenance and drydocking expenses, and become the de facto manager of the vessel. The owner is kept informed of the movements of the ship, and periodically receives the agreed payments which, as in the time charter, are based on the deadweight tonnage of the ship (or, if mutually agreed, a lump sum per day).

Both time and bareboat charters normally contain certain restrictions concerning the types of cargo which may be carried. At the minimum, the stipulation is that "any lawful merchandise not injurious to the vessel" may be put aboard. Some contracts are more specific: one document states that "No livestock [or] sulphur and pitch in bulk to be shipped." Should the owner wish to protect the ship from damage by certain goods, an exclusionary clause would be inserted to limit the quantity of such goods to be transported. A typical clause reads: "No livestock nor injurious, inflammable or dangerous goods (such as acids, explosives, calcium carbide, ferro silicon, naphtha, motor spirit, tar, or any of their products) to be shipped."

The time or bareboat charterer directs where the ship shall sail. Because marine underwriters are very specific as to the areas of the world where they will accept responsibility for damage sustained by ships they insure, the time and bareboat charter parties provide a space in which the limits of the ship's voyaging are stipulated. Furthermore, the charterer is prohibited from ordering the ship to "any place where fever or epidemics are prevalent," nor may the charterer direct the ship into places where there is danger of being frozen-in for the duration of the winter. A typical "ice clause" reads thus:

> The Vessel is not to be ordered to nor bound to enter any ice-bound place or any place where lights, lightships, marks and buoys are or

The owner invoked the "ice clause" when his ice-strengthened bulk carrier encountered these conditions. Photograph courtesy of A/S Hydraulik Brattvaag

are likely to be withdrawn by reason of ice on the Vessel's arrival or where there is risk that ordinarily the Vessel will not be able on account of ice to reach the place or to get out after having completed loading or discharging. The Vessel is not to be obliged to force ice, nor to follow icebreakers when inward bound. If on account of ice the Master considers it dangerous to remain at the loading or discharging place for fear of the Vessel being frozen in and/or damaged, he has liberty to sail to a convenient open place and await the Charterer's fresh instructions. Detention through any of the above causes to be for the Charterer's account.

If the contemplated employment of the ship entails voyages to ports where the above-described conditions may be encountered, the terms and conditions under which that activity will be performed must be negotiated and set forth in minute detail in the charter party.

Any charterer who takes a ship for a period of time faces the possibility of disputes with the owner over the performance of the ship (fuel consumption, sea speed, reliability) and the carrying capacity of the vessel, as well as other details of the contract. To protect both parties, the specifics of ship performance and the amount of space below decks must be set forth and mutually agreed upon before the charter party is signed. The ship-owner provides, and is responsible for, accurate data, and gives assurance that they reflect the facts of the ship. These stipulations are known as the "warranties," and failure to live up to them makes the shipowner liable for breach of contract.

Most of the warranties are provable without difficulty, but speed and fuel consumption are affected noticeably by weather conditions. Should a dispute arise over either or both of these stipulations, there will be discussions between the contracting parties until a satisfactory adjustment is made. Should no compromise be reached in these areas or in any other part of the charter party, the dispute may be referred to arbitrators. Their decision will have the same force as a judgment handed down by a court of law.

A typical time charter, as reported in the maritime press, provided this information, including the warranties:

> Delivery Rotterdam, transatlantic round voyage, redelivery Havre/Amsterdam range, May 5 to 10, *Belmount,* Norwegian flag, built 1975, 110,444 metric tons deadweight, 4.6 million cubic feet grain, 12 knots on 43 tons heavy fuel oil plus 1.5 tons diesel, $11,600 daily.

The warranties for the big Norwegian motorship are that she has a total deadweight of 110,444 metric tons, her enclosed cargo stowage space equals 4.6 million cubic feet (grain measurement), and that she will travel at a speed of 12 knots on a daily consumption of 43 tons of high viscosity fuel oil and 1.5 tons of marine diesel oil.

The charter party always stipulates the port in which the ship is to be delivered or, in the terms of the trade, "tendered" by the owner. It also specifies the beginning and the ending of the period of days during which tender of the ship may be made. This period is known as "lay days." In addition, the charter party sets forth the date terminating the right of the charterer to cancel the agreement and to refuse to accept tender of the vessel. The owner is protected from arbitrary action by the charterer by this clause in the contract:

> If the vessel cannot be delivered by the cancelling date, the Charterers, if required [by the Owners] are to declare within 48 hours (Sun-

days and holidays excluded) after receiving notice thereof, whether they cancel or will take delivery of the vessel.

Should the contract be for a single voyage, the exact commodity to be carried and the charter hire payable per ton of that commodity actually loaded are designated, as are the loading and discharge ports. These details are important to the owner not only for the obvious reasons but also because they make certain that there will be time to look ahead for other employment following the completion of the present charter. Experience and knowledge guide the owner in estimating the number of days the ship will require to carry out the contract; a judicious guess must be made as to possible delays. With this foundation, the owner can make long-range commitments.

Among other provisions of the voyage charter are statements concerning the number of days allowed for loading and discharge (also known as "lay days,"[16] the penalty (demurrage) for holding the ship in port beyond the period stipulated for working cargo, and the premium (dispatch) for reducing the time spent in port. Demurrage is intended to compensate the owner completely for time lost in port as a result of some failure on the part of the charterer. Dispatch is paid by the shipowner to the charterer, usually at one-half the demurrage rate, to reward reduction in port time. It is a stipulation found in voyage charter parties only when there is great demand for ships.

Because the voyage charter imposes the least operational responsibility upon the charterer and is convenient for the movement of bulk commodities, it is the most common form of contract. The owner of the ship, under the "gross" form, pays for every item of expense, including loading, discharging, port fees, canal tolls, and all expenses in connection with the cargo, as well as the operating charges such as crew wages, subsistence, and fuel.[17] Under the "net" form, the owner pays all the normal ship operating costs, and the charterer is responsible for charges accrued for loading and discharging the cargo as well as for port fees (except those related directly and solely to the crew) exacted against ship and cargo. The owner retains the full burden of managing the ship.

A voyage charter, as has been pointed out, is concerned with moving a particular cargo between designated parts. The charterer is obligated to provide sufficient cargo to fill the entire ship unless the contract stipulates otherwise. The master is responsible for the correct and seaworthy loading of the vessel. The charter party almost always gives to the master the authority to require the charterer to decrease or increase the quantity of cargo offered, if such action is necessary to assure proper trim and stability of the vessel.

The charterer must pay the agreed sum for each ton of the commodity to be shipped; if the ship is loaded to less than its capacity, the charterer is liable for "dead freight," the difference between what should have been loaded and what actually was put into the cargo holds. To obtain maximum revenue from the voyage, the owner directs the master to accept as much cargo as the safety of the ship will permit. The charterer, having set the day when the ship is to be tendered, is expected to have the cargo waiting so that no time is lost once the ship has been delivered to the charterer. Any delay for which the charterer is responsible raises the possibility of having to pay demurrage.

Under a time charter, the charterer provides cargoes for the ship, keeps her busy, and pays the owner the agreed charter hire regardless of whether the ship is active or lying at anchor. The owner is fully responsible for the operation of the ship: provides the crew, stores, and all necessary equipment for the vessel; pays all port charges incurred for and on behalf of the crew; and is responsible in all respects for the navigation and main-tenance of the vessel and the stowage, care, and safety of the cargo. In addition to charter hire, the charterer provides the fuel and pays port entry, clearance, agency fees, pilotage charges, tug hire, costs of loading and dis-charging cargo, including wharfage and dockage, and arranges for appro-priate representation in ports of call.[18]

To illustrate the theory of the time charter, here is a simplified form of agreement for the use of a ship:

This charter party is made and concluded in New York, N.Y., the first day of June 1994 between Olav Bjornsen A/S, of Bergen, Nor-way, Owner of the good Norwegian motorship *Queen Ingrid,* and Ocean Trading Corporation, of Newark, New Jersey, Charterers of the said motorship (described as being classed 100-A-1 at Lloyd's Register of Shipping, of about 1,893,000 cubic feet [57,210 cubic meters] grain capacity, 30,093 gross register tons, 14,720 net regis-ter tons, and about 49,228 tons of 2,240 pounds deadweight on a summer draft of 40 feet 5 inches [12.118 meters], with a diesel mo-tor of 9,562 kW [13,000 brake horsepower] and a service speed of 14 knots on a consumption of about 41 tons of high viscosity fuel and about 3 tons of diesel oil per twenty-four-hour day. Permanent bunker capacity is 2,014 tons of high viscosity fuel and 208 tons of marine diesel oil) now in service and trading. These particulars are not guaranteed, but are supplied in good faith, and are believed to be correct.

1. *Delivery.* The vessel is to be delivered in Galveston, Texas, not earlier than July 13, 1994, and not later than July 30, 1994, between the hours of 9:00 A.M. and 6:00 P.M. (Sundays and holidays excepted), at such available berth where she can safely lie always afloat as may be directed by Charterers, for a period of fifteen months from date of delivery.

2. *Trade.* The vessel is to be employed in lawful trades for the carriage of lawful merchandise only, between good and safe ports where she can safely lie always afloat. No livestock, nor injurious, inflammable, or dangerous goods such as acids, explosives, calcium, ferro silicon, naphtha, motor spirit, tar, or any of their products, are to be shipped.

3. *Owners to provide.* The Owners are to provide and pay for all provisions and wages, insurance of the vessel, all deck and engine-room stores, and are to maintain her in a thoroughly efficient state in hull and machinery during the term of this contract.

4. *Charterers to provide.* The Charterers are to provide and pay for all fuel, port charges, pilotage (whether compulsory or not), lights, tug assistance, consular charges (except those directly related to the master, officers, and crew), taxes, dock and harbor and tonnage dues at ports of delivery and redelivery, agencies, and commissions. Owners also are to arrange for and pay for loading, trimming, stowing (including dunnage and shifting boards), unloading, weighing, tallying, and delivery of cargo, and all other charges, including detention.

5. *Bunkers.* Charterers at port of delivery and Owners at port of redelivery are to take over and pay for oil fuel remaining in the vessel's bunkers, at the current price at the respective ports. The vessel is to be redelivered with not less than 100 tons and not more than 150 tons of heavy fuel and 40 tons of marine diesel oil.

6. *Hire.* The Charterers are to pay as hire the sum of $9,250 per day, or $5.98 per deadweight ton per month, in cash and without discount, every thirty days, in advance.

7. *Redelivery.* The vessel is to be redelivered on the expiration of the charter in the same good order as when delivered to the Charterers (fair wear and tear excepted), at an ice-free port in the Charterer's option between Cape Hatteras and Portland, Maine, between the hours of 9:00 A.M. and 6:00 P.M. (Sundays and holidays ex-

cepted). Charterers are to give Owners not less than ten days notice at which port and on which day the vessel will be redelivered.

8. *Cargo space.* The whole reach and burthen of the vessel, including lawful deck capacity, shall be at the Charterer's disposal, reserving proper and sufficient space for the master, officers, and crew, and all tackle, apparel, furniture, provisions, and stores.

9. *Master.* The master shall prosecute all voyages with the utmost dispatch and may render customary assistance with the vessel's crew. The master shall be under the Charterer's orders as regards employment, agency, or other arrangements.

10. *Directions and logs.* The Charterers are to furnish the master with all instructions and sailing directions. The master and chief engineer are to keep full and correct logs accessible to the Charterers and their agents.

11. *Suspension of hire.* In the event that the vessel is unable to perform for any reason for a period in excess of twenty-four consecutive hours, no hire shall be paid for such lost time. The Owners shall be responsible for delay during the currency of this charter only if such delay or loss has been caused by want of due diligence to make the vessel seaworthy and fitted for the voyage.

12. *Ice.* The vessel shall not be required to enter any port where there is immediate risk of being frozen-in, nor shall the vessel be required to force ice. The master shall have liberty to leave a port when, in his judgment, there is risk of being frozen-in, whether or not the cargo has been fully loaded or discharged.

13. *Overtime.* The vessel is to work day and night, if required. The Charterers will reimburse the Owners for the cost of overtime paid to officers and crew.

14. *Liens.* The Owners shall have a lien on all cargoes and subfreights belonging to the Charterers for all claims under this charter. The Charterers shall have a lien on the vessel for all moneys paid in advance and not earned.

15. *Sublet.* The Charterers shall have the option of subletting the vessel, giving due notice to the Owners. The Charterers shall remain always responsible to the Owners for due performance of the charter.

16. *Canceling.* If the vessel cannot be delivered by the canceling date, the Charterers, if required, are to declare within forty-eight hours after receiving notice thereof, whether they will take delivery or will cancel.

17. *Arbitration*. Any dispute arising under the charter is to be referred to arbitration in New York or such other place as may be agreed upon. One arbitrator shall be designated by Charterers and one arbitrator shall be designated by Owners. If arbitrators cannot agree, they are to appoint an Umpire, whose decision shall be binding upon both parties.

18. *Commission*. The Owners shall pay a commission of $2\frac{1}{2}$ percent to the brokers involved.

<table>
<tr><td>Olav Bjornsen A/S</td><td>Ocean Trading Corporation</td></tr>
<tr><td>by Harold Saylor</td><td>by Joseph Merchant</td></tr>
<tr><td>as broker only</td><td>as broker only[19]</td></tr>
</table>

The bareboat (or demise) charter is similar to the time charter in that it involves the use of the ship for a period of time. The full responsibility of operation, however, is transferred from owner to charterer, who would have to be supported by the appropriate organization to manage the vessel. Quite often, the bareboat charterer is a steamship company which requires augmentation of its fleet, but does not wish to purchase a ship. In other cases, the owner may be a financial institution, such as a bank, which seeks an operating company to run the ship. As a matter of fact, relatively few bareboat charters are consummated.

Perusal of the different charter parties is rewarding, for the numerous provisions of the documents reflect the experience of shipowners and charterers through the years. Drawn by working members of the shipping community and by experts in maritime and commercial law, the charter parties represent a working compromise between the demands of the shipowners and the insistent requirements of the charterers. Negotiations for a particular transaction usually start with one of these standardized and readily available forms. As the specific terms are agreed upon by the contracting parties, the printed form may be amended—some clauses may be deleted—to reflect the meeting of minds.

"Working the market" requires that both charterer and shipowner be alert to many factors. The charterer needs to know a great deal about the availability of ships and the consequent fluctuations of the freight and charter markets. Likewise, the charterer must take note of how rates vary for the same commodity on different trade routes and at different seasons of the year. The operator must be aware of practically everything the charterer should know in addition to mastering a wide assortment of facts and details which are part and parcel of business life. Attention must be given to conditions in ports and harbors around the world, the charges made for handling ships, the efficiency of longshoremen, and the availability of cargo-working equipment. The peculiarities of harbors—their depths, tides, winds, ice, fog anchorages, and local customs concerning the use of pilots and tugs—are essential elements of information. Because ships frequently need repairs, it is important that the owner be aware of what facilities are available in the ports to which the ships may be sent. Establishing contacts in anticipated ports of call will ease the acquisition of pertinent data and reports of developments affecting shipping in those waters. Certainly high on the list of concerns of the shipowner is where and how to procure the proper grade of fuel at times when quality is highly variable.

When it comes to cargoes, the tramp shipowner must be intimately acquainted with the characteristics of practically every commodity in the world which moves in bulk, so that when it is necessary to set a rate, it will be one which will return a reasonable revenue. Additionally, the owner must know how these bulk commodities are handled, for in some ports everything is mechanized and therefore fast loading or unloading is assured, while in other places the whole process is dependent upon human labor alone.

It is small wonder that mastering the intricacies of the tramp shipping business is a full-time career.

CHAPTER THREE

The Management of Tramp Shipping

To provide timely and efficient transportation from a producing area separated from a consuming region by thousands of miles of ocean is a severe test of the judgment and skill of those responsible for the effective employment of tramp ships. Matching ships to cargoes, selecting the most advantageous routings, ascertaining accurately the costs of performance under different types of contracts, and balancing present opportunities against future prospects, are a few of the areas of concern in the profitable and effective management of these workhorses of the sea.

The commodities which move in greatest quantity, and therefore offer the best opportunities for employment of ships, are ores, grains, and coal. Of these, grain is the most likely to experience fluctuations in demand, and therefore to have a significant impact upon the tramp shipping industry. As a basic requirement in feeding the population of the world, grain—the term includes a wide variety of cereals such as wheat, corn, oats, barley, rye, sorghum, and soyas—is in constant demand. It is grown in many regions, but only the United States, Canada, Argentina, and Australia (in that descending order of magnitude) have significant quantities for export. As a cargo, grain can be carried in many different types of ships, and because it moves almost exclusively in bulk, it is susceptible to mechanized handling, with resultant short loading and discharging times. Until the advent of containerships and the introduction of the very large bulk carriers, grain was an attractive "filler" cargo for ships in liner service, and therefore became the target of intense competition between "regular traders," as liners sometimes were termed, and tramps.[1]

A different aspect of competition became manifest when tankers and bulkers of at least 50,000 tons deadweight capacity began actively to seek cargoes. Both these types, because of their size and lower unit cost of transportation, were able to offer freight rates which were significantly below those which the conventional tramp of 25,000 tons deadweight could accept.

The general-purpose dry cargo tramp, however, has not been eliminated. The versatility of this vessel, which can enter ports too shallow for the deep draft bulkers, has assured its employment in a variety of cargo movements. Grain continues to be a commodity which these smaller ships can, and do, transport as they battle to survive in an increasingly competitive environment. Many other bulk cargoes move in international commerce, and provide year-round opportunities for bold and aggressive owners of tramp ships. Metallic ores, fertilizers, coal, and forest products, to name only a few, account for a substantial tonnage which must be transported across the seas. To meet the incessant demand for cargo space requires vigorous action on the part of producers of these materials, traffic managers of import and export corporations, ship brokers, and shipowners. Each of these groups needs to have, in varying degrees, a broad range of information on which to base decisions.

It is not surprising, therefore, to discover that both the users of tramp ships and the owners of those hard-working carriers become avid readers of the daily news, with special emphasis upon accounts of weather in different areas, economic conditions, political events, and crop reports. An unseasonal and unpredicted series of very heavy rains in midsummer, when crops are ripening, may have devastating effects on the final harvest. Not only is the farmer involved immediately, but the sellers and importers have to make adjustments in their marketing plans. Carriers—both land and oceangoing—discover that the flow of cargo requiring their services is reduced to a trickle. The worldwide patterns of tramp ship operations may be altered drastically as a result of this untimely change in the weather. Relating news events to transportation activities is a requisite for those who would participate in this fascinating and ever changing activity.

For the owner and operator of tramp-type shipping, every effort must be directed toward the most effective employment of the units of the fleet. The ultimate criterion of achievement is the profit or loss sustained from the voyages undertaken during a given accounting period. Whether the color of the ink used by the bookkeeper is black, announcing a profit, or red, admitting a loss, depends upon the ability of the managers of the fleet to reduce voyages in ballast to an acceptable minimum, to control the number of idle days between active voyages, to find the most suitable cargoes for the ships, and to obtain the best freight rates and the most favorable terms.

To be able to arrange for a series of charter commitments which will follow one upon another with little or no intervening time during which the ships do not earn any revenue is the ambition of every manager. Should the policy of the owner be to keep the fleet in the market for voyage charters, where the returns are higher but the risks of finding continuous employment are greater than in the longer term time charter activity, it is necessary to be extremely selective in the commitments made. For example, a high rate may be offered to carry a cargo of grain from New Orleans to Calcutta, but unless there is some assurance that a load can be found within a comparatively short distance from Calcutta, the business may be a money loser because of the high cost of sending the ship to the area of her next employment. Ideally, as each voyage charter is ended and the ship is redelivered to the owner, a new assignment is waiting, and the time between revenue-producing voyages is minimal. In practice this happens only occasionally; all too often it is necessary to send the ship on a trip of several thousand miles to pick up the next load. The profits, if any, from the first voyage may be absorbed in the cost of repositioning.

To illustrate the various possibilities for employment of a tramp ship, this hypothetical example is offered: a 25,000-ton general-purpose vessel is assigned to lift grain from New Orleans to India. By the time she completed discharge at the port of destination, these were the possibilities under consideration by the owner:

1. To proceed in ballast to Australia to pick up wheat for delivery in either the United Kingdom or the Bordeaux-Hamburg range of the European continent; or
2. To proceed in ballast from India to Mauritius to load a full cargo of sugar for a port on the Atlantic coast of either Canada or the northern range of the United States; or
3. To proceed to Mormugao, India, to take on a load of ore for Japan. From Japan, these were the potential opportunities for employment: (a) to sail in ballast to the Philippines to load copra for Europe; (b) to go to the Philippines for a cargo of sugar for a U.S. port on the Gulf of Mexico or the Atlantic coast; or (c) to proceed in ballast to British Columbia for either a cargo of grain for Europe or a full load of lumber for the Atlantic coast of the United States.

In the real world of tramp shipping, the terms and conditions demanded by the charterer must be fair and reasonable from the viewpoint of the shipowner. What at first may seem to be a very profitable rate may turn out to be a guarantee of a heavy loss unless there is protection against excessive delays incident to port congestion. For instance, when a cargo of grain is offered at an attractive rate from Churchill, a Canadian port on Hudson Bay, where the weather is notoriously uncertain and often shuts down the port altogether for several consecutive days, the owner must insist on compensation for time lost in such an eventuality. Otherwise, the voyage might result in a deficit.

As a tool with which to formulate decisions relating to the future employment of a tramp steamer, the computer has proven its value. It can provide a great amount of data, but the final decision as to the type of charter to accept depends upon the owner's ability to evaluate the calculations and to foresee the demands for ships. If it is likely that there will be a significant increase in cargo movements in the near future, relatively short-term voyage charters are preferable in order to have the ships available when the expected higher rates will be paid. Should the indications point to a protracted period when rates will be held at the current level, a series of voyage charters of moderate length might be desirable. If, however, the forecast is for a severely depressed market which will bring freight rates to a low level, it would be prudent to accept time charters paying enough to meet capital and daily operating costs with either no profit or a very small difference between revenue and expenses.

Although any forecasts regarding the trend of world freight markets contain a high degree of conjecture, there are certain developments which serve as guideposts on which considerable reliance may be placed. When, for example, prominent grain-trading organizations charter ships to be tendered several months in the future, or fix ships under long-term time charter, these actions indicate that freight rates probably will remain at their current levels; if they do drop, the decline will not be very great. If major charterers are making neither short-term nor long-term commitments, it is a sign that these usually well-informed merchants expect ocean freights to drop significantly in the not-distant future.

Tramp shipowners, seeking always to find profitable employment for their ships, use these indicators to determine what kind of charter is desirable, given the circumstances they face. Frequently, the owner must decide between two offers, one to place the ship under a voyage charter, in which the compensation is payable for the actual tonnage of cargo loaded, and the other to commit her to a time charter on which the hire is an agreed price per deadweight ton, summer draft, per month, or a lump sum per day. An example of the comparison suggests the method followed.

A voyage charter paying twelve dollars a ton is under consideration for a ship of 64,000 tons deadweight capacity. The estimated time to complete the charter is forty days, and operating expenses for the contemplated voyage (including fuel and port fees) amount to $16,400 a day. After deducting requirements for fuel, water, and stores, a total of 61,800 tons is available for cargo. The calculation is:

Cargo revenue, 61,800 tons @ $12.00	$741,600
Voyage expense, 40 days @ $16,400	656,000
Earnings from the voyage	$ 85,600

The alternative is to place the ship under time charter at a rate which recognizes the charterer's responsibility for fuel and port fees. To determine what the charter hire should be for this venture, this calculation is made:

Net voyage expense, 40 days @ $12,000	$480,000
Earnings from voyage charter	85,600
Revenue required from 40-day time charter	$565,600
Charter hire per day	14,140
Rate per deadweight ton per 30-day month	6.63

A ship under voyage charter is always under the total control of her owner. The contract calls for transporting an agreed quantity of a certain cargo between named ports, is limited to the time required to load, to travel from port to port, and to discharge, and is fulfilled when delivery of the cargo is completed. Should the voyage be lengthened by unexpected heavy weather, the added expense must be borne by the owner. Unless otherwise provided by the contract, interruptions to cargo-working operations due to adverse weather conditions such as heavy rains, snow, or exceptionally high winds are charged to the owner. For self protection, the owner may stipulate the number of days allowed to load and to discharge the cargo, or may require a certain number of tons to be handled in each twenty-four hour period. Notwithstanding the aforementioned hazards, which are not all-inclusive, the great inducement for an owner to offer a ship for a voyage charter is that the hire usually is greater than that of a time charter, and the opportunity remains with the owner to take advantage of heightened demand for ships and consequent higher freight rates.

The owner of a vessel who is working the voyage charter market must always be on the alert for new opportunities. Ideally, as one charter is terminated, another is waiting for the ship, and the ports in which the ship discharges and loads are separated by very short distances, so that little time is lost between assignments. The reality is far removed from this ideal, and quite often an interval of several days elapses between completion of one charter and commencement of the next. This time of idleness is almost unavoidable, and if it does occur, it must be accepted as a hazard of tramping.

A notable example of excellent management is to be seen in the case of the *Scandic Wasa,* a motorship of 20,280 tons deadweight. On fuel consumption of 25 tons per day of intermediate fuel oil, the ship had a speed of 14 to $14\frac{1}{2}$ knots. In addition, she used an average of $1\frac{1}{2}$ tons of diesel fuel per day.

The first charter of the *Scandic Wasa* took effect at Amsterdam, when she went under time charter for a voyage to the Arabian Gulf at a rate of $7,350 per day. She was tendered in September. When this charter expired in November, the vessel was placed under another time charter from the Arabian Gulf to Japan via India. The rate was $12.50 per deadweight ton per month, equivalent to $8,300 per day. The duration of the charter was the time needed to accomplish the single voyage.

On her arrival in Japan, the owners of the *Scandic Wasa* welcomed the ship with instructions concerning another time charter. This called for a voyage with cargo from Japan to a grain loading port on the Rio de la Plata of Argentina; the routing was by way of the Cape of Good Hope. The time charter hire was $10.70 per deadweight ton per month, equal to $7,100 per day.

The voyage from Japan to the Argentine was accomplished in due course, but some delays were experienced on arrival in the river. The next employment for the *Scandic Wasa* was a time charter from Argentina to Italy, at a rate of $13.75 per deadweight ton per month ($9,100 per day). Discharged in Naples, the hard-working tramp proceeded in ballast to the nearby port of Casablanca, Morocco, to pick up a cargo of phosphate rock destined to Avonmouth, England. On completion of that assignment, she sailed in ballast for Detroit, Michigan, where further employment awaited her.

A frequent experience in tramp shipping is the necessity to send the ship on a fairly long voyage (as in this case, when the *Scandic Wasa* went to Detroit) at the owner's expense to reach the port where the next charter becomes effective. Sometimes the charterer can be induced to pay a "ballast bonus" to assist in meeting the cost of the voyage to the loading port. This desirable circumstance normally occurs, however, only when there is an existing or anticipated shortage of ships at the loading port, or the voyage is to commence at a place off the normal routes.

As has been noted earlier in this chapter, owners of tramp ships must observe the fluctuations of the charter market. While the hope is always present that it will be possible to capitalize on opportunities, it is true that there are many periods when all trades are depressed, and both liner and tramp freight rates are extremely low. Many ships lie idle, unable to find employment at any rate. When this situation arises, the oldest and least competitive ships are withdrawn from service and are placed in what the owners hope will be temporary lay-up. This action is taken only after careful consideration, because the cost of returning a ship to full commission can be very great. It is a melancholy fact of shipping that not all the laid-up ships are always restored to operation. Some of the oldest, slowest, smallest and, therefore, least productive ships, will be sold to the shipbreakers, because reactivation is too costly.

Whereas the liner service operator has a regular route and carries a predictable variety of cargoes proffered by a comparatively small number of shippers who use his or her vessels repeatedly, the tramp shipowner is required to find new clients almost every voyage.[2] Given the world-ranging nature of tramp ship employment, this would be an impossible task for an individual owner. The difficulty is resolved, as has been described in another chapter, by the brokers who are found in almost every port of commercial importance.

In the complex world of tramp shipping, there are brokers who have principals whose ships are engaged in many different trades, and therefore must have an extensive knowledge of the entire field of marine transportation. Inevitably, there also are individuals who handle one type of business more and more frequently, and who find themselves becoming specialists in a particular trade. In this manner brokers become specialists in matching ships with the movement of liquid petroleum cargoes or in finding charters for tankers; similarly, concentrating upon fixing ships to handle full loads of grain leads other experts to devote their attention exclusively to ships seeking grain cargoes, or the reciprocal relationship. There are, as might be expected, many large ship brokerage houses which serve the entire industry but have subdivided their activities and assigned specialists appropriately so that the greatest efficiency in negotiating charters can be attained.

Most chartering procedures commence with discussion of the acceptability of the standard charter party for the particular trade to which the ship is to be committed. These standard agreements have been drawn up, primarily by shipowners' groups such as the Baltic and International Maritime Council,[3] a multinational association of many tramp ship owners which has its headquarters in Copenhagen. These contracts incorporate the experience gained from hundreds of voyages in individual trades. While these standard charter parties are revised and brought up-to-date as frequently as possible, it is true that circumstances prevailing at a particular moment will bring about agreement on minor modifications in some clauses, changes of substance in other clauses, and deletion of inapplicable or unwanted terms. Great care must be exercised to assure that the changes do not run counter to court rulings, established practices of the trade, or other clauses in the contract. Brokers, of course, are responsible for safeguarding the interests of their principals.

Not only must brokers be well informed on those practices of the trade which are reflected in the terms and conditions of the charter party, but they also must be aware of the level of freight rates prevailing day by day in the trades in which their principals desire to participate. Fortunately for all concerned, the great majority of fixtures of ships under charter are published daily in bulletins compiled by large brokerage houses or in maritime trade journals. Although the specific terms which may have influenced the acceptability of a particular rate may not be known, the experience of the broker makes possible extremely accurate guesses about these matters.

In addition to these "open market" quotations, a number of ship fixtures never receive publicity. This situation arises most often in the case of long-term charters where unusual or unique circumstances have impelled substantial modification of standard terms and conditions. The other possibility for desiring to keep the deal out of the news is that neither party wishes to reveal the figures—the charterers for fear it will reveal their profit, and the shipowner because of reluctance to disclose the low rate, or vice versa. Complete secrecy is rarely maintained for any great length of time; the constant interchange of information about the market which occurs between brokers will serve, willy-nilly, as the medium of communications about these private deals.

An earlier chapter has included comment on the existence of standard charter parties covering a great number of trades. These documents have been criticized occasionally by charterers as being the exclusive handiwork of the shipowners, and do not provide adequate protection for the interests of the parties contracting to use the ships. The explanation for this criticism lies in the tramp shipowning profession's basic concern with the problems of operating ships in a great variety of circumstances. The owners have a common need to find solutions and to protect their financial positions. Shipowner organizations consequently have been formed to draw up contracts acceptable to their members.

The users of tramp ships, to the contrary, are not organized, nor is it likely that the wide disparity of their interests can be reconciled to the extent that a particular position can be taken and held against opposition.

This is not to denigrate attempts which have been made to bring charterers together to form proposals to present to the shipowners; in a number of instances, they have been successful and better relations between the two interests have come about. The limited successes, however, emphasize the fact that individual charterers often have problems which can be solved only by paying attention to those acknowledged difficulties.

So it comes about that the standard charter parties drawn up by the shipowners serve as the basis for negotiation of a contract. Every clause must be examined by the contracting parties to be sure that it applies in its entirety to the contemplated use of the ship; if it does not, it is common practice for the principals, advised by their brokers, to make mutually acceptable adjustments. One voyage charter party covering grain movements from Argentina was not rewritten for years. A number of its clauses became unacceptable and replacements, which became almost standard, were typewritten and pasted over the obsolete passages. Eventually a modernized version was adopted and printed, to the relief of all concerned.

This vignette of shipping history is cited to show that shipowners, by choice, operate under charter parties which are well known and have withstood the analyses and interpretation of courts of law and decisions of arbitrators. They believe, with considerable reason, that as each employment requires, it is better to make a few changes in the familiar contract than to draw up a completely new document which invites interpretation by a court in the event a dispute should arise. When new charter parties are proposed, they receive the most careful and searching scrutiny on the part of the owners, their lawyers, and the brokerage profession, to be sure that, insofar as possible, the interests of the shipowners are safeguarded. It is a highly commendable fact, therefore, that new, rewritten, or substantially revised charter parties, usually for specific commodity movements, emanate from many sources on a fairly regular basis. The tramp shipping industry may be called conservative, but it is not stagnant.

It is fitting, in rounding out this sketch of how tramp shipping is managed, to include a number of case histories of ships which operated under time and voyage charters. The following four examples illustrate many of the principles discussed in the preceding pages.

Western Australia to Antwerp/Hamburg Range. Motorship *Scotspark*, 25,000 metric tons, $21.50; 3,000 tons discharge free, barley. April 13-25.

This extremely brief report of an uncomplicated voyage charter is an example of the shorthand used in trade journals. The details, derived from other sources, make an interesting story.

The motorship *Scotspark* was a bulk carrier of 27,175 tons deadweight, with a below decks capacity for grain of 1,400,000 cubic feet (42,000 cubic meters). On a daily consumption of 40 tons of heavy oil and 2 tons of diesel fuel, she had a service speed of 15 knots. Her fuel tanks had a capacity of 2,152 tons, adequate for a fifty-one-day voyage without refueling.

In the grain trade from Australia to Europe, it is customary for charterers and owners to agree that the cargo will be loaded at the expense of the ship, at a minimum rate of 1,000 to 1,500 tons per weather working day. The cost of discharging in Europe is to be borne by the charterers, unless specific contractual provision is made to a different effect. In the case of the *Scotspark,* the shipowners undertook to defray the expense of unloading 3,000 tons of the barley cargo.

Barley is one of the lighter grains, and has a stowage factor of 56 cubic feet (1.68 cubic meters) to the long ton. The entire cargo space of the *Scotspark* would be filled when 25,000 tons had been taken aboard. To determine the tonnage available for fuel, the following computation was made:

Deadweight capacity at summer load line	27,175 tons
Barley cargo loaded	25,000 tons
Available for fuel, water, stores, etc.	2,175 tons
Estimated weight of water, stores, etc.	500 tons
Net tonnage available for fuel	1,675 tons

The record of this voyage shows that the ship arrived in Esperance Bay, Australia, on April 12, and tendered under the charter at the earliest permissible date, April 13. She departed Esperance Bay on April 14, arriving in Fremantle two days later. Cargo operations were finished and the *Scotspark* cleared for Antwerp via Table Bay (Cape Town, South Africa) on April 20. She arrived in Antwerp on May 31, after a forty-one-day voyage. Her average speed was 11 knots on a daily consumption of 30 tons of fuel. Her owners apparently decided to travel at the most economical speed for the dual purpose of reducing the cost of fuel and also eliminating the need to purchase replenishment fuel at Cape Town.

On completion of discharge, the *Scotspark* was time-chartered to Continental Lines for a voyage from Antwerp to the United States north of

Cape Hatteras, at a rate of $2,500 a day. The containerships of the charterer's line were unable to handle a bulk cargo. Rather than lose the business, the *Scotspark* was obtained for this one voyage.

> Vancouver to Antwerp/Hamburg Range. Motorship *Regina Oldendorff*, 37,150 tons deadweight cargo capacity; 1,620,000 cubic feet grain space. Lump sum $330,000, basis one discharging port, with option for two discharging ports $10,500 extra. Free in and out and trimmed. Eleven weather working days all purposes, Sundays and holidays excepted. Grain/seeds. April/May.

The *Regina Oldendorff* was a diesel-powered bulker of 37,150 tons deadweight on her summer load line. The charterer planned to use her to transport any kind of grain or a cargo of oilseeds, or a mixture of both, from Vancouver, British Columbia (Canada), to a port on the western European coast between Antwerp and Hamburg. From the fixture report, it is clear that when the ship was chartered the precise nature of the cargo was not known, and therefore the owner demanded that the charterer pay a fixed sum for the hire of the ship. The agreed lump sum payment was $330,000, which was owed regardless of how much grain or oilseed might be put aboard. To meet possible requirements to deliver the cargo in two ports, the charter party stipulated that this could be done for an additional $10,500. With these arrangements, the owner of the *Regina Oldendorff* was guaranteed a satisfactory revenue regardless of what kind of grain or seeds, or both, might be loaded.

It must be noted that there are various kinds of grain which have different stowage factors, some being light and others heavy. The oilseeds also vary in weight from light to heavy. Unless the charterer can assert positively what the tonnage and type of grain or seeds will be, the shipowner has no alternative to asking for a lump sum payment. It would be logical for the charterer to apportion the grain and oilseeds to make the most effective use of the ship's cargo space and deadweight.

The report of the *Regina Oldendorff's* performance under the charter party shows that she arrived in Vancouver on May 1, and sailed on May 9. She made the transit of the Panama Canal on May 21, and on June 5 arrived in Rotterdam, where she discharged her entire cargo. The charterer did not elect, by paying the additional fee, to have the vessel call at another port. Loading and discharging consumed a total of seventeen calendar days, including Sundays and holidays, which were not counted as part of the "all purposes" allowance of eleven days. The charter party also provided that only "weather working days" would be debited against cargo working time. The available data do not indicate whether adverse weather hindered cargo operations, so it is impossible to establish whether demurrage was incurred.

The *Regina Oldendorff*'s cargo was wheat ("heavy grain") which stowed at 45 cubic feet (1.32 cubic meters) per long ton. Her cargo space of 1,620,000 cubic feet (48,600 cubic meters) would be filled completely by 36,000 tons of grain. The record shows that the ship actually loaded 35,370 tons, a figure derived after taking these facts into consideration.

The ship was directed to sail from Vancouver direct to Panama, transit the Canal, and proceed by the shortest route to Rotterdam at a speed of 15 knots. At her summer load line, the *Regina Oldendorff* was permitted a total lift, including fuel, water, stores, and cargo, of 37,150 tons. The resulting calculation was:

Deadweight at summer load line		37,150 tons
Fuel (27 days @ 40 tons per day, plus safety		
reserve equal to 5 days' consumption)	1,280	
Water and stores	500	
Tonnage for ship's needs		1,780 tons
Quantity of wheat to be loaded		35,370 tons

Toledo, completing St. Lawrence, to Antwerp/Rotterdam. Motorship *Moordrecht,* Heavy grain, 15,500 tons from Toledo, $15.50, completing in St. Lawrence up to 21,500 tons, $8.50; option to load only in Toledo, $2.50 extra; option to discharge German North Sea port, 25 cents extra; option to discharge Avonmouth/Glasgow/Belfast, 50 cents extra. Free in and out and trimmed; 7 days all purposes, basis 4 days load if "top off" or 3 days without "topping off." 3,000 tons discharge. April.

The *Moordrecht* was a bulker with a deadweight capacity on summer load line of 22,430 tons. Her beam was less than the $75\frac{1}{2}$ feet maximum width of the locks on the St. Lawrence Seaway. Because the greatest depth in the channels of the Great Lakes is about 26 feet, the cargo to be loaded in Toledo was limited to 15,500 tons. The actual capacity of the ship, after deductions for fuel, water, stores, and equipment was 21,500 tons.

This charter party contains interesting options. The rate on the heavy grain (wheat) loaded in Toledo, Ohio, was $15.50 which, on a full cargo of 15,500 tons, would produce revenue to the ship of $240,250. By "topping off" in a St. Lawrence River port with 6,000 tons of wheat freighted at $8.50, the ship's earnings would be increased by $51,000 for a total of $291,250. If only the 15,500 tons lifted in Toledo were carried to Europe, the freight rate would be raised by $2.50 to $18.00 per ton, and would bring $279,000 to the ship. this would be $12,250 less than if the "topping off" cargo were taken aboard. A measurable part of this difference would be offset by the saving in ship time attained by not stopping in the St. Lawrence River port.

At the same time the ship was fixed for this business, the charterer was uncertain where delivery would be required. Flexibility, therefore, was written into the contract: the ship could be sent to a German port on the North Sea, a day's steaming distance from Amsterdam, on payment of twenty-five cents a ton above the stipulated freight rate. Should delivery be required in a port on the West Coast of the British Isles or in Belfast, Northern Ireland, the additional payment would be fifty cents a ton.

An essential part of the charter party was the statement that the charterer pay the cost of loading, trimming, and discharging the grain (free in and out and trimmed). Seven days were allowed for both loading and unloading; if more port time were used, the charterer would be subject to a bill for demurrage. Finally, the charterer guaranteed that the wheat would be discharged at the minimum rate of 3,000 tons a day.

The record of the voyage revealed that the *Moordrecht* sailed from Liverpool in ballast on April 7, and arrived in Toledo on April 28. She loaded her cargo and sailed for Montreal on April 30. Topping off was accomplished between May 2, when the *Moordrecht* arrived, and May 5, when she was cleared for Europe. Delivery of the cargo actually was made at Leith, on the east coast of Scotland; obviously special arrangements between the charterer and the owner were required for this development.

River Plate to U. K./Gibraltar–Hamburg Range/Mediterranean not east of the Adriatic. Motorship *North Emperor* 46,427 tons deadweight, and 1,893,000 cu. ft. grain space. 15 knots on 43 tons fuel oil, plus 2 tons diesel oil. $3,100 per day plus $127,500 ballast bonus. Trip, delivery River Plate, redelivery dropping pilot, U. K., Gibraltar–Hamburg range, or Mediterranean not east of the Adriatic. Charterers: Continental Grain Corporation. April.

To put the ship in position to carry out this time charter, it was necessary for the owner to send the *North Emperor* in ballast from Koper, near Trieste, in the former Yugoslavia, where her previous charter had terminated, to Argentina. The full cost of the voyage was for the owner's account, but the circumstances of the charter were somewhat unusual. From the statement in the fixture report that a payment of $127,500 would be made to the owner for the ballast voyage, it may be deduced that the market for ships at the time of the fixture was very competitive, and only a few vessels were available. To meet its own corporate commitments, Continental Grain Corporation was willing to assume part of the expense of the transatlantic voyage. The agreed charter hire of $3,100 per day was not to be paid until the ship had passed Recalada lightship (off Montevideo, Uruguay) on the way to Rosario, 191 miles up the Rio de la Plata (River Plate) from Buenos Aires.

The ship was time chartered for that period required to make the trip from the loading port in the River Plate to a port in the United Kingdom, or in Continental Europe between Gibraltar and the eastern shore of the Adriatic Sea. As is customary in time charters, the charterer was to pay not only the daily hire of $3,100 but also the cost of fuel consumed, which the owner warranted would not exceed 43 tons of intermediate grade fuel oil (1,000 seconds Redwood) plus 2 tons of diesel fuel for each twenty-four hours under way. The deadweight on its summer load line was stipulated to be 46,427 tons, and 1,893,000 cubic feet (56,790 cubic meters) of space below decks were guaranteed for a grain cargo.

To establish the precise moment when the ship would go "off hire," the charter party contained the provision that when the pilot was dropped as the ship was commencing her outbound voyage from the destination port, payments under the charter would cease.

The record of this voyage shows that the *North Emperor* departed from Koper on March 24, called at St. Vincent for bunkers on April 4, and arrived in Rosario on April 16. She was unable to depart from that port until April 23 because of congestion. On arrival in Buenos Aires, she experienced the same type of difficulty, and was delayed in finding a berth until May 5. Topping off operations were finished in time for the ship to sail for a port in Italy on May 7. The delays incurred in connection with loading were charged against the time charterer, whose responsibility, according to the terms of the charter party, commenced when the ship passed Recalada lightship and continued until she was redelivered at the end of the voyage in Italy.

Tramp shipping can be highly remunerative to owners when there is a brisk demand for transportation of cargoes moving in bulk, and can be disastrous when, for reasons beyond any possibility of control by the owner, there is a sudden reduction in requirements. Inherent in this situation is the fact that ships normally working in a certain trade will be reassigned to different routes whenever the need for carriers diminishes. In such circumstances, the competition becomes very intense, freight rates drop precipitately, and the older, less efficient ships may have to be laid up for lack of employment.

In a sense, the tramp ship's owner is nearly always at a disadvantage in the marketplace, because only very rarely is there so small a supply of ships that owners can set their prices on a "take or leave" basis. In the words of one economist, the shipowner is a "price taker," which means that the charterer usually dictates the maximum for ocean freights. Even granting that bold and venturesome carriers may send their ships to new geographical regions, or reassign them to a different trade, for the most part the owners' freedom to demand high rates is circumscribed by a variety of limitations.

Despite the problems which owners of tramp ships must face, it remains true that tramping is an enterprise in which the rewards can be extremely good, and therefore it attracts both individuals and corporations to invest their capital. Whereas in the years before World War II it was possible to purchase a ship for a sum not beyond the capability of one person (or a small group of investors) to raise, the great increase in the cost of ships resulting from their larger size, higher speed, more elaborate and hence more expensive accommodations for the officers and crew, and often the provision of costly cargo-working gear such as deck cranes, mechanically operated hatch covers, and better cargo ventilating equipment, have combined to reduce the number of individual adventurers. The number of ships has diminished in the post-World War II years, but total carrying capacity has grown as vessel sizes and speeds have increased in the ceaseless effort to achieve greater efficiency and therefore greater profit.

In the decades since 1945 the emergence of the large bulk carrier has had a profound impact upon the tramp shipping business. Formerly iron ore, coal, grain, and lumber moved in comparatively small ships which were interchangeable between these trades. When demand for steel, and consequently iron ore, suddenly exploded, the limited capacities of the general-purpose tramp, even though this ship had grown by almost 100 percent in its deadweight tonnage, proved to be unacceptable to industry,

The size of the 163,760-tons deadweight ore-oil carrier *Garden Green* (built 1973) is clearly evident. She was 280 meters long, 47.4 meters wide, with a draft of 17.7 meters. Photograph courtesy of Overseas Shipbuilding Group.

and the semispecialized bulk carriers became more and more prominent. In January 1993, there were 4,789 bulk carriers over 10,000 tons deadweight; their average deadweight was 44,414 tons. The biggest ships, of which there were 139 in 1993, had an average deadweight of 187,769 tons.[4] They require cargo-handling facilities in both loading and discharge ports because they have no cargo gear. Meeting more effectively the demands of the shippers, these vessels have very nearly preempted the trade in metallic ores. Some of them have been designed to carry alternative cargoes such as grain or fertilizers, and have become formidable competitors of the small general-purpose, dry cargo tramps.[5]

A further handicap which the conventional tramp must overcome is the invasion of the grain trade by tankers. It was only after the conclusion of hostilities in 1945 that it became practical to transport wheat in the cargo spaces of a tanker. This eventuated from the perfecting of a portable suction device which would remove wheat and other grain by pneumatic action rather than having to rely upon the conventional discharging equipment of the "marine leg" with its endless chain of buckets and a conveyor belt leading to the shoreside receptacles. Once the "vacuveyors" had demonstrated their effectiveness, literally scores of tankers were assigned to

Built in 1992, the 322,941 metric tons deadweight bulk carrier *Bergeland* was 338.7 meters (1,137.9 feet) long, 55 meters (184.8 feet) wide, and had a draft of 23 meters (77.2 feet). Her speed was 14.5 knots. Photograph courtesy of Bergesen d.y. AS.

carry grain. They were attractive to shippers because the cargo tanks were comparatively small, the hatches were of minimum size, and neither shifting boards nor feeders were needed. These advantages were translated into actual cash savings not only in the cost of these fittings, but also in ship time. Modern dry-cargo bulkers have compromised by installing portable shifting boards which are part of the ship's outfit and can be set up or removed in a short time, usually by the ship's crew.

Between the loss of iron ore and the keen competition for grain cargoes, the owners of conventional tramps have found it difficult to keep their ships employed, but they have earned higher profits during those times when demand has been strong for the type of tonnage they controlled. It remains true that most ports of the world have a limiting depth of between 30 and 35 feet, and it is to these shallow harbors that the modern, efficient, and economical tramps make their voyages.

Tramp shipping today requires, as does the entire steamship industry, a higher degree of managerial skill than formerly, as well as the tools of good management such as the computer, the satellite-relayed telephone, the fax machine, and the complex automation found more and more aboard ships as owners seek to enhance their profit-making capability by the use

Bulk wheat is delivered by the supply pipe and spread through the ship's hold. Photograph courtesy of Port of Sacramento, California.

of sleepless and tireless monitoring devices. This sophisticated type of supervision permits more effective control of ship use, more accurate cost determination, and superior overall performance. The essential requirements remain for a keen awareness of where the business can be found and when the freight rates are favorable for time charters rather than for voyage charters, and only skilled and careful owners are able to place their ships where they will meet the demands of the industrial world. There is now, and there always will be, a vital role for the tramp ship to play in the continuing drama of the commercial community.

CHAPTER FOUR

Chartering and Tramp Ship Operation

To nations with a maritime heritage—England, Norway, Sweden, Greece, Italy, and Japan are among the leaders—transporting people and goods across the seas has been an important economic activity for decades. No single country today dominates the world's shipping trade as did England before 1914, but seafaring, with all its ramifications, in many instances is a family occupation passed from generation to generation.

This tradition of life at sea helps to explain how men—and increasingly women, as careers at sea become available to them—can face patiently, courageously, and with spiritual satisfaction the labors involved in tramp ship operation. A typical voyage is marked by hard work and prolonged absence from the home port as the ship finds employment in the "cross trades," i.e., on routes that cross the oceans without touching the shores of home. In fact, it is somewhat exceptional when the vessel is assigned a voyage back to the land of her registry.

That protracted voyages are anything but unusual gives rise to a variety of problems in management. There are, for instance, the ever present necessities of fueling, provisioning, and putting the ship into ports never before visited. The master must cope with personnel changes occurring by reason of death, desertion, or illness; if crews are repatriated periodically, there are significant alterations in the composition of the ship's company. Although the cargo transported nearly always is one of the commodities moving in bulk, there still are cargo-loading problems to be solved. Port entrance and clearance routines for remote or infrequently visited places must be envisioned and anticipated. While some of these details may be handled from the owner's office in the distant homeland, many of them inevitably are delegated to the master of the ship. Throughout the voyage, the master must serve as the representative of the owner, and thus becomes to a measurable extent the custodian of that often shadowy figure's fortunes.

The competitive nature of the tramp trade, previously described in some detail, is such that no permanent system of government subsidy has been developed in any country. A very interesting and quite successful venture into this field was made by the British government in 1935, when world shipping was critically depressed. A law was passed setting up a fund of two million pounds sterling to help British tramp operators, on condition that the industry devise the means to administer the scheme. A Tramp Shipping Administrative Committee was formed to work toward the goals of minimizing domestic competition, improving freight rates and chartering conditions, and promoting the fullest employment of British ships in competition with vessels which received some form of governmental assistance. British tramps were rationed to prevent uneconomic competition, and through the efforts of cooperating owners the rates of charter hire were fixed at levels which prevailed in 1934. These were sufficient only to keep the ship in operation, without allowance for depreciation or interest. The stability that resulted did improve market rates about 15 percent in the first year, even though the volume of cargo moving remained unchanged. The scheme was continued until 1938. No similar comprehensive plan has been instituted in the post-World War II decades.[1]

Tramp ships receive no undisguised subsidy today, nor are there regulations governing where the ships shall go, or how many voyages must be completed each year. Fleets vary in size from one to many ships, depending upon the financial status of the individual owners.[2]

The home office of the tramp relies upon brokers around the world for representation in the constant search for cargoes. Daily, and sometimes hourly, cables and faxes come from many regions with information or offers of business. Decisions are reached and shipmasters, agents, brokers, and governments are informed of what the owner deems best in a wide variety of circumstances. Modern communications have changed the customs and procedures of the trade to the extent that the master no longer is expected to find employment for the ship when a charter expires. The master, however, must be not only an excellent seaman, but also a good administrator, an expert in personnel management, and a conscientious representative of the owners.

Tramp owners depend upon ship brokers to provide opportunities for employment of their ships. To describe the relationship between them, it is fitting to simulate the daily drama of chartering vessels, and to follow the actions of the participants. The following situation is entirely fictitious, but the methods depicted are those in current use.

King Corporation is a wheat exporting firm in Chicago which purchases grain in the American market and then sells it to European customers. It does not, however, own any ships, leaving the burdens of vessel operation to specialists, and relies upon brokers to find suitable ships, invariably taken on voyage charters.

A French importer has purchased 200,000 tons of American wheat (heavy grain) through King Corporation, and has directed that delivery of the first shipload of at least 60,000 tons be made by March 30. King is to make and pay for all arrangements to transport the wheat. Both King and the importer require that the vessel chartered must hold the highest rating from the ship classification organization.

Through its broker, James Sharp, in New York, King seeks an acceptable ship at the lowest possible freight rate. Sharp canvasses the other brokerage houses, but finds nothing listed in New York which meets King's requirements. Sharp therefore cables his London counterpart, Thomas White, to ask for assistance, well aware that White can go to the Baltic Exchange and will in short order be able to offer a suitable ship. The cable to White is phrased in these words:

```
RELIABLE PRINCIPAL OFFERS FIRM CARGO OF
60,000 TO 70,000 TONS HEAVY GRAIN NEW
ORLEANS TO ONE PORT BORDEAUX-HAMBURG RANGE,
LOADING NEW ORLEANS FIRST HALF MARCH. WILL
USE GRAINVOY CHARTER.
```

White understands from this cable that a ship able to carry not less than 60,000 tons of cargo in addition to fuel, stores, and water must be in New Orleans ready to load between the first and fifteenth of March. The charter party to be used is a well-known document developed to meet the peculiarities of grain shipment. White has a copy of the Grainvoy charter party in his office.

Perusal of the list of ships represented by White discloses that none of these vessels will be ready within the time limits. White therefore proceeds to the floor of the Baltic Exchange, where he meets brokers seeking cargoes for their principals' ships and other brokers looking for ships to transport cargoes. White quickly makes contact with Harrison Burnett, who represents Olav Berg, a Norwegian owner domiciled in Bergen. Burnett tells White that Berg's big motorship *Great Viking* will be off-hire in a Texas port near the end of February. White requests a firm offer of this ship, and Burnett accordingly cables Berg, his principal, as follows:

```
FIRST CLASS CHARTERER MAKES FIRM OFFER OF
CARGO OF 60,000 TO 70,000 TONS HEAVY GRAIN
```

NEW ORLEANS TO ONE PORT BORDEAUX-HAMBURG
RANGE. LOADING NEW ORLEANS MARCH ONE THROUGH
FIFTEEN. USING GRAINVOY CHARTER. PLEASE
OFFER FIRM BY FIFTEEN HUNDRED HOURS LONDON
TIME TODAY.

Berg is pondering how to work his ship back to Norway. White's
invitation to offer the *Great Viking* fits his desires exactly, so he immediately responds to Burnett with this cable:

NORWEGIAN MOTORSHIP GREAT VIKING, SERVICE
SPEED 15 KNOTS, 70,000 TONS DEADWEIGHT,
79,500 CUBIC METERS GRAIN CAPACITY. SEVEN
HOLDS, GEARLESS, CLASSED HIGHEST AT DET
NORSKE VERITAS, NOW DISCHARGING HOUSTON AND
EXPECTED READY TO LOAD AFTER MARCH SECOND.
SUBJECT TO REPLY REACHING US BY SEVENTEEN
HUNDRED HOURS TOMORROW BERGEN TIME,
AUTHORIZE YOU TO NEGOTIATE FOR FULL CARGO
HEAVY GRAIN 62,000 METRIC TONS, FIVE PERCENT
MORE OR LESS AT VESSEL'S OPTION FROM ONE US
GULF PORT TO ONE PORT BORDEAUX-
HAMBURG RANGE. DISCHARGING PORT DECLARABLE
ON SIGNING BILLS OF LADING. CANCELING DATE
MARCH TENTH. FREIGHT EIGHTEEN DOLLARS FIFTY
CENTS PER METRIC TON, FREE IN AND OUT AND
TRIMMED, LOADING AND UNLOADING SIX WEATHER
WORKING DAYS, SUNDAYS AND HOLIDAYS INCLUDED.
LAYTIME REVERSIBLE. DEMURRAGE FOURTEEN
THOUSAND THREE HUNDRED DOLLARS PER DAY,
DISPATCH HALF DEMURRAGE. ALL DOLLAR
QUOTATIONS PREDICTED ON EXCHANGE RATE US
DOLLARS TO NORWEGIAN KRONER PREVAILING CLOSE
OF BUSINESS ON DAY BILLS OF LADING ARE
SIGNED. GRAINVOY CHARTER ACCEPTABLE EXCEPT
LAYTIME FOR LOADING TO COMMENCE AT NINETEEN
HUNDRED HOURS IF NOTICE OF READINESS
TENDERED BETWEEN THIRTEEN AND SEVENTEEN
HUNDRED HOURS. DEMURRAGE TO BE PAID PER DAY
OR PER HALF DAY AND NOT OTHERWISE PRORATED.

BROKERAGE COMMISSIONS PAYABLE MAXIMUM THREE
PERCENT OF CHARTER HIRE.

Burnett immediately visits White's office, and the two brokers ana-
lyze the message from Berg. The ship can lift the minimum quantity of
grain specified by Sharp, and she can be in New Orleans within the time
limit. The obligation to declare the port of discharge at the time the bills of
lading are signed by the master is consistent with good chartering practice:
the master must know the destination of the voyage about to be undertaken.
The freight rate assigns all costs of handling the grain at both loading and
unloading ports to the charterer. Time allowed to take grain aboard and to
discharge it is adequate given the facilities at the port of New Orleans and
the probable destination ports, and covers the possibility that one port may
be superior to another in its ability to work ships rapidly. By permitting
whatever time is saved in one port to be credited toward the allowed
working days in the other port, the charterer is encouraged to use the
hours effectively. Demurrage—the charge for keeping the ship in port
beyond the permitted number of working days—is an essential part of
any voyage charter, and usually represents the owner's costs and a very
small margin of profit. Berg obviously is eager for the business, since he
offers to pay brokerage commissions a little higher than the normal rate
of $2\frac{1}{2}$ percent.

White considers the terms of the offer fair and reasonable when compared to the current charter market, and sends a cable to Sharp in New
York, relaying everything except the rate of commission, which for Sharp's
information is quoted as 1 percent. For his part, Sharp notified King Corporation of the offer and is instructed to make a counter proposal, which is
presented to White in this cablegram:

REFERENCE YOUR CABLE OF YESTERDAY OFFERING
GREAT VIKING SUBJECT TO REPLY REACHING US BY
SEVENTEEN HUNDRED HOURS TODAY NEW YORK TIME.
CHARTERERS ACCEPT OWNERS OFFER EXCEPT LAY
DAYS TO BE MARCH FOUR TO TWELVE INCLUSIVE.
FREIGHT RATE TO BE SEVENTEEN DOLLARS AND
TWENTY FIVE CENTS. LAY TIME TO BE SEVEN DAYS
SUNDAYS AND HOLIDAYS EXCLUDED. DEMURRAGE TO
BE THIRTEEN THOUSAND SEVEN HUNDRED DOLLARS
PER DAY PAYABLE DAY BY DAY AND PRORATED FOR
ANY PART OF A DAY.

On receipt of this message, White presents the modifications to Burnett, who, as a broker, has no authority to accept or reject the proposed changes. He therefore relays the cable to Berg by fastest means.

Berg in the meantime has noted that the charter market is weak, and that his original offer of $18.50 is out of competition. A recomputation of the cost of the anticipated voyage shows that a rate of $17 would yield an acceptable profit. He knows that once grain loading and discharging operations commence, they proceed without stop. He is aware that he is under pressure to pay dispatch money when the charter asks for seven days cargo-working time. There also is the demand for the ship to stand idle on Sundays and holidays, which would cut into the profit remaining when the rate is reduced to the proposed figure per ton. All these factors having been given due consideration, Berg sends this cable to Burnett:

```
REFERENCE YOUR CABLE REGARDING GREAT VIKING.
CHARTERER'S COUNTER OFFERS ACCEPTABLE EXCEPT
LAYTIME REMAINS AT SIX WEATHER WORKING DAYS
SUNDAYS AND HOLIDAYS INCLUDED.
```

Burnett notifies White of this response, and the information is transmitted immediately to Sharp in New York, who recommends to King Corporation that the terms set by the shipowner be accepted without further negotiation. King is pleased that the freight rate has been reduced, and concedes the other modifications. Sharp therefore is instructed to close the deal, which is done by the following cable to White:

```
REFERENCE YOUR CABLE. GREAT VIKING ACCEPTED.
CHARTERERS ARE KING CORPORATION OF CHICAGO.
AUTHORIZE YOU TO SIGN CHARTER ON CHARTERER'S
BEHALF BUT AS BROKER ONLY. AIRMAIL SIX
COPIES OF COMPLETED CHARTER. THANK YOU FOR
YOUR EFFORTS.
```

White passes the word to Burnett, who notifies Berg that his ship has been fixed for the voyage. Berg acknowledges the message in this cable:

```
REFERENCE YOUR CABLE CONCERNING GREAT
VIKING. THIS CONFIRMS THAT TERMS AS APPROVED
BY CHARTERER ARE ACCEPTABLE.
```

SHIP WILL BE ORDERED TO NEW ORLEANS TO
ARRIVE MARCH FOURTH. AUTHORIZE YOU TO SIGN
CHARTER AS MY BROKER. SEND ME THREE COPIES
OF CHARTER. THANK YOU FOR THIS BUSINESS.

Burnett relays this confirmation of the charter to White, who closes his file with this cablegram to Sharp:

RECONFIRM FIXTURE OF GREAT VIKING. SHIP
ORDERED TO ARRIVE NEW ORLEANS MARCH FOURTH.
THANK YOU FOR THIS BUSINESS.

Negotiations having been brought to a successful conclusion, the charter party is filled out by White's staff, and copies are distributed as directed by the principals. The original document, duly signed by Burnett and White, is filed in the vault at White's office and is available to authorized persons at any time.

Berg composes a brief message instructing the master of the *Great Viking* to sail for New Orleans to arrive in that city during the forenoon of March 4, so that loading can commence that same day. This cablegram is followed by an airmail letter enclosing a coy of the charter party and specific instructions for the conduct of the voyage. In the gracious tradition of shipping, this letter is concluded with the statement: "We take this opportunity to express the hope that you will have a pleasant and satisfactory voyage."

For their part in the transaction, the three brokers will each receive 1 percent of the net earnings of the *Great Viking* under the charter, after demurrage or dispatch is paid.

A new development in chartering made its debut in 1985 when the Baltic International Freight Futures Exchange (BIFFEX) began operation. Through buying and selling "index points," it now is possible for shipowners or charterers to protect themselves against the likelihood that charter hire will decline or rise before the ship is available to lift a cargo, or the cargo is ready for transportation.

Thirteen significant ocean trading routes on which dry cargo moves in chartered vessels have been chosen by the exchange, and weighted according to their relative importance in the world tramp market. Each day, the members of a panel of ship brokers who belong to the Baltic Exchange, individually and without consultation, submit the spot rates which they consider applicable to the thirteen routes. The panel's recommended rates are entered into a computer which has been appropriately programmed. From the computer is derived the so-called Baltic Freight Index, which is published in maritime and commercial journals:

BALTIC FREIGHT INDEX

1473 (June 30, 1993) Previous day—1484

The Baltic International Freight Futures Market in London offers owners and charterers in the bulk shipping community a forum for futures trading of a freight rate index. The contracts are based on the Baltic Freight Index, announced daily, of 15 routes listed below.

Routes	Commodity	Weight	Dollars/ Metric Ton	Index
U.S. Gulf-North Continent	L. Grain	10%	13.567	1494
Trans-Atlantic Round	Time Charter	10%	10,583*	1615
U.S. Gulf-Japan	H. Grain	10%	24.208	1695
Skaw Passero-Taiwan-Japan	Time Charter	10%	14,083*	1901
U.S. North Pacific-Japan	H. Grain	7.5%	13.675	1482
Trans-Pacific Round	Time Charter	7.5%	10,592*	1575
U.S. Gulf-Venezuela	H. Grain	5%	19.042	1631
Skaw Passero-Far East	Time Charter	5%	14,225*	1759
Hampton Roads-Richards Bay-Japan	Coal	7.5%	13.325	1292
Hampton Roads-Rotterdam	Coal	5%	5,733	1178
Queensland-Rotterdam	Coal	5%	10.433	0949
Far East-Europe	Time Charter	5%	7,692*	1015
Tubarao-Rotterdam	Iron Ore	5%	6.008	1171
Casablanca-West Coast India	Phosrock	2.5%	38.208	1070
Aqaba-West Coast India	Phosrock	5%	19.217	1419

*Dollars per day.

Each Baltic Freight Index point has been assigned an arbitrary value of $10.00. Any shipowner or charterer may purchase or sell points by arranging with a member of the BIFFEX to represent them on the floor of the Baltic Exchange. A deposit from the trade is required, and if the market moves contrary to expectations, the broker will demand payments equal to the decline in the market value of the index. As each transaction is accomplished, the information is transmitted for inclusion in the computer of the International Commodities Clearing House, Limited, which daily produces a record of all dealings. The dealings are then confirmed by the members of the BIFFEX. The clearing house also serves as the banker for the BIF-

FEX, and provides a guarantee that the contracts will be fulfilled. Contracts are fulfilled by either purchase or sale of the futures contracts, or by a cash payment at stipulated times during the year.

Simplified examples of the use of futures to protect against the fluctuations in charter hire will demonstrate the working of the plan.

A ship of 100,000 tons capacity will be available in three months for a voyage from Hampton Roads to Japan, carrying high grade coal. On October 1, the freight rate for this trip is $12.00 per ton, producing an income of $1,200,000 for the voyage. The BIFFEX index on October 1 is 1,000, and the index forecast for January 1 also is 1,000. One contract on the BIFFEX, at $10.00 per point, has a correspondent value of $10,000. The owner sells 120 contracts at the rate of $10.00 per point, and gains the equivalent of the ship's earning. In October, the owner was pessimistic, and predicted that the market would decline by January 1. This expectation was realized when rates dropped by 10 percent to $10.80 per ton. The owner bought back the 120 contracts for $1,080,000. This resulted in a net profit on the futures transaction of $120,000, which offset the loss of an equal amount of the vessel's charter hire.

In a similar manner, a charterer might hedge a commitment for future movement of cargo. On October 1, the charter rate for heavy grain shipped from New Orleans to Rotterdam was $9.00 per ton, with reliable indications that the level would drop before January 1. The shipper of grain planned to send a parcel of 50,000 tons to Rotterdam, loading on January 1. On October 1, the BIFFEX index stood at 1,000. The charterer therefore bought fifty contracts at the price of $9.00 per point, paying $450,000 for the lot. As anticipated, the market did rise, and on January 1, the quoted rate was $9.90 per ton of grain. The contracts were sold for $9.90, and realized $495,000 for the charterer, who thus had adequate funds to pay the increased freight rate.[3]

The competition mentioned earlier in the analysis of tramp shipping manifests itself principally in the rates charged by different shipowners for transporting the same commodities. A superficial glance at the reports of ship fixtures might suggest that these rates are established in a casual fashion. To the contrary, much thought and skill are required to develop the rates of charter hire. Fluctuations reflect the circumstances facing both owners and charterers at the precise moment that a decision must be reached. The first step in determining the price is to estimate the cost of performing under the charter. Success or failure—both in the sense of obtaining the business and in earning a profit—may hinge upon the difference of a few cents a ton.

Of the numerous factors influencing the formation of freight rates, it is generally acknowledged that the value of the commodity has the greatest significance. In theory, the shipper of a ton of gold is able to pay $2,000 for its transportation, while the exporter of coal, which has a value at the mine of only $10.00 a ton, often cannot accept a rate of $3.00 a ton. Economically, tramp shipping exists to provide the transportation required by those articles of low value exemplified by coal. To do this, the tramp shipowner must set freight rates which are low enough to encourage the movement of goods yet high enough to cover the expense of operating the ship and, ideally, to earn at least a small profit.

Knowing costs down to the smallest detail is one way in which the owner attempts to achieve this objective. "Costs," in this connection, means more than simply the obvious out-of-pocket expenses involved in ship operation; also included must be the less conspicuous items such as amortization, interest, and overhead. For example, a general-purpose tramp with operating costs of $300 an hour is chartered to carry a load of 25,000 tons of coal. Loading at the rate of 750 tons an hour will absorb thirty-four hours. Only 250 tons are discharged per hour, for a total of one hundred working hours. The charter rate must include a charge for 134 hours at $300 per hour ($1.61 per ton) to recover costs.

Some owners develop comprehensive tables of ship costs per deadweight ton which include crew wages and subsistence, vessel maintenance and repair, insurance, amortization, interest, and a contribution toward overhead. Whether the ship is lying in port waiting for assignment or steaming across the ocean, these items do not vary substantially. The costs that do change with the employment of the vessel are fuel, port fees, pilotage, towage, dockage and wharfage, and cargo handling. When all costs are compiled, the owner should add a sum sufficient to cover all unforeseen contingencies and to provide a profit. If the market is "strong," meaning that there are many cargoes and few ships, these cost figures can be used without trimming when negotiating for a charter. If, however, the market is considered "weak" because there are many ships and few cargoes, the owner must exercise the most exquisite judgment in cutting the estimates of cost to meet the figures quoted by competitors. Sometimes it is necessary to accept business at an actual loss rather than incur the expense of laying up the ship.

Under a gross form voyage charter, for example, a bulk carrier is chartered ("fixed") to carry 50,000 tons of coal from Norfolk, Virginia, to Rotterdam at the agreed rate of $10 per ton. The shipowner must pay $5 a ton for loading and discharging the coal. Ship operating expenses are $12,500 a day; for the fifteen days required to load, sail, and discharge, the total cost is $187,500. Cargo handling and ship costs aggregate $437,500, leaving a profit to the owner of $62,500. Any delays in the ship's passage, or unexpected increase in the cost of fuel or cargo handling reduce the margin of profit significantly.

Computer technology has given the modern shipowner the capability of sophisticated examination of all the elements of cost and potential profit involved in a proposed voyage. Every item of expense can be identified as it relates to the total venture. For instance, the ship's speed is seen as a function of her fuel consumption at different cruising speeds, the smoothness of her hull, and the price of fuel at various bunkering ports. The rapidity with which the proposed cargo can be handled in the ports of loading and discharge affects significantly the calculations concerning the length of the voyage. The actual number of tons of a given commodity which can be stowed below decks must be related to the amount of space needed to accommodate 1 weight ton. Detentions may be individually unimportant, but cumulatively can be disastrous. The profitability of the voyage can be profoundly affected by the availability and willingness of longshoremen to work overtime or on holidays and religious festivals, the number of hours needed to prepare the ship to accept the proposed load, delays in putting the ship alongside the cargo-working berth, and loss of time resulting from shortages of pilots or tugs in the harbor. This detailed analysis provided by the computer provides the owner with solid bases for the required decisions.

In working out the finances of the voyage or voyages, the computer can develop, in any desired detail, such items as these: costs of the ship lying in port at anchor and at the berth working cargo; costs of the ship steaming fully loaded at designed speed; fuel consumption at different speeds and drafts; costs of fuel when purchased at different points along the route, compared with the time needed for refueling; port and harbor charges, with particular reference to harbor dues on entering the port and accrued day by day until departure; costs of loading and discharging the cargoes contemplated for the complete voyage; and the costs of overtime paid to the ship's crew when cargo is being worked.

Once these data are available, it is possible to determine the details of the proposed employment of the vessel: the itinerary of the ship, showing for each port the arrival time, waiting time, predictable lost time, and anticipated departure time; costs for each port where cargo is worked, includ-

This shipboard gantry crane can be fitted with different specialized cargo-handling devices to expedite loading and unloading. Photograph courtesy of Munck International.

ing stevedoring and overtime expenses; and total costs of harbor dues and fees. From these basic figures, management can obtain summaries of the cost to transport 1 ton or a full shipload, the total revenue to be earned on the contemplated voyage, and an analysis of the financial results of the planned employment. This last presentation would include depreciation, interest, overhead, ship operating costs, port charges, cargo-handling expense, and the net profit (or less) at the offered freight rate.

Just as the computer has made management much more systematic and less dependent upon instinct and experience, so the advances in naval architecture and marine engineering have influenced profoundly the development of the tramp fleets of the world. The importance and versatility of the general-purpose tramp already have been set forth. The preferred carrier in the bulk trades, except in ore, in 1993 was one which had a cargo deadweight between 25,000 and 40,000 tons, had adequate cargo gear to be self-sustaining, and had a sufficiently shallow draft to permit entrance into almost any port.

The medium-sized bulker is a vessel of approximately 50,000 to 60,000 tons deadweight. This ship has no cargo gear, and is popular in both the northern transatlantic and the northern transpacific routes hauling coal and grain.[4]

In the specialized iron ore service, the ship most favored in 1993 was the bulker with a capacity between 100,000 and 125,000 tons of cargo. By assigning these ships to voyages between deep-draft harbors, their utility and inherent economy of scale have been exploited successfully.

CHAPTER FIVE

Organization of a Liner-Service Company

Every steamship company, regardless of country of origin or location of corporate headquarters, is organized to meet its own particular needs and its own specialized functions. Therefore, no uniform pattern of organization exists in the workaday world of shipping. Nevertheless, the functions of the different officials, by whatever title they may be known, are sufficiently similar to permit their identification within the corporate structure.

The top of the pyramid is the *board of directors*, usually made up of persons who have a financial or managerial interest in the company. The board may consist of from five to twenty or more people elected by the stockholders and responsible to them for proper management of the business. Always included as a voting member of this board is the chairperson. Increasingly, in American corporate practice, this person also is the chief executive officer, meaning that he or she takes an active part in the affairs of the company and makes major decisions within the authority conferred by the board. The president of the company, who in modern American business also serves as the chief operating officer, is exactly what that descriptive title indicates, and therefore is a member of the board. The treasurer, as the financial advisor, and the secretary, who keeps the minutes of the meetings and authenticates all official documents, very often serve as members of the board. In all matters of magnitude, especially those involving massive expenditures (as, for instance, the purchase or construction of ships, or entering into or withdrawing from a trade route) and the selection of senior executives, the board makes the final decision.

The *president*, as the chief operating officer, is responsible to the board for the proper functioning of the entire organization. This person may have come up through the ranks of the company, or may have been brought in at or near the top. As the supervisor of all activities, the president does not become involved for any protracted period of time in the detailed working of any specific division. As ships and their supporting operations have become more expensive, the office of the president inevitably has been concerned primarily with the financial aspects of the company, and a primary consideration in the choice of a president is the soundness of past financial judgments made in difficult circumstances.

The demands upon the president's time imposed by these fiscal burdens have resulted in the delegation of much of the supervision of daily activity to the *executive vice president*, who may be described accurately as the chief of staff. This officer is responsible for seeing that the policies promulgated by the board and the president are carried out. Within the scope of authority of the position, the executive vice president makes all appropriate routine decisions and sends to the president's desk only those matters requiring special consideration. The executive vice president is able to assume the duties of the president whenever that official is absent from the office, and in this capacity as "alternate president" must be as well informed as the president about the affairs of the company.

The *secretary* maintains the official records of the corporation, supervises transfers and issuance of stock certificates (if the corporation is publicly held), accepts service of legal papers drawn against the corporation, and can represent it in any court when identification of records or other similar data is an issue. The secretary also is responsible for preparing the annual report to the stockholders, usually in conjunction with the treasurer and the executive vice president.

Many of the secretary's duties involve legal matters, and consequently it is not unusual for this person to be a lawyer. Should it be consistent with company policy, the legal section (sometimes known as the house counsel) may be placed under the secretary's supervision. This important segment of the organization usually consists of one or more lawyers who provide legal advice, comment on the significance of court decisions and the impact of new laws, assist trial attorneys in preparing court cases, and take part in negotiations where interpretation of contract terms may be needed.

Acting primarily as financial advisor to the board chairperson and the president, the *treasurer* obtains the requisite information from the comptroller, cashier, accountants, and auditors. The treasurer is able, at any time, to report on the complete financial position of the company and to discuss areas of fiscal strength and weakness. In some steamship organizations, the offices of secretary and treasurer are merged into one.

To keep control over the multitude of financial records which must be maintained by a steamship company (especially if it holds a subsidy contract with the U.S. government), some organizations include in the executive structure a *vice president for finance*. The auditors, accountants, and bookkeepers, as well as pursers aboard ship, come under this officer's su-

CHART NO. 1   ORGANIZATION OF A TYPICAL AMERICAN LINER-SERVICE COMPANY

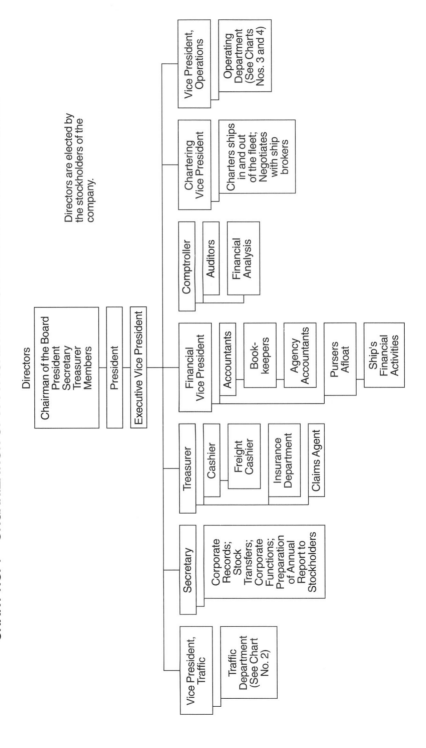

pervision. As a master accountant, the vice president for finance cooperates with the treasurer in keeping the president, the board of directors, and stockholders informed on financial matters. Because of the obvious overlap of functions, it is not unusual for the offices of treasurer and vice president for finance to be merged.

Analyzing the significance of accounts and supervising the operating budget are rather exact sciences, especially as computer technology is applied to financial management. Larger companies today recognize the need for qualified specialists in this area, and have established the office of *comptroller* to handle all aspects of fiscal control. This officer is assisted by the auditors, who oversee accounting procedures and inspect financial records. In general terms, the comptroller supervises expenditures in accordance with the budget while overseeing routines of fiscal administration. In smaller companies, the treasurer performs the duties of the comptroller, assisted by the auditor and chief accountant.

From time to time, liner-service operators have occasion to charter ships into and out of their fleets. As has been described in detail elsewhere in this volume, chartering is a specialized form of endeavor, and in those organizations where it occurs with some frequency, full responsibility for this activity, with authority to make final commitments, is assigned to a vice president. Regardless of title or location within the corporate structure, the official handling charters must keep abreast of the employment of the company fleet and the potential demand for additional tonnage or the development of a surplus. As circumstances warrant, the *chartering vice president* provides extra ships or finds charters for those which are temporarily redundant.

Aside from chartering, the functions of the officials described above are substantially the same as those of senior executives of any corporation. Essential to their success are high moral character, inspiring leadership, and sound business judgment. It is an advantage if these officials have the widest possible familiarity with the maritime industry, since this will assure them of respect in the business community while providing a sound foundation for their decisions.

Maritime transportation is a business with specialized aspects, but is not unique as an economic enterprise. It exists to make a profit, and must sell its product (transportation) to the public in precisely the same manner that the tire manufacturing industry must find markets for automobile and truck tires. Terminology differs, of course, but the realities of competition, cost, plant modernization, and promotion are as clearly defined in the shipping firm as they are in any manufacturing firm. The techniques of management are, in their essentials, the same as in other forms of business. Circumstances and factors influencing the activities of a steamship company often are remote from, and completely beyond the control of, the maritime community, but even here there are similarities with other types of commercial enterprise.

As a case in point, the traffic department of the liner-service company has the same goals as the sales division of a tire manufacturer. Both must sell their respective products, transportation and tires. The techniques of salesmanship, adapted to the maritime industry, can be applied successfully to "merchandising" transportation. The vice president, traffic, is responsible for keeping a constant flow of cargo coming to the ships just as the director of sales must find buyers for the tires.

The operating department of a shipowning corporation should be viewed in a similar manner to the production division of a manufacturing concern, to which it bears a striking resemblance. Just as the production vice president is required to oversee all details relating to the manufacture of the rubber tires previously mentioned, and must adjust output to meet the requirements of the sales force, so the vice president in charge of marine operations must insure that the ships are kept in good condition, on schedule, and in all respects able to provide the service promised by the sales staff to the shippers.

In shipping, as in manufacturing, the traffic (sales) and operating (production) departments are complementary and interdependent. The transportation sales staff must be assured that ships will be available to lift the cargoes they procure; the operating department must have the cargoes to fill the ships they have brought into port. As one executive explained, "The best traffic department in the world cannot survive without a good operating department; the finest operating group has no reason for existence unless it is supported by a good sales force."

TRAFFIC DEPARTMENT

The *vice president, traffic*, directs the department charged with generating the cargo to fill the company ships.

This officer reports to the president through the executive vice president, keeping both these officials informed on all matters related to both outbound and inbound cargo. Within the department, the vice president, traffic, sets policies to achieve the goals assigned by the president and the board of directors. As an expert on traffic, this vice president may be called upon to work with carriers to solve matters of mutual concern, or to consult

CHART NO. 2   TRAFFIC DEPARTMENT

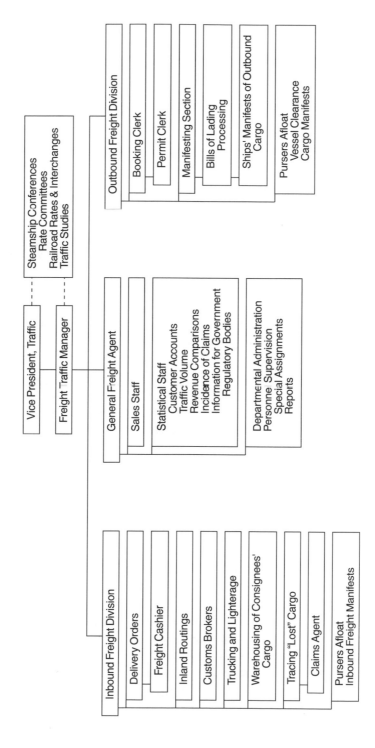

Vice President, Traffic

Steamship Conferences
Rate Committees
Railroad Rates & Interchanges
Traffic Studies

Freight Traffic Manager

Outbound Freight Division

Booking Clerk

Permit Clerk

Manifesting Section

Bills of Lading
Processing

Ships' Manifests of Outbound
Cargo

Pursers Afloat
Vessel Clearance
Cargo Manifests

General Freight Agent

Sales Staff

Statistical Staff
Customer Accounts
Traffic Volume
Revenue Comparisons
Incidence of Claims
Information for Government
Regulatory Bodies

Departmental Administration
Personnel Supervision
Special Assignments
Reports

Inbound Freight Division

Delivery Orders

Freight Cashier

Inland Routings

Customs Brokers

Trucking and Lighterage

Warehousing of Consignees'
Cargo

Tracing "Lost" Cargo

Claims Agent

Pursers Afloat
Inbound Freight Manifests

with important shippers whose problems are of a magnitude so great that they merit attention from an executive in the organization.

The vice president, traffic, must spend considerable time conferring with fellow executives, especially from the operating and chartering departments, as to the proper scheduling of ships, seasonal changes in demand for shipping space, better employment of the fleet, improvements in design for projected new or modernized tonnage, plans for the acquisition or disposition of vessels, and ways and means of minimizing stevedoring expense. The vice president, traffic, also deals with the claims agent, the insurance manager, and the financial manager to develop better ways to handle claims for compensation for damaged or lost cargo. From time to time this officer will confer with the terminal manager and the stevedore to consider techniques of cargo handling which might lead to fewer claims. Now and again he or she will be involved in formulating, with the comptroller, freight cashier, and vice president for finance, a policy dealing with the collection of freight charges. In a company handling all of its cargo in containers, the vice president, traffic, will confer with the terminal manager to ascertain that access to the terminal is satisfactory, that control procedures are working properly, and that receipts and deliveries are meeting company promises to shippers and consignees.

Outside the company, the vice president, traffic, may serve as a member of an industry group studying ways to improve packaging of goods or to standardize practices of booking full container loads of cargo. As the patterns of business place greater emphasis on intermodal transportation, much time is devoted to making rates which will cover the costs of inland transportation, and which therefore must be acceptable to railroads, trucking contractors, and the government regulatory bodies.

If the company belongs to an association of steamship lines which regulates competition and sets uniform freight rates, the vice president, traffic, may represent the organization at times when a firm commitment to a certain principle or policy is required. He or she may also be part of a special committee of the association responsible for adjustment of freight rates to meet changing conditions and shippers' requests. In addition to these "troubleshooting" assignments, the vice president must always be alert to better ways to carry out the mission of the company, to gain larger shares of the available business, and to augment company profits.

The *freight traffic manager* is the deputy to the vice president, traffic, and is qualified to substitute for that executive when the office is vacant for any reason. As the supervisor of the freight traffic department, this manager assures that departmental policies are carried out in the most effective manner. The freight traffic manager considers shippers' requests for special calls at ports not on the regular schedule, or to transport large quantities of unusual cargo, and makes appropriate recommendations to higher authorities when necessary. Troublesome bookings, as, for example, unexpectedly large offerings for a ship already almost filled, or proposals to delay a ship's sailing to accommodate a customer, also are referred to this manager.

Immediately under the freight traffic manager is the *general freight agent*, who directs the sales staff (sometimes called solicitors) and handles departmental administration. Sales staff members are the contacts between the carrier and the shipping public; the company's prosperity depends upon their ability to convince these clients that the company deserves their patronage. The coordination of their efforts, and the establishment of policies with regard to sales, are of great importance, and represent a major part of the general freight agent's work. This agent supervises the day-to-day appointments made by the sales staff, suggests approaches to difficult customers, and makes sure that the capabilities of the company are set forth correctly. When subordinates make suggestions which have merit, but which involve changes in departmental or company policy, the general freight agent transmits these suggestions, together with a recommendation, to the appropriate executives. As additional information is obtained which may be useful in selling the services of the company, the agent calls in the sales staff and develops, with them, ways to use this knowledge to induce shippers to give their business to the company. Clients who benefit by this effort may become supporters of the line since they appreciate that the sales staff personnel often bring suggestions which, if accepted, can be financially advantageous to the shipper.

In addition to these responsibilities, the general freight agent directs the keeping of records which show the business received from individual shippers, the seasonal variations in the volume of cargo offered by shippers and in the tonnage carried by the ships, and even comparisons between voyages and calendar periods. These records have many uses. They may furnish data for some governmental agency concerned with international shipping. Perhaps the president has directed that certain aspects of traffic activity be analyzed and the most readily available information would be in these statistical records. Should a traffic study (a forecast of future business trends, based on past experience and present practice) be in progress, the data from these records could be of major importance. They also may suggest to the reviewing official trends in traffic which have not been obvious to the less diligent examiner, and which have great potential for increasing business.

The statistical section's reports show the volume of business handled, revenue earned, demands for service to named ports, the desirability of certain commodities in the light of the cost of handling them, and the frequency with which claims for damage are made. These reports are circulated to the senior executives, the comptroller, the operating department, and any other officials who may require them. They are useful as the basis for judgments relating to all aspects of freight traffic.

An important activity of the general freight agent is to maintain close contact with the claims division to learn what commodities and what shippers are involved in claims for damages and the probable causes of the alleged damage as well as the validity of the claims.

As the departmental administrative officer, the general freight agent makes routine and special assignments, sets up training programs for new members of the department, transfers persons within the department for the most efficient use of their capabilities, recommends promotions when earned, and dismissals when necessary. Incidental to these supervisory functions, the general freight agent maintains appropriate personnel records.

The freight traffic department is divided into two major segments, the *outbound freight division* and the *inbound freight division*, of which the outbound is by far the larger. The chief of each branch usually holds the rank of assistant freight traffic manager, and reports to the freight traffic manager.

The *booking clerk* is a senior member of the outbound department and controls the space in a cargo ship, allocating that space to individual shippers as they make their requests. The booking clerk obtains the basic information from the operating department, such as the amount of fuel, water, stores, and equipment to be aboard the ship on the proposed voyage, and the actual space, in cubic feet, and capacity in tons, available for cargo. As reservations for space in a break-bulk vessel are received, the booking clerk computes the stowage factors and allots the required number of cubic feet. The sales staff works closely with the booking clerk to assure that customers are extended the treatment they have been promised. Conversely, when the booking clerk finds that a vessel needs either high-volume lightweight cargo or dense cargo, an appeal is made to the sales staff to assist in making a balanced load by arranging visits to shippers of the kind of cargo desired. The booking clerk is in regular contact with the terminal and notifies the stevedore about the cargo that has been booked and when it will be arriving. On the basis of the booking clerk's daily reports, the stevedore plans the stowage of the ship, and the terminal manager tentatively lays out the transit shed.

For fully containerized ships, it is not necessary to compute stowage factors for individual shipments, nor is the stevedore dependent upon the booking reports. Instead, the booking clerk reserves undesignated "cells" for the containers offered by the shippers, and relies upon a carefully programmed computer to determine exactly where the box will be stowed. The booking clerk notifies the terminal of anticipated receipts of containers, making certain that all necessary data are furnished for proper identification of the trailer, and is in frequent contact with the gatehouse of the terminal to update and clarify earlier information.

Working directly under the booking clerk is the *permit clerk*, who notifies shippers of large lots of cargo (usually defined as 10,000 pounds or more from a single originator), directing them when to send their consignments to the terminal. The "permit system" is designed to favor the shipper of large lots and, by spacing the arrivals of trucks at the terminal, to eliminate the heavy expense of truck waiting time. In companies carrying nothing but containerized cargo, the receiving process at the terminal is highly sophisticated and computer directed. The same principles noted in break-bulk shipping apply, however, and the goal is to save both customer and carrier time and money.

Cargo which moves in small lots (often described among break-bulk carriers by the railroad term of "less than carload lot" or "LCL" cargo) normally does not come under the permit system. Experience has shown that little, if any, time is saved for the small lot shipper as a result of attempting to schedule truck movements to the terminal, and a good deal of clerical work can be eliminated. Cargo which requires special handling (a heavy-lift item, for instance) or must be brought to the ship's side by barge or lighter, has to be scheduled to prevent congestion, confusion in the loading operations, and perhaps great expense to the shipper who would be charged for the delays at the terminal.

Patrons of steamship lines handling all cargo in containers, but whose individual offerings are in comparatively small lots (referred to by the carriers as "less than container loads" or again "LCL" cargo), are encouraged to send their consignments to a section of the terminal reserved for this type of traffic. At this "consolidation station," known as a container freight station (CFS), small lots are processed and loaded into containers by terminal personnel. There is no significant difference between the handling of these shipments on a break-bulk terminal and at a container yard.

The manifesting section, under the *chief bill of lading clerk*, is the busiest and largest of the segments of the outbound freight department. Here the shipper delivers, for processing, the bills of lading he or she has prepared. These are matched with the dock receipts from the terminal to obtain the actual measurements of the parcels in the shipment, together with their actual count and condition (or the size, number, and weight of the container(s) in the shipment), and are freighted by the *rate clerk*, listed on the ship's outbound cargo manifest, signed by the chief clerk for the master, and routed to the freight cashier to hold until the shipper prepays the freight charges and picks up the "freighted" bills of lading.

The *inbound freight division* is a service agency responsible for the consignees' obtaining their cargo without delay, and in an orderly manner. The carrier requires that the original bill of lading be surrendered before the cargo is released. This procedure necessitates the timely notification of the consignees of the anticipated arrival of the vessel. The consignees also are informed, by personnel of the inbound freight department, of those pertinent regulations with which they must comply prior to taking delivery of their goods. When the goods are removed from the ship, the consignees call at the inbound department offices and exchange the original bill of lading for a "delivery order," which authorizes the terminal to release the cargo to the consignee or a designated representative. Should the goods be destined for an inland city, the department makes arrangements for transportation pursuant to the consignee's instructions. If required, cargo will be warehoused until this transportation is available. No charge is made for this assistance unless the cargo is left on the terminal too long; the expense of trucking, warehousing, customs broker's service, and transportation to the ultimate destination is for the customer's account. If the consignee believes that some, or all, of the shipment has gone astray, the inbound department initiates the search and keeps the claims agent at the loading point informed of its efforts. Finally, since pursers on the homeward voyage often make up the inbound cargo manifest, the inbound department maintains constant liaison with them to make certain that their work satisfies company and governmental requirements.

OPERATING DEPARTMENT

Supervising the operation of the fleet is the *vice president, operations*. While a seafaring background is not mandatory for this official, it is highly desirable because of the intimate contact with the personnel who run the ships, perform the essential stevedoring functions, and make the repairs. Broad experience in management directly related to ship operations may be a satisfactory alternative to service in merchant vessels.

CHART NO. 3 OPERATING DEPARTMENT

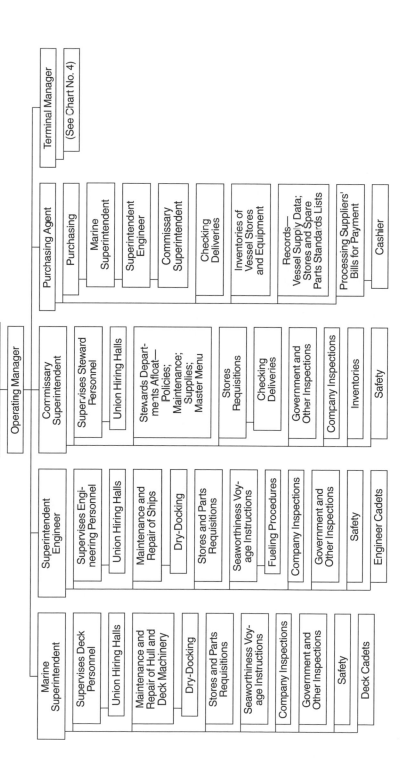

The vice president is responsible to the president, through the executive vice president, for all matters concerning ship construction, operations, stevedoring, and labor relations. If the company is small, the vice president usually is the negotiator with shipyards for building and repair contracts, with stevedores on details of handling cargo in the various ports served by the company fleet, with suppliers of ship stores and outfit, and with representatives of all types of labor unions on many aspects of the working agreements. The larger the company, the greater is the likelihood that specialists will handle each of these activities, but final decisions on these matters are the vice president's. To assist in the many duties required to run the department, and to assume the direction of the department whenever the vice president is absent, an *operating manager*, who administers the department, is appointed.

In many companies, final appointment of masters and chief engineers of the ships is made by the vice president. The marine superintendent initiates the recommendations for promotion to the rank of master and forwards this through the operating manager to the vice president. Similarly, the superintendent engineer selects the person considered best qualified for the position of chief engineer. After study of these proposals, the operating manager lays them on the desk of the vice president. The reason for this action is to assert, in unmistakable terms, that these two seafarers enjoy the full confidence of the highest echelons of management. It also authorizes them to talk to anyone below the vice president, when representing the interests of the ship, as equals.

The operating manager is the departmental executive officer and co-ordinator of all activities in the department. Within the very broad limits of authority of the office, the operating manager makes those decisions needed to carry out company and departmental policies. A most important facet of the duties is the evaluation of the periodic reports prepared by the various divisions of the department. Covering the actual performance of assigned functions, these reports afford a means of determining the efficiency with which the work is accomplished, and offer opportunities for improvement in the techniques of supervision and management. The results of these evaluations always are made known to the vice president.

MARINE DIVISION

At the head of the Marine (or Deck) Division is the *marine superintendent*, who is responsible to the vice president for the seaworthiness of the ships in all particulars except for the engineering department. The marine superintendent necessarily is both a qualified shipmaster with long experience and a person with demonstrated ability as an executive. The marine superintendent supervises the performance of deck personnel of the fleet through study of vessel logs, conferences with ship's licensed officer, and personal observation. Before each voyage is begun, the marine superintendent issues instructions to the master which include the latest information relating to conditions along the route, appropriate details of special requirements, and pertinent comments on carrying out company policies as they may apply to the forthcoming voyage. The marine superintendent may also inspect ships on their arrival in the home port to insure that governmental and company standards of maintenance are upheld. All licensed deck officers, except the masters, are hired by the marine superintendent who also supervises, through these officers, the performance of the unlicensed personnel. Because of these personnel activities, the marine superintendent must establish and maintain a good working relationship with officials of the maritime unions.

Safety of personnel afloat is of major importance. Some of the larger companies have *safety directors*; smaller organizations often designate the marine superintendent as the official in charge of the safety program for the deck department.

Requisitions from the ships for repairs to hull and deck machinery within the purview of the deck department, and plans for scheduled dry-dockings, inspections, surveys, and other examinations of the hull pass through the marine superintendent's office. The marine superintendent (or an assistant sometimes known as a *port captain*) always is present when the bottom is sighted, and accompanies all inspection parties on their tours. Requisitions for spare parts and consumable supplies for the deck department must be approved by the marine superintendent before they are forwarded to the purchasing agent.

Training of deck cadet-officers is under the supervision of the marine superintendent, who sets company policy concerning their duties and responsibilities while aboard ship.

ENGINEERING DIVISION

Occupying a position of importance equal to that of the marine superintendent, but concerned solely with the engineering activities of the fleet, is the *superintendent engineer*. Like the deck counterpart, this official has a background of years of service afloat and has demonstrated the qualifications desirable in an executive. Many of the responsibilities of the office parallel those of the marine superintendent: seaworthiness of the engineering department; supervision of personnel afloat, including training of cadet-engineer officers; relations with the maritime unions; inspections and surveys; safety; and oversight of repairs and procurement of spare parts. Engine abstract logs and voyage reports are submitted to the superintendent engineer by the chief engineers as their ships return to the home port. Examination of these documents reveals, with notable accuracy, the efficiency of engineering practices of the ship, and serves to delineate those areas where improvements are in order. From the listings of repairs accomplished by the ships during their voyages, both by ship's company and contractors in ports of call, the superintendent compiles individual histories of each ship's maintenance programs. Some large steamship companies have a maintenance and repair section which is charged with all details relating to accomplishing repairs beyond the capability of shipboard personnel. The superintendent engineer in this case serves as the liaison between the ship and the specialists of this section.

The chief engineer of a ship is the maintenance and repair officer who has overall responsibility for the physical condition of the vessel during a voyage. All requisitions for work exceeding the capability of the ship's crew are channeled through the chief engineer, and are delivered to the superintendent engineer in the home port. Once contracts for the requisite repairs have been let, actual performance thereunder is monitored by the chief engineer and the department heads concerned (e.g., deck repairs by the chief mate, commissary department by the chief steward, etc.).

When a vessel is scheduled for drydocking, the marine superintendent and the superintendent engineer cooperate fully to take maximum advantage of the time on drydock and in shipyard. Repair lists from the ship serve as the basis for writing the specifications for the work to be performed. The importance of verifying that the specifications have been carried out fully and competently cannot be exaggerated; these superintendents are the technicians responsible to the highest echelons of management for the seaworthy condition of the ship. The protection of the owners' interests, especially in regard to meeting standards of the classification societies, underwriters, and governmental agencies, must always be a paramount consideration. To this end, appropriate liaison must be maintained with the technical representatives of these bodies to assure that their inspectors will be on hand at the appropriate times.

Supervision of vessel fueling, instructions to the ship concerning keeping records of fuel consumption, and establishing the tests to be conducted on fuel taken aboard elsewhere than in the home port are particular responsibilities of the superintendent engineer and have attained new significance as the uniformity and quality of marine fuel and diesel oil became questionable following the petroleum crisis of 1973. In some instances, the office of the superintendent engineer may prepare the plans for bunkering the ship during a voyage; in any event, the bunkering records kept by this office may be consulted by staff members whenever necessary.

COMMISSARY (STEWARD'S) DIVISION

Supervising all aspects of activities related to the care and feeding of the shipboard personnel is the *commissary superintendent*. This official, who invariably has a background of seafaring experience as a ship's chief steward, establishes policy for the operation of all aspects of the steward's department (often designated as the catering department) afloat. As ships come into the home port, the commissary superintendent inspects them to assure that they meet company standards of cleanliness, storage, and record-keeping, and that the physical condition of the accommodations and food preparation spaces is satisfactory. Ships' chief stewards are guided and instructed in the most efficient and effective ways of preparing and serving food; frequently a master menu will be furnished by the commissary superintendent for use during the voyage. All requisitions for foodstuffs are submitted to the commissary superintendent for approval before being sent to the purchasing department. All matters relating to safe operating practice are of major concern, as are instructions for the proper and safe performance of duties of steward's department personnel.

A major activity of the commissary division is the procurement of competent seafaring personnel, and therefore the superintendent maintains good relations with the maritime unions. In the absence of government certifications of competence and standards of proficiency in the performance of the duties of steward personnel, the commissary superintendent is free to establish (within the framework of the agreement with the maritime union) appropriate qualifications for selection, promotion, and dismissal.

A very important part of the routine of the commissary superintendent's office is checking supplies when they are delivered to the ship. This entails coordination of schedules with the purchasing division and the assignment of inspectors to examine foods as they are brought to the ship. It is standard practice in U.S. shipping companies to have a qualified inspector from the U.S. Department of Agriculture examine and approve all meat, poultry, eggs, butter, and vegetables before they are accepted by the ship.

PURCHASING DIVISION

The duties of this office are set forth in detail in Chapter 9.

TERMINAL DIVISION

The *terminal manager* is in charge of all activities directly related to handling the cargo into and out of the ships at the company's terminal. Whether the carrier is engaged in the break-bulk or container trade, the terminal division must employ scores of skilled artisans as well as numerous clerks, and expends large amounts of money for rent of facilities, operation of equipment, and compensation of personnel. Necessarily, the terminal manager has had extensive experience in all phases of cargo handling, and has also demonstrated unusual competence as an administrator and supervisor. The terminal manager is the company's technical advisor on all matters dealing with cargo handling, stevedoring, and management of the marine terminal. The manager's immediate seniors in the executive structure are the operating manager and the vice president, operations.

Functionally, the terminal division has four sections: receiving and delivery of cargo, stevedoring, administrative, and protective and custodial. Chart number 4 shows the assignments of responsibility and control within the division.

The *receiving clerk* is one of the key assistants to the terminal manager. This person is in charge of the office through which pass all papers connected with outbound cargo brought to the terminal for loading aboard ship. Under the receiving clerk are clerks who prepare the necessary reports and draw the diagrams showing how and where the cargo has been stowed in the ship. The actual examination of the cargo is performed by *checkers*, who are hired by the day as they are needed. When cargo arrives at the terminal, a checker is assigned by the receiving clerk's office to inspect, count, and measure the packages, and to insert the appropriate data on the dock receipt. The completed form, initialed by the checker, is returned to the receiving clerk for authentication. The original goes to the delivering carrier as proof that the cargo has been accepted in the condition noted on the dock receipt. Throughout the process of loading the ship, a member of the receiving office staff makes frequent surveys of the cargo spaces to ascertain the exact area in which lots of cargo are stowed.

In addition to handling the documentation described above, the receiving clerk assists the terminal manager in laying out the transit shed for the next ship. Copies of the booking clerk's daily reports serve to indicate

CHART NO. 4   TERMINAL DIVISION

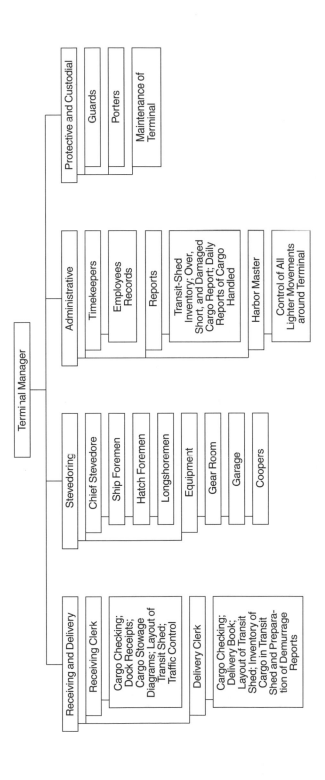

the quantity of cargo for each port of call, and thereby suggest the amount of floor space to reserve for those ports. Truck traffic into the terminal area is controlled by the receiving clerk, who issues gate passes to drivers in the order of their arrival and consistent with the number of checkers available to oversee the unloading of the cargo from the vehicles.

Terminals operated by containership companies follow almost the same routine, except that the role of the checker is minimized. The exterior condition of the container is inspected carefully, the condition of the seal on the container's door latch is examined, and appropriate data to identify the container are recorded. Containers are weatherproof, and are stored in "container yards" (CY), sometimes on wheeled chassis (this operation is known as a "wheeled operation") and sometimes dismounted and stacked two or more high (this operation is known as a "grounded operation"). Thousands of containers are assembled in a large terminal, and control of their receipt, inspection, locations in the yard, movements within the yard and to the ship's side, and stowage aboard ship depends upon the existence and constant use of a highly sophisticated computer based system. The basic responsibility for the condition and location of containerized cargo is identical to that of the break-bulk carrier.

The *delivery clerk* has functions similar to those of the receiving clerk, except that the delivery clerk is concerned entirely with inbound cargo. As the consignees claim their goods, a checker is assigned to inspect the packages to ascertain their condition at the moment of transfer to the consignee. The checker's report is filed in the delivery office, and the trucker or other inland carrier signs for the cargo in the delivery book, which shows the date and hour when the ocean carrier released the goods. The delivery clerk also aids the terminal manager in laying out the terminal for incoming cargo, using information transmitted from the overseas ports to the inbound freight department. The delivery clerk takes periodic inventory of the transit shed to determine what cargo has not been claimed, and what lots have been on the transit shed's deck in excess of the allowed free storage time. From these records, charges for storage (demurrage) are compiled.

For container terminals, the responsibility imposed upon the delivery clerk is the same as in the break-bulk terminals, but the details of operation are incorporated into the computer system.

Loading and unloading ships employed in break-bulk service is a specialized activity normally performed by contractors rather than by the steamship company. Once awarded the contract, the stevedoring firm assigns a supervisor to the terminal. This *chief stevedore* or *stevedore super-*

intendent, although on the contractor's payroll, functions as a de facto member of the terminal manager's staff. This individual oversees the performance of the longshoremen. The details of each day's work, as required to meet the schedule set forth by the terminal manager—number of gangs to be employed, supporting equipment needed, specialized workers to be assigned, and safety precautions to be followed if unusual cargo is to be handled—are the concerns of the stevedore superintendent, not of the terminal manager. The terminal manager assures that the terms and conditions of the contract are carried out, that longshoremen are not idle, and that the responsibility for damage to cargo which occurs in the terminal is fixed at the earliest practical moment.

Many stevedoring contracts stipulate that the contractor shall furnish all gear and equipment. Usually the stevedore company also supplies the mechanics and carpenters necessary to maintain these items in proper condition. The terminal provides the space for shops. Where the contract requires the shipowner to provide and maintain the gear and equipment, the terminal manager must exercise positive supervision to make certain that all requisite materiel is in dependable, operating condition.

Container terminals represent very large investments of capital because of the space needed to store and to maneuver the containers, the multimillion-dollar cranes used to hoist the containers into and out of the ships, and the highly specialized equipment employed to shift containers from chassis to the ground and vice versa, or to stack them in the container yard. Few container companies own these terminals, preferring to lease them from public bodies (port authorities, cities, or state agencies). Relatively few laborers are needed, and those who are hired are considered as skilled operators rather than manual workers. Some containership operators manage their terminals completely with their own personnel, while others contract for everything; terminal space, labor, equipment, and supervision.

Administratively, a great deal of paperwork is processed by the terminal division. Among the numerous reports submitted in connection with each loading and unloading operation of a break-bulk ship, those prepared by the *timekeeper*, the safety engineer, and the stevedore superintendent are most useful in evaluating the competence of the labor force. The timekeeper's records are compiled daily and show how many workers were employed at any time; the number of hours of straight time and overtime work; and the number of hours, and the workers, assigned to handle premium or penalty cargo (commodities for which longshoremen receive extra compensation). Reports filed by the safety engineer (or the official charged with responsibility for safety of personnel) supply details of safety meetings, accidents, injuries, or equipment failures which occurred and have been placed under investigation. From the stevedore superintendent come data on the actual performance of longshoremen in terms of tons of cargo handled per hour, stoppages and the reasons therefor, problems encountered in the stowage or discharge operation, and related details.

Each morning, a report is drawn up to show the amount of cargo handled by the terminal during the preceding twenty-four hours. As a vessel is finished, a report of any cargo which has been over-carried, short-delivered, or damaged is prepared. Inventories of unclaimed lots of cargo are inspected and brought up to date. All these documents are channeled through the terminal manager's office before being disseminated to the divisions concerned. By inspection of these papers, the terminal manager is able to gain a summary of activity during the period covered.

In containership terminals, although the computer is used to bring together all the details, the same types of reports must be prepared regularly to provide the basis for evaluating the performance of the terminal organization. The enormous cost of the ships makes rapid turnaround essential, and maintaining control of the terminal activity is a vital part of attaining that goal.

Some ports have a significant quantity of cargo moved within their limits by lighters. Any terminal which has a steady flow of lighter traffic may have among its supervisors a *harbormaster*, who controls the arrival, moorings, and departures of these non-self-propelled craft. All lighters come under the harbormaster's supervision as soon as they are moored in terminal waters and are shifted when and where the harbormaster directs in order to fulfill the cargo working plans. When the lighter is emptied, the harbormaster notifies the owner, and orders the lighter to be moved to a point where it can await its owner without interfering with other operations. It is important that prompt notification of the release of the lighter be given to that craft's owner in order to fix the exact time when the steamship terminal's responsibility comes to an end.

Maintenance of the physical plant is a necessary and important activity. Security guards often are assigned the duty of reporting to the maintenance office whenever they observe something that needs attention: a deck plank which should be replaced, an electrical conduit which has been damaged, a break in the protective fencing around the terminal, or piles of debris ready for removal. The maintenance workers who respond to these reports sometimes are placed under the supervision of the protective division for administrative control and routine assignments of work. Large-scale projects, such as repainting the interior of the transit shed, resurfacing the working area, or installing new lights, automatically invite the terminal manager's personal attention since they entail major financial expenditures and a possible rearrangement of all terminal activity during the job.

The terminal manager, as the overall supervisor, must be alert at all times to poor working practices which reduce efficiency or increase the risk of injury to employees. In addition, the terminal manager must always be seeking better and more economical ways, both in terms of time and of money, to handle cargo. As appropriate, the terminal manager makes suggestions for modification or construction of terminal facilities. Finally, and perhaps most importantly, the terminal manager participates in the formulation of all programs and policies relating to the terminal and terminal personnel.

The organization of a liner-service company can be as varied as the number of companies that exist. What they all have in common, however, is that their particular structure is designed to allow them to operate efficiently as they carry out their mission. The functions required to carry out the mission will be identical no matter what size the company may be, but individual titles may vary somewhat from company to company. Close examination of any one company's structure will give the observer insight into the management philosophy of the company.

CHAPTER SIX

Terminal Management

A marine terminal exists for the purpose of effecting the efficient transfer of cargo between a ship and other modes of transportation. It is a service facility with its structure and operation designed and organized to be flexible and responsive to the needs of the shippers. Its operations are planned and carried out based on these fundamentals: to assure that cargoes are handled safely, at the lowest cost, and in the least possible time. Achieving these objectives is a day-to-day concern of the terminal management team, which must provide for economical and efficient operation.

Terminal management requires systematic assignments of standardized duties to staff members to accomplish expeditiously the many functions of the terminal. The management structure of the marine terminal, although differing somewhat from terminal to terminal, is always structured so that the terminal's objectives are met.

In charge of the whole operation is the terminal manager, who is responsible for coordinating and controlling the day-to-day activities on the terminal. The principal assistants to the terminal manager are the chief receiving clerk, who supervises all routines relating to cargo being brought to the terminal for loading on board outbound vessels; the chief delivery clerk, who performs the same duties for cargo being turned over to consignees; the security chief, who is responsible for the physical safety of the plant and its contents; the timekeeper, who keeps detailed records of the employment of every laborer hired on an hourly basis; and the stevedore or vessel superintendent, who directs vessel loading and unloading operations. Often the superintendent is employed by the stevedore contractor, rather than the terminal, but serves as a member of the terminal manager's staff and advises on all matters directly connected with the labor force and actual handling of cargo into and out of ships.

The security chief is responsible to the terminal manager for the physical safety of the plant and its contents. A force of guards is directed by the chief of security, and has a number of important duties: to control access to the terminal area, to visit routinely all parts of the terminal at peri-

A modern, well-designed terminal built on a wharf. Wide aprons, numerous doors, and skylights enhance efficiency. Photograph by Sutton, courtesy of The Port of New Orleans.

odic, but irregularly scheduled intervals, and to prevent theft and fire. The security force is also responsible for these ancillary functions:

1. Inspecting refrigerated containers to assure that their machinery is operating and the proper temperatures are being maintained.
2. Connecting and disconnecting refrigerated containers, as required, when they are in the storage areas.
3. Observing the operations of tying up or letting go the mooring lines of a ship.
4. Operating an intra-terminal personnel bus service to minimize or even eliminate all pedestrian traffic.
5. Controlling the maintenance and porter units to assure that hazards to safety resulting from damage or accumulation of waste are removed quickly and efficiently.

The logic behind these additional assignments is that security guards constantly patrol the transit sheds, storage yards, container marshaling yards, and the piers and wharves. They must be alert to any deviations from safe and accepted practices which endanger the physical safety of the plant or cargo.

Refrigerated cargo requires closely controlled temperatures, and the frequent rounds of the patrolmen provide an excellent means of monitoring the performance of the cooling units on each container. If a unit is observed to be functioning improperly, the patrolman notifies the appropriate office which can effect necessary repairs.

Observing the tying-up and letting-go of lines between the ship and the berth is an outgrowth of preventing theft. All too often, smugglers among the ship's company will attempt to pass their contraband to shore-side confederates during the confusion which can exist when a ship is being moored or unmoored. The security force does not handle the lines; they observe and monitor performance by the assigned personnel. The actual responsibility for handling the lines belongs to the ship's master and the line handling gang.

Because modern container terminals usually cover a very large area, a regular bus service, using security personnel as drivers, connecting major locations is efficient and economical. A ban on any pedestrian traffic in the terminal enclosure enhances safety of personnel and equipment. It also reduces the possibility that unauthorized persons might gain access to the cargo storage areas. Assigning security guards as drivers serves a dual function, in that the guard is a trained observer, and on the bus route will be alert to any unusual circumstances. The guard also has the authority to take action if any deviation from accepted practice or routine is encountered.

By giving the security chief supervisory responsibility for cleanliness and maintenance of the terminal, when trash accumulations are reported by the patrolmen, a cleanup gang can be dispatched immediately. Burned-out light bulbs, breaks in the transit shed deck, potholes in truck lanes, and damage to the chain link fence all pose hazards to personnel or cargo, and prompt attention is thus assured.

None of the foregoing comments, however, should suggest that the primary mission of the security chief is other than the safety and security of the terminal premises and the cargo stored therein. Contingency plans must be prepared to cope with emergencies such as fire, hurricane, hazardous material spills, and major equipment failure which could lead to loss of cargo or injury to personnel. To prevent theft and pilferage, routine guard patrols must be established and monitored constantly. Continuous vigilance and resourcefulness are needed. For instance, if truck drivers are suspected of stealing cargo, it is good preventive technique for terminal management to study the movement of trucks within the terminal, the persons with whom the driver has a legitimate reason to do business, and the possibilities for theft which exist. The procedures at each stop in these "danger zones" therefore should be scrutinized:

1. *Gatehouse.* The driver surrenders all documents to the gatekeeper, who verifies that this truck and cargo are expected.
2. *Inspection area.* For break-bulk shipments, the truck stops to pick up a checker who will supervise the unloading and the condition of the cargo at the moment it is accepted by the terminal. For containerized shipments, the checker inspects the box for evidence of actual or potential damage to the contents. The condition and number of the seal on the container doors are observed and recorded by the checker.
3. *Unloading area.* Break-bulk cargo is examined and tallied by the checker, who initials the dock receipt. The exact location in the transit shed is identified, so that plans can be made for the most efficient use of time and equipment loading the cargo aboard ship. Containers brought to the terminal for outward loading in ships are trucked to the designated slots to await transfer to the ship. Once the container is released from the truck-tractor, the driver returns to the gatehouse.
4. *Gatehouse.* The driver presents all papers to the gatekeeper, who inspects the truck (if it carried break-bulk cargo) before releasing the vehicle.[1]

Other measures which the security chief takes to protect the cargo include liaison with police units, and contact with major shippers to learn if the protection system devised imposes undue delay or expense, or is in any way objectionable to these customers.

The timekeeper is another important member of the terminal manager's staff. Detailed records must be kept of the employment of every laborer hired on an hourly basis. Longshoremen work in gangs hired for four-hour shifts; their names must be inscribed individually on the time sheets at the beginning of each shift. If they handle obnoxious commodities ("penalty cargo") and are entitled to additional compensation for such work, the timekeeper is to note the actual time during which the extra money is payable. Workers employed to do the many tasks around the terminal, but not members of longshoremen's gangs, are listed under the heading of "dock labor" or "extra labor," and are paid according to the number of hours they work. It is essential that the timekeeper periodically determine that the records show exactly who is working, and that the pay accounts are consistent with the labor actually performed.

Underlying every consideration of good terminal management is the awareness of the need for safety. Not only is safety important for the good morale of employees, but it is vital if the goodwill of shippers and consignees of goods is to be retained. Working practices which endanger the lives of the laborers are intolerable both morally and financially. Equally intolerable are habits of handling cargo which result in damage or loss of customer's goods.

Enforcing safety rules and preventing accidents among longshoremen and other terminal workers are major responsibilities of terminal management. Three areas of concern require constant scrutiny on the part of supervisors: personnel and vehicular traffic patterns, physical safety (i.e., structural and plant conditions), and operation of equipment and vehicles.

On many pieces of cargo-handling machinery the driver has very limited vision when actually working cargo. By designating specific pedestrian walkways, or eliminating pedestrian traffic altogether in areas where cargo is being worked, exposure to accidents can be reduced. Due to the size of loads and machinery used nowadays, accidents between machines and pedestrians can be of major consequence.

Terminal management is equally concerned with the possibility of accidents between cargo-handling machines. To minimize the risk, it is prudent to set specific traffic patterns in transit sheds as well as in the marshaling or container yards. In addition, these precautions become important: enforce safe speed limits, properly train equipment operators, require pre-start safety inspections of the equipment, eliminate cross traffic at intersections, and install mirrors at all blind corners. Preventing accidents protects personnel, cargo, and machinery.

The physical structure of the terminal itself has significant impact on safety. If the terminal is dirty, or improperly lighted, ventilated, or heated, or if the deck surface is in poor repair, there is risk to personnel and cargo. Everyone working on a marine terminal shares in the responsibility of insuring that the condition of the physical structure and plant is in good order. The terminal manager, of course, has final responsibility for seeing that all is safe.

The search never ends for better and less costly methods of handling the packages crossing the marine terminal. There is a pressing need for economy, because the cost of running a terminal often approaches the total of all other ship operating expenses. A saving of only one cent per ton can make a noticeable contribution to overall company profits.

Spools of barbed wire, stacked on wooden pallets, are transported by a crane truck. Lifting bridles and spreaders and the design of the pallet are clearly visible.

Although speed is essential in all the processes of receiving, stevedoring, sorting, and delivery of the cargo, the ideal terminal manager never accepts the report that work was accomplished at "maximum speed." Managers are always under pressure to find ways to reduce the time the ship has to spend in port, for when vessels cost $500 or more an hour to keep in commission, few operators can afford the luxury of idle ships at the terminal. Everyone must be aware that ships earn money only when they are actually transporting goods from one port to another. The shorter the port time, the more voyages a ship can make in a year, and the greater her earnings.

An efficient, economical marine terminal is well maintained, clean, and orderly. It should be the intent of the manager to make it a place where the workers are treated humanely. The office should be neat and in good order, cargo gear should be stacked neatly, and dunnage should be conveniently located, but not in the main stream of traffic. Debris and dirt should be removed promptly, as a matter of safety rather than esthetics.

The provision of good, well lighted, and spacious toilet and washroom facilities for terminal employees reflects excellent management. In this regard, it is good practice to have, somewhere in the terminal, proper shelter for the laborers, so that they may be protected from the elements during bad weather. Not only is this humane, it is also efficient, because it keeps the labor force together, and permits immediate resumption of work when conditions are favorable. It also eliminates having a large number of workers wandering aimlessly through the transit shed, with the possibility of injury. A further advantage to providing a shelter is that smoking can be controlled, and the chance of a fire being started by a carelessly discarded cigar or cigarette is reduced.

In the United States, modern break-bulk terminal operation is predicated upon two facts: manpower is very expensive, and machines can do more work than people. There are many types of mechanical equipment available to use in handling cargo, but the determination of how many pieces of machinery shall be purchased and operated, and the ratio of workers to machines, is the responsibility of the terminal manager. In the ceaseless efforts to reduce vessel port time and the costs of handling cargo, it is imperative that the manager be alert to the possibility of replacing obsolescent machinery with more efficient equipment. At the same time, the division of costs between investment in equipment, expense of equipment operation, and the wages of laborers must be taken into account. Naturally, every decision as to replacement of equipment has to be based on the determination that more work will be done at lower cost if more efficient machines are procured.

The proper use of cargo-handling machines is of major concern to the terminal manager, who is guided by these basic principles of material handling:

1. *Safety of personnel is of first importance.* Every piece of machinery and every work technique must be analyzed to determine what, if any, danger there may be for the operators assigned to the job. If danger is detected, the machine must be altered or the technique corrected to eliminate, insofar as is humanly possible, the threat to the worker. Experience has shown that these analyses are worthwhile because safe work practices permit faster and better performance by the employees. Along with safe equipment and safe work practices goes proper training of operating personnel. This training should include checking equipment for safety, safe equipment operation, and standardized work practices.
2. *Safety of cargo.* Maximum effort must be made to insure that the

Mechanized cargo handling. *Left:* Rolls of newsprint are hoisted aboard ship with vacuum-cup grips, while a fork-lift truck uses clamps. *Upper right:* A short-masted, propane-fueled, solid-tired fork-lift truck of 8,000 pounds capacity stuffs cargo into a seagoing container. *Lower right:* A high-masted fork-lift truck, equipped with a spreader, removes bagged rice from a truck. Photographs courtesy of Port of Sacramento, California.

cargo is stowed and segregated properly, inspected diligently, and protected from theft or damage.

3. *Operations must be balanced between workers and machines.* To take maximum advantage of the capabilities of a machine, one or more workers must be assigned to work with it. The judicious determination of the exact number of workers required to produce maximum efficiency from a machine is a major responsibility of the terminal manager. The manager must guard against the possibility that too many—or too few—people are put on a job at the expense of efficiency. It often happens that, even with the will to work, too many people in a gang will interfere with each other, and the result of their collective labors is not as good as would have been the case had fewer workers been assigned.

4. *Work practices must be standardized.* To calculate costs in terms of money, manpower, time, and machinery, it is necessary that standard work practices be followed throughout the terminal. There will

Sacks of rice contained in large bags are lifted by a "bagged rice spreader" for stowage in a ship's cargo hold. Each unitized lift of fourteen bags retains its lifting cables, expediting discharge. Photograph courtesy of Port of Sacramento, California.

be minor variations depending upon the personality and experience of the individual supervisor, but the pattern of activity in handling a particular commodity should be nearly identical in all parts of the terminal. The manager must guard against complacency and has to be alert to suggestions for improvements in the techniques employed. Until a new procedure is approved, however, all subordinate leaders are required to perform their tasks in the accepted manner. It is common practice for the majority of longshoremen to work at a different terminal each day, or every few days. Therefore, practices must also be standardized between terminals for the same task in order to maximize the efficiency of labor. The purpose of this standardization is to assist management in controlling output and expense.

5. *The proper type of equipment must be assigned to the job.* It is generally accepted that it is inefficient to use heavy equipment for light work, and light equipment for heavy work; it is the function of management to select the machinery to be employed by the longshore-

As an economy measure, this pier was built with just sufficient width to serve vessels with a small cargo-working area. The pier extends from shore to a depth needed to berth the ship. Bow and stern are not secured to the cargo pier. Photograph courtesy of Stolt-Nielsen Inc.

men and to direct the types of equipment to be used for designated types of work.

6. *Movement must be direct.* Circuitous routes are longer and require more time, both for operator and machine, than direct routes. From management's viewpoint, the routes followed by wheeled materials-handling equipment should be the shortest possible to keep to the minimum the time involved in transporting loads. Lengthening the distance inevitably increases machine time and hence requires additional equipment if the same rate of tonnage movement is to be continued.

7. *Handle cargo as little as possible.* Each time cargo is handled there is potential for damage due to rough handling.

In general, terminals are designed and built for some specific purpose without much input from the people who will ultimately manage them. Once built, managers come to a terminal and must make the operation work with existing resources.

Some factors that affect the design and operating characteristics of a marine terminal are: the size and type of vessels that will call at the terminal, the types of cargo that will be expected at the terminal, the volume of cargo anticipated, the mechanical cargo-handling equipment to be used; the space available for use as a terminal; the availability and access of land transportation; the degree and type of federal, regional, and local regulations; and the impact that the terminal will have on the environment.

TYPES OF MARINE TERMINALS

While the principles of good terminal management remain the same no matter what kind of terminal is being operated, there are seven distinct types of terminals, and each has its own unique management challenges. The seven types are described below.

1. *Break-bulk* or *general cargo* terminals are designed to accommodate several kinds of ships and a variety of cargoes packaged by the shipper. This type of terminal has large transit sheds close to the face of the dock and large open areas adjacent to the transit shed to collect cargoes which are not weather sensitive. These terminals can be capital intensive and labor intensive.

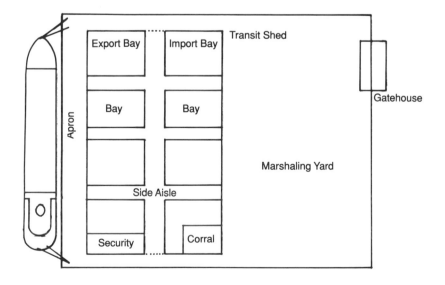

Typical break-bulk terminal configuration.

The manager of a break-bulk terminal is concerned that the limited terminal space is used wisely, that cargo is being received and delivered on time, that the proper mix of labor and machinery is maintained, and that the different types of equipment are all maintained properly.

2. *Bulk product* terminals are designed to accommodate cargo which is not packaged. There are two kinds of bulk terminals: dry bulk, which consists of cargoes such as grains, ores, and wood chips; and liquid bulk, which consists of cargoes such as petroleum products, vegetable oil products, and any other liquid product shipped in bulk form. Bulk terminals are designed to accommodate dry-bulk ships and tankers. They have fixed cargo-handling systems (pipelines, conveyors, etc.) which run from the berth to large storage facilities ashore. Due to the deeper drafts of bulk carriers and the nature of the fixed cargo-handling systems, the berths are generally extended farther into the waterways. These terminals are generally very capital intensive but not very labor intensive.

The manager of a bulk product terminal is concerned that the quality of the cargo being received or delivered is that which is specified, that the fixed cargo-handling systems are properly main-

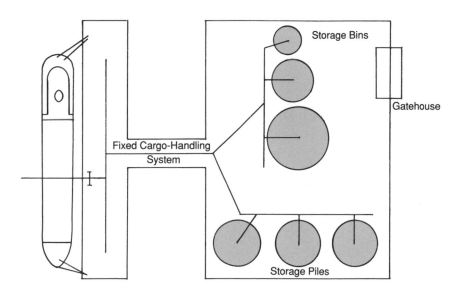

Typical dry-bulk terminal configuration. *Note:* Storage area must support very heavy weights and is usually on land for this reason.

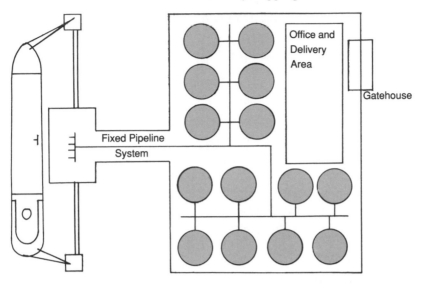

Typical liquid-bulk terminal configuration. *Note:* Storage tanks must support very heavy weights and are usually on land for this reason.

tained, and that the storage facilities are ready to meet the requirements of the customer.

3. *Neo-bulk* terminals are designed to accommodate homogeneous cargoes that cannot be loaded or discharged using fixed cargo-handling systems. Some examples of neo-bulk cargoes are logs, scrap
steel, or automobiles. Neo-bulk terminals are designed to accommodate specialty carriers such as: car carriers, bulk carriers (i.e., scrap
steel), and break-bulk carriers (i.e., logs). They have no transit
sheds and very large open areas. These terminals are less capital intensive then a bulk terminal, but are more labor intensive.

   The manager of a neo-bulk terminal is concerned that there is
ample yard space for the cargo, that the specialized cargo-handling
equipment is properly maintained, and that there is a sufficient
number of laborers available to take care of the work (especially
car carriers, where the terminal may need more than one hundred
drivers).

4. *Container* terminals are designed to accommodate cargo which has
been containerized for transportation in containerships. They have
very large open areas known as container yards (CY), specialized
container-handling equipment, and no transit sheds. The terminal
may contain a container freight station (CFS), which looks like a

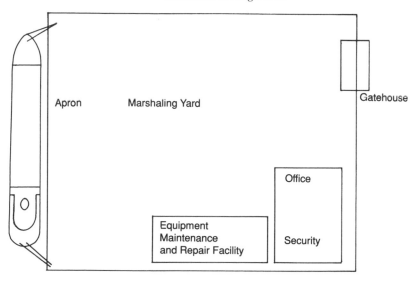

Typical neo-bulk terminal configuration.

transit shed and serves many of the same functions of a transit shed. The major difference is that the CFS is not located near the face of the terminal. This type of terminal operation is very capital intensive and requires a work force that is highly trained.

The manager of a container terminal is concerned that the large number of transactions that take place on the terminal and the detailed paperwork associated with each transaction are recorded accurately, that the computer is operating properly, that the container yard is laid out properly, and that the highly specialized container-handling equipment (cranes and straddle carriers) is properly maintained.[2]

5. *Passenger* terminals are designed to accommodate human "cargo."[3] They are built to accommodate passenger ships, and have large, often double-decked buildings. There are no open areas. The terminals feature large and well lighted waiting rooms designed for the comfort of the passengers, with rest rooms, baggage areas, ample communications equipment, and easy access to land transportation.

The manager of a passenger terminal must assure that passengers can be processed by passenger traffic department personnel quickly and efficiently, and embarkation is facilitated by the availability of sufficient numbers of porters and baggage handlers. When

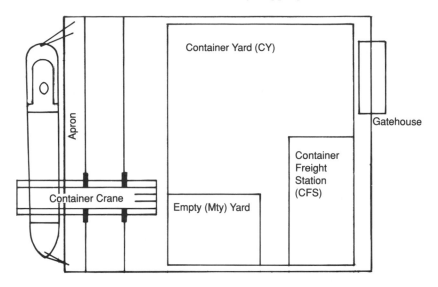

Typical container terminal configuration.

passengers are disembarking, provision must be made for customs and immigration inspection, and adequate numbers of baggage handlers must be on duty. Loading areas for land transportation must be clean, neat, and under constant surveillance by the security force. A manager would do well to remember that the passenger terminal is the first and the last thing that the passenger sees. The experience in the terminal can set the tone for the voyage and can leave a lasting impression (good or bad) in the mind of the passenger. Obviously, the passenger ship company has a great interest in the proper operation of the terminals where its ships call.

6. *Combination* terminals are designed to accommodate cargoes of various types (i.e. bulk, general cargo, container, passenger). This is perhaps the most challenging type of terminal to operate. The terminal must be designed to accommodate all types of ships, and must have ample transit shed space of high quality, as well as sufficient open space to handle a variety of cargoes.

The manager of a combination terminal must be notified as to the type of ship which will be using these facilities. If a passenger ship, a break-bulk ship, and a bulk carrier are at the terminal at the same time, it will be necessary to segregate operations, and to assure that the shippers and passengers are served properly and effi-

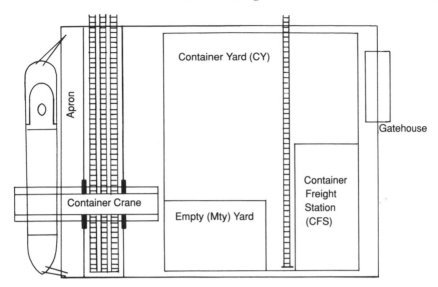

Typical intermodal terminal configuration.

ciently. A number of problems relating to cleanliness of the terminal and arrangements for processing passengers will absorb the attention of the manager and key staff members. All equipment must be maintained and kept in readiness to work.

7. *Intermodal* terminals are designed to accommodate cargo that is involved in a "through container movement." These terminals are built to accommodate containerships and have very large open areas, specialized cargo-handling equipment, and convenient access to land transportation (primarily rail). Many of these terminals have provided rail access to handle double-stack rail cars and are referred to as intermodal container transfer facilities (ICTF).

The manager of an intermodal terminal is concerned with speed and proper land use. It is imperative to coordinate the cargo moving from one mode to another in time to make the connecting mode's schedule. This requires a very skilled labor pool and a carefully designed mix of labor and machinery.

STEVEDORE CONTRACTOR TERMINALS

In some cities, large stevedore companies will lease terminals from the local port authority and operate them as independent terminals. At these terminals the stevedore will provide full terminal service for the ocean carrier, or a substantial portion of that service.

Magic Stevedore Company, for example, has leased and staffed a fine, modern terminal which it equipped with new, highly efficient machinery to handle break-bulk cargoes, palletized goods, and containers. It also has large refrigerated spaces for fresh fruits, vegetables, and meats.

Magic wins a contract from Blue Sea Lines to perform all terminal activities, with the proviso that Blue Sea will have a representative, qualified to make major decisions, on duty when one of its ships is being worked. The agreement also specifies that the freight traffic department will establish and maintain channels of communication during working hours. Blue Sea will notify Magic not less than four hours before any cargo is scheduled to arrive at the terminal.

It is interesting to note that in this type of terminal operation the terminal manager has little control over the types, or amounts, of cargo being booked to the ships calling at the terminal. These decisions are made by the steamship company, in this example Blue Sea Lines, and the terminal is merely informed what cargo to expect. In these instances, the only area that the terminal manager can control is the actual movement of the cargo through the terminal. This control, and the subsequent efficiency of the movement, is a function of proper space allocation on the terminal, and proper balance between labor and machinery as dictated by management prerogative and labor contracts. Today, with ever growing concern for the environment and safety, some terminals are beginning to state restrictions in their tariffs on certain cargoes.

Once cargo is booked to a Blue Sea Line's ship, the booking clerk will notify the terminal and provide all the cargo specifics. This process allows the terminal to begin making arrangements for the delivery of the goods to the terminal and also permits terminal management to allocate space for the cargo. Once the ship leaves its last port prior to arriving at the Magic terminal, Blue Sea Lines will provide the terminal with a complete cargo plan and manifest. All this information is used by the stevedore to plan for the most efficient discharge and load sequence. It also allows the stevedore to plan for the proper allocation of equipment and labor to complete the job and get the ship back to sea in the shortest possible time.

This may seem quite straightforward, but imagine that this terminal operation is complicated by having four different steamship companies contracting with Magic Stevedore Company, and each company has three or four ships calling at the terminal each month. Now the challenges to management become significant and the following types of questions must be answered: How do you allocate space appropriately on the terminal? How do you schedule vessel berthing so that no ship is kept waiting? How do you balance personnel and equipment when working multiple vessels? How do you coordinate cargo receiving and delivery operations and still work the ships? How do you standardize paperwork so that each of the four companies will accept the same paperwork? (It would be a nightmare if each company wanted something different.) How would you assess the exposure to risk that your company is assuming in this situation? These are all good questions and it is the terminal management team that must have answers to them all.

Increasingly, all terminal managers are being faced with new challenges they must address. These new challenges include such things as how to dispose of dredged spoils recovered in the never-ending task of keeping enough water alongside their docks to accommodate the larger ships; how to manage the hazardous materials passing through the terminals each day; how to keep current on hazardous material regulations as the list of those materials changes and grows; how to maintain the delicate balance between the protection of the environment and the needs of the shipper to move goods and the shipowner to get ships out in minimal time; and how to address adequately the needs of labor as they relate to terminal efficiency.

The proper management of a marine terminal is an exciting and demanding challenge for anyone. The person who fills the position of terminal manager must have good written and oral communications skills; good interpersonal skills; an eye for detail; an analytical mind; must be an innovator; and must be calm, patient, and willing to work long hours when needed. In short, this person must have general management knowledge and skill as well as specific maritime knowledge about ships, terminals, and labor.

CHAPTER SEVEN

Terminal Operations

As stated in the last chapter, a marine terminal is a transfer point and exists for the sole purpose of effecting the efficient transfer of cargo between the vessel and other modes of transportation. It is a service facility whose structure and operation is designed and organized to be responsive to the needs of shippers.

Marine terminals are operated on the following principles:

1. Personnel must be protected from injury while in the terminal area.
2. The ship must be unloaded, reloaded, and made ready for sea in the least possible time.
3. Cargo must be handled efficiently and economically between the ship and a variety of inland transportation modes.
4. Cargo must be protected from loss or damage while on the terminal.
5. Paperwork necessary for the movement of cargo must be completed quickly and done accurately.
6. Terminals are not long-term storage areas. The goal is to move cargo through the terminal as rapidly as possible.

Terminal operation depends upon the availability of a large force of workers whose skills and productivity set the level of efficiency. These workers are proud of their craft, and are fanatically loyal to their unions. Few terminals in the world today can be operated without due appreciation of the role of the labor unions and their members.

Of the seven types of terminals (break-bulk, bulk [dry and liquid], neo-bulk, container, passenger, combination, and intermodal) the break-bulk terminal is probably the most complicated operation. For that reason, the operations of a typical break-bulk terminal will be examined in detail.

The terminal manager is the director of cargo operations for the steamship company and responsible for the efficiency and economy of all terminal activities, and is expected to keep the ships on schedule insofar as port working time is concerned. The actual supervision of loading and unloading vessels is delegated to the chief stevedore with other key tasks being delegated to the security chief, the chief receiving clerk, and the chief delivery clerk. The manager, however, is called upon to make decisions on specialized aspects of cargo handling, the number and skills of laborers needed to perform an unusual job, and the procedures to be followed by clerks, checkers, longshoremen, watchmen, and other personnel in the performance of their assigned duties. A major concern of management is that the ship sail on time, and the entire working schedule of the terminal is adjusted toward that end.

Terminal operation is affected by the fact that longshore labor is almost universally unionized, and union customs and working agreements must be taken into account in planning how the cargoes are to be handled. A few examples from the port of New York will make this clear.

By long-standing agreement between employers and union, longshoremen working a break-bulk ship are hired in units of twenty-one people. These units (gangs) are worked intact and may not be divided. Even when insufficient work exists for all twenty-one people in No. 3 hold, it is not permissible to leave ten there and send the other eleven to No. 2 hold, where expansion of the gang would expedite cargo outturn. Any gang, however, may be augmented by hiring additional personnel for that particular gang.

The period of work for longshoremen also is governed by union agreement. These workers are hired for a minimum of four hours, except in carefully defined circumstances. If a ship is not expected to berth until nine o'clock in the morning, and work is to commence immediately, the gangs must be hired and paid from eight o'clock. During the waiting time, the gangs may be used for any work the terminal may assign, such as piling cargo, shifting equipment, or sweeping the decks of the transit shed.

No work of any sort, except berthing a ship, handling the mail, or handling an emergency, will be performed on Labor Day, and no work is done after five o'clock on Saturday afternoons, except to "complete" a ship. To complete means finishing a job, if it can be accomplished in a maximum of four hours' time.

The other laborers on the terminal belong to a group collectively known as "dock labor," hired from the ranks of union members as individuals, rather than as a gang. Varied skills such as those of the carpenter, cooper, wire splicer, and cargo checker are found in the dock labor force. When it is determined that four carpenters, two wire splicers, three equipment operators, and six checkers are needed for the day's work, these fifteen people are hired individually. Their wages, hours, and conditions of working are set forth in detail in the union agreements.

Many terminals, especially in the larger ports, have sufficient activity to keep a nucleus of longshoremen and dock laborers regularly employed. This group (known as "steady men") comes to the terminal each day, and although unionized and subject to the working agreement, is not compelled to apply each morning and afternoon for work. The very nature of terminal operation, however, makes it necessary to hire additional people of those grades and skills which the particular needs of the different ships make apparent. These supernumeraries are hired for periods of four hours and may be released at the end of any shift. In most American ports, it is customary for supernumeraries to be obtained through some sort of hiring hall. The normal routine calls for notifying the hiring hall, which may be operated by the union (as in San Francisco), or by a governmental agency (as in the port of New York), of the needs for the next day. The hiring hall, in turn, has its own arrangements for making contact with gang foremen and individual craftsmen. At the appointed hour, the desired contingent of longshoremen and craftsmen reports to the terminal for assignment.

A guiding principle in determining the financial advantage of using labor in overtime periods is derived from accurate knowledge of the true cost of ship's time. This is a complex subject; it involves not only the tangible, out-of-pocket costs of ownership, such as wages, insurance, and fuel oil, but also the intangible "earning potential" of the vessel on her assigned trade route. To fix the earning potential, it is necessary to compute the actual demand for the services of the ship, represented by the number of tons of cargo offered at each port of call, as well as to estimate the number of voyages which could actually be made in the time saved by working after normal hours. Unless it can be shown that the shipowner derives a measurable gain, good management dictates that the vessel lie idle rather than pay laborers at the overtime rate.

For example, a break-bulk cargo ship of about 16,000 tons deadweight might have operating costs of $350 an hour and in port would be charged wharfage and dockage fees to bring the aggregate cost of port time to $400 an hour. The differential between straight time and overtime costs of a single longshore gang in an Atlantic coast port of the United States is $246 an hour. Additionally, checkers and the clerical staff supporting the overtime operation would have to be paid at the prevailing rates. If the total cost of the proposed overtime work did not exceed $400 per hour, and quicker turnaround of the ship, with the consequential benefit of more productive voyage days, is assured, the decision to work the ship in overtime hours would be justified.

The terminal manager who seeks to improve the overall efficiency of the operations can capitalize upon the longshoremen's loyalty to the gang and the importance attached to the position of gang foreman. The careful observance of protocol by management is necessary if the authority and dignity of the foreman are to be maintained. The manager, for instance, may be dissatisfied with the performance of some members of a gang. Rather than correcting the loafer personally, the manager lodges the complaint with the stevedore superintendent. The superintendent discusses the matter with the walking boss (ship foreman) who is instructed to handle the problem. The walking boss explains the problem to the gang foreman (gang boss), who takes the necessary action.

It is essential to recall that the gang members look to the foreman for practically everything: the place and time of the next job, the rotation of work within the gang, promotion to less arduous and more responsible work, the acceptability of excuses for absences, and recommendations for retention in or dismissal from the gang. The foreman has earned this peculiarly privileged position by superior ability to perform the work of each person in the gang and by demonstrated ability to enforce discipline. The foreman has only supervisory duties when the gang is working and is usually on deck where all that transpires can be observed. Ordinarily, the foreman oversees the work of the hatch tender, who directs the exact spot where a draft of cargo is to be placed, and makes certain that the workers understand where and how they are to stow the individual packages of cargo. If a difficult parcel is being handled, the foreman may be in the hold to coordinate the work efforts. As the need arises for dunnage, separation paper, and other supplies, the gang foreman notifies the walking boss.

The hatch tender is the signalman who directs the winch operators and serves as the means of communication between them and the hold or the apron, using a code of hand signals to transmit orders to the winch driver. Excellent depth perception is required since the work station is on the uppermost deck of the ship and it is necessary to judge accurately when a draft of cargo is approaching the last inches above the landing point perhaps 50 feet below. The hatch tender should be of a placid temperament, not easily excited, and able to give undivided attention to the movement of a single cargo draft. The safety of the other workers, and that of the cargo, depends upon those hand signals and decisions.

Winch operators are chosen from members of the gang on the basis of their ability to work with the hatch tender. They control the motors turning the drums on which the cables connected to the cargo hook are wound. In U.S. Atlantic coast ports, there is an operator for each of the two winches on a conventional rig; in Pacific coast ports, one operator controls both motors if they are close to each other. Perfect timing and teamwork are mandatory when two operators are employed. In any event, undeviating attention to the travel of the hook and the signals of the hatch tender is absolutely mandatory.

Dockmen are those members of the gang designated by the foreman to work alongside the ship. In the port of New York, there are eight dockmen; their counterparts are eight holdmen. The dockmen make up the drafts of cargo and hook them to the crane for loading aboard ship. If the ship is discharging, they guide drafts to the platform, and after unhooking the gear, distribute the packages to appropriate piles. Holdmen perform the same duties, except that they work in the ship's cargo spaces. Comparatively, the hold work is more arduous and requires more skill, but since gang members are rotated from pier to hold at the discretion of the foreman, there is no difference in wages.

Complete mechanization of the handling process, in the manner found in a soft drink bottling plant, has not yet come to the break-bulk terminal, nor does it appear to be economically feasible to attempt to develop such systems because of the nature of general cargoes. Since packages are uniform neither in size nor in weight, they cannot be handled as are the bottles and cases in a bottling plant. In addition, vessel stowage must be planned to give the ship adequate stability and proper trim when she is at sea. The constantly changing makeup of a vessel's load means that rarely is there the same distribution of weight from one voyage to the next. Additionally, packages must be stowed compactly below decks so that they will not be damaged when the ship rolls or pitches in a heavy sea. A major problem is to keep commodities which could cause damage to each other, such as marble and redwood, from coming into contact. Finally, lots of cargo must be segregated by ports and consignees to prevent misdelivery. So far, a mechanical installation with adequate flexibility, ruggedness, and economy has not been devised to solve all the problems of cargo stowage.

Cargo on a break-bulk terminal is worked by hand with some mechanical assistance. The principal machines used in terminal operations in U.S. ports today are the forklift truck (sometimes referred to on the waterfront as the "hi-lo"), the mobile crane, the straddle truck, and the tractor-trailer trains. Of these, the forklift truck, traditionally powered by either a gasoline or diesel engine, but increasingly found with battery-operated electric motors to reduce environmental pollution and to enhance safety from fires or carbon monoxide poisoning, is the most versatile and most widely used. It is able to lift its burden high in the air to stack it for storage,

Skilled longshoremen complete securing a heavy locomotive against the perils of sea passage. Photograph courtesy of Delta Line.

or to deposit it on the ground. The versatility of the forklift truck is amazing, and a competent operator can accomplish near miracles with it. The forklift most favored by terminal operators has a capacity of 2 tons and can lift as high as 7 feet. Alternate models are also available with lift capacity of 15 or more tons and a stacking height in excess of 16 feet.

The mobile truck crane has a gasoline engine and pneumatic tires. At the rear of the four-wheel vehicle is a winch, actuated by a power takeoff unit. A wire rope, shackled to a 3-foot length of chain terminating in a cargo hook, runs from the winch along a steel boom projecting several feet beyond the front wheels, and over a roller sheave. When carrying a load, the hook is pulled up almost in contact with the sheave; the draft of cargo hangs from the hook. From the driver's seat, the operator controls the winch, which has a capacity of 3 tons. The truck crane can travel any distance and is almost as maneuverable as its shorter wheelbase partner, the forklift truck. For handling commodities like bagged mail, loose rubber tires, sacked beans, and other items which can be placed in a cargo net, the truck crane is unrivaled.

Some terminals have found that they handle enough timber or long lengths of steel, piping, or packages to justify procuring one or more straddle carriers. These specialized carriers were built originally to handle stacks of lumber, but have proved useful for other items of considerable length and great weight, such as containers. As is true in the case of the forklift truck, the straddle carrier depends upon having its "lift" on a special type of pallet which its mechanism can grip. It is a costly machine, and investment in so specialized a piece of equipment is warranted only by the volume of appropriate cargo which must be handled. Modified to handle very large and heavy containers, the straddler carrier today is used primarily on container terminals.

The tractor-trailer train provides an excellent means of moving cargoes over a considerable distance. It consists of a power unit, or tractor (commonly known as a "jitney"), which tows a train of two or more trailers loaded with either palletized or loose packages or sacks. Although it can be used to advantage in any terminal where hauling distances are great, it is most efficient where wide aprons extend beyond the sidewalls of the transit shed, and trailers can be brought directly under the ship's cargo hook. Most authorities agree that the optimum benefit from this type of equipment is obtained where the design of the terminal includes both wide aprons and long travel distances. The train is also useful in moving cargo from the truck dock to a place of rest in the shed, and from that place to the ship's side. A forklift truck usually is needed to handle the pallets. Trailers at the ship's side are loaded or emptied by means of the ship's cargo gear.

Trailers are comparatively inexpensive, and large numbers are found in terminals utilizing the tractor-trailer system, The tractor, an expensive unit with a highly paid driver, should be kept moving as much of the time as possible. Ideally, a train of loaded trailers is delivered under the ship's hook and uncoupled from the tractor. The tractor is then moved to a point where it hooks on a train of empty trailers and tows them to the loading point, where another exchange is made between "empties" and "loads."

Pneumatic tires are favored for most materials-handling equipment, which is designed to provide maximum simplicity of operation combined with safety and comfort for the driver. Experience has shown that employee morale and efficiency decrease in direct ratio to operator fatigue.

Proper operation of a terminal requires that vehicular traffic patterns be planned with great care. In laying out traffic patterns within the terminal, cross traffic should be avoided. Eliminating the hazard of collision at a crossing makes possible greater vehicle speed. With no crossings, no fields of observation need be provided, thereby saving deck space.

A major problem in terminal operation is truck traffic. If large motor vehicles are permitted to enter the transit shed, roadways and turnaround spaces must be provided. Some terminal managers exclude trucks altogether, and receive and deliver cargo at the headhouse. By excluding trucks, maximum deck area is reserved for cargo. The forklift trucks and other motorized terminal equipment require only narrow alleys, and can move more rapidly when they do not have to watch for moving trucks. If trucks are unloaded at the headhouse, maximum benefit is obtained from the labor of the people assigned to this job because they spend their working time on the truck line, handling cargo as fast as trucks can be put into position. Cargo is discharged from trucks to pallet boards or cargo nets and is taken directly to the ship for loading or is transported to the place where it is to rest until loading time. Goods are delivered to the trucks of the consignees after being sorted in the transit shed and placed on pallets or in nets. Appropriate equipment is used to transfer cargo to and from the truck loading platform.

This same pattern of traffic control can be followed on the wharf. Instead of bringing trucks to the headhouse, they are driven to the loading platform which parallels, on the land side, the ship's berth. The shed is reserved exclusively for materials-handling equipment and cargo. An advantage the wharf enjoys over the typical finger pier is that trucks may be directed to the loading platform most nearly opposite the ship's hatch where the cargo is being worked. The movement of cargo is limited to the short distance across the wharf. This plan is especially successful where a wide, sheltered platform is provided at truck-bed height.

In ports where railroad lines extend to the waterfront, it is usual for the tracks to parallel the ship's berth. This arrangement permits railroad cars to be placed under the ship's hooks, and for their contents to be transferred directly into the hold of the vessel. Conversely, the goods carried in the ship may be discharged into waiting railroad cars. Terminal management techniques for operations of this sort are the same as for lighters bringing cargoes to the offshore side of the ship. Delivery of cargo by rail cars to be "spotted" at ship's side must be scheduled to conform to switching schedules of the railroad. Many terminals have their own means of moving cars after they are spotted on the tracks. Where no method of moving cars is provided by the terminal, the railroad company must be asked to make a switch locomotive available.

Ideally, materials-handling equipment hauls payloads in both directions (known as "cycling"), but the average marine general cargo terminal affords little opportunity for such efficiency. Consideration should be given to the possibility of back-hauls when routes are laid out. In all cases, the goal of the routing must be the maximum movement of tonnage per machine-hour.

Attention has already been drawn to the importance of controlling the circulation of vehicles within the terminal enclosure. In break-bulk transit sheds, pedestrian traffic, if allowed, should be restricted to conspicuously marked walkways. Container terminals, partly because of their size and partly because of the density of truck traffic, should exclude pedestrians from the area in which containers are stored. For workers and others authorized to be within the terminal enclosure, transportation should be provided and its use made mandatory for everyone, without exceptions. These measures enhance personnel safety as well as the security of cargo.

In conjunction with the equipment just described, powered and non-powered gravity roller conveyors are found in many terminals. They are excellent for transferring packages of uniform size over relatively short distances, such as from a delivery truck to a cargo stack. They are also useful in expediting the movement of small packages from the wings of a hold to the square of the hatch, or in the reverse direction. Conveyors in service on marine terminals are easily portable and are shifted as required. The more extensive employment of these two types of conveyors in general cargo operations is not deemed practical for the reasons advanced to explain the lack of complete mechanization in a break-bulk terminal.

Whether thinking in terms of people or machines, the terminal manager has to remember that working cargo is the sole reason for the organization. Ideally, the terminal manager, or a skilled representative, takes part in forming the plans for receiving cargo which is to be unloaded from the ship and also to be brought to the terminal for movement overseas. The assignment of precise locations for designated lots of outgoing cargo is usually a function of the stevedore superintendent, who recommends to the terminal manager certain patterns for laying out the transit shed. This layout is planned to assure that there will be sufficient space in the shed for those goods to be discharged from the ship which are most likely to be held for several days before delivery. When the terminal handles cargo in only

Railroad passenger cars are unloaded at a gantry-crane equipped open pier. The ship's whirly cranes and exceptionally large hatches are noteworthy. Photograph courtesy of F.J. Duffy.

one direction, either outgoing or incoming, it may be possible to allocate permanently certain spaces in the shed to cargo for each port of call. This arrangement is satisfactory where the quantity of cargo moving does not vary greatly from voyage to voyage; where there is not much pressure resulting from frequent arrivals or departures of ships; and where floor space so assigned, and not used, can be spared.

A more flexible plan usually is followed in sheds where two-way traffic must be processed. Outbound requirements are ascertained from study of the cargo booking sheets to determine how much space is needed to accommodate consignments to each of the ports of call. Examination of the incoming ship's cargo stowage plan and manifest reveals approximately how many square feet must be allocated to each of the major blocks of her cargo. With this information, the available space in the terminal enclosure can be assigned for most effective use. It must be noted, in this connection, that the layout must be adapted to any congestion which may exist in the transit shed because consignees of cargo delivered by earlier arrivals have not picked up their goods.

The actual layout of the transit shed necessarily depends upon its design. If the shed is long, narrow, and cluttered with many stanchions, there will be a significant loss of working area because of these stanchions. Modern terminal design provides for wide sheds and stanchions as far apart as possible so that the available floor space may be put to the most efficient use.

A wharf lies parallel to the shoreline and is easier to work than a finger pier. It has two advantages over the pier: there is accommodation for ships on the one side only, and traffic has access to the transit shed at each end as well as at intermediate points of the wharf structure. The finger pier, as the name suggests, projects into the waterway at an angle to the shore. Ships usually are berthed on both sides, and some long piers provide moorings for two or even three vessels in tandem. Cargo operations in such circumstances are impeded because all wheeled traffic must enter and leave through a single gateway at the land end. A major cause of lost floor space in this type of installation is the need to provide clear areas where trucks can turn around.

The rule of thumb for the amount of transit shed floor space needed to work a ship's cargo is 9 square feet per ton. Ideally, the shed should have only one level in order to use modern terminal and materials-handling techniques to their highest levels of efficiency. Wheeled vehicles of any description are able to move anywhere, and traffic control is comparatively simple. Routine inspection and inventory procedures are made easy. An important, but occasionally overlooked, gain is that desirable illumination of the working area may be obtained through installing skylights in the roof.

Nevertheless, many of the older transit sheds are two-story structures, built to obtain the largest possible number of ship berths on limited water frontage. These sheds are usually narrow and not well adapted to mechanized cargo-handling operations. The disadvantage of the upper deck lies partly in the restricted weight allowance per square foot on the upper deck, and partly in the difficulty of access for large trucks and the consequent necessity of rehandling packages. Using the second deck for incoming cargo, however, does eliminate confusion with the outbound shipments.

As a device to offset the higher cost of handling cargo on double-deck piers, a few of these sheds have been built with truck ramps connecting the street level with the upper level. The theory is that trucks can be driven from the street to the upper level to discharge or to load. This obviates the need to move cargo from the upper deck before it can be put into trucks.

Interior of a well-designed and well-lighted transit shed. Photograph courtesy of the Port Authority of New York and New Jersey.

The floor space devoted to the ramp, however, does interfere with efficient operation of the entire terminal.

No double-deck transit sheds are equipped with elevators to lift trucks to the upper level. Installing them would be prohibitively expensive, and while they would take up less space than a ramp, they still would absorb room which can be used more profitably for other purposes.

Materials handling of break-bulk cargo on the waterfront today depends almost entirely on the cargo pallet. This invaluable piece of equipment is a light, double-faced platform of wood, usually 4 feet long by 40 inches wide. It is inexpensive considering the number of times it is reused. As cargo is received at the terminal, it is general practice to place the goods on pallets to build up a "handling unit" weighing 1 or 2 tons. This "palletized" unit must be moved by machine and is not broken up until the individual containers are removed for stowage in the ship.

The principle underlying the use of pallets is simple: it provides a more economical method of employing the resources of the terminal (space, manpower, and money). The greatest expense in terminal operations lies in the requirement to handle literally thousands of packages (bales, boxes, bags, crates, and loose items such as automobile tires) each day. By combining many packages into a single large handling unit at the time they are received by the terminal, and then using a machine operated by one person to perform all movement within the terminal, obvious economies are effected. Concurrently, increased efficiency is obtained by the use of terminal shed space, always critically short of requirements, and better service can be rendered the shippers by reducing the time needed for either loading or unloading cargo.

Many ocean carriers have been able to convince shippers that this palletization and containerization of their cargoes should be accomplished at the warehouse or factory where the shipment originates. The shipper builds up and straps the load into a single unit which remains unbroken until the consignee has received it at destination. There are notable benefits from this practice.

1. Individual packages are not subject to handling at the terminal, and therefore breakage and other types of damage are reduced, if not eliminated altogether.
2. The opportunities for pilferage and loss of individual packages are minimized, especially if the entire shipping unit is enclosed in a protective cover. A sheet of heavy plastic serves very well.

3. Cargo checking by all parties is simpler, more rapid, and more accurate because fewer units have to be counted.
4. Economies of time can be effected at every transfer point.

Over the years, pallet sizes have become more or less standardized, but no formal agreements as to dimensions have ever been reached between carriers or shippers. It is true, however, that as the use of pallets has been extended beyond the confines of the terminal, the size and type of pallet used for transportation has become more and more conventional, until today the most generally used pallet is 48 inches long by 40 inches wide, as previously mentioned. The material used for facings is almost invariably lumber 1 inch thick, while the so-called stringers are 4 inches square.

Where pallets are used extensively in the terminal, a number of important determinations must be made by the manager. Roadways and passages for the forklift trucks are basic requirements, and space for them must be allocated first in the general layout of the shed. Then the load-bearing capacity of the shed's deck must be ascertained, and rules promulgated as to the number of tiers of pallets which may be permissible. The tiers will vary with the weight of the commodity piled on the pallet, and therefore guidance must be given to the labor force if structural damage is to be avoided. The nature of the packages in each pallet also will influence the number of tiers because the bottom pallets must be protected from crushing. If cargo is palletized by the terminal, then adequate quantities (often numbering in the thousands) must be kept on hand. Provisions for storing, repairing, and issuing or receiving pallets become part of the routine of cargo operations.

After completing these arrangements, it is necessary to select the sizes, types, and capacities of materials-handling equipment to be used in moving pallets economically and efficiently around the terminal. This machinery is expensive; only those units required, plus spares to insure good maintenance, should be procured.

A clean and neat terminal demonstrates that a good safety program is in effect. In cold climates where snow and ice may accumulate on wharf or pier aprons or in marshaling yards, it is good management practice to have appropriate plans and equipment available to remove these hazards. Oil spills on working surfaces must be cleaned up immediately; otherwise, the oil will become a serious hazard as it is spread throughout a wide area by vehicles operating within the terminal. All motorized equipment therefore should be inspected daily for leaks, and defective units withdrawn until needed repairs have been effected.

All equipment, both aboard ship and in the terminal, is inspected before work begins to assure that detectable deficiencies are remedied, and all unsafe machinery must be barred from use. The most rigid standards must be established and adhered to in the inspection of cables, wire rope, cargo nets, slings, and any other devices employed to lift cargo. Questionable items must be replaced as soon as a potential weakness is detected. Supervisors at every level—gang bosses, foremen, supervisors, and management personnel—must be aware at all times that they are personally responsible for safe working practices within their sphere of authority, and must understand that they will be held individually accountable for accidents.[1]

Safety concerns are not limited to personnel; they can have considerable economic force when applied to cargo entrusted to the carrier. The ship operator is obliged to handle a consignment so that the condition at the moment of delivery to the consignee is no different from that when presented by the shipper. Unless it can be shown that the damage or loss occurred as a result of a cause for which the law grants an exemption, the carrier is responsible and must pay the shipper or consignee the agreed value of the goods. Often the settlement of a single claim for one broken article can absorb the profit earned on the transportation of several hundred tons of other cargo. The terminal manager must strive constantly to insure that cargo moving through the terminal receives the best possible treatment.

Care of the cargo requires two things: skillful and gentle handling of packages to prevent even superficial damage, and thorough inspection of packages to verify the condition in which the cargo is presented by the shipper to the carrier. The terminal manager must assume that the longshoremen and their supervisors are competent to handle the individual packages properly, and periodic inspections are made to assure that no one deviates from approved standards of performance. The inspection of goods, it must be emphasized, is a task of utmost importance since the carrier will base any defense against a claim for damage or loss on the completeness and accuracy of the examination of each package. It is mandatory that the receiving clerk and the staff of checkers be instructed in desired procedures, that inspections be performed conscientiously and efficiently, and that adequate records of the inspection be entered on the dock receipt. The same significance attaches to the careful inspection of cargo removed from the ship. The delivery clerk is responsible for this activity. At the time the consignee accepts the shipment, the condition of each identifiable unit must be noted and appropriately recorded.

Checker measures an item of cargo with his four-foot rule.

Checkers are very important in terminal operation. In most ports, they are employed by the hour. In U.S. ports, they receive the same hourly compensation as longshoremen but are guaranteed eight hours' pay, rather than the four hours assured longshoremen when they report for work. Usually there is a checker assigned to each gang of longshoremen, and thus employment opportunities for checkers vary with those of the longshoremen. In those terminals where a ship is on berth practically all the time, a fixed number of longshoremen and checkers is certain of steady employ-

"Taking exceptions": A cargo checker examines steel pipe on arrival at a marine terminal. Photograph courtesy of North Carolina State Ports Authority.

ment. These "regulars" or "steady workers" can be instructed in the terminal's procedures of checking, and their integrity and accuracy can be established in fact. Additional checkers are obtained, in U.S. ports, by notifying the longshoremen's union hiring hall. Although these temporary employees are competent to inspect, measure, and weigh packages, the accuracy and completeness of their records may not always be in accordance with established terminal practice. Furthermore, there is no satisfactory system for determining the personal integrity of these individuals before they begin their work. This aspect of operation poses a serious, recurring, and nearly insoluble problem in the economy of terminal management.

Checking cargo in a typically busy two-way break-bulk general cargo terminal is of the utmost importance. The carrier must inspect the cargo as it is received and record any defects noted. In terminal parlance, this is known as "taking exceptions," and refers to the phrase in the bill of lading that cargo is accepted for shipment "in apparent good order and condition, except as noted hereon." The exception is the carrier's defense against the charge that the damage was inflicted after the package was turned over to him or her. Ideally, the shipowner should refuse to accept any damaged cargo, and should insist that perfect packages be substituted for damaged ones, or the bill of lading should be corrected to show the number of perfect packages actually received. Practice is short of the ideal, and the carrier may have to accept articles which have already been somewhat damaged. The carrier is responsible only for damage in excess of that noted at the time of receipt of the goods. Unfortunately for the shipowner, it often transpires that the shipper or consignee blames the carrier for damage that was sustained prior to its receipt by the marine terminal. The more complete the carrier's record of exceptions, the better the legal position.

Efficient terminal management requires that notations made by checkers be accurate, definite, and complete. It is not necessary to define further the word *accurate*. The term *definite* refers to the identification of the particular item, the exact description of the damage, and the reason therefor, if readily detectable. *Complete* means that when the checker turns in the notation, there will be no need to seek further information. A few examples follow:

A bag of coffee is noted to be only partially filled ("slack"). Further examination shows that the sack has been torn and resewn. There is no ready explanation for how the bag was torn or when it was resewn. The checker's entry should be: "SACK No. 4, torn and resewn. Stamped weight, 110. Actual weight, 78 lbs."

A sack of flour is observed to have a large brown stain on the lower portion of the bag. It is not possible to determine what damage has been caused to the flour. The entry should be: "SACK No. 22. Water-stained, lower half, front of bag."

An unboxed automobile is discharged, and one fender is found to have been scratched and dented. The entry should be: "Ford Sedan No. 332. Right front fender, deep scratch, 9 inches long, beginning 14 inches from headlamp, running diagonally to bottom beading. Small dent, 3 inches in diameter, on top of fender 8 inches behind headlamp. Paint not broken."

Efficient operation of a break-bulk cargo terminal requires care in planning each stage of activity, and nowhere is this more true than in the layout of the transit shed(s). The booking clerk keeps the receiving clerk informed as cargo commitments are made, so that adequate space may be allotted to handle the consignments to the different ports. In the case of a company maintaining a service to a number of ports of call, as, for example, through the Mediterranean, or to the southeast coast of Africa, or the Pacific coast of South America, not only must there be an area reserved for each port, but there must be a plan for properly segregating the various types of cargo destined to each port. The following categories must be so placed within each port space that they do not contaminate any goods:

1. Wet cargo (liquids in barrels or drums) to be stowed in the bottom of the ship's holds.
2. Long steel, timber, or other pieces to be stowed on the bottom or in the wings of the cargo holds.
3. Odoriferous or obnoxious commodities requiring special stowage.
4. Hazardous articles (acids, gases, inflammables, and explosives) which must be stowed on deck or in special lockers aboard ship.
5. Packages containing commodities like lamp black, flour, and cement which sift out and may damage other cargo.
6. Refrigerated or other perishable cargo.
7. Fragile goods, such as glassware.
8. Valuable packages requiring security stowage (this sometimes is known as "mate's cargo").
9. Heavy-lift items. Port equipment or the ship's heavy-lift gear must be used to handle this type of cargo, and therefore careful scheduling of details incident to the use of this specialized equipment is essential to eliminate lost time.

Of equal importance to the terminal for planning purposes is information concerning cargo on incoming ships. The quantity, nature, and disposition of the load must be known since space for storage has to be provided somewhere within the terminal enclosure. When a considerable portion of the inbound cargo is to be transshipped into barges or lighters working on the offshore side of the vessel, there is an immediate easing of the requirement for accommodation in the transit sheds. If the cargo must be brought into the shed for sorting and delivery to consignees, a corresponding amount of space will be needed. These arrangements depend upon careful coordination of all the divisions of the terminal to achieve the desired goal of efficient and expeditious turnaround of the ship.

Once the terminal has been laid out for the incoming and outgoing cargoes, the receiving clerk becomes responsible for placing the outbound cargo in the designated areas within the shed for terminal enclosure. When a consignment of cargo is delivered to the terminal, it must be accompanied by the dock receipt, which is prepared by the shipper and contains these data: name of shipper and consignee; port of destination; description of the goods, including type(s) of package and weight; and the booking number. This form, in some steamship company practice, is prepared in five copies. When the truck arrives at the gatehouse, the driver surrenders the dock receipt to the receiving clerk, who stamps it with the date and time of arrival, and inserts the name and voyage number of the vessel into which the cargo is to be loaded. The original of the five copies is the official dock receipt, and on it are made appropriate notations concerning the condition of the cargo or the container, and the actual measurement and weight of the consignment. The second copy, after processing, is returned to the driver as proof that the cargo was delivered as ordered. The third and fifth copies are placed with the cargo; from this customary usage, the third copy is known as the "pile tag." As the consignment either is packed into a container or is stowed aboard ship, this tag is given to the chief mate for record and for planning the outturn of cargo at the port of destination. The fourth copy remains with the receiving clerk, where it is available to the stevedore for use in preparing the stowage plan. After the cargo has been placed aboard ship, the fifth copy, with all appropriate notations, is returned to the receiving clerk's files, where it is kept as a permanent record of the handling of the consignment.[2]

The receiving clerk assures that outgoing cargo is marked so that everything for one port will be easy to locate in the holds of the ship. Usually this is accomplished by means of "port marks" or symbols applied to every box, bag, crate, or other container received for shipment. For example, Genoa might be designated by a red circle, while Istanbul would be symbolized by a green square. There are no fixed rules for port marks, except that they be simple in design, distinctive, and easy to see. They may be affixed at the convenience of the terminal, sometimes in the transit shed and sometimes after the cargo is stowed in the ship. Affixing the mark after stowage makes it certain that it will be visible during discharging operations. Regardless of where or when put on, the mark must not harm the container, and must not rub or wash off. Unpackaged articles such as lumber or steel are marked with a quick-drying paint; some bagged or baled goods on which painted marks are not practical are tagged, using the same color scheme as for painted marks.

Cargo discharged by the ship is picked up by the consignee on notification by the carrier that it is available. Normal routine of delivery is in accordance with the following pattern.

The truck driver presents the steamship carrier's delivery order to the gatekeeper, who verifies that the papers are in order. The process includes obtaining clearances from the customs officers on duty, and also ascertaining that all freight, terminal, and demurrage charges have been paid. If everything is in order, the driver is dispatched to the slot where the cargo is located. A checker will count the packages, to assure that the number matches what is designated on the delivery order. Discrepancies are noted, and reconciled if possible. When the truck is loaded, the driver returns to the gatehouse, acknowledges receipt of the cargo, and is given a gate pass.

A cardinal principle of terminal management is that transit sheds shall not be converted into warehouses. One device widely employed to accomplish this is to charge consignees who are slow in picking up their shipments a punitive storage fee, called demurrage. In the United States, the general rule is that the consignee has five working days after the ship completes discharge during which to take delivery of the goods. After the expiration of this "free time," demurrage is charged on an accelerating basis. After two days, for instance, the rate is doubled; after four days, it is tripled; after five days it is quintupled. A necessary corollary of the demurrage plan is the efficient operation of an inventory system that will reveal daily what cargoes have been left on the terminal beyond the allowed free time, and what packages have been picked up. An incidental benefit to the terminal operator is that the systematic examination of cargo piles within the terminal enclosure often uncovers items discharged at the port by mistake. A box destined to Baltimore that is removed from the ship in New York will be "short delivered" in Baltimore, and a claim will be filed. Locating the box in New York removes the basis for the claim. Occasionally a box, previously reported as missing or lost, will be found to have been placed on the wrong pile in the transit shed. Only as deliveries are accomplished is the missing package discovered.

To control the flow of cargo, and to establish a system for locating a 50-pound package in the midst of 15,000 tons of assorted commodities, the terminal maintains a variety of records. The first of these, in order of compilation, is the receiving clerk's *list of cargo received*, on which are recorded, by dock receipt numbers, the various consignments of cargo delivered by truck. A separate list is opened for each ship to be worked, and stays open while that vessel is in port. When loading is completed and the ship is ready to sail, the list is closed. In appearance, the list is very simple since it shows only the serial number of the dock receipt in one column and the cubic footage and weight of the shipment in adjacent columns. In normal circumstances, it is used only by the receiving clerk to keep informed of what consignments have been brought to the terminal. It has no circulation outside this office.

A similar list for cargo delivered by barge or lighter is maintained by the receiving clerk. It differs slightly from the truck record, because it is the permanent notation of when the lighter was delivered by the harbor carrier, when work was started, and when the lighter was released to its owner.

There is a column in this *lighter record* to show where the cargo is stored in the terminal, or stowed in the ship, as appropriate.

Each morning at eight o'clock, the receiving clerk compiles a report of cargo work completed during the preceding twenty-four hours. A separate report is submitted for each ship and contains these details: number of tons of cargo booked into the ship, tons of cargo actually delivered by shippers during the day, tons loaded, and the quantity still to be worked. The *daily cargo report* also shows hatches worked, number of laborers engaged, actual time they were employed, and commodities handled during the period.

The daily cargo report can be used for many purposes: it is the basis for forecasts of commodity-handling speeds, and the comprehensive record of the actual gang-hours required to unload and reload the ship. If there has been any period of "detention" (time lost from the cargo-working period), the length of the detention and the reason for it are shown. The state of the weather is also set down, as well as any unusual incidents that might explain the rate at which cargo was handled. The report provides information on both discharging and loading operations. It is circulated to the vice president, operations; the vice president, traffic; the freight traffic managers; and any other persons concerned with the data contained in this document.

The *wharfage report* is the inventory of all cargo on which demurrage is payable because it has been left on the pier beyond the allowed free time. It is compiled for each ship by the delivery clerk and shows for every shipment the commodity, consignee, marks, bill of lading number, and the reason for nondelivery. The report is made initially at the expiration of allowed free time and periodically thereafter as each demurrage period ends, until the cargo is removed from the terminal.

When a vessel's discharge has been completed, the terminal manager gathers into one report all data relating to cargo for which no documents are on hand and which investigation shows should have been delivered to another port. These are known as "over-carried" or "short-delivered" cargo. There will be consignments in which shortages have been noted. Inevitably there will be some damage, to be followed by claims from consignees for restitution of the loss. These data are assembled into the *over, short, and damaged cargo report*, commonly referred to as the O. S. and D. report. This document is of great value in determining the actual efficiency of the terminal and the carrier's operations, for it helps to pinpoint actual damage; it puts losses, overs, and shorts into their proper perspective; and it serves as a convenient means of notifying all other ports on the company's route that certain cargo is missing or seeking an owner. The O. S. and D. report is disseminated to the master of the ship, the terminals in every port of call, the claims department, the vice presidents for operations and traffic, and the terminal's receiving and delivery clerks.

Terminal efficiency is gauged generally by the number of tons of cargo handled in one hour by a gang of longshoremen, or alternatively by the total annual throughput. This rating is not based upon individual performance, nor does it show how fast or how slowly particular commodities are loaded or discharged. It does, however, set up a reasonable standard by which to compare terminals in a port and is useful in evaluating relative efficiency in the different cities where a steamship company may operate general cargo terminals. Comparisons, to be valid, must take into account the use of machines by the gang. All too often, expensive tools become simply effort savers. In the port of New York, for instance, at least one forklift truck is required to support a gang, but the number of tons of cargo handled per hour is not much greater than it was in the days when manpower alone was used.

Break-bulk cargo terminal operations are more efficient, and port turnaround time is reduced, when the pier or wharf has a wide apron between the shed and the ship's side. Railroad and motor vehicles can be brought directly under the ship's hook for delivery or receipt of goods. Terminal equipment can be used effectively to spot or pick up cargo drafts. Ships' booms extend over the apron to deposit or pick up their loads. Two or more drafts can be deposited on the apron and still be within reach of the single ship's hook. If the terminal provides shoreside cranes, as is true in most European ports, all the above listed advantages apply, with the addition of a larger radius of operation. Either several trucks or railroad cars can be served concurrently, or a number of piles of cargo can be built up while the materials-handling units are working to and from the interior of the transit shed. These factors are recognized in modern terminal design, and aprons varying in width from 15 to 50 feet are found in the new structures.

The value of cargoes piled in a transit shed, or in the area immediately adjacent to the entrance, is great, and the terminal manager must provide for its safety. Just inside the shed, where it will be clearly visible at all times to the gateman, is the locker for especially valuable cargo. In this space, commonly referred to as the "corral" or "crib," are stored items such as bales of furs and valuable skins, perfumes, liquor, watches and watch movements, cigarette lighters, guns, narcotics, and costume jewelry. When

Derrick (whirly) cranes hoist palletized, bagged cargo. Note wide apron of marine terminal. Photograph courtesy of Port of Sacramento, California.

the terminal is in full operation, the most reliable and trustworthy guard is assigned to duty inside the corral. Patrolmen make frequent inspections of the entire terminal area, seeking evidence of theft and irregularities which suggest actual or contemplated pilferage, and indications of fire. Alertness, willingness to take a second look at anything, and facilities for prompt communications with the roundsman are essential to satisfactory performance of the duties of the patrolman.

The minimum staff for the security of any transit shed is a gateman, a patrolman, and a roundsman. During the working day, it may be necessary or desirable to increase the staff by a large number who will be assigned posts in accordance with the plan proposed by the security director or the roundsman. If pilferable cargo is to be worked in a ship, a uniformed guard in the hold has a deterrent effect upon would-be thieves. If passengers are to be embarked, a number of guards must be assigned to assure that baggage is not stolen, passport routines followed without disturbance, and traffic of both vehicles and people is directed properly. If a ship is moored alongside for some time, a gangway watchman is provided to limit access to authorized persons. All these extra people are ordered from the agency holding the contract for guard service and are assigned by the roundsman or the security director, in accordance with the capabilities and experience of each guard. In the United States, security personnel are unionized and their working hours and conditions are set forth in appropriate detail in the agreement between the employers and the union.

The terminal manager depends upon the superintendent to supervise the actual labor of handling cargo to and from ships, upon the security director to take care of cargo while it is in the transit shed or the area immediately adjacent, and upon the receiving and delivery clerks for accurate performance of their duties. Without these assistants, it would be impossible to operate the terminal.

As can be imagined, operating a marine terminal is a twenty-four-hour-a-day job. The level of detail required to discharge and load a ship successfully is almost incredible, and each detail must be completed accurately and on time in order for the terminal's objectives to be met. A key element in the smooth operation of a terminal is for all terminal workers to realize that they are an integral part of a special team whose task is necessary for proper growth and operations of international trade. It is a good feeling to watch a ship sail on schedule and know that the terminal made the sailing possible.

CHAPTER EIGHT

The Stevedore Contract

Among the documents enumerating the duties and responsibilities of shipowners and shoreside specialists, none is of greater importance than the contract between the steamship company and the stevedore. Fundamentally, this is an agreement delineating the charges, terms, and conditions under which the arduous, skilled, and highly essential labor of loading and unloading ships is to be performed.

The usual contract to handle break-bulk cargo at a conventional terminal contains a list of the commodities that will be handled and the charge per ton or other unit of each of the listed items. The fee is predicated upon normal working hours of the longshoremen, and includes all necessary handling of goods, clerical work, checking cargo into or out of the ship, and routine recoopering (sewing torn bags, securing loose boards in boxes and crates, and similar minor repair work), and watchman service. A sample of the listing of different items handled in a break-bulk terminal follows:

Large unboxed automobiles	Charged per unit
Compact unboxed automobiles	Charged per unit
Bagged cargo stowing at more than 60 cubic feet per weight ton	Charged per 2,240 lbs.
Bagged cargo stowing at less than 60 cubic feet per weight ton	Charged per 2,240 lbs.
Cocoa beans in bags	Charged per 2,240 lbs.
Wet hides in bundles	Charged per 2,240 lbs.
Dry skins in bales	Charged per 2,240 lbs.
Copper, slabs	Charged per 2,240 lbs.
Cement in bags or strapped to pallets	Charged per 2,240 lbs.

The method by which these different rates are set is worthy of study. Many of the "old-timers" in the stevedoring business used intuition, experience, and the barest minimum of rudimentary calculation to determine what they should charge to handle a particular commodity. Today, rates are made somewhat more scientifically and are computed to the fourth decimal place, reflecting with greater accuracy the actual cost of performance under the contract.

The stevedore's efforts to obtain a contract to work conventional break-bulk ships at a terminal in the United States normally commence by learning, as accurately as possible, the details of the trade of the carrier under consideration. First, the stevedore must know how frequently and in what form (bundle, bale, bag, carton, slab, or whatever packaging is customary) each item moves, and approximately how many tons are included in each ship's load. Access to, and careful study of, a number of inbound and outbound cargo manifests will provide this essential information. Inasmuch as vessel characteristics, particularly hatch sizes and the capabilities of cargo gear, affect the rapidity with which the vessel may be worked, the stevedore must become acquainted with the ships of the fleet under consideration. The terminal where the vessels will load and unload merits expert scrutiny since the physical features of the plant can influence the speed with which longshoremen are able to transfer cargo from shore to ship and vice versa.

At this point in the investigations, the contracting stevedore must talk to the shipowner to reach agreement on what each will be required to furnish. If the contractor is to provide the equipment and gear used in the operation, the bid must reflect the investment in the equipment. If, on the other hand, the shipowner is to supply the machines, slings, nets, and other items of equipment, the stevedore's bid should be correspondingly lower.

A number of unchangeable factors, however, must be taken into account by the contractor as the computations are being made. For one thing, the size of the gang of longshoremen to be employed cannot be altered by an individual contractor since it has been fixed by negotiation between the union and all the employers of longshoremen in the port. The wages to be paid, and the working conditions in which the laborers perform their tasks, have a decided effect upon final rates for individual commodities. Necessarily, the stevedore's bid is the result of determining all the hourly costs of labor (including fringe benefits paid by the employer as well as actual wages, insurance premiums, and related taxes), and estimating as accurately as possible the number of tons of the commodity the standard gang of longshoremen can load or unload in one hour. An error of a half-ton an hour in the performance (or production, as it is known in the trade) of the gang can be financially disastrous to the stevedore, should the commodity under study begin to move in quantities exceeding expectations.

The following clauses, quoted from a standard contract used in a major U.S. port, set forth the responsibility which each of the two parties to that contract must assume:

Commodity Rate Inclusions. As part of the foregoing specified rates, the Contractor agrees to include in the commodity rate the following described services:

a. Transport Contractor's gear and equipment to and from the pier where the ship is berthed, excepting to locations that are inaccessible to motor trucks.

b. Provide all necessary stevedoring labor, including winchmen, hatch tenders, tractor and dock crane operators, also foremen and such other stevedoring supervision as is needed for the proper and efficient conduct of the work.

c. Adjust rigging of booms and guys, etc., at hatches where work of discharging and/or loading will be conducted and unrigging when completed; also removing and replacing beams and hatch covers.

d. Discharge cargo from or load cargo into vessel's holds, 'tween decks, on deck, shelter or bridge spaces, deep tanks, cargo lockers and lazarettes, also temporary bunker spaces, but excluding fore and aft peaks and bilges.

e. Shift gangs as required between inshore and offshore, also from lower to upper floor (or vice versa) on double-deck piers. Shift lighters into working position after they have been placed alongside vessel, when this can be done without tugs.

f. Sort (by longshoremen) and stack cargo man-high on pier upon discharge of vessel or break down cargo from man-high upon loading of vessel.

g. Perform such long trucking as required within the limits of the pier where the vessel is berthed; limited to the section occupied by the vessel, should the pier have multiple sections.

h. Load and lay dunnage board (except freighted dunnage lumber) as required during loading for proper stowage of cargo.

i. Work two gangs simultaneously in hatches when required and when practical to do so, provided necessary additional booms, falls, and winches are supplied by vessel or from shore facilities.

Vacation, Welfare and Pension Allowances. Assessments charged to the Contractor to carry out the requirements of paid vacations, welfare benefits and pension fund plan under the prevailing Wage Agreements with the International Longshoremen's Association are

not included in the commodity rates quoted herein, unless otherwise stated, and such assessments shall be charged for by the
Contractor at the percentage factors prevailing in the port. When
charges are to be rendered by the Contractor on the basis of the
labor wages incurred, these assessments shall be added at cost.
Equipment. The ship is to supply booms, adequate winches, in good
order and with sufficient steam or current for their efficient operation; blocks, topping lifts, guys; wire or rope falls of sufficient
length and strength, hatch tents, lights for night work; tugs, derricks
or cranes for such heavy lifts as exceed the capacity of the ship's
gear, and cranes in the absence of ship's winches. The ship is also
to supply dunnage, paper, and all material for shoring and lashing
cargo as well as grain bags and separation cloths.

The Contractor is to supply all other cargo handling gear and
equipment, such as hooks, pendants, save-alls, nets, trays, bridle
chains and slings (except slings for heavy lifts when hoisted by
heavy-lift floating or shore derrick), also hand trucks, mechanical
trucks or tractors, also dock tractor cranes as needed for efficient
stevedoring work.
Insurance. The rates quoted include the cost of, and the Contractor
agrees to maintain in full force and effect, Workmen's Compensation Insurance covering the Contractor's statutory and common law
liability for injury or death sustained by its employees and Public
Liability Insurance covering the Contractor's liability for bodily injury, including death, sustained by third parties, arising out of operations performed hereunder, such Public Liability Insurance to be in
the amount of $50,000 for death or injury of one person and
$150,000 for death or injury of more than one person in a single
accident.

The rates specified herein also include Social Security Taxes
and Unemployment Insurance as presently payable by the Contractor. Whenever labor wages are to be charged for by the Contractor
under this agreement, the Social Security Taxes and Unemployment
Insurance incurred thereon shall be added to charges for Workmen's Compensation and Public Liability Insurance, and all such
charges shall be termed "Insurance."
Responsibility for Damage or Loss. The Contractor will be legally
liable for damage to the ship and its equipment, and for damage to
cargo, or loss of cargo overside, through its negligence. When such
damage occurs to ship or its equipment, or where loss or damage oc-

curs to cargo by reason of such negligence, the Ship's Officers or other authorized representatives will call this to the attention of the Contractor at the time of accident. With respect to claims for loss or damage to cargo and/or baggage, the liability of the Contractor shall be limited to physical damage, caused by the negligence of the Contractor and to such claims that result from fraud on the part of employees of the Contractor engaged in the delivery, receiving, and watching of cargo.

Detentions, Waiting, Lay Time. Whenever work is interrupted after starting and detentions of not over 20 minutes' duration occur, the Contractor will make no charge for reimbursement therefor. Should such detention time exceed 20 minutes' duration, the Contractor will charge for the full detention time at cost plus insurance. When men are employed and unable to work through causes beyond the Contractor's control, or when men are to be paid for a minimum working period in accordance with the wage agreement, the cost of such waiting or idle time will be charged for by the Contractor at cost, plus insurance.

Overtime. When overtime hours are worked, the additional wages thereby incurred and paid to all labor and other stevedoring personnel so employed will be charged for by the Contractor at cost, plus insurance.

In the event that, under any Government Order or final determination by a court of competent jurisdiction, labor is required to be paid wages in excess of the wages paid under the Federal Fair Labor Standards Act as presently interpreted throughout this port, such wages plus insurance and social security and unemployment taxes together with any additional amount other than wages for which the Contractor may be legally liable under the Act, shall be reimbursed to the Contractor by the Owners, Agents, or Charterers, at cost.

Increase or Decrease in Wages. All rates specified are based on and subject to the employment of present longshore labor at the rate scale and working conditions existing in the port in the month of _____ 19____ under the International Longshoremen's Association Agreement. In the event of an increase or decrease in such wage scale or change in the present longshore labor or working conditions, the rates specified herein shall, as a consequence, be proportionately increased or decreased.

Rehandling or Shifting of Cargo. The rates specified herein apply to one handling of cargo. When rehandling, resorting, or shifting of cargo is necessary through no fault of the Contractor, the time required for such work will be charged for at cost, plus 10% for overhead and gear, plus insurance.

Damaged Cargo. When handling cargo damaged by fire, water, oil, etc., and where such damage causes distress or obnoxious conditions, or in all cases where the men are called upon to handle cargo under distress conditions, the Contractor's charges are to be based on the cost in accordance with the International Longshoremen's Association Agreement, plus insurance and 20% for overhead, depreciation of gear, and profit, in lieu of the rates specified herein, together with the cost of the gear destroyed and the cost of the equipment for the protection of the men as may be required.

This agreement shall not include the furnishing of terminal facilities by the Contractor to accommodate damaged cargo or in connection with any services for which wages are the basis of charges, nor where a contract of affreightment exists which interferes with the carrying out of this contract.

Condition of Cargo. If the condition of the cargo or packages is other than in customary good order, thereby delaying prompt handling, special arrangements shall be agreed upon in lieu of the rates herein specified.

Acts of God, War, Etc. No liability shall attach to the Contractor if the terms of this agreement cannot be performed due to the Act of God, War, Governments, Fire, Explosion, Civil Commotion, Strikes, or other labor difficulties.

It must be remembered that the stevedore contractor is selling labor, usually reinforced with machines and equipment but often just strong arms and skilled hands. The contract merely mirrors wages, working conditions, and legal requirements imposed upon the employer by union agreements or governmental decree. An indication of this fact is found in the clause on "Increase or Decrease of Wages," which binds the contractor to the contract only so long as the wage scale and working conditions existing on the effective date of the contract continue in force.

There is much more to the stevedoring process than can be accomplished by the people who comprise the longshore gangs that work aboard and alongside the ship. This complementary activity is known as "extra labor," and usually is performed by additional personnel obtained by the contractor for the purpose. The definition of the tasks constituting "extra labor" is set forth in the contract in these words:

Extra Labor Services. When required to supply extra labor, the Contractor will render its charges therefor at cost plus 10% and insurance for the following described services: (a) handling ship's lines and gangways; (b) cleaning ship's holds; (c) discharging excess dunnage or debris; (d) tiering cargo on pier above man-high upon discharge of vessel or breaking down cargo on pier to man-high upon loading of vessel; (e) loading or discharging ship's stores, material or equipment, mail, baggage, specie, bullion, livestock, animals, live poultry and birds; (f) carpenter or coopering work of any nature; (g) handling and placing flooring or timbers for heavy lifts or for use by carpenters; (h) services of Harbormaster for the berthing and unberthing of lighters; (i) lashing and shoring cargo; (j) bolting and unbolting tank lids; (k) battening down hatches when called upon to do so upon completion of the vessel; (l) rigging and unrigging heavy lift booms and hatch tents; (m) supplying extra labor for any other services when authorized.

Overtime work, when performed, always is compensated at a rate— usually 100 percent on weekdays and 150 percent on holidays—higher than that paid in normal working hours. In setting the commodity rates, the stevedore does not allow for the higher wages of labor in the overtime hours but agrees to perform any overtime work authorized and directed by the shipowner, on the basis of actual wage cost plus taxes and insurance. Actual wage costs means the monetary difference between the cost of labor in the straight time period and the compensation paid laborers (plus insurance and taxes directly related to earnings) in the overtime hours. If the contractor, for example, were to determine that the wage costs for a gang, including the foreman, were $492.99 per hour, the overtime cost would be double that, or $985.98. The differential would be passed along to the shipowner, without any markup except for the added cost of taxes and insurance.

Taxes are assessed by the government and apply to social security benefits and unemployment compensation, as set forth in the contract. Insurance is designed to provide for workmen's compensation, public liability, and property damage. The insurance premium is a function of the wages paid to the laborers and varies in cost as a result of factors which might contribute to accidents: for example, frequency of claims against the assured, the hazardous nature of certain commodities, and the environment in which the work is to be performed. The percentage figure used by stevedore contractors to estimate the cost of insurance may be as little as 11 percent of the wage cost and as high as 45 percent, depending upon the location of the port in the world. In some large ports, the rates charged contractors by underwriters may differ as much as ten percentage points, depending upon their loss experience.

These provisions of the contract are reasonable since the stevedore computes all cargo-handling expenses and allows an appropriate margin of profit on the assumption that all wages will be paid at the straight time rate. So long as the differential between straight time and overtime wages and related cost is for the account of the shipowner, it is immaterial to the stevedore when the work is performed. This arrangement permits the shipowner to control the use of overtime.

The commodity charges stipulated in the contract are the result of careful consideration of a number of interrelated matters. Each element in the rate is identified, and a cost for that element, prorated to the freighting unit (e.g., weight ton, measurement ton, or individual unit), is calculated as accurately as possible. There is no prescribed method for accomplishing this task; each contractor follows its own scheme of computation predicated upon the wages paid at any given time.

The contractor's estimated profit must be sufficiently large to make the contract worthwhile, but at the same time not so great that it takes the proposal out of competition. There is no rule for the percentage of profit, which ranges generally between 12 percent and 25 percent of all costs.

Labor is, by all odds, the most expensive single element in the commodity rate. It is, moreover, an element that consists of both wages and those items tied directly to wages. The components of the labor cost are illustrated by the following hypothetical schedule which is intended to demonstrate theory only:

Labor cost				
18 laborers	@ $14.00 per hour		$252.00	
1 foreman	@ 14.50 per hour		14.50	
		Subtotal	266.50	
Insurance	@ 45.8% of wages		122.06	
Social security	@ 7.5% of wages		19.99	
Workmen's compensation, state and federal unem-				
ployment taxes	@ 14.0% of wages		37.31	
		Subtotal	179.36	
	Total direct labor costs per hour			$445.86

Fringe benefits

Vacation	@	$2.10/man/hr	39.90
Welfare	@	1.05/man/hr	19.95
Pension	@	1.50/man/hr	28.50
Guaranteed income	@	0.22/man/hr	4.18
Port security	@	0.05/man/hr	.95

Subtotal	$ 93.48	
Total labor costs per hour		$539.34

Using this determination of the total hourly wage cost for a gang of longshoremen, the contractor must forecast what production will be: i.e., how many tons of a given commodity this gang can handle in one hour. Having established this figure, it is relatively simple to put a price on each of the components of the rate, somewhat in the following manner:

Commodity: Coffee beans, in bags *Handling rate: 28 tons per hour*	
Basic labor cost: $539.34 per gang hour	
Labor cost ($539.34 divided by 28 tons)	$19.2621
Checker's services @ $28.38, prorated per ton	1.0138
Equipment costs (2 forklift trucks @ $14 per hour,	
supporting equipment @ $8 per hour), prorated per ton	1.2857
Supervision @ 10% of labor and checking costs,	
prorated per ton	2.1562
Overhead @ 15% of all above prorated costs	3.5577
Profit @ 8% of all above prorated costs	2.1821
Commodity rate, per ton	$29.4576

From this illustration, it may be seen what factors must be taken into account, and how carefully each commodity must be considered in establishing this rate schedule. In deciding which stevedore shall be awarded the contract, the shipowner devotes special attention to those rates applying to the commodities transported in largest quantities. Suppose, for example, that the records show that of all cargo carried, four commodities accounted for the major tonnage lifted in the ships: bagged cargo, 32 percent; automobiles, 23 percent; copper slabs, 11 percent; and dry skins, 4 percent. The shipowner's concern for obtaining the lowest possible bid for handling these particular items is understandable. If the remaining 30 percent of the goods handled were distributed among twenty or thirty commodities and nonc individually accounted for more than 2 percent of the total tonnage, the price of handling these assorted items would be comparatively unimportant in the final selection of a stevedore contractor.

The container revolution has simplified the computations involved in establishing stevedore contract rates. Because goods now can be delivered to the terminal in a large van preloaded and sealed by the shipper, the stevedore is freed of the need to determine the characteristics of the items moving, the customary stowage practices, and the number of tons of each commodity that the laborers can handle in an hour. Instead, the entire computation is directed toward the rapidity with which the available cranes, whether on land or aboard ship, can hoist, transport laterally, and lower containers. Basic wage conditions and overtime provisions are unchanged. Should the stevedore contract to provide the complete container terminal, it would be necessary to calculate the huge investment in cranes and real estate as well as ship berths. Relatively few stevedore firms have assumed this financial burden, and therefore the contract generally covers only the supply of labor, crane operators, and such supervisory and security personnel as may be dictated for the operation. Consequently, in bidding to service a container terminal, the stevedore's labor costs will outweigh other considerations even more than they do for break-bulk cargoes.

Many containership operators offer their customers the opportunity to send goods to the terminal in break-bulk fashion, and to have them packed into containers for a certain fee per ton of each commodity. In this event, the stevedore will be asked to provide the information on which the carrier may base its charge to the shipper. The determination of the labor cost would involve the same process as was followed in fixing the individual rates for break-bulk operations, and would entail considering some of the elements that affected the break-bulk rates. For instance, it would be necessary to know the rapidity with which the laborers could stuff the commodity into a van, or strip the container, measured in terms of tons per hour per gang, or per individual, depending upon how the laborers were employed. The characteristics of the commodity that influence handling (fragility, awkward shape, heavy weight, or similar factors) would have to be established. Other items of expense would include details like the cost of separating small lots to assure correct delivery to consignees, the disbursements incurred in checking goods into the container, the charges paid to move containers to and from the loading dock, and the investment in a safe and weatherproof loading shed. Overhead, insurance, taxes, and fringe benefits must also be computed as essential elements in the fee per commodity ton.

The sophistication introduced by containers is paralleled by the widespread use of computers which permit much more elaborate calculation of costs than has been illustrated in these pages. The basic principles of identifying every item of expense and prorating it against the unit, whether that unit be a ton, a pallet, or a container, remain unchanged. The major benefits resulting from the use of computers are the significantly greater detail of calculations, the enhanced awareness and appreciation by management of all those elements that contribute to the true cost of terminal operation and service, and the ability to identify immediately those areas to which the attention of management should be directed for greater efficiency and economy.

In a highly competitive industry, partially dominated by factors beyond the control of the contractor, the methodical determination of stevedore costs is of immense importance to both the shipowner and the contractor. The more each party to the contract understands the problems of the other, the more likely it is that the final agreement between the two will be fair and reasonable.

CHAPTER NINE

Procurement of Vessel Stores and Supplies

It is difficult to overemphasize the importance of proper procurement of stores, spare parts, and supplies for ships. The seaworthiness of a ship depends, in part, upon having on board at the outset of the voyage adequate quantities of replacements, manila or nylon line, and food—especially the last. These items cumulatively are costly and represent a significant portion of vessel operating expense. Close control over both their procurement and expenditure therefore is a major responsibility of management.

Procurement of all ship needs normally is centralized in the purchasing department, the manager of which often is called the *purchasing agent,* who has the same status as the heads of the deck, engine, and commissary departments, and reports to the vice president, operations, through the operations manager. Along with these supervisors, this department head participates actively in the establishment of standards of quality and quantity of the stores to be placed aboard ship. Of equivalent magnitude is the obligation to procure all material called for in requisitions in accordance with company policy, at the best available prices. Good management dictates that the heads of the engine, deck, and commissary departments, *not* the purchasing agent, make all decisions as to what shall be deleted from, or added to, requisitions from the ships. Only by strict enforcement of this principle can the procurement policy function effectively and efficiently.

For generations, the chief engineer of a ship has served as her maintenance and repair officer, through whom all requisitions for spare parts or material used in repairs of any sort are channeled to the offices of the cognizant departments ashore. In many cases, the superintendent engineer and the marine superintendent, drawing upon their own seagoing experience, have followed the unwritten but time-honored policy expressed in the phrase, "If the chief wants it, give it to him." In recent years, however, this uncritical acquiescence has come under attack because of the greatly increased cost of spare and replacement parts and the considerably improved performance records of present-day shipboard equipment. More attention is being given to the history of breakdowns to ascertain whether there is any justification for the fears of seagoing engineers that failure to carry a particular part, or a certain quantity of parts, will result in unsatisfactory ship operation. Shoreside management also has begun to be concerned with the problems associated with the physical possession of a large inventory of equipment. Much of what is placed on ships as original spare parts is not used; one estimate is that, in terms of monetary value, approximately three-quarters of the investment in original spare parts is wasted because the parts never are used.

The formation and enforcement of policy concerning the quantities and locations of spare parts to be purchased and held either aboard ship or in warehouses ashore are functions of the highest echelons of the operating department. The logistical support policy is developed only after considering such matters as the availability of parts from suppliers, the frequency with which mechanical units break down, the advantages of replacing the entire unit compared with substituting new components for old ones, and the cost of maintaining substantial inventories of spares in one or more ports in contrast to acquisitions only when an item is needed and for which a premium price may be charged.

Modern steamship management demands that attention be given to every level of cost control and to the development of a system by which the needs of the ships are met efficiently and with appropriate consideration of the impact upon the financial stability of the shipowner. To illustrate this point, a typical (but hypothetical) situation involving the availability and use of replacement parts is offered.

A special survey of the *Bounding Main,* as directed by the classification society and requiring a number of days to complete, was planned originally for September. An unexpected reduction in cargo offerings forced a reduction in the frequency of sailings by the owners, and made it possible to withdraw the *Bounding Main* in June. The survey was ordered immediately following the release of the ship from her commitments, and only one week's advance notice was given to concerned officials. No procurement of replacement parts had been initiated in June, although the superintendent engineer intended to order a new set of blades for the rotor of the turbine powering the ship's electrical generator. Operations records from the *Bounding Main* indicated that while the blades probably might pass the survey, they were losing efficiency as a result of normal wear. When the turbine casing was lifted during the course of the survey, it was found that the blading was lacy, but still within the minimum standards of the classification society. Everyone agreed that the blading could be kept in service for another year, but at some cost in the efficiency with which steam was utilized. At the prevailing and anticipated price of fuel oil, it was calculated that continuing with the old blades would add about $8,000 to ship operating expense. New blades could be obtained in three days, but only by paying a premium of $3,500 above the normal price. The decision was to pay the premium, and to install the new blades. At the same time, the vice president, operations, launched an inquiry to discover why a spare set of these blades had not been purchased and held in the warehouse against the probability that it would be needed by the ship. He also wished to establish whether the frequency of replacement and the lead time required for most economical procurement justified the cost of keeping so expensive an item in the spare parts inventory.

This example demonstrates that whenever policy is made relative to the acquisition and retention of expensive spare parts, it is the function of wise management to have each of the executives concerned—marine and engineer superintendents, repair specialists, accountants, and purchasing agent—contribute from their knowledge and experience. When all analyses are examined, it may be found that the cherished notion that "if the chief wants it, he gets it" is justified in some cases but in others there is no reasonable basis for investing that amount of money in certain parts and becoming responsible for their proper care and custody. For example, the pumps installed in six ships of a company fleet are shown to have performed without a breakdown for ten consecutive years. That same make of pump is to be installed in a new ship. It is deemed unnecessary to acquire a spare pump, either to keep in the shoreside warehouse or to put aboard the vessel. The compressor on a refrigeration unit, however, has an operating life of about six months before it must be replaced. The chief engineer's request for a replacement to be carried by the ship is granted because it is supported by the facts.

In January 1979, the Maritime Administration (then part of the U.S. Department of Commerce) revised its specifications concerning the requirements for spare parts on ships built with construction differential subsidy. The shipbuilder was directed to furnish, and to put aboard ship, the quantity of repair parts required to meet the minimum dictates of the regulatory and classification bodies. The shipowner was authorized to select, in addition, those spare parts it wished to have the builder supply as part of the original outfit of the vessel. For the owner's guidance, a monetary limit for such parts was fixed, rather than a stipulated number of items. Every item of equipment was assigned to a category, and each category had a fixed percentage of the equipment's base cost which could be used to pay for spares. The categories, in ascending order of percentages allowed, were:

Limited to 1 percent (of base cost of equipment):
    Engineer's workshop
    Condensers
    Boilers
Limited to 2 percent:
    Ventilating and heating equipment
    Hull piping
    Cargo oil system
Limited to 3 percent:
    Air conditioning machinery
    Main engine
    Feed heaters and other heat exchangers
Limited to 4 percent:
    Fuel oil service piping
    Steam piping
    Feed, condensate, circulating, and drain piping
    Lubricating oil piping
Limited to 5 percent:
    Electricity generation and distribution equipment
    Electronics
    Deck machinery
Limited to 6 percent:
    Shafting and propeller(s)
Limited to 7 percent:
    Saltwater evaporator system
    Miscellaneous auxiliaries
Limited to 15 percent:
    Instruments and gauges

When a new ship is delivered to her owners by the builder, she has on board a year's supply of spare parts, based partially on the manufacturer's estimate of need. The Maritime Administration conducted a study in 1979 of the procurement of spare parts by a number of U.S.-flag steamship operators.[1] It found that the manufacturers' estimates of the requirements for spare parts could not be relied upon without any question, because they were predicated upon fragmentary information coming back from ships actually in service. A contributing factor to this unreliability was the latent desire of some manufacturers to sell spare parts. In addition, the study suggested that other manufacturers were reluctant to admit that their products were subject to breakdown after a relatively short time. Ideally the manufacturer of each item of equipment would be informed every time a repair was made and would be able to compile from such notices an accurate history of operational experience and the need for replacement of components. The impracticality of this ideal is obvious, especially in view of the many occasions when ships are sold, often from one national registry to another, or converted into new types of transportation capability with demands upon shipboard equipment totally different from the original purpose for which it was installed.

At the time they are delivered by their builders, new ships have on board a library of manuals that give complete information on each and every piece of machinery. The purchasing department should assure that all "name-plate data" and appropriate additional information from the manuals are recorded in each ship's file and kept readily available to furnish to suppliers whenever replacements or spare parts are ordered.

It is important to note that the regulatory agencies (like the U.S. Coast Guard or the British Department of Trade) set certain minimum standards of spare parts and reserve supplies that must be carried by ships. The classification societies likewise establish requirements for spare parts. These stipulations, however, have little impact upon the actual number of spare parts carried because each steamship operator has established its own levels for these items. This disparity results from the fact that the regulatory and classification agencies are interested primarily in assuring that the ship will be able to make port in the event of an emergency, whereas the owner is concerned that the ship remain in full operating condition when away from the home port.

An indispensable element in company policy concerning the quantity of spare parts to be placed aboard ship is the "allowance list." There is no uniformity in the way this list is developed by individual companies; each one reflects the experience of the owner in a particular type of service. The Maritime Administration study determined that the following considerations, of which the first three are predominant, influence the formation of the list:

1. Engineering experience.
2. Fleet and vessel experience for this class of ship.
3. Manufacturers' and equipment suppliers' recommendations.
4. Shipbuilders' allowance list.
5. Usage data, wear, and failure rates.
6. Regulatory and classification society requirements.
7. Loss of ship time incident to failure of a given component.

8. Availability of spare parts (i.e., lead time required for procurement).
9. Cost limitations.
10. The trade route on which the ship will be employed.
11. Where the ship was built (i.e., foreign or domestic yard, with foreign or domestic components).
12. Types of equipment installed.
13. Reliability records provided by manufacturers of shipboard equipment.

It is almost axiomatic that spare parts for machinery can be procured most cheaply if they are ordered at the time the machinery is being manufactured and assembled. When these same parts are purchased years later, it may be necessary for the manufacturer to stop normal production routines in the factory and to tool up expressly to fabricate the required item. In this connection, the Maritime Administration learned, during its study of procurement of spare parts, why replacements cost so much when ordered years after the initial run of manufacturing had been completed.

Most of the manufacturers surveyed stated that they did not cease production of a particular item, but instead they either upgraded that item or provided a satisfactory substitute. One fabricator reported with pride that it continued to put out spare parts for older equipment, some of which was found in ships built thirty years earlier. These statements, however, could not be interpreted as indicating that these individual components were kept constantly in stock and were available immediately, but rather that the company retained the capability to manufacture the product on demand, by interrupting current output. An example will make this clear.

A wholesale supplier purchased a large stock of coupling pins during a three-year period when many ships of similar type were under construction. At the time of acquisition, the price was $2.50 per pin. Twenty years later, a shipowner ordered six of these pins and was charged $110 for each one. In explaining the tremendous increase in price, the wholesaler said that the manufacturer had reported that every minute and every operation involved in researching and producing these six pins were charged against this single order. It was necessary to hunt for the engineering drawings, to identify the material used, to procure the very small quantity of the specialized material at a high price, to set up the turret lathes to make the six pins, and then to reset these lathes for the job from which they had been diverted for the special order.

A less extreme situation exists with those manufacturers who do keep a small reserve of older spare parts in stock. Whereas at the time of original fabrication, the output might have been in terms of five or six hundred units, the restocking order would be for twenty or thirty. Even if there were a sufficiently steady demand to keep the research and procurement procedures current, there still would be the cost of interrupting the production cycle on current orders.

A major concern for those dealing with the logistics of providing spare parts is the fact that some equipment installed in new ships is of an obsolete design, and spare parts may not be available throughout the operating lifetime of the vessels. The reason for this often is that an improved model of that piece of equipment is under design and test but is not yet ready for production. To meet the builder's time schedule, the obsolescent part is supplied. Production of this older piece is terminated perhaps five years after the ship has been placed in service, with resultant problems for those associated with the working of the ship. It is desirable, but not always practical, to demand from the shipbuilder a warranty that spare parts for all component machinery in the ship will be available for not less than twenty years after delivery from the shipyard. The advantages of obtaining a statement of this kind of logistical support are obvious.

If the shipbuilder cannot provide the assurance of spare parts availability for the life of the vessel, the alternative of buying sufficient spare parts to meet all demands for that period of time poses the twin problems of making a very large investment of funds that will be frozen for upwards of two decades, and of properly caring for and safeguarding this large inventory.

When a ship is purchased secondhand and brought into a different fleet, it is the part of good management to take a thorough inventory not only of spare parts and consumable supplies, but also of all equipment installed in the ship, so that the purchasing department will have complete name-plate data for future reference. The results of this scrutiny should establish what must be acquired to have the levels of stores, spare parts, and supplies brought into conformity with the new owner's standards. Taking an inventory on this scale is a major task; one operator estimated that it took a team of ten experienced persons one full week to complete this task. Thereafter, ideal ship husbandry would repeat the process annually, but this is very nearly impossible in the circumstances of fast turnaround that surround most ship operations today.

The Maritime Administration requires that inventories be taken when an American-flag ship is placed in subsidized service, when the operating differential subsidy contract expires, when the accounting period ends for determining the amount of subsidy subject to recapture, and when the vessel is withdrawn permanently from subsidized service. These inventories are required for inclusion in reports on the financial operations of the company. They must make reference to the stores levels fixed in the *standards book,* which regulates the expenditures of spare parts. The regulations pertaining to these inventories also stipulate that the condition be reported of any equipment for which spare parts are provided. For instance, a refrigerator compressor is part of the original equipment installed by the builder and is estimated to have a working life of five years. Annually, therefore, the condition of this compressor must be listed in a manner that would permit its elimination from the records when it was worn out and a replacement had been made.

Because of the complexity and detail associated with inventories of spare parts, the availability of a computer and its proper use to keep constant and updated records of procurement, storage, expenditure, and replacement of each item is of major benefit to all concerned. One operator of ships registered in the United States has developed a highly automated, computer-based inventory control system that is extremely simple in its fundamentals. Every spare part is tagged individually, and from those tags the needed information can be supplied to the computer, which then provides the following:

1. An inventory of what each vessel in the fleet has on board;
2. An inventory that combines the spare parts on the ships with the spare parts in the company's warehouse;
3. A report showing the usage (consumption) of parts by vessel and by voyage; and
4. An automated purchase order for procurement of replacements that have been used.

All tags on spare parts are coded for the computer program and show the company's identification number for the part, the exact location of the place where the part is stored, and the name of the ship(s) on which the part is carried. Spares kept in the warehouse ashore are tagged in the same manner, except that the name of the ship is left blank. The warehouse itself is divided into five sections, one for each of the four ships in the fleet, and one for general storage. Spares purchased while a ship is on a voyage are placed in the designated area to await the return of that vessel to the home port. Storage shelves are indexed to the ship's boxes in which those spare parts will be stowed when they are turned over to the custody of the chief engineer.

Whenever spare parts are needed by the ship, the chief engineer removes and retains the tags. At designated ports of call, the local agent of the line is given a list of the spare parts that have been issued from stock. This list is mailed to the home port by the agent. At the end of the voyage, the chief engineer personally delivers the tags to the supply office. In this way, a careful and up-to-date inventory is maintained, and resupply material is available in ample time for the next scheduled voyage.

Aboard ship, spare parts, as already indicated, are stored in appropriately marked boxes, which then are sealed until there is a requirement for whatever is in the box. This greatly facilitates control of inventory; it also makes it comparatively easy to verify the supply of spares in the custody of the chief engineer. Boxes that have been unsealed are inspected and their contents, if any, counted. The quantity used should correspond to the number of tags retained by the chief engineer.

Once all the data have been assembled and the computer has processed the material, the superintendent engineer is in a position to decide how to bring the inventory up to standard. The process may involve inter-ship transfer, shifting from warehouse to ship, or direct purchase from a supplier. If either of the first two steps is taken, the tags are marked accordingly, and the computer record is updated immediately. If procurement is ordered, the computer is programmed to prepare the requisite purchase documents.

At the beginning of each outbound voyage, the ship's chief engineer is furnished with a report showing the status of the spare parts aboard the ship, including the exact location of each part and each box. This report replaces the one used on the preceding voyage, and eliminates any possibility of error from omission or transcription.

A system of this sort has significant advantages from the viewpoint of management. In the first place, there is a continuous record of shipboard requirements for each and every spare part. The superintendent engineer is able to order replacement parts for the shipboard stock on the basis of the experience of each ship. Thus, if an air compressor runs 1,400 hours during a voyage, and requires a new drive belt after 350 hours of operation, the minimum support level can be set accurately at four belts. At the same time, if a new brand of belt is tested in service, the relative merit may be determined on the basis of actual performance, which is duly recorded and is available for later study. Another benefit is that supply personnel can keep an accurate list of the lead time required for procurement of replacements. Additionally, because there is continuous control over the parts, noticeable economies can be effected in the logistical support of the ships.

The basis for all procurement, as well as for long-range planning for acquisition, storage, and control of both spare parts and consumable stores, is the requisition submitted by the chief engineer. If the vessel is assigned to a long voyage—two or more months between calls at the home port—it is customary to process requisitions so that everything needed for the forthcoming trip will be placed aboard ship well in advance of sailing time. If, however, the ship returns to her home port every two weeks, good management would suggest that the ship submit one requisition every third or fourth voyage, and while the ship is on the fourth or fifth trip, the appropriate examination of and adjustments to the requisition may be accomplished and procurement completed.

A fairly standardized pattern of procurement is followed by steamship operators. The cognizant department analyzes the ship's requisition, makes changes as required by company policy or records of experience, and then passes the requisition to the purchasing department. Replacement of "proprietary" items, meaning parts unique to a particular manufacturer, is accomplished by ordering the desired quantity from that source. Material that, like tools, valve packing, and interchangeable parts, can be acquired from a number of suppliers, is procured only after bids from several (three or more) sources have been solicited and compared. In each case, the goal is to meet the needs of the ship most efficiently, promptly, and economically.

A problem of significant dimension is encountered in the procurement and warehousing of what may be called "insurance items." These are items that are expensive, usually require long lead time for delivery, and are needed only rarely. Typical of this category are propellers, tail shafts, turbine rotors, major propulsion-unit spares, reduction gears, electric motors, turbogenerator sets, pumps, and valves. Where two or more steamship operators have the same port and their ships use the same equipment, it is quite possible that a sort of informal "pool" may be set up. If a ship suddenly needs a replacement tailshaft and the owner has expended the one in his inventory and has not yet received the replacement ordered from the manufacturer, the other shipowner(s) will be asked to "lend" a shaft until the replacement is delivered. The advantage of this arrangement is that these expensive and rarely required items may be stocked as single, rather than multiple, units in a warehouse. Were the fleet owner to attempt to keep a complete complement of these spare parts for the ships in the warehouse, it might represent an investment of approximately two million dollars for each large containership. For smaller and less complex vessels, the cost of a complete collection of spare parts could be close to a half-million dollars per ship. The importance of keeping the number of insurance items as low as possible is self-evident when the amount of money invested in them is taken into account.

A noteworthy facet of spare parts procurement was cited in the Maritime Administration's study of the subject. This is the procurement of insurance items on what might be termed a speculative basis. Often a part, and sometimes a complete unit, will be offered for sale by a manufacturer at a bargain price. For example, imagine that a shipowner signed a contract to build two ships and had an option to build two more. The shipyard, at its own risk, constructed three sets of reduction gears, on the chance that at least one of the two ships under option would be ordered. Because of adverse business conditions, however, the shipowner waived the options, leaving the shipyard with one complete set of reduction gears for which it had no prospective need. Rather than store this surplus item in its warehouse for an indefinite time, the shipyard offered it for sale at approximately two-thirds of its normal cost. On learning of this action, an operator of ships equipped with these gears immediately purchased the set, because records showed that one in ten ship-years a replacement was required. The combination of the lower acquisition price and the advantage of having the item on hand to meet a predictable demand made it worthwhile for the shipowner to assume the burden of possession.

It is not always necessary that the part required by a ship be new. Many pieces of equipment outlast the ships in which they are installed, and when those vessels are dismantled the used parts dealers acquire these items, and offer them for sale at prices which invariably include some premium markup. Shipowners who need this equipment, however, often find that the dealer's price results in a cost which overall is lower than if the material had been bought new and warehoused for a period of time. Additionally, as ships get older and the original suppliers of machinery components either cease production or go out of business altogether, the only source of replacement parts may be the secondhand dealers.

A notable consideration in procurement is whether to insist upon the use of "genuine" replacement parts—that is, parts manufactured by the original maker of the major component. These parts, as might be expected, are precisely machined to the dimensions and tolerances fixed by the designer and specified in the engineering drawings. They make perfect replacements, but they also may be more expensive than "non-genuine" parts made by an independent. In most cases, non-genuine parts are copied slavishly from genuine originals, and will perform satisfactorily in the equipment for which intended. Because they are copies, rather than made from the engineering drawings, there always is the possibility that some clearances or cuts may be slightly different from the genuine part, and could cause operational difficulties. Some operators, however, believe that the difference in cost more than offsets the possible damage that might result from a rare instance of poor machining. Ideally, good management would insist upon the use of genuine parts, because the buyer gets the correct design, proper material, and expert fabricating procedures. In addition, by using genuine parts, the buyer deals with a source that maintains engineering and design departments, a quality assurance group, and an inspection team, all of which combine to give to the buyer exactly what has been ordered.[2]

Some steamship owners have elected to follow what might be designated as the "zero-based spare parts policy." Rather than maintaining fixed levels of spare parts, these companies keep on hand, both afloat and ashore, as little reserve material as experience justifies. They make a determined effort to anticipate the need for replacement parts and to procure these early enough to forestall breakdowns or delays to ships necessitated by waiting for the required items. Perforce, procurement officers must keep track of the availability of equipment, both old and new, to meet unexpected failures. This often involves the practicality of substituting equipment similar to, but not identical with, that which is installed in their ships. Additionally, the purchasing department must be alert to the possibility of using parts that can be modified to fit the needs of a particular repair job. It is obvious that this zero-based policy can be effective only if there is a sustained review of requirements from the ships and a systematic maintenance and repair program.

An essential element in purchasing department routine is the establishment and continuous updating of an active and accurate list of spare parts, both on board ship and in company storage places, supplemented by a current list of manufacturers and distributors who have various types of equipment readily available. Purveyors of surplus and used machinery are indispensable sources of both replacement and spare parts for those items no longer in the manufacturers' stocks. Great reliance is placed upon distributors of equipment who have been authorized by the manufacturers to handle their products. The advantage of dealing with distributors is that items obtained from them meet specifications, both as to fabrication and material. Although not necessarily typical, the practice of one fleet operator's procurement division indicates, by the percentage of resupply acquired from each source, the relative importance of each:

Authorized distributors	50%
Original equipment manufacturers	20%
Wholesalers	15%
Jobbers	10%
Custom manufacturers	5%

In liner service, where the same voyages are repeated again and again on closely monitored and rigidly followed schedules, experience and established rates of consumption make preliminary planning for purchasing relatively simple. The principles to be observed in these circumstances are:

Length of the proposed voyage. The quantity of consumable stores and spare parts to be placed on board is regulated by the length of time the ship will be away from the home port.

Route and ports of call of the proposed voyage. Because of the critical situation prevailing in many nations in regard to international balances of payments, the tendency in many ship operating companies is to purchase as much as possible in the country in which the operator is domiciled and of which it is a citizen. Vessels engaged in the cross-trades, which do not return to their home ports, are stored in the areas where the most satisfactory arrangements can be made after quality, variety, quantity, and dependability have been evaluated. Ships operated under subsidy contract with the Maritime Administration are required to obtain all stores in the United States, except for perishable foodstuffs needed by ships on protracted voyages. The ports where supplies of these commodities (especially meat, milk, vegetables, and fruit) are available should be made known to the purchasing agent in time to establish the procurement program for the voyage. Passenger ships assigned to long cruises (sixty to one hundred days) usually are scheduled to take on fresh fruits and vegetables at a number of ports of call; meats, cheese, wines, and staples like flour normally are stored for the entire cruise at the port of origin. It is mandatory, regardless of whether the ship be a passenger or a cargo carrier, that the quality of supplies obtained along the route be acceptable. Many American owners have found it advantageous to obtain the greater proportion of their needs in U.S. cities rather than to expect foreign sources to meet their standards. One operator, for instance, discovered that canned fruit juices met with greater favor among his seafaring employees than did frozen concentrates, because the potable water available along the route varied too greatly in flavor.

The number and nationalities of crew and passengers. In procurement of food supplies, it is necessary that the purchasing department be well informed as to the number of persons, both passenger and crew members, to be fed, and insofar as possible their nationalities and racial backgrounds. Dietary customs and restrictions can become very significant in personnel management, and consideration must be given to these facts. The following examples represent typical cases:

A ship with her home port in New York and manned by persons from that part of the United States will have to provide a substantial quantity of potatoes. A ship sailing from New Orleans, and carrying a crew from Gulf communities, must offer rice in preference to potatoes.

A German-flag vessel must cater to her people's appetites by providing such specialities as sauerkraut, knockwurst, and rye bread; a vessel with an Italian crew would require quantities of spaghetti, macaroni, and similar products as well as supplies of tomatoes and seasonings.

Chinese and Indian seamen traditionally are fed diets in which rice and fish play a prominent part.

Passenger ships carrying large numbers of Jewish people must not only offer kosher food but must be able to assure the travelers that Jewish dietary laws are observed in the preparation of food.

Incidental to planning commissary offerings is the time of the year in which the voyage is to take place. If the ship is to run from northern to equatorial latitudes, it would be desirable for an American ship to stock abundant salad-making materials, fruits, and the lighter foods. On the other hand, if the ship is to proceed to extremely cold areas, the heavier, more warming foods will be in demand. Should the voyage take the ship through various seasons, then procurement of food must be designed to meet the changing tastes and demands of the personnel aboard.

From time to time, operational delays will be encountered by a vessel employed in liner service. To make up for the days lost during the voyage, and to sail the ship on the advertised departure date, frequently the turnaround time in the home port is reduced drastically. If the decision is to meet the scheduled departure at the expense of time in port, those responsible should notify the ship of the curtailment of turnaround time, and should instruct the master to send estimates of required stores and spare parts by airmail or radio, as circumstances dictate. The alternative is for the purchasing agent, in consultation with the superintendents of the engineer, deck, and catering departments, to prepare tentative requisitions, and to use these as the bases for soliciting bids from suppliers. The successful bidders are notified of their selection, but exact quantities to be delivered are not made known until the ship arrives and details are cleared up. When this is accomplished, the purveyors receive final instructions by telephone, and deliveries are effected in accordance therewith.

As already noted in discussing procurement of spare parts, it is the part of good management for requisitions to be compared with the standards established for the ship to be supplied, and to make whatever adjustments may be appropriate to the anticipated employment of the vessel. In the liner services, which entail close supervision of ship movements, the actual quantity of goods purchased for each voyage becomes almost a routine, and normally should be the difference between what is on board and what is needed to bring the stores level up to company standards.

The goal of good stores procurement is to provide everything for the ship that reasonably may be expected to be needed and used, without stockpiling large inventories either afloat or ashore. Items deemed necessary for the efficient operation of the ship and the personal comfort of the ship's company should be supplied in adequate but not excessive quantity. To put too much of any consumable item on board a ship is to promote wasteful extravagance while working capital is tied up unprofitably.

Spare parts for shipboard machinery, maintenance supplies like paint and housekeeping equipment, and other nonperishable items sometimes are ordered periodically in sufficiently large quantities to supply the entire fleet. While this may result in discounts because of the wholesale lots in which procurement is made, it is important that the investment in these large inventories be compared with alleged savings to assure that working capital is being used efficiently. Perishable foodstuffs must be purchased with special care to eliminate, insofar as possible, the losses from spoilage resulting from long periods of storage.

Items on requisitions are divided by the purchasing department into the appropriate categories (fruits, vegetables, meats, hardware, cleaning gear, paints, etc.) and interested suppliers are invited to submit proposals. Ordinarily the lowest responsive bid consistent with good quality and economy over the long run will win the business for a purveyor of a single category, even though prices of some items within the category may be a trifle higher than those of a competitor. Quality is under constant scrutiny, and whenever a particular brand is found to be uneven or otherwise undependable, it is dropped from the list of approved products. Dealers—whether manufacturers, agents, or wholesalers—are held to exact compliance with specifications, and failure to meet the terms of the contract as to brand and quality may be judged sufficient reason for cancellation.

A major exception to the practice of purchasing by categories exists in the procurement of meats, especially for passenger ships. The cost of meat represents a substantial proportion of total food expense, and quality

Passengers' tastes are reflected in this cruise ship's buffet table. Photograph courtesy of Cunard Line.

is of critical importance. To assure minimum cost and highest quality for a particular grade of meat, proposals from suppliers are analyzed to determine which merchant offers the lowest price, consistent with the quality stipulated, for individual cuts such as rib roasts and filets mignons.

To encourage competition both in price and in service, some purchasing agents follow the practice of dividing food purchases to give the lowest bidder about 85 percent of the total, and to award the remaining 15 percent to the second lowest bidder.

Purchases sometimes are made from large-scale shippers whose products can be used by the fleet. This "reciprocal buying" is a decided asset to the traffic department in maintaining the goodwill of these customers who frequently pay more in freight charges than the value of the purchases made by the procurement office. For example, a carrier earns $5,000 a year in freight revenues from handling the cargo of a varnish manufacturer, and buys in return only $750 worth of that company's product. So long as the varnishes are of good and consistent quality, and the prices are competitive with those of other offerers, the fact that the supplier is a valuable customer may tip the scale in favor of that firm. Occasionally there may be a slight premium paid for the merchandise procured from these large-scale shippers, but in most cases the tender made by the shipper is at the market price. In any event, the quality and long-term economy of the merchandise must be equivalent to that available from other bidders.

Procurement of stores and supplies, other than spare parts, is from manufacturers, authorized distributors, jobbers, and ship chandlers. Generally, purchasing agents of the larger steamship companies attempt to deal directly with the manufacturers of those items used in large quantities. Canvas, paints, oils, and greases are typical of such items. Should the manufacturer set prices at the same level as those quoted by the jobber (a wholesale merchant who buys in very large lots and sells in quantities to retailers and heavy consumers), it is simpler to order from the jobber who has offices in the home port. In addition to the convenience of location, dealing with a jobber facilitates purchases in smaller quantities than the manufacturer might require. Another, less visible and therefore less measurable, advantage of dealing with the jobber is that business contacts are kept at the local level, with resultant goodwill toward the shipowner.

Ship chandlers are called upon to supply the miscellaneous small lot items needed by a ship. Large steamship companies do not buy paint, pipe, canvas, rope, or meat through the chandlers. They do place orders with these merchants, however, for those articles required in lots of one, six, or ten units, and thus simplify their own bookkeeping, receiving, and inspection procedures. Some small shipowning companies do not maintain purchasing departments, and use the services of the chandlers instead. An alternative is to engage a "purchasing house" to perform the functions of the supply section. In either case, the burden remains with the shipowner to provide very explicit specification and instructions because there will be no personal acquaintance with the ships or their personnel, and no access to owners' records.

Ships, especially those engaged in the tramping trade, often are supplied through the offices of the agents who represent the owners in the various ports of call.[3] Customarily, these people are engaged in the routines connected with the arrival, working, and departure of the ships, and are not necessarily experienced in supply procedures. Should the ship require stores or supplies of any sort, the various department heads (chief engineer, chief officer, chief steward) should consult with the agent to assure that the requisitions are understood and that the exact nature of whatever is to be procured is explained fully. This is of particular importance where the requisition must be translated into a different language. Exceptionally careful inspection of all goods so procured must be made at the time of delivery, and shipboard personnel should be thoroughly instructed by the owners prior to the commencement of the voyage as to the procedures to be followed, especially if some deficiency or shortage is discovered. Because ship chandlers are in the business of filling ship requisitions, it may prove to be more satisfactory for ships engaged in tramp operations to deal directly with some reputable chandlery than to attempt to work through the agent.

Ship chandlers, especially in the larger ports, offer an extensive range of goods, usually in the form of a carefully prepared catalog issued once a year. Changes in prices often are made by means of a separate sheet distributed periodically. An alternative is for the chandler to submit bids on the basis of the catalog price minus a discount or plus a surcharge. If no catalog is supplied by the chandler, offerings may be made to shipowners by referring to the manufacturer's catalog and quoting a fixed price or the manufacturer's price minus a discount.

Purchases for vessels employed in the long trades usually are made in large quantities and often in containers of the largest size provided by the manufacturer or processor. It is poor economy, however, to acquire everything in these very big containers, because wastage is almost inevitable. This is true in food supplies; for example, rice bought in one-pound bags really is less costly than rice bought in one-hundred-pound sacks, because the cook will use one, two, or five pounds for a meal, will not spill any, and will not tend to overestimate liberally what is the designated quantity. Although the unit price of rice in one-pound packages may be somewhat higher than if the sack is purchased, the saving from the reduced wastage more than offsets the greater cost.

To establish an efficient supply program for a fleet of ships requires attention to many details. It is essential, as has been noted previously, that the purchasing department be furnished by the requisitioning department with complete information (for example, name-plate data for machinery and equipment) concerning anything that is to be purchased. To eliminate mistakes in ordering, one carrier devised a system of preprinted cards for every item on the ship's allowance lists. The cards had three parts, each of which contained the complete nameplate data, manufacturer's information, and engineering drawing numbers, together with any other pertinent data. Whenever an item was withdrawn from the storeroom or taken off the shelf, the card was annotated to show the date and reason for its use. The chief engineer retained one part of the card when the item was put into service, and at the first opportunity mailed the other two parts to the home office. The purchasing department was able to order replacements with the assurance that it was acquiring exactly what was needed, and retained one of the two parts of the card. The other part was sent to the data processing unit to be worked into the computerized record system.

Preparing a procedure of this sort is a major undertaking. If the ship is acquired from the shipyard, full details accompany the vessel when she is delivered, and should be made available to the purchasing and data processing departments as soon as possible. If the ship is purchased from another operator and does not have full documentation aboard when title is transferred, a stem-to-stern and keel-to-truck inventory may be needed to establish the basis for logistical support. Ships taken on bareboat charter should be inspected in the same way that an old ship is examined, so that appropriate records can be set up, ideally before the commencement of the first voyage.

The hull plan and vessel layout must be studied with care, since procurement of supplies will be affected by structural features of the ship. In particular, the purchasing department must determine the location, size, accessibility, and interrelation of storerooms of all types (paint and other deck stores, engine room spares, commissary dry stores, refrigerated foodstuffs, and hotel equipment). It must also ascertain what facilities have been built into the ship which simplify or complicate the handling of stores. This information will be useful in selecting sizes and weights of packages. For example, if the boatswain's storeroom is located near a hatchway through which delivery can be made with the ship's cargo-hoisting gear, it may be feasible to order manila or nylon line on large spools. If the store-room is accessible only through a narrow doorway, and everything must be man-carried down a ladder, the obvious limitation on spool sizes is to that which can be handled by one or two workers.

A steamship line engaged in transporting large numbers of passengers, whether on cruises or overnight ferry runs involving feeding, must procure, among other items, large stores of linen, china, glassware, and silverware house-marked according to company practice. This means that orders for these articles must be placed months in advance because of the time required to weave or mark the material. Sheets and towels can be obtained in one or two months, whereas china and glassware will not be delivered for a half year or longer. Stocks of these long-lead items usually are kept in shoreside storerooms under the supervision of the purchasing agent, and ship requisitions are filled immediately. This method of replenishing what has been lost or broken during the voyage is both convenient and efficient; at the same time, it justifies procurement in very large quantities with the resultant economy of scale.

It is worth noting that just as hotels have found it to be almost an invitation to souvenir hunters to carry off house-marked items, so ships have encountered the same problem. A predictable result has been the abandonment of the time-honored practice of having the house-flag appear on every item used by the travelers. Insofar as the purchasing agent is concerned, this has all but eliminated the waiting time for these items.

Cargo liners with a capacity of twelve or fewer passengers usually are supplied with standardized table services; linens in some instances may be marked with the house-flag. Depending upon the frequency of sailings, the length of the voyages, and the policy of the owners, procurement may be in lots large enough to supply the entire fleet, or it may be on a ship-by-ship basis. If ordinary restaurant and hotel supplies are used by the vessels, and no problems are encountered in obtaining the items requisitioned by the ship, it is convenient to purchase whatever is needed for each vessel as she returns to her home port.

Perishable foodstuffs (meats, fruits, vegetables) are obtained on contracts which, in New York, are let each week. The suppliers submit their bids on Tuesday to cover the week ending with the close of business the following Monday. The lowest overall bidder, as previously explained, normally is awarded the contract for the week. As requisitions are received from ships during that seven-day period, the successful bidder is notified of the items and quantities desired, and these stores are delivered in accordance with pertinent instructions.

The quality of food offered to passengers, especially on luxury cruises, is of major concern to the operator. Competition in the cruise trade is so intense that any deviation from the highest standards may have a disastrous effect on the prestige of the operator. As a result, some companies keep foodstuff buyers in the market constantly, seeking the finest quality of fruits, vegetables, and meats. Meats purchased in the United States are graded by the Department of Agriculture and inspected by the buyer to assure that cuts and weights correspond to specifications and invoices. Passengers normally are served those meats that are graded "prime," while those provided to crew members are graded "good." If inspections are made at the purveyor's warehouse, the delivery trucks may be loaded and sealed in the presence of the shipowner's representative, to eliminate a final inspection when purchases are taken aboard ship. An incidental benefit from this warehouse inspection is that the longshoremen who handle the foodstuffs are not held up by the need to have each item examined for quality and quantity.

Ships registered in the United States are subject to the terms of the agreements between shipowners and the maritime labor unions. Among other provisions of these negotiated arrangements is the stipulation that the meat proffered to crew members shall be equal to the Department of Agriculture standard for the classification of "good." Those cargo ships that carry twelve passengers are permitted by those same union agreements to serve only one menu for all persons embarked. This simplifies the procurement, inspection, and delivery process to a notable degree.

Deliveries to the ship of commissary and other stores and supplies are made pursuant to schedules set up and made known to purveyors by the purchasing department. In many ports of the United States, as already indicated, stores are placed aboard ship by longshoremen, and therefore delivery schedules must be coordinated with cargo operations to cause as little interruption as possible in the handling of cargo. In terms of the working day, this means that the terminal manager should be consulted prior to instructing the various suppliers as to the time they should have their goods at the ship's side. The shipboard department heads also must be included in the planning and scheduling of deliveries, so that storerooms and verifying officers may be ready to receive the orders. It has been found to be good practice to have the supplier furnish the truck driver with manifests in quadruplicate. The original is signed by the responsible ship's officer when the count, quality, and condition of the goods have been determined to be satisfactory in all respects. The truckman returns this original to the supplier as evidence that the delivery has been made and accepted; eventually, it becomes the supporting document for the bill sent to the steamship company's disbursing office. The duplicate copy goes to the ship, to provide an exact record of what has been placed in the storerooms. The triplicate is retained by the purchasing department and filed with the other papers relating to procurement for that voyage, and the quadruplicate is routed to the accounting office for verification that all charges are in accordance with the contracts and are consistent with that which has been delivered. This system assures that everyone concerned is informed immediately of any deviation from the requisition as submitted by the ship and the quantity ultimately stacked in the storeroom.

Although complete inventory of a vessel's stores at the end of each voyage is ideal, it has been found impractical when turnaround time has been reduced to a matter of hours. To offset the possibility that elimination of the inventory may result in waste and extravagance, various expedients have been devised by senior management. Among these "checks and balances" are the following:

1. Engine room stores, particularly spare parts for individual machines, are inventoried, boxed, and sealed. Until the seal is broken, or there is reason to suspect that the contents have been tampered with, it is not necessary to do more than note that the box is in the proper place. As parts are used, the required replacement is obtained and put into the box, which is resealed and the updated packing list is displayed conspicuously. In this manner, unreported expenditure of spare parts is prevented.
2. Inventories may be made by ship's personnel during the voyage and mailed to the home office from an intermediate port of call. When this is done, stores-control supervisors determine whether the expenditure of stores is consistent with their anticipations. If usage exceeds expectations, and is appropriately justified, procurement standards can be adjusted to meet the facts. At the same time, preliminary plans for "spot inspections" and partial inventories may be formulated.
3. Spot inspections of vessel stores are made at irregular and unannounced times, but always in the presence of the responsible officer.
4. Requisitions are compared with vessel standards, and any unexplained deviations become the subject of investigations and inquiry by the appropriate department head. Where the standards are found to have been based on unrealistic assumptions, they should be ad-

justed to conform to actual experience.

5. File folders are prepared for each ship, and into them are inserted all requisitions, purchase orders, approved and signed invoices, and delivery receipts. These records show the actual expenditures for each class of supplies, and the cost of procurement of all items authorized by the appropriate managers. These records furnish the basis for comparisons between standards and expenditure of supplies, and also for planning future procurement.

Operating differential subsidy contracts between the United States Maritime Administration and operators of ships of that nation's registry prohibit purchases of stores or supplies in foreign countries except on long voyages that require replenishment of fresh stores. Emergency procurement of parts or stores is accomplished as the need arises, but must be explained fully by memoranda from all ship's personnel concerned. In any case, subsidized operators must maintain careful records of every purchase made outside the United States both to satisfy the Maritime Administration and to justify applications for exemptions from customs duties.

Some carriers do not procure stores abroad because quality is variable, there are health hazards, and the supply is not dependable. If meat is bought outside the United States, it must be sealed in refrigerated lockers before entering the territorial waters of the United States, or be inspected by the U.S. Public Health Service to ascertain that it is free of disease.

Some large steamship operating companies have concluded that because several of their ships may happen to be in the home port at the same time, or their turnaround time is very short, or they arrive at odd hours, it is neither convenient nor practical to rely upon the normal routine of procurement from merchants and manufacturers. To meet the demands of the ships without delaying their movements, these companies have established warehouses and buy in wholesale quantities. Requisitions from the ships are filled from stocks maintained in the warehouse. The warehouse, in turn, follows normal procedures for resupply.

The warehouse must be distinguished from the storeroom maintained by each division of the operating department. The storeroom contains, in the case of the marine superintendent, charts and other aids to navigation, and a few of the most critical pieces of navigational equipment. Similarly, the superintendent engineer will have a storeroom with a small supply of those parts that experience has shown are most likely to be needed as soon as a ship returns to the home port. The commissary division's storeroom, especially for cargo liner companies, will contain sufficient glassware, crockery, and linen to meet the immediate demands of a ship.

There are certain definite advantages that accrue from operating a warehouse; the principal ones are:

1. Ship requisitions may be filled in accordance with vessel schedules, regardless of the business hours of the purveyors of goods.
2. The exact item desired or needed may be furnished the ship without the delay associated with normal purchasing routine.
3. By procurement in large quantities, greater discounts may be obtained from the suppliers, with resultant enhanced savings.
4. Articles difficult to acquire, or in short supply on the market, may be stockpiled against future requisitions.
5. Seasonal purchases may be made at considerable savings, and occasionally greater savings may be effected by the ability to take advantage of fluctuations in market prices.
6. Wholesale procurement of linens, china, glass, and silverware, marked or designed to company specifications, often results in lower costs of those items.
7. Savings from wholesale purchases may offset all or a major portion of the cost of operating the warehouse.
8. A "pedigree card" showing the history of each major part kept in warehouse stock may be maintained. Items like tailshafts, turbine rotors, generators, gears, and propellers would be recorded on these cards to show the source of procurement, name of manufacturer, original certificate or forging number, the ships on which the component (if rebuilt or refurbished) had been installed, and the date when that component was removed from the last ship, together with the name of the vendor that performed the repair or refurbishment. Attached to the pedigree card are the applicable certificates from the classification society. This is especially valuable if the certificate shows any restriction for the installation or use of the item. The advantages of having this kind of information to pass along to those concerned aboard ship are self-evident.

There are some disadvantages to the warehouse system of vessel supply, of which the following are significant:

1. A complete warehousing operation must be established, with the accompanying problems of inventory, records, and security of goods.
2. Qualified warehouse operatives must be added to the company pay-

roll.

3. The investment in inventory is high. Depending upon the size of the fleet supported, the capital required for a warehousing program will range from a million dollars to fifteen or twenty million dollars.
4. The warehouse must be bought or rented (or, alternatively, space in a commercial warehouse must be leased from its operator), and some mechanism must be devised to send the goods requisitioned to the ship. Few warehouses are located right on the waterfront.
5. Warehouse stocks, in some of the fifty United States, are subject to taxation either by the state or the community in which the warehouse is sited. The impact of this potential burden must be measured carefully before a decision concerning the establishment of a warehouse can be reached.

One containership operator devised a modification of the warehouse system to fit the peculiar needs of his ships and their short turnaround schedules. Several 40-foot containers were fitted as storerooms, and supplies and spare parts were packed on the shelves and placed in the bins and lockers as they were received from the purveyors. Complete control over every phase of the procurement process was achieved. When it was time for the ship to sail, the loaded container-storerooms were hoisted aboard and placed where they would be convenient for all concerned to have access to them. There were obvious savings in the actual process of transferring stores from shore to ship; what was more significant was the complete storing of the ship which was accomplished by this development.

Whether procurement practices be based upon using a ship chandler, a purchasing house, or a division of the operating department of the steamship company, the shipowner carries the heavy burden of responsibility that, at the outset of a voyage, the ship is adequately supplied with everything that will be needed while she is at sea. It is, as has been brought out in these pages, a matter of good management that careful control be exercised over all facets of the procurement program. It also is a matter of assuring that the lives of the mariners who take the ship across the trackless oceans are protected by having at hand the material that experience and foresight indicate will be required while the vessel is "off soundings."

CHAPTER TEN

Containerization: The Beginning

April 26, 1956, was a rainy, cold day in Port Newark, New Jersey, not unlike many other spring days in the New York area. The departure for Houston, Texas, of the partially converted World War II vintage T-2 tanker *Ideal X* was very much a routine affair, except for one thing. That one thing was destined to change deep-sea shipping practice around the world but like other strokes of commercial genius it was not recognized at the time as being of any real significance.

As Malcom P. McLean waved farewell to his ship, he could not have been aware that he was initiating a revolution in shipping which would have as great an impact upon that business as did the coming of steam. For what McLean was watching was the first movement of cargo in which carriage by truck and ship was purposefully combined to form an integrated transportation system. As in other demonstrations of commercial genius, the achievement of McLean lay not in the mechanics of the operation but in the wholly new approach to relating diverse modes of transportation to each other and to the shipper. What had been a series of disconnected haulings by rail, highway, and waterborne equipment was converted into a coordinated and mutually supporting procedure which made the most efficient and economical use of the potentials and capabilities of the different modes.

Very briefly described, what McLean had done was to modify the standard 35-foot-long highway trailer used by trucking firms in the United States to permit the cargo-containing box (which almost immediately came to be called simply the "container") to be separated from the chassis. He then placed these trailers at the inland warehouses of shippers who filled them with their goods and sealed them in the same way that railroad boxcars were sealed. A trucker was summoned to haul the loaded trailer directly to the side of the oceangoing ship, where a crane lifted the container from the chassis and deposited it on the especially constructed "spar deck" of the tanker. At the port of discharge, the process was reversed, and the trailer was delivered to its consignee in an inland city. Most important to the whole scheme was the fact that a single contract of affreightment covered the entire movement from the shipper's loading dock to the consignee's warehouse.

The "container revolution," as the McLean conception of an integrated transportation system was denominated, originated in the mind of a man who had spent over twenty years in the intercity trucking business, building up his enterprise until his big trucks linked many cities in coastal states between New York and Florida.[1] He was well aware that a large portion of what was hauled in his vehicles came from shippers who filled trailers with goods consigned to single addresses. Systematic analysis of this one-shipper-to-one-consignee business revealed that there was a substantial proportion moving between those cities along the Atlantic and Gulf coasts which had good facilities for handling oceangoing ships. Furthermore, it was learned that a considerable quantity of other cargo came to or went from points some distance inland from these port cities. It was clear, therefore, that if the means were developed to carry the trucks by ship along the coasts, and simultaneously to simplify the paperwork involved in a multimedia system of transportation, at least some of the complexities which bedeviled the interstate movement of merchandise by truck might be alleviated.

As a possible answer to the dilemma, McLean remembered earlier proposals to put trailers aboard ships built expressly for the purpose. The ships themselves resembled in many details a single-deck garage. Once loaded, the relatively high-speed ships were to proceed to major coastwise ports where truck-tractors would be waiting to haul the trailers to their destinations. Preliminary considerations of these schemes intrigued the veteran truckman, who directed his staff to make detailed studies, including careful financial analyses, of the proposals. After determining accurately the characteristics of the flow of cargo—the main cities of origin and destination, the tonnages, the commodities carried, the frequency with which lots of cargo moved, the length of time needed to effect delivery, and the freight revenue earned—it became evident that a ship running between New York and Charleston, South Carolina, would serve the route very well. The consulting naval architect was commissioned to draw preliminary plans for the "floating garage" ship and to ascertain its performance capabilities. As the conception was studied in greater depth, it seemed desirable to consider the economic practicality of using the alternative ports of Providence, Rhode Island, in the north, and Wilmington, North Carolina, in the south. To meet the demands of the anticipated trade, it was determined that four of these floating garages would be required.[2]

Concurrently, the economic analyses were disclosing some startling facts which dampened the enthusiasm of the champions of the garage ships. Although the trailers could be rolled on and off the vessels in a very short time, and port turnaround therefore was at the optimum, too much of the available space in the ship was absorbed by the nonrevenue-producing chassis of the trailers. Only the goods *inside* the container were charged for transportation. A standard 35-foot highway trailer might carry 41 tons of cargo measuring 40 cubic feet to the weight ton, but mounted on the chassis the space occupied was equivalent to about 94 measurement tons. Identifying the problem suggested the solution. The containers must be separated from the chassis and loaded aboard ship in no more time than the roll-on process required. Additionally, the number of container-carrying spaces in the ship had to be great enough to earn both operating expenses and a reasonable profit.

McLean redirected the energies of his staff to devise the means to accomplish the goal envisioned by the economic analysis. The first move was to initiate technical discussions with the trailer manufacturer, who was asked to create a new type of highway trailer. This new unit was to consist of a flat-bottomed box with vertical strength to withstand stacking, longitudinally reinforced so that it could be lifted by a crane when fully loaded, and capable of being separated quickly from or connected to the chassis. The next step was to put aside the proposal for a garage ship and to concentrate upon the design of a ship to accommodate the especially constructed container.

It became obvious at this point that a full-scale test had to be conducted to determine the reaction of the shipping public to the innovation. This meant acquiring ships to transport the containers. Because they would be operated in the coastwise trade, certificates of public convenience and necessity from the Interstate Commerce Commission were essential. To design and build container-carrying ships was a multiyear project, entailing a very large investment while the process of obtaining original certificates from the commission was a tedious and protracted undertaking. With what proved to be characteristic boldness, McLean solved the problem by purchasing the seven-ship fleet of the Pan-Atlantic Steamship Company, a subsidiary of the Waterman Steamship Corporation, of Mobile, Alabama, which held valid certificates for operation in both the coastwise and the intercoastal trades.[3]

The conventional break-bulk cargo carriers obtained in his bold move were not adapted to McLean's new idea. Rather than delaying the test until the ships could be converted, four standard T-2 tankers built during World

Top left: A container goes aboard the *Ideal X.* Note the "feet" to fit into securing sockets. *Top right:* Spar deck of the *Ideal X. Bottom left:* Containers are secured to the spar deck. Note sockets for securing containers' "feet." *Bottom right:* The *Gateway City* was the first ship converted to carry containers in cellularlized spaces. Her gantry cranes made her independent of port facilities. Photographs courtesy of Port Authority of New York and New Jersey.

War II were bought from their operators, and spar decks were installed above their main decks. The containers were secured to the spar deck for the ocean voyage between New Jersey and Texas. McLean and his technical staff thus capitalized upon a wartime expedient devised to transport fighter aircraft to the European theatre of combat. A steel skeleton deck was erected above the tanker's main deck, and the airplanes were lashed to this structure. The only difference between the two conceptions was that the McLean spar deck was solid, with sockets inserted at appropriate loca-

A container is lowered to its cell in the *Gateway City*. Photograph courtesy of Port Authority of New York and New Jersey.

tions to accept the legs of the containers, and to lock the boxes to the deck by means of devices built into the socket-leg combination. The payload of each ship's "suit" of fifty-eight containers was about 1,160 tons.[4] Because the revenue from this tonnage was insufficient to pay all costs incident to initiating the new service, McLean planned to carry full loads of petroleum products from Texas to New Jersey to augment vessel earnings.[5] The U.S. Coast Guard negated this scheme, citing regulations prohibiting the mingling of dry cargo and bulk petroleum. Undeterred by this setback, McLean filled the cargo tanks with ballast water, and carried out his plans while accepting the losses as unavoidable "start-up" expenses.

The two potential obstacles to development of this idea having been removed by the acquisition of the certificates of convenience and necessity and by the purchase and modification of the four tankers, McLean was free to devote his energies to working out the details of moving the containers to and from shippers and consignees. It was simple enough to get the container to the ship for loading; it was more of a problem to assure that there would be a chassis and a truck-tractor awaiting each container when it was lifted off the ship by the dockside crane. By a series of contracts with truckers, these details were brought completely under McLean's control. At last, he was able to solicit business on the basis of a single bill of lading which applied to the whole movement from the point of origin to the final destination of the goods regardless of the number or type of participating carriers.

To Malcom McLean, therefore, must go full credit for conceiving and developing the integrated transportation system. An examiner on the staff of the Interstate Commerce Commission included this comment in his recommended decision submitted to the full commission on November 27, 1956:

> Malcom McLean is pioneering in the integration of sea-land transportation and in the application of the latest technological developments. A man of vision, determination, and considerable executive talent, he is making a valuable contribution.[6]

McLean placed a chassis-mounted container at the inland warehouse of the shipper, where that individual loaded (or "stuffed," as the term came to be) the goods into the container and sealed its doors shut. A truck-tractor then hauled the trailer directly to the ship's side, where the box holding the cargo was separated from its chassis and hoisted aboard the vessel by a dockside crane. At destination, another crane lifted the container off the ship and lowered it to a waiting chassis, following which it was towed to the consignee's warehouse. The consignee broke the seal, emptied (or "stripped") the container, closed its doors, and released the trailer to the truckman. A single bill of lading covered the entire movement.

Anticipating at this point the developments which came about some years later, it is appropriate to observe that, in time, a more complex interchange was arranged. The container was stuffed and sealed by the shipper who directed the truckman to haul the trailer to the railroad yard. There the container was transferred to a flatcar on which it moved from the inland city to the seaboard. When the flatcar reached the seaport, the container was shifted to a chassis and towed by a truck-tractor to the ship's side. In this manner, most efficient use was made of three distinct methods of transportation, without costly and time-consuming rehandling of the goods. This combination eventually was designated as "intermodal transportation."

As often has been the case when a totally new procedure is adopted, those casual observers who happened to be present at the moment when the action occurred saw nothing of overwhelming interest. The magnitude of what was transpiring on that cloudy, cool April day lay not so much in the visible scene but rather in the uncounted hours of thinking, experimenting, and establishing the most effective means by which to accomplish the objective.

So it was that, on April 26, 1956, the sailing of the modified tanker *Ideal X* with fifty-eight loaded containers stowed on her recently installed spar deck, seemed very little out of the ordinary. The waterfront watchers saw only the unusual feature of a slotted deck erected above the tanker's main deck with its maze of pipes and valves, to which were secured the special boxes that had been placed on the spar deck by shoreside cranes. The enormous importance of the procedure could not be detected because much of it was represented by what *did not* happen to the cargo stowed in the boxes.

Traditionally, the over-the-road trailers would have been unloaded in the transit shed of the terminal, and the separate packages would then have been moved to a consolidation point before being taken to the side of the ship to be hoisted aboard and then stowed in the appointed cargo space. McLean's procedures by-passed this time-honored routine by bringing the container directly under the crane and hoisting the entire box, unopened, aboard ship. In five minutes, some 40,000 pounds of revenue cargo would have been shifted from a highway vehicle to a seagoing vessel. To the farseeing observer, the implications were tremendous. Quite literally, a new era in transportation of goods by ship had dawned.

To appreciate fully the loftiness of this stroke of commercial genius, it is necessary to sketch, in an admittedly highly oversimplified manner, the whole procedure involved in what was known technically as "break-bulk carriage," and what later was called "conventional" handling of seaborne goods. For convenience, a single crate of furniture will be followed as it is moved from Grand Rapids, Michigan, to the inland city of Tours, France, about 100 kilometers from Paris. The same pattern of activity would be followed for a thousand packages, regardless of their contents, so long as each package could be identified.

The shipper crated the furniture with great care to assure its safe delivery despite the numerous handlings that lay ahead. The first movement was by truck from the warehouse to the railroad yard in Grand Rapids, where the crate was transferred to a boxcar for the trip to New York. On arrival at that point, the crate was removed from the boxcar and placed in a truck to be carried to the marine terminal. The truck was unloaded at the steamship operator's transit shed, and the crate was shifted to a "place of rest" where it waited until time to be loaded in the ship. At the designated moment, the crate was picked up by a forklift truck and brought to the ship's side. It was hoisted aboard the vessel and lowered into the hold. Longshoremen set it securely in its predesignated place where it remained until the unloading process began at the port of Le Havre. What transpired until the crate was delivered to the consignee in Tours was the reciprocal of what had occurred between Grand Rapids and New York. A minimum of twelve handlings was needed from the moment the crate was placed in the shipper's truck until it was taken into the consignee's warehouse. It is unnecessary here to expand upon the expenditure of time and money, as well as the possible damage to the crate and its contents, which these multiple handlings entailed.

Certain steps required by the shipowner for his own protection against unwarranted claims, but which did not involve additional handling, have been omitted from the foregoing skeletonized account. These steps, however, took the time and effort of well-paid employees, and recording what, if anything, was discovered then and at the time it was placed at the ship's side, when it came off the ship, and when it was turned over to the consignee's truckman. Individually, this series of examinations was justifiable and represented only a small amount of paperwork, but cumulatively, for a ship being loaded with 10,000 or 15,000 tons of heterogeneous cargo, it escalated into a major aspect of terminal management.

McLean, in a flash of genius, saw a means of simplifying the whole process. When the shipper loaded the container and then sealed it, he filled out a bill of lading and thereby certified to the carriers concerned that certain items, and only those items, were within the box. So long as the seals were not broken, McLean reasoned, the shipper's declarations were binding, and no verification was needed. All documentation required by the steamship operator therefore could be in terms of the big box, considered as a single package. Instead of four inspections of each individual package, there would be one when the container was received at the marine terminal and one when it was released to the consignee's truckman. Labor, money, and, above all, precious ship's time would be saved.

What distinguished McLean's thinking from previous efforts to improve the procedures followed in break-bulk shipping was this appreciation of the whole process as a single distribution system in which every part was interrelated and had a definite function. Another American ship-owner had come close to this idea but never brought it to the full fruition which occurred under McLean's guidance.

On January 12,1929, Graham M. Brush placed in service a seagoing railroad-car carrier which he appropriately named *Seatrain*.[7] The ship was devised by Brush, while the technical details of design and engineering were worked out by William Spofford, vice president and chief engineer of Brush's organization, known initially as Over-Seas Railways, Inc., and later renamed Seatrain Lines. What made the *Seatrain* unusual, if not unique, was the manner in which her hull was arranged to accommodate the railroad cars. One very large hold, extending from the forward collision bulkhead to the engine-room bulkhead near the stern, had three decks, each fitted with four sets of parallel railroad track. The hold and the lower deck each could accept twenty-six cars; the upper deck had space for thirty cars, while the superstructure deck, because of its lighter supporting elements, was restricted to a maximum of thirteen empty cars. Altogether, the ship could carry from ninety to ninety-five cars on a trip.

An essential part of the Seatrain operation was the ingenious crane which Brush, a civil engineer by training and background, had designed. The cables of the crane were secured to a massive steel "cradle" which served as the means of lifting the railroad car. When the cradle had been raised to the level of the superstructure deck, it was moved athwartships to the designated "slot" and lowered to the appropriate deck. Here the car was connected to a wire rope linked to a steam winch and was pulled in this manner from the cradle to the place where it was chocked securely for the voyage.

Brush set up his steamship as an adjunct to the railroads. His thinking was set forth in an advertising booklet issued by the company in 1932, and appropriately entitled, *Out to Sea on Rails*. Seatrain Lines sought out those shippers who normally would use railroads, and offered a financial saving if the car were routed so that a portion of the total transportation was performed by the ship. This was a very successful procedure until competition from McLean began to assert itself. Seatrain, by this time no longer controlled by Brush, attempted to adapt to the new methods, but was too conservative. Unable to survive in the new climate of competition, the company sold its fleet and name to a group of investors who followed McLean's lead and carried all cargo in containers.

In an earlier chapter, the complex and expensive operation of a break-bulk marine terminal has been described. The great expense of this activity always was of major concern to senior executives, terminal managers, stevedore superintendents, and ships' officers, and over the years many suggestions were offered to improve the traditional practices. There was, for instance, the logical proposal that cargo piled on pallet-boards should be strapped to permit each loaded pallet to be placed aboard ship as a single unit. Out of this idea developed the thought of placing certain types of cargo, especially fragile items, in large boxes which would be transported to the overseas destination without rehandling the contents.

Immediately following World War II, a Great Lakes businessman named Leathem D. Smith devised a steel container approximately 8 feet square and almost 8 feet high. Smith was concerned with the persistent problem of containers: the return voyage, usually without any cargo, involved substantial expense to the owner of the container. To reduce this back-haul cost, Smith's containers were intended to be folded so they would measure only 8 feet square by approximately 3 feet high. Unfortunately, the rough handling given to the boxes made the folding feature unworkable, and the idea was dropped.

Along the waterfront, meantime, gradual improvements in the techniques of cargo handling were being tried. Traditionally, packaged goods were received at the terminal by longshoremen who loaded the packages on hand trucks and trundled them to the place of rest to await moving to the ship's side. The actual process of hoisting cargo from dockside platform to ship's deck was no different from that used by the Phoenicians, except that steam or electric power had been substituted for human muscles. The individual packages were stowed by hand into the appropriate spaces in the ship. The whole operation was infinitely laborious and consumed much time for which the ship was not paid: it is axiomatic that a ship earns money only when at sea actually moving cargo from one point to another.

About 1935, the forklift truck was introduced without fanfare to the marine terminal. Its use required that packages be piled systematically on pallets so that the truck could fit its forks under it and lift it before transporting the load to any designated point. So successful was this development that the hand truck disappeared from the waterfront within a few years, and a whole new technique of materials handling was adopted. It was the fulfillment of a prediction when a pallet load of packages destined to the same port was strapped with steel bands and loaded aboard ship, eliminating the tedious process of individually stowing every box.

The use of containers in the movement of goods did not originate with McLean. As far back as 1911, several commercial enterprises engaged in the packing, crating, and shipping of household goods began to stow these valuable items in heavy steel boxes for intercity movement by rail. Overseas shipments of household goods in these steel boxes occasionally was accomplished, but in each case it was a matter of a series of disconnected movements arranged for and supervised by the shipper. Insofar as the carriers were concerned, the container was nothing more than an oversized and sometimes excessively heavy unit that was handled as any other package would be. The number of these shipments was small and cannot be considered as anything more than a minor part of conventional break-bulk carriage.

Following the end of World War II, the idea of stowing certain commodities in containers for transportation by ship began to spread rather widely. Great Britain, Denmark, Belgium, the Netherlands, Germany, and France were the western European nations where the practice received greatest attention; concurrently, there was some increase in the use of containers in the United States. The boxes varied in dimensions according to the notions and experience of the carriers who owned the equipment and made it available to shippers. Generally, the containers were small, ranging in capacity from about 5 to 15 cubic yards (4 to 10 cubic meters). Shippers who had sufficient goods to fill a container sometimes were given the option of having the container sent to their premises for loading, or delivering their cargo to the marine terminal where the carrier's personnel stuffed the container. By 1949, it was not unusual for a ship to sail with the square of one or more hatches filled with these steel boxes. An immediate advantage to shippers was that these containers were the last packages to be placed aboard ship, and the first to be taken off, which thereby shortened total transit time for the goods.

In the United States, the Alaska Steamship Company and the Bull Line, operating respectively out of Pacific northwest and Atlantic northeast ports to noncontiguous U.S. possessions, were among the leading advocates of containers to reduce ship turnaround time. Alaska Steamship used metal boxes in 1949, added what it called "collapsible cargo cribs" in 1952, and began carrying loaded trailers aboard its seagoing ships in 1953. The "cribs" were developed from the standard wooden pallet and consisted of a base with lattice sides and a plywood top; capacity was 1.68 cubic meters. Cribs were made available, on request, to shippers who could pack and strap them. If they were received by the terminal in this condition, they were delivered to the consignee in that same condition.

The Bull Line commenced its experiment with containers about the same time as Alaska Steamship. Because shippers to Caribbean destinations used packaging for their goods that was too fragile to withstand the rough handling involved in movement by ship, the carrier was interested in methods to reduce the inevitable damage. Large steel boxes in which the fragile cartons could be stowed appeared to be one solution. In time, the company developed a box of 19 cubic meters capacity. Somewhat later, a larger unit was devised that was 4.6 meters long, 2.4 meters wide, and approximately 2.4 meters in height. These dimensions were suggested by the need to fit two boxes on a standard flatbed truck-trailer, which was 9.75 meters long. These containers, which Bull Line called "vans," were stowed in the holds of conventional break-bulk ships. Their handling below decks was facilitated by casters permanently fitted at the corners, and also by rugged frames which permitted lifting by forklift trucks.[8]

While it is undeniable that there were steamship operators who placed cargo in large containers, as described above, it cannot be deduced from this fact that the container revolution antedated the first sailing of Malcom McLean's *Ideal X* in 1956. The practices noted in the preceding pages were the results of efforts to improve the techniques of marine terminal operations and thereby to reduce the time required to discharge and reload a conventional break-bulk carrier. Concurrent with this objective was the desire to bring about better outturn of cargo in order to cut down on costly claims by shippers for lost and damaged goods. The containers used by shipowners prior to McLean's day rarely, if ever, left the terminal premises. Shippers apparently preferred to send their offerings to the terminal where, at the discretion of the superintendent, they might be stowed in a container or they might be put aboard ship as individual packages. The essential component in the structure of the container revolution was McLean's introduction of the integrated transportation system. It was the flowering of this conception which made the sailing of the *Ideal X* on April 26, 1956, of lasting importance in the development of marine transportation.

A fully integrated distribution system, in theory, puts under one management all the participating modes of transportation and handles the business under a single contract of carriage. This makes possible the most efficient employment of each component of the system, and produces the most economical operation. A practical, but not insuperable, problem is to assemble in one corporate structure the diverse talents required to manage the different types of transportation. The day-to-day practices of railroading are not necessarily similar to those of long-distance trucking, and the supervision of inland waterways tugs and barges varies in many details from that of oceangoing vessels. The senior executive must possess an unusual background of experience to provide rational and evenhanded administration, including allocating financial resources among the carriers.

In the United States, existing law regulating interstate commerce forbids the proprietor of one mode of transportation to own a competing method. Until recently, no railroad, for instance, was permitted to control an inter-city trucking enterprise. A coastwise steamship company may not own a railroad that parallels its route and competes for the same business. The ideal of a single corporate unit controlling and using most efficiently the various kinds of transportation available in the United States therefore remains more of a dream than a reality.

McLean saw the potential of his conception of the shipping industry, and in September 1955 divested himself of the trucking enterprise. Thereby he freed himself to devote his energy and his vision to the development of the new system of transportation. History has shown that his decision to channel all his interests toward maritime matters was correct, for his new method of sending goods between seaports spread throughout the world and influenced, in the most profound manner imaginable, the carriage of merchandise by sea.

Shippers responded with enthusiasm to the new development, and provided the empirical proof that was required if further growth and evolution were to occur. To be profitable, however, at least two hundred loaded containers had to be transported on each trip. This was beyond the capabilities of the spar deck tankers. New construction was deemed unwise at this stage of the fledgling steamship company's existence, and therefore conversion of ships was the only alternative.

Anticipating this turn of events, McLean completed negotiations on May 5, 1955, to acquire the remaining assets of the Waterman Steamship Corporation for the sum of $41,567,000. Among the properties purchased were thirty standard C-2 cargo ships built between 1942 and 1945.[9] Only ten of these vessels were retained; all the other Waterman holdings were sold within the next four months.[10]

George G. Sharp, an outstanding American naval architect, planned the conversion of the ships acquired from Waterman. At a cost of approximately $3\frac{1}{2}$ million dollars each, the ships underwent a major rebuilding. All interior bulkheads and decks were removed, and weather deck hatch openings were enlarged to a uniform length to accommodate the 35-foot-long containers. The cargo spaces were fitted with an elaborate steel framework to form cells into which the containers were lowered and stacked one atop another to a depth of five units. Two additional tiers of containers could be carried on deck. By installing a 30-ton gantry crane forward of the midships house, and another abaft this structure, the ships were made self-sustaining, and could be sent to any port which had a dockside apron wide enough to permit a truck-tractor to maneuver a trailer on which to place the container. The cranes traveled back and forth on tracks laid on sponsons which were built on each side of the hull for a total additional width of 9 feet. A diesel-driven generator provided electric power for each crane, which had arms that, in port, projected about 20 feet over the side of the ship and were folded down to touch the hull when the vessel was ready to sail.[11]

When the ships were placed in service, initially in the coastwise run from New York to Houston, Texas, they astounded observers by the rapidity with which a full cargo of inbound containers could be removed and replaced by a complete set of outbound boxes. In 1958, a newspaper report noted that only fourteen hours of ship time were needed for this procedure, and altogether forty-two longshoremen were hired, compared with about 126 for a break-bulk vessel.[12] Admittedly, the ship operator was able to economize on cargo-handlers' wages, but the more important saving was in ship time. It is axiomatic that the hours a ship spends in port working cargo are not revenue-producers. By reducing cargo handling time from the eighty-four hours needed for break-bulk operation to the fourteen used to handle the containers, the number of ships required to maintain a specified frequency of service on a given route was reduced significantly.

The following comparison between the operation schedule of the *Gateway City,* the first McLean ship to be converted to carry containers exclusively, with a conventional break-bulk ship of the same basic design and an identical power plant, will demonstrate how the saving in stevedoring time benefited the shipowner.

The *Gateway City* was assigned to sail between Port Newark and Houston, a distance of 1,928 miles. At her normal cruising speed of 14.5 knots, the one-way passage required 133 hours, without allowing for possible delays and the inevitable slow transit through inner harbor channels. In Houston, she used 14 hours to discharge and reload, and then spent another 133 hours steaming back to Port Newark. Port time in the New Jersey terminal was 14 hours, bringing the total time for the round trip (from departure on Voyage No. 1 to departure on Voyage No. 2) to 294 hours. To assure against breakdowns, it was established that the *Gateway City* would be withdrawn for maintenance purposes at the end of each twenty-five-week period of operation. During the fifty weeks of the operating year, the ship was able to complete 28.56 round voyages. If every one of the 226 containers carried a full load of 20 revenue tons, ship earnings would be based on 4,520 tons per one-way passage.

The *Fair Isle,* a conventional break-bulk ship comparable in all respects to the *Gateway City,* was operated on the same route. Her sea time was identical with that of the containership, but discharging and reloading required 84 hours in Houston and a similar period in Port Newark. Total voyage time came to 434 hours. In fifty weeks, the *Fair Isle* completed 19.35 voyages. Her earnings also were based on carrying 4,520 tons per one-way passage.

Translated into fleet size, the calculations reveal that two containerships had the theoretical capability of maintaining sailings every 6.14 days through the 351 days of their operating year. The longer turnaround time for the break-bulk ships meant that three vessels would be required to make possible a sailing every 6.05 days. Because no more revenue would be earned by the three break-bulk ships than by the two containerships, it is obvious that the reduction in total voyage time was of major financial importance.

(It must be emphasized that the above calculations are entirely theoretical and do not reflect actual ship operations. The purpose of the computation is to show the disparity between the performance potential of the two types of ships and to suggest the relative earning power of the vessels.)

With experience, the McLean management team learned that equipping each ship with gantry cranes, while it made possible calls at ports which lacked the facilities needed to handle containers, resulted in more drawbacks than advantages. The cranes were idle while the ship was at sea; they were very heavy and therefore reduced the tonnage of cargo which could be carried; they added greatly to the cost of ship building; their presence aboard ship restricted the load of containers to two tiers on deck; and the maintenance of the cranes was an expensive aspect of ship operating cost. Dockside cranes, on the other hand, could be used continuously, serving one ship after another. They also provided a much wider outreach than that of ships' cranes and thus increased the efficiency with which containers were handled alongside the ship. Although the land-based cranes were purchased and installed by the operators of the ports (usually public bodies like the Port Authority of New York and New Jersey or the Board of Commissioners of the Port of New Orleans), their great cost—the first ones were acquired for 1 million dollars each, and later versions were priced two or three times higher—was reflected in the rentals charged to ships for the berthing spaces they occupied. These increased charges, however, were less than the investment required to provide cranes aboard every ship. All of McLean's later ships, both conversions and new construction, were designed to depend upon dockside cranes. Worldwide, containership operators have followed this precedent almost without exception.[13]

As an inducement to shippers to use the new method of transportation of goods by sea, McLean made the specially designed containers available to his customers. This expensive expedient was necessitated by the fact that the standard over-the-road trailer used by American trucking fleets did not have a detachable box, nor was it built with the reinforced corners required for stacking the boxes aboard ship. McLean vessels, perforce, loaded and carried only McLean-owned containers. In this way it came about that initially the containership operators assumed full responsibility for procurement, maintenance, and control of containers, and only those boxes that belonged to, or were leased by, a particular steamship company were transported by that company. The financial burden imposed upon the shipowner may be gauged by the fact that when McLean sold his interest in the shipping company in 1969, the inventory listed 27,000 containers which cost about $3,500 each—an investment conservatively estimated at nearly 100 million dollars.

It was not long after the maiden voyage of the *Gateway City* that other operators began cautiously to explore the new method. This attitude was based in part upon consideration of the capital investment required, changes in terminal operating practices and the resultant conflict with the longshoremen's unions over reduced employment opportunities, and possible legal problems connected with extending the carrier's liabilities beyond the marine terminal. It also reflected the conservatism characteristic of much of the shipowning fraternity which accepted change only after proof that what was proposed was both practical and necessary.

In fairness to operations in the international overseas trades, it must be conceded that conditions encountered on these routes were very different from those prevailing in the coastwise service between two U.S. ports. If the overseas area were well developed with internal highway and railroad networks, and the ports were equipped to handle the big boxes (which might weigh 25 or more tons), it was feasible to adopt the new mode of integrated transportation. If, however, the overseas nation were still in the process of internal development, it would be a major error in judgment to convert to containers. Some operators were quick to perceive the long-range benefits of an integrated system and ventured into the new era by modifying one or more hatchways to accommodate containers, while retaining the capability to handle large amounts of break-bulk cargo.

To understand the attitudes toward the novel system, it is appropriate to examine some aspects of the economics of containerization.

First, but not necessarily most importantly, the process of stowing merchandise in the container was a logical step on the part of carriers in their never-ending search for more efficient and more economical ways to handle cargo. The increasing number of uniform-sized packages offered for shipment made the use of the pallet feasible, and the introduction of the forklift truck made it possible to move the loaded pallets economically and conveniently from place of rest in the transit shed to the ship's side.

It took some years for the next step to be adopted rather widely, but the practicality of the notion eventually won adherents. Lots of uniform-sized packages destined to either the same consignee or the same port were assembled, under the watchful eyes of a cargo checker, on a pallet, and then secured with steel straps so that thereafter the whole collection could be handled as a single unit. This had several advantages: (a) it was more difficult to pilfer the individual package; (b) checking on the condition of individual cartons was reduced; (c) stowage in and breakout from the ship's hold were more expeditious and efficient; and (d) the goods themselves were less susceptible to breakage and damage. From the use of the steel-banded palletboard to the all-weather container was a simple and almost predictable step.

Second, containerization transferred the task of stuffing and stripping the container from the carrier to the shipper and consignee, and thereby reduced significantly the shipowner's cost to check the condition of cargo when received and delivered.

Handling merchandise in the marine terminal, prior to placing it aboard ship and after it was removed from the vessel, represented a major portion of terminal expense. By transferring this charge to the shipper and consignee of the goods, the ocean freight rate could be restated to reflect more accurately the actual cost of port-to-port transportation. Additional benefits in which all parties shared were the allocation to the shipper of responsibility for proper stowage of the goods in the container, a marked reduction in the total transit time from warehouse to warehouse, and the elimination of numerous rehandlings of the merchandise. When the container was turned over to the ocean carrier, all that was required was to inspect the exterior for evidence of possible damage and to establish that the original seal attached by the shipper was intact.

Third, containerization saved time by having cargo brought to the ship's side in boxes that could be loaded directly into the vessel. The benefits to the shipowner of the shortened stay in port already have been delineated. To the shipper, the reduction of the time needed to deliver the goods to the ultimate consignee meant receiving payment with less delay.

Fourth, marine terminals were made much more productive and efficient when they were completely mechanized and operated around the clock whenever a ship was at the berth. This shortened the ship's turnaround time and thereby effected savings for the ship operator. Relocating terminals to areas convenient to major highways and railroad lines helped to eliminate delays in delivery and pickup of containers, with resultant economies to the shippers.

The operation of a modern, well-outfitted container terminal requires fewer longshoremen, checkers, and coopers, but remains a major item of shipowners' costs because of the large number of expensive machines needed to handle the containers. Straddle trucks, very high capacity forklift trucks, mobile cranes, and similar equipment are indispensable. Their operators, being especially skilled, command premium wages.

Finally, the containerized shipment of goods has resulted in better outturn of cargo, with a consequent reduction in claims for loss and damage. There also has been less pilferage of cargo since containers have come into general use.

Up to this point, little attention has been devoted in these pages to the question of the sustained sea speed of containerships. One reason for this seeming neglect of an important subject is that the velocity of vessels is of less importance to both shippers and consignees than reducing the length of time the cargo has to be in the custody of the shipowner. When the *Gateway City,* which had a maximum speed of $14\frac{1}{2}$ knots, made her first voyage as a carrier of containerized cargo exclusively, she traveled at approximately the same speed as did all other cargo ships. What gave McLean a major advantage over his competitors was that his method reduced the time required to load the cargo aboard, remove it from the ship, and make it available to the consignee. It was as though he had raised the speed of a conventional break-bulk ship by at least 25 percent.

It was not until ships were designed and built to handle all their cargo in containers that significant increases were made in their cruising speed. As pointed out earlier, the fewer the days needed for a single voyage, the more revenue-producing trips a ship can complete in a year. There are, however, only two ways in which to reduce the duration of a voyage. One is to cut the time to discharge and reload. The other is to decrease the number of hours spent in transit between ports. To justify the cost of greater speed, it must be shown positively that the revenue earned by the additional voyage exceeds the cost involved. The speed of the container-carrying ship therefore must be related to the integrated transportation system and evaluated for its contribution to that system.

A partial view of the enormous area of Port Elizabeth's containerized cargo terminal. Photograph courtesy of Port Authority of New York and New Jersey.

To anticipate later developments, it may be observed that the cost of building the newer containerships, which were much larger, faster, and more complicated in structural details than the pioneering originals, escalated during the second decade of the container era, and reached almost incredible levels. As a natural consequence, the necessity to reduce to the minimum the number of units required to maintain the acceptable frequency of sailings became a matter of survival. Sea speeds were raised, and cargo working schedules were established on a round-the-clock basis.

Concurrent with these developments, there have been continuous modifications in terminal management ever since that day when the *Gateway City* inaugurated fully containerized shipping service. In those early days of the revolution, the problem of providing an adequate terminal was of comparatively minor importance. The *Gateway City* and her sisters were equipped with their own cranes and therefore could be berthed at any wharf or pier with a wide apron. As techniques improved and awareness increased of the potential of container transportation, it was perceived that specialized terminals equipped with appropriate cranes were essential.

This load of the multi-measurement containership *Cape Hatteras* demonstrates how variable lengths of containers may be stowed. Photograph courtesy of Columbia Shipmanagement Ltd.

Traditionally, berthing for ships has been made available by the government authority having jurisdiction over the waterfront. Piers and wharves, with supporting transit sheds and head houses, have been constructed by this authority and leased to steamship companies serving the port. Almost invariably, features requested by the oceangoing carriers have been incorporated into the facilities built for their use.

The role of these public agencies has not changed, and owners of containerships still look to them to design and construct satisfactory terminals. The enormous expense of creating container terminals requires the financial resources of port authorities, which can issue bonds backed by the full faith of the state or municipality. Shipowners have been hard pressed to pay the high prices of their ships without having to assume in addition the burden of costly terminal construction.

At the time the completely cellularized ships were introduced into McLean's operation, computer technology was in its earliest stages. It was clear to the management team guiding the growth of the integrated transportation system that only by taking advantage of the computer and exploiting it to the maximum could the goal envisioned by McLean be attained. What emerged, after appropriate study and testing, was a computer-oriented technique of control which provided the information essential to good management. It is true that the emergence of computer technology made possible the fruition of the container revolution. It also must be acknowledged that this achievement was owed in part to the willingness of the McLean team to abandon traditional methods in favor of the computer procedures that were being introduced, and to adapt the "electronic brain" to the requirements of the McLean enterprise.

An almost classic example of the application of progressive management techniques may be found in the solution to the problem of keeping track of the containers controlled by McLean. When the *Ideal X* sailed in 1956, the data relating to the fifty-eight containers aboard had been assembled and posted by hand. This method was still in use when the *Gateway City* made her inaugural voyage in 1958. When, however, she was joined by five more ships, each outfitted with at least three sets of 226 containers, and boxes were scattered the length of the Atlantic and Gulf coasts of the United States, it was apparent immediately that only a completely computerized record system would serve to prevent these expensive units from going astray through either delay in getting information or clerical error in using it. As the McLean fleet grew and expanded into worldwide operation, the value of such a control device was magnified.

A retrospective examination of Malcom P. McLean's role in the development of the containership and its essential function in the integrated transportation system reveals that he was bold but never reckless or foolhardy. The consequences of every step, insofar as it was possible to do so, were evaluated methodically and pragmatically before any action was taken. It will be recalled that the first idea was to load wheeled trailers aboard ships, and to roll them off at destination. The economics of this scheme were found, after exhaustive analysis, to be unfavorable. The alternative suggested by the study was to carry the boxes without the chassis. McLean approved the idea and forthwith acquired the necessary certificates of convenience and necessity by purchasing the Pan-Atlantic Steamship Company, an established coastwise operator. The full-scale laboratory experiment then was carried out with four modified tankers.

McLean proved, by the initial voyage of the container-carrying tankers, that the theory of the containership was valid, and that its potential would be achieved when an integrated transportation system was developed around the indispensable vessel. The almost storybook success that crowned McLean's pioneering efforts is now history and justified in every respect the basic premises on which he had proceeded.

Looking back to April 26, 1956, it is easy to comprehend that one of the great technological events of modern times, the beginning of the container revolution, occurred on that date. It is much more difficult to establish the moment when McLean first had the inspiration of an integrated transportation system using existing railroads, trucks, ships, containers, and contracts of carriage to obtain the greatest possible efficiency and economy. Whenever the inspiration was translated into a cohesive idea, it became the driving force that led to the practical success of the new method. That McLean had both the imagination and the financial resources to convert his dream into hard reality is one of the fortunate twists of history. Had it been otherwise, there is basis for endless speculation as to when the container revolution would have come about—if ever.

What is of paramount importance is to realize that without the combination of practical wisdom, commercial genius, and unwavering audacity, the events which today are described as the container revolution might not have occurred. That wisdom was joined to genius, and that audacity supported them both is, in final judgment, the reason that Malcom P. McLean may and must be hailed as the initiator and the leader of a revolutionary business system which he put together and made function perfectly the day it was unveiled to the world.[14]

CHAPTER ELEVEN

The Ramifications of Containerization

Once the feasibility of the container movement had been proven by Malcom McLean's success in the U.S. coastwise trade, shipowners in the international services began to look with interest on the new method. For many reasons, including the entirely pragmatic one that there was a shortage of the proper containers, it was not until early 1966 that any regular transportation of containerized cargo was offered to shippers on the busy North Atlantic route. In February, Moore-McCormack Lines began to dispatch containers in their fast break-bulk ships, emphasizing as an inducement to exporters and importers that these boxes were the last to be loaded aboard and the first to be taken out of the ship, thereby saving a considerable amount of time over and above the reduction in conventional handling. The United States Lines followed suit the next month by assigning four break-bulk ships to carry containers. Fully cellularized containerships transporting all cargo in the big boxes were introduced to the North Atlantic by McLean's Sea-Land Service in late April of the same year, when the *Fairland* and three sister ships were placed on berth to operate between Baltimore and Port Newark in the United States and Rotterdam, Grangemouth, and Bremerhaven/Bremen in western Europe.

From this 1966 beginning, the conversion of international shipping on the main trade routes to full use of containers was rapid and dramatic. Loaded international dry container trade volume increased from a total of 2.1 million 20-foot equivalent units (TEUs) in 1970 to 27.6 million TEUs in 1990, with compound annual growth averaging 15 percent over the period. Further, projections for the year 2000 are for an annual volume of 40 million TEUs.[1]

This natural evolution in transportation, which took place so rapidly that many refer to it as a revolution in transportation, was almost indescribably expensive. In the period between 1958 and 1973 alone, shipowners, terminal operators, and port agencies in the United States invested $7\frac{1}{2}$ billion dollars in ships, containers, and port facilities. The concurrent growth of container operations throughout the world caused similarly high levels of expenditures elsewhere as well. This was pointed out by the New York *Journal of Commerce* report of June 20, 1977, publishing the results of a survey of the expense involved in converting to the new method. These facts were emphasized:

1. Containerships cost twenty-five to thirty dollars per cubic foot to build, compared with seven to eight dollars per cubic foot for conventional break-bulk carriers;
2. A standard steel container, 20 feet long by 8 feet wide and 8½ feet high, represented an investment of $3,500, while a fully refrigerated container might be priced four times higher;
3. A 30-ton-capacity container-handling crane involved a minimum outlay of $1,750,000 before it lifted its first box; and
4. Waterfront property for marine terminals and marshaling yards could be obtained only by paying between $250,000 and $300,000 an acre.

Added to these formidable figures was the harsh economic fact that the new method of packaging and transporting goods was forced upon shipowners only a few years after they had commenced a very expensive replacement program for their obsolescent break-bulk vessels. These new ships embodied the latest and most efficient ideas of cargo handling and stowage and had been acquired with the expectation that their costs would be amortized in fifteen to twenty-five years. Furthermore, a number of operators had expended very sizable sums in modernizing and equipping their break-bulk terminals both in home ports and overseas. It is easy to understand their reluctance to write off, somewhat abruptly, the many millions of dollars (or pounds, or yen, or other appropriate currency) they had put into what had been intended as a long-range fleet modernization plan. The tide of change, however, was irresistible, and adaptation to the container method was a matter of simple survival. It is a sad commentary upon the relentless and remorseless pressures of economics that a number of reputable but small-scale operators found it necessary to withdraw from the shipping business and to liquidate their holdings.

The burden that was suddenly thrown upon shipowners by the technological advance was immense. New containerships not only cost much more to build than did the break-bulk vessels they were displacing, but they were capable of higher speeds and had significantly greater capacity. The duration of sea voyages was shortened and port turnaround time was reduced radically, contributing to the heightened performance of these big

The enormous size of container-handling cranes may be gauged by comparing the 4-meter (13 foot) high trucks and trailers with the towering cranes. Photograph courtesy of Ray Soto, Port of Houston Authority.

ships. In theory, one modern cellularized container carrier of about 26 knots speed and a deadweight of approximately 29,000 tons, carrying close to 2,000 20-foot containers, could transport the same quantity of cargo in a year that five or six conventional break-bulk ships could handle. Had it been possible to effect a simple reduction of ship numbers according to that ratio, it would have resulted in a reasonably satisfactory solution to many of the problems spawned by containerization. Shippers had become accustomed, however, to a certain frequency of service, such as one sailing a week by a favored operator, and looked askance upon any suggestion to change this to one sailing every third or fourth week. To harassed shipowners, this intractable attitude might have seemed most unfriendly, but in the end they acknowledged that, as always, the requirements of the shipper determined the nature of the trade. It was a case of satisfy the customer or go out of business.

To provide that satisfaction, shipowners were forced to accept the idea of building and operating whatever number of large, fast, high performance, and extremely expensive carriers might be needed to provide the service demanded by their customers. It worked out, in practice as opposed to theory, that the new fleet would replace the older vessels in the ratio of one to three. This meant that shipowners were compelled to build almost twice as many ships as the trade would support financially. In terms of potential revenue tonnage, there was only one interpretation of this fact: there was a great deal more capability (or cargo space) than there was cargo.

The obvious solution was the one adopted by many operators. They joined forces with one or more of the other carriers on the same trade route to form a sort of composite management of that number of ships which would be justified economically while still meeting the demands of shippers and consignees. In effect, what happened was that four owners might band together and each supply one ship to the consortium. Every week there would be a sailing, thereby satisfying the shipping public while at the same time assuring revenue cargo adequate to pay the expenses of the voyage. This arrangement between carriers required prior approval by the Federal Maritime Commission before any operators participating in the foreign commerce of the United States could become active in the association.

An example of a consortium was the formation, in 1967, of the Atlantic Container Line. Three Swedish firms (Swedish American Line, Wallenius Shipping Company, Transatlantic Steamship Lines), the Holland America Line (a Netherlands organization), the Compagnie Générale Transatlantique (a subsidiary of the French Compagnie Générale Maritime), and the Cunard Steam Ship Company (part of Trafalgar House, an English conglomerate) each contributed one or two ships of approximately the same size, speed, and characteristics to a new company in which the six operators had equal holdings. Named the Atlantic Container Line, this organization operated between European and British Isles ports and U.S. Atlantic coast cities from Boston to Norfolk. The first sailings were made in the fall of 1967, but it was not until some months later that the planned number of ten ships was placed on a twenty-one-day cycle; not all ships called at all ports, but dependable schedules for the different routes were set and maintained. A computer-oriented system controlling the loading and discharging of containers assured that consignees could obtain their boxes with a minimum of delay. Full containers for a single consignee were ready for pickup not later than thirty hours after the ship arrived, while cargo shipped as part of a container load and requiring more attention was available to the consignee in less than seventy-two hours after the ship was berthed.

The essence of the consortium was to substitute cooperation for competition, and to form a single unit in which the good of each participant was the predominant principle, rather than a frantic scramble by individuals for the greatest possible share of the available business. An association of this sort could be successful, however, only if the members provided equipment of substantially the same capability, and a single management handled the enterprise. Carriers were disposed favorably toward this idea, in view of the enormous cost of setting up a complete container service (ships, containers, acquisition of appropriate terminal facilities, and the necessary supporting network of agents) to say nothing of the problems inherent in the training and oversight of qualified salesmen, office personnel, and supervisors at every level.

Success crowned the idea of the consortium, if results are the proper criteria by which to judge. It proved eminently practical on trade routes having a sound economic base and a reasonable balance between incoming and outgoing cargoes. Not every prospective consortium, it must be noted, was able to achieve its goals. Some associations were proposed, but died aborning; others were put together with every prospect favoring the scheme but had to be dissolved in the face of insurmountable obstacles, many of which were not of the carriers' making. Still others began their existence with a number of operators but in short order were narrowed down to as few as two partners.

An alternate method used by shipowners to help them control costs is the current practice of chartering space on containerships owned by other companies on the same trade route. This practice allows the shipowner to maintain its company identity and company recognition by customers, and at the same time allows capacity to be increased without acquiring additional ships. The reciprocal of this practice also applies. Excess capacity on its ships could be chartered out to other carriers seeking shipping space.

Two concerns of management assumed unprecedented importance as containerships became relatively standardized, very large, extremely expensive, and somewhat inflexible units.

The first of these concerns dealt with what accountants designate as "variable costs." Variable costs are important in determining the lowest possible rate that may be legally charged for the services rendered. In the steamship business, these are the items of expense related directly to the specific voyage on which a ship is engaged at a given time. Wharfage and dockage and other fees charged by the port authorities, pilotage fees, tugboat hire, stevedoring expense, watchmen's services, and agents' commissions are examples of these variables. To illustrate how they fluctuate in break-bulk shipping, consider the hypothetical example of a vessel which called at the same port on two consecutive voyages. On the first visit, the ship lifted only 1,000 tons of cargo, and incurred total charges of twelve thousand dollars. On the second call, she loaded 15,000 tons of cargo and spent $109,000. Variable costs in break-bulk shipping usually represent about one-half of total voyage expense; the other half is allocated to capital and overhead charges, which must be met regardless of what the ship carried or even whether she earned any revenue.

In containership service, it soon became apparent that several items of costs which had been considered as variable had become so uniform and regular that they no longer had any flexibility, and had little relationship to vessel employment. Genuinely variable costs, it was perceived, had been halved by the very nature of containership operation. For instance, the dockside cranes charged the same to hoist empty containers as they did to handle filled ones; the draft of the ship on arrival and departure was almost always the same, so the pilot fees (which were based on the draft of the ship) scarcely ever changed significantly. The same ports were visited in the same rotation voyage after voyage, and except during times of adverse weather conditions at sea, fuel charges were very nearly identical for every trip. These expenses, although technically variable, in fact had become so constant that they were as predictable as capital costs of amortization, interest, depreciation, insurance, and overhead.

The other area of special interest to management was related to the dawning awareness that the container was in reality an integral part of the ship, and therefore it was possible to "put the ship alongside the cargo" even when that cargo was in a warehouse a thousand miles from the sea. A most significant corollary of this new definition was that geographical limits for cargo solicitation (known as the hinterland) were extended enormously. With this movement inland by the steamship company, it also quickly became clear that keeping track of marine equipment once it left the terminal would be difficult, that there was a problem in finding trades that had a balance of cargo in both directions so that equipment would not have to be repositioned empty, and that the differences between inland and deep sea transportation were substantial enough to preclude immediate adoption of any truly uniform contract of carriage applicable to all parties involved in the transportation movement.

One of the noteworthy developments of the container age, spawned at least in part by this new theory of placing the ship alongside the cargo, was the emergence of an "infrastructure" for container shipping. This term implies a whole catalog of supporting functions and responsibilities on the part of the shipowner which explains the complexities of the container system. Of primary importance in this supporting organization was the indispensable network of agents, freight forwarders, and cargo brokers, known generically as "third parties," who represented the water carrier throughout the inland territory, and who, in effect, served as its local sales and delivery staff. On their diligence, enterprise, and judgment depended, to a great extent, the ultimate success of the shipowner.

INTERMODALISM

As the complexities and tremendous potential of containerization came to be understood, there was a concurrent movement within the industry to capitalize on the inherent advantages of other modes of transportation to create an economical and effective system. This movement was given the name of "intermodalism."

Intermodal transportation is defined as a systems approach to transportation in which goods are moved in a continuous through movement between origin and destination using two or more modes of transportation in the most efficient manner.[2] That is to say, a shipper located a thousand miles from the seacoast may pack goods in a standardized container and send the box by truck, barge, ship, and railroad to an overseas destination under a single contract of carriage which adequately protects all parties concerned at any given moment while the goods are in transit. Admittedly, there are no technical or mechanical difficulties associated with the process of shifting the container from one form of transportation to another as long as the container will fit into the designated cell aboard ship. The problem is entirely a legal matter.

As stated earlier in this chapter, it was clear that the differences between deep sea and inland transportation were substantial enough to preclude immediate adoption of any truly uniform contract of carriage applicable to all parties involved in the intermodal movement. A uniform contract required the shipowner to furnish the shipper a bill of lading stipulating acceptance of full responsibility for any loss or damage sustained during the entire transit. By separate agreements negotiated between the carriers, the liabilities of inland carriers for loss or damage were established, and appropriate remedies were set forth to protect the shipowner in cases where the inland carrier might be found at fault. This somewhat ponderous method did accomplish what was required, and made it possible for the shipper to receive a single document and to have one carrier accept complete responsibility for the care and custody of the cargo while it was in transit.

In the transportation of goods the relationship between shipper and carrier is set forth in the contract of affreightment (sometimes referred to as the contract of carriage, and more generally known as the bill of lading). Unlike the conventional contract, which is the result of a meeting of minds following negotiation, the maritime contract of carriage is drawn up unilaterally by the shipowner and is not subject to negotiation except in unusual circumstances. It becomes binding upon the shipper when it is accepted and no signature is required. The act of acceptance is construed as agreement to all the terms and conditions of carriage. The maritime contract of carriage reflects the experiences of the individual shipowner who issues it. There is no necessary similarity between contracts issued by different operators on the same route, except insofar as legal prescriptions apply. That the contracts drawn up and used by two competing carriers on the same route do contain a number of identical phrases is both a fact and coincidence, because only very rarely will there be consultation between shipowners on the wording of their individual contracts.

In the movement of goods by containers, it has become standard practice for the shipper (rather than the carrier) to stow the goods in the container. When it is filled, the shipper closes the container and secures it with a seal. This seal is practically identical with the one used by railroads, and consists of a thin metal band fitted through a slot in the locking mechanism of the door. It terminates in a weighted knob into which the band is threaded and held by a type of cement. It has a serial number, which becomes part of the permanent record of the movement, and thereby assures that no substitution can be made without detection. No key is used because of the practical impossibility of the consignee possessing this key when the container is delivered.

Containers filled by the shipper ordinarily are not subjected to inspection of the goods inside when custody is accepted by the carrier. The description of the goods provided by the shipper must be accurate, under penalty of legal action. Unless the container is received in a condition which shows that some damage probably has been sustained, the carrier and the shipper agree that they will be bound by the contractual stipulation that the package, i.e., the container, is "in good order and condition." The consignee is obligated to set forth in detail any damage discovered when the container is opened, and may be invited by the shipper to prove that this damage was not the result of faulty stuffing.

Participants in an intermodal movement which crosses one or more national boundary lines must take notice of the rules and regulations applicable to their business. The shipowner, and the party responsible to the shipper, must be well informed on these points, and of necessity depends upon the inland carriers for notification of any changes which affect the intermodal arrangements.

The idea of intermodal transportation is to give shippers those routings which will result in the fastest and least costly carriage of their goods. A typical case might require the services of an intercity trucker to haul the container to a feeder-barge collection point, transit by feeder barge to the ship selected to take the container to a foreign port, and a railroad trip to an inland point where a trucker would accept the container for transportation to the ultimate consignee. The shipper is interested only in three details: the party to whom claims for loss or damage during transit should be presented, the rapidity with which the container is moved from origin to destination, and the total cost of transportation. Intercarrier relationships are of no concern to the shipper, which helps to explain their pressure for a single, comprehensive bill of lading.

One of the obstacles to developing an intermodal contract of carriage acceptable to all participating carriers has been the question of financial responsibility for loss of or damage to the goods. Participants in the intermodal movement understandably are reluctant to become involved in claims actions when there is no evidence of their culpability. Added to this reluctance is the fact that in most circumstances the container is not opened while it is in transit; so the true condition of the contents at any given time is unknown to any of the carriers.

The following description of a hypothetical intermodal shipment of a container loaded by the manufacturer of high-grade porcelain tableware will illustrate the problem.

A consignment of 106 cartons of finest quality tableware, valued altogether at approximately $200,000, and with some cartons worth as much as $5,240 each, was loaded by the manufacturer into a new and carefully inspected container supplied by direction of a steamship line operating from Oakland, California, to Honolulu, Hawaii. The purchaser demanded that the goods be sent by the fastest possible surface means. Pursuant to this instruction, the shipper's traffic manager decided to move the container by intercity trucking service from Trenton, New Jersey, to the railroad yards in Newark and thence overland to Oakland, where the transfer to a fast containership would be effected. Transportation was accomplished accordingly, with no external evidence that the container had been subjected to any forces that might cause damage, or had been the victim of pilferage. Inspection of the exterior of the container confirmed the original statement by the initiating carrier that the container was in good condition, and the contents in apparent good order and condition.

When the container was delivered to the consignee in Honolulu, it was discovered that one carton, worth $1,000, was missing, a void space near the door of the container giving incontrovertible evidence that the cargo had been loaded. Two other cartons, each with a declared value of $5,240, had been crushed into rubble. They were loaded at the forward end of the container, and even had the doors been opened by a carrier for an inspection, their condition would not have been detected. The total claim by the consignee amounted to $11,480, a sum sufficiently large to make it important for those not involved to prove their lack of responsibility for the loss and damage.

Inquiries were initiated by the steamship line as the delivering carrier. In the order of their contact with the shipment, these facts were assembled by the claims agent:

1. The manufacturer in Trenton stated in an affidavit that everything listed in the manifest had been placed in the container, that expert packers handled the stowage, that no careless or rough treatment was accorded to any of the cartons, and that the container had been sealed after a final inspection to assure that all was in good order within the container.
2. The intercity trucker declared, also under oath, that delivery had been effected to the railroad yard in Newark without incident. The

driver of the truck was identified by name and license number, and his record for safe driving was confirmed by the state police. Furthermore, the driver testified that he personally had examined the seal at the time custody was transferred to the railroad, and the seal had not been damaged in any way.

3. The railroad set forth in its notarized comment that the container had been lifted off its chassis by a skilled and dependable operator of a mechanically perfect crane, and there was no record of improper handling at the time of loading or unloading of the railroad flatcar. Examination of the train crews' reports did not lead to any conclusions that those cars making up that particular train had encountered any abnormal circumstances or been treated in an unusual manner.

4. The steamship operator had its own records of the container from the time it was brought by the trucker who accepted it from the railroad until it was turned over to the consignee's drayman and he was cleared for departure from the Honolulu container yard. The external appearance of the container was satisfactory, and the condition of the seal corroborated the drayman's statement; there had been no basis for questioning the accuracy or veracity of the shipper's description of the contents, and therefore the container had not been opened for inspection.

The determination of who was responsible for the loss and damage clearly posed a problem. Because of the high value of the claim, and the unusually complete data relating to the transfers, it was impossible to place responsibility on any one carrier. Negotiations between all the participants were conducted by the steamship company's claim department, and it was agreed that the consignee would be reimbursed by assessing each of the carriers in direct proportion to the amount of freight money which had been earned.

The illustration has been simplified deliberately by keeping the entire transaction under U.S. jurisdiction, which permitted one of two solutions: (a) to initiate legal action in a U.S. court, pursuant to laws and regulations known to and binding upon all participants; or (b) to permit negotiations within the framework of the pertinent regulations. It takes only a little imagination to comprehend the practical difficulties resulting from an intermodal shipment in which, for instance, an American railroad was the initiating carrier, a Dutch ship provided the ocean transportation, and a German barge service moved the container inland and turned it over to a Swiss trucker for delivery to the consignee.

True intermodal transportation as described above is still in the process of evolution. A major step toward realization of the ultimate goal of intermodalism—the most efficient use of the available means of transportation without the requirement for special intercarrier contracts—has been taken. The single bill of lading has become a reality. The ocean carrier is willing to issue the bill of lading because that carrier controls the inland movement. That is to say, the shipowner already has contracted for use of the inland carriers, and knows exactly what the relationships are with them. Drawing up the bill of lading for shipments involving inland carriers is, therefore, a comparatively simple legal exercise.

The essence of the intermodal contract is an agreement among carriers of different types, such as barge lines, railroads, and trucking firms to perform certain carefully described and defined services for agreed rates of compensation. Ideally, the ocean carrier offering intermodal service should be free to negotiate the most favorable rates, terms, and conditions for the type of service required. The resultant intermodal rate is the total of what must be paid to connecting carriers plus the shipowner's compensation. There are persuasive reasons why the carriers in the same trade (for example, Japan to the U.S. Pacific coast) would find it advantageous to negotiate with the intermodal operators to establish the charges for inland transportation. Although this appears to be a logical element in the conception of intermodal transportation, the Shipping Act of 1984 bars any association of ocean carriers domiciled in the United States from negotiating "on any matter relating to rates or services provided to ocean carriers within the United States by those non-ocean carriers." Ocean carrier groups, however, are permitted to set "joint through rates" for cargo destined to inland points. From the text of the law, it would appear that the intent is to permit the individual ocean carrier to negotiate a rate for intermodal service and then to meet with the other carriers in the group to agree upon a combined sea and land rate which would be common to all members.

A major growing pain of the container age has been the conflict over the size of the containers. When Malcom McLean began his operation with the sailing of the *Ideal X*, he modified for shipboard stowage the standard 35-foot trailer used by the U.S. trucking industry. As other steamship owners cautiously entered the new phase of seaborne commerce, they designed containers that seemed most appropriate for the trades they served. Before many years had passed, but well before there was the almost complete conversion of liner-service shipping to container transportation, there was a profusion of containers. All were 8 feet wide and approximately 8 feet high, but in length they ranged from 10 to 40 feet, although not in uniform increments. There were, for instance, boxes that were 20, 24, 27, 28, 35, and 40 feet long. Each was excellent for one particular route, but as shippers began to accept the new method and to demand that their goods be moved in the big boxes on many trade routes, shipowners faced the gigantic problem of making containers interchangeable in the same way that railroad cars in the United States, Canada, and Mexico are moved across international boundary lines without mechanical hindrance. Shipowners also had some interest in having uniform container sizes because they found that more inland routes were available to them if they had standardized containers that were compatible with more types of carriers.

In 1961, the International Standards Organization (ISO) strongly recommended that containers be designed and built to "standard" specifications. Many carriers adopted the idea. The basic ISO module was 10 feet; approved containers therefore were 10, 20, and 40 feet long and 8 feet wide by 8 feet high. McLean stubbornly clung to the 35-foot boxes for the reason that they fit the chassis used by the American trucking industry and therefore could be handled most efficiently and effectively to any point in the nation. He built into his ships cells for this size unit regardless of ISO proposals. Over the intervening years, the battle of size appears to have been won by the proponents of 20- and 40-foot units, and most of the containerships built today are designed to accommodate either of these sizes. The worldwide yardstick for determining the capacity of containerships as well as expressing the statistics of container traffic is the "20-foot equivalent unit." Even Sea-Land Service modified many of its ships to handle 40-foot boxes as well as its own 35-foot containers. Its newest ships were designed for both 20- and 40-foot boxes.

(The trend in the design of containers, especially in the United States, is toward longer, higher, and in numerous instances wider, boxes. All, however, are constructed to meet ISO standards of strength, regardless of whether intended for land or marine use. Some boxes are as long as 53 feet; others, described as "high cube," are up to 53 feet long, 9 feet 6 inches high, and 8 feet 6 inches wide. They are used only in domestic land movements in the United States, and are not seen on ships.)

The question of making containers interchangeable between steamship lines and between other modes of transportation (an essential element of intermodalism) has resisted rapid settlement. Pioneer containership owners had to buy their own boxes and make them available to shippers. Inevitably, they tended to load their ships only with goods packed in these company-provided containers. In overseas and foreign trades, the dispersion of containers to destinations quite remote from the ports at which the ships called quickly assumed the dimensions of a major problem. Significant losses of boxes were sustained by some operators, and elaborate measures had to be devised for tracing them. Some were discovered to be serving as warehouses for consignees, who explained that it was cheaper to take the goods out of the containers as their counters needed replenishment than to empty the big boxes into warehouses and then shift the goods to shelves and sales racks. Other owners learned that the containers were used not only as warehouses but as the stores themselves. In many instances, in the more impoverished regions of the world, containers were converted into houses by cutting windows and doors into them and placing them on hard stands.

As a result of these findings, complex and expensive systems for keeping track of containers were developed, but the high cost of buying, maintaining, and tracing the boxes has encouraged the formation and growth of companies with no interest except to buy containers and lease them to shipowners. The emergence of these entities has brought closer to fruition the dream of interchangeability, and attention now is directed toward forming "neutral pools" of containers. The term is a shorthand reference to those boxes owned by leasing companies which are used for one-way movements, and then turned over to an agent. This functionary places the containers in central collecting points where they form a pool from which individual units can be drawn to meet the needs of shippers within geographical range of that central point. Because they are specialists in the procurement and management of containers used in worldwide trade, the leasing companies have devised elaborate, computer-based systems by which they are able to keep informed of the location of every one of their containers and chassis at any time.

The probability is that shipowners will withdraw gradually, as their investments in containers are amortized, from owning the boxes, and will depend entirely upon the leasing organizations except for perhaps some of the very specialized containers that their customers may require. There are three compelling reasons for this trend. The first is that the new containerships are so expensive that little capital is left to the shipowner for purchase of the required thousands of containers. The second reason is that the need for interchange is growing day by day, and the folly of attempting to force shippers to use only carrier-owned containers is increasingly evident. The third reason is that the requirement for tracking and balancing equipment is a very expensive operation both in terms of labor and computer equipment. By using leased containers the burden of tracking and balancing is shifted to the leasing company.

Crane operator's view of a container ready to be hoisted aboard ship. Photograph courtesy of North Carolina State Ports Authority.

One major user of containers complained that "empties" had to be returned to the shipowner within a fixed number of hours, and then ensued a wait of a day or longer for the same shipowner to bring a container in which to pack the next outbound consignment. Said this traffic manager, "Sometimes my returning 'empty' passes the incoming container, which also is empty. It's a very wasteful and extravagant way of doing business."

With the advent of the neutral pool of containers, the old system by which Deep Sea Line would send a container to consignee X in Sacramento, and then bring it back empty to Oakland, while Blue Water Line was dispatching a container to Sacramento for trader Q to load with goods for Australia, will come to an end. Instead, Deep Sea Line will move a container to Sacramento, and simultaneously notify the leasing company that Box 123 is now in the custody of consignee X. The leasing company becomes responsible for keeping track of Box 123 when it is unloaded and turned over to the neutral pool. Blue Water Line, meantime, will have informed the pool that trader Q accepts the box, and becomes responsible for notifying the pool when the container is delivered to the steamship company. In turn, the carrier tells the pool agent in Australia when the consignee has taken custody. The consignee is obligated to return the container to the pool depot.

The advantages of this system are obvious. Intermodal transportation requires the adoption of a uniform-sized container that can be loaded with equally productive use of space in ships, aircraft, barges, trucks, and railroad cars. Already wide-bodied, all-cargo aircraft accept one or two 20-foot boxes. Railroad technology covers a spectrum including: the old 89-foot flatcars which handle two 40-foot containers or over-the-road trailers, the newest double-stack cars which can handle 53-foot containers, the lightweight spine cars which can carry 48-foot containers one high, and the new carless technology which allows the over-the-road trailers to be moved on rails without traditional rail cars. Trucks habitually employ flatbed trailers to haul containers for which they do not have chassis. Physically and mentally, there are no obstacles to using all types of carriers for containerized cargo.

Looking ahead, future growth and acceptance of the container as a means of packaging goods for transfer from one point to another depend upon the establishment of true intermodal systems. Before this can be achieved, all the different users and carriers who would be involved in the system must agree on the following points:

1. The standardization of container sizes.
2. Complete interchangeability of containers between carriers.
3. Establishment, maintenance, and control of container depots by an agency or agencies which would be neutral (unaffiliated with the carriers) and dedicated to working only with containers.
4. The formulation of a uniform contract of carriage binding upon all participants. This is necessary to handle claims and to facilitate negotiations concerning clauses of the contract.

5. Reduction in the present number and complexity of documents required for cargo shipped in containers. The ultimate goal must be one document that will be accepted by commercial and governmental interests as meeting legal and other stipulations relating to origin, value, ownership, and routing instructions.

6. The introduction and widespread use of highly sophisticated computer systems to support the interchange program. This would include acceptance and use of electronic data interchange (EDI) which involves the electronic transfer of commercial transactions using an agreed standard with which to structure the transaction or message data.[3] This would also include the use of automatic equipment identification (AEI) which involves electronically tagging all equipment used in intermodal movements, thereby making the tracking of the equipment easier.[4]

7. Efficient, economical collection and distribution of containers from and to the marine terminals, monitored by all parties concerned. In the United States, this may not be possible without legislation exempting the cooperation inherent in the intermodal principle from existing antitrust law.

8. Uniform rules concerning responsibility for the condition of containers while in the custody of a given person.

9. Agreement on a uniform method of processing and adjudicating claims.

LANDBRIDGE

It is true that, although containerization depends upon fast, efficient ships for the ocean passage, the growth of the conception of landbridge service is rooted in the land. The shipowner has no choice but to become involved in every phase of transportation if there is to be a smooth, uninterrupted flow of cargo to the ships.

As the use of containers for international shipping expanded following the first voyages in 1966, it was logical for both operators and shippers to think of ways in which to obtain even greater benefits. A look at the map showed that from Tokyo to New York there were two routes: one routed the ship through the Panama Canal, an all-water trip which might take up to thirty days, depending upon the speed of the ship, while the other routed the ship to a port on the west coast of the United States and sent the cargo overland to the eastern metropolis. With the goods already packed in a container, the time and risk factors involved in transferring from ship to railroad were minimized and between seven and ten days could be saved.

The landbridge conception simply uses a landmass as a "bridge" in what otherwise could be an all-water routing. There are three basic types of landbridge services; landbridge, mini-landbridge, and micro-landbridge. Landbridge service is characterized by the use of a major landmass to bridge two water routes. An example of this would be the movement of cargo from Japan by ship to a U.S. West Coast port, then across the United States using a mode of land transportation (usually rail), followed by a ship movement from an east coast port to its final destination in England. Mini-landbridge service is characterized by the use of a major landmass to bridge an all-water route where the final destination is on the opposite coast. An example of this would be the movement of cargo from Japan by ship to a port on the West Coast of the United States, then across the United States using a mode of land transportation (usually rail), to its final destination at Boston, on the east coast. Micro-landbridge service is a little different, being characterized by the use of a landmass to complete/begin a voyage that involves water. An example of this would be the movement of cargo from Japan by ship to a port on the West Coast of the United States, then across the United States to Kansas City. There is no all-water alternative in the micro-landbridge service as there is in the landbridge or mini-landbridge service. Properly developed, landbridge or mini-landbridge services offer time, money, and energy savings.

Seatrain Lines generally is credited with being the initiator of the landbridge services, with the first shipments completed in 1971. The idea, however, was neither new nor original with Seatrain but rather revived what had been a successful operation during the 1920s when a very interesting service (mini-landbridge) was offered by steamship operators. Known informally as the "silk express," the service connected Yokohama and New York via Seattle, carrying bales of raw silk as primary and premium cargo. Express steamers loaded their valuable consignments in Japan, followed the great circle course to Seattle, and transferred the silk to waiting railroad baggage and express cars that were dispatched at high speed to the market in New York. This coordinated arrangement was offered to shippers whenever the need arose and therefore was not a regular feature of transpacific steamship operations. It was popular and lucrative and was terminated only as economic conditions and international rivalries created circumstances inimical to its continued existence.[5]

The silk express was a coordinated operation of the steamship carriers and the transcontinental railroads. Two separate contracts of carriage were issued, one by the water carrier and one by the land carrier. The only reason for the service was to reduce transit time between Japan and the New York silk market. Each transporter functioned in its own area; there was mutual support without any attempt to establish single control. Both the steamship owner and the railroad company benefited, but aside from adjusting schedules and assigning equipment so that there would be no delays in transshipment, the silk express was the result of two distinct activities.

What differentiated the Seatrain scheme from the earlier arrangements was that Seatrain assumed and retained full responsibility for all transportation and made its own subcontracts with the transcontinental railroads. The shipper dealt only with Seatrain, which added to the attractiveness of the new method. As the number of containers booked to this service increased, Seatrain arranged for "unit trains" to transport the boxes across the United States. A sixty-car train, loaded with two 20-foot containers on each car, was dispatched not more than forty-eight hours after the ship docked in a West Coast port, and then proceeded under special orders to Weehawken, New Jersey, the Atlantic coast container terminal maintained by Seatrain.

There was one illogical feature about this operation. Containers might originate as far west as Pittsburgh or Chicago but had to be sent to Weehawken, at the expense of the shipper, before the water-rail arrangement and freight rate became effective. It was a waste of time and railroad car space to insist on this routing, but it was necessary because the unit train was made up in Weehawken and was taken as an unbroken element directly to the Pacific coast. Stops were made only for the convenience of the railroad to relieve crews or to refuel or change locomotives. A special contract was negotiated between the railroad and Seatrain for this transportation; no exceptions were permitted or requested.

In 1979, as part of its strategy to expand its hinterland, American President Lines initiated a "liner train" service from Seattle to Chicago and New York. Compared to the all-water route, this saved seven days of transit time. Capitalizing on the success of this venture, the company in 1984 introduced its individually designed railroad flatcars which carried containers stacked two high. A contract was negotiated with the railroad to provide unit train service transporting a total of two hundred 40-foot containers, with two departures a week in each direction. So effective was this operation that two additional "liner trains" per week were scheduled from Los Angeles to Chicago and New York. A freight forwarding company, Trans-way International Corporation of New York, served as the company's representative in the Midwest and Northeast.

As often occurs in business, a successful venture encourages others to emulate the pioneer. In the case of American President Lines, the port authorities in Seattle purchased sufficient double-stack flatcars to commence a common carrier unit train operation from Seattle to Chicago and New York. This was available to any steamship company using the port of Seattle. By the middle of 1985, the Danish-owned Maersk Line had duplicated in every detail the pattern of service from Seattle by American President Lines. Orient Overseas Container Line announced in June 1985 that it was initiating liner train service from the West Coast to Houston and New Orleans.

Any survey of the extension of landbridge service must include reference to the activities of the Russians in developing the trade between Germany and Japan, using the trans-Siberian railway as the link to the ships. In March 1971, the Russians sent a few containers from Moscow to Nakhodka, where Japanese-flag ships were waiting to transport the boxes to Yokohama. A year later, the service was extended to Germany in what became known as the Trans-Siberian Container Service. This trade grew significantly, and not only was the port of Nakhodka modernized and enlarged, but a nearby harbor, Vostochny, was converted into a container terminal. Both Japanese and Russian ships handled the water phase of the movement. Despite problems inherent in moving containers through the extremely low temperatures of a Siberian winter, the saving of seven to ten days in transit time and also a lower cost for freight were approved by the shipping public. The only difficulty of any magnitude resulted from the greater number of loaded containers moving toward Germany as compared to the traffic flow toward Japan.[6] Returning the containers to their respective owners has been a problem, however, since the dawn of the container age and promises to remain a matter of concern well into the future.

In the United States, landbridge operations have been the source of controversy. Atlantic and Gulf Coast ports that formerly handled cargo destined from the coastal states to the Far East complained that the new system was "diverting" business from regions that were "naturally tributary" to those ports (their hinterland). They contended that for decades before the advent of the container revolution, exporters domiciled within a certain radius of a port had sent their goods to that city's waterfront to be loaded into ships that then proceeded through the Panama Canal to ports of the Orient. With the introduction of containers and the adoption of the landbridge scheme by Seatrain and other carriers, the containerized cargo was placed on railroad flatcars that went directly to Los Angeles or Oakland,

California, or to Seattle, Washington, for transfer to the containerships. This disrupted the economy of these ports. The dispute was brought before the Federal Maritime Commission in 1973, and after prolonged hearings involving many facets of administrative law, a decision was promulgated on August 8, 1978, which held that landbridge service did not violate any laws.

In commenting on the long-held doctrine of "cargo naturally tributary" to a given port, the commission laid down two "general principles" for the future guidance of all concerned.

The first of these principles was that "certain cargo may be naturally tributary to a port, but any naturally tributary zone surrounding a port is constantly changing." In a particular case, the tributary zone would be determined by considering (1) the flow of traffic, including the points of origin or destination of the cargo, through the port prior to the introduction of the new practices of the carriers; (2) the relevant freight rates for inland transportation; (3) the natural or geographic patterns of transportation and the most logical and efficient use of those patterns; and (4) the needs of the shippers and the characteristics of the goods being moved.

The second principle was that "a carrier or port may not unreasonably divert cargo which is naturally tributary to another port." Judging by the factors listed under the first guideline, certain cargoes may be designated correctly as "naturally tributary" to a particular port. Should any or all of this cargo be diverted from that port, the logic and reasonableness of that diversion would have to be established. "Reasonableness" of an individual routing of cargo is to be determined by considering (1) the quantity of cargo being diverted and whether substantial injury is being sustained by the bypassed port; (2) the cost to the steamship operator of providing direct service to the complaining port; (3) any practical and demonstrable difficulties in ship operations or other factors, such as the small quantity of cargo offered for scheduled sailings, or inadequate facilities for handling the proffered cargo, which would influence the water carrier's ability to provide direct service; (4) the competitive conditions existing in the trade; and (5) the fairness of the method or methods employed to effect the diversion, including, for example, the absorption of certain costs or the techniques of soliciting business.

The commission further noted that the contention that a region was naturally tributary to a given port "cannot be extended to the point where a port or a range of ports can claim a multi-state inland region as its exclusive 'territory.' This, however, is precisely what the complainants are attempting to do in this case."

Cargo was found to be originating in states far removed from the Gulf Coast. The commission observed in its ruling:

> Even if it were assumed that all minibridge [mini-landbridge] cargo originates in Texas and Louisiana, the Gulf Coast ports all lay equal claim to those areas and no individual port has established an area locally tributary to it alone. . . . The theory that an entire region of the country might "belong" to a range of ports is not a tenable basis upon which to build a regulatory framework of fair competition between the interests of ports and carriers. Historical movements of cargo are not without some relevance, but it cannot be seriously maintained that Congress intended [the port-protecting] Section Eight of the 1920 Merchant Marine Act to freeze international transportation movements into their 1920 patterns.

An indication of the sense of financial injury that a port sustained by the diversion of cargo resulting from landbridge operations may be gained from that portion of the commission's decision dealing with the claim by Houston, Texas, that three-quarters of a forty-million-dollar bond issue had been assigned to build facilities to handle containers in the expectation that Seatrain would continue to provide direct port-to-port service from Houston to Europe.

The commission held that:

> Absent clear proof to the contrary, it must be assumed that a local investment decision of this magnitude was dependent upon a number of factors other than the unsecured assurances of continued vessel calls by a single containership operator. It has long been recognized that, absent unique circumstances, the Shipping Act does not require ocean carriers to provide service to a particular port.[7]

A reexamination of this decision several months later prompted these comments from the vice chairman of the commission:

> Historical and geographical considerations (relating to naturally tributary cargo) may still be applied, but they should not serve as rigid criteria in defining any port's naturally tributary zone. Competitive conditions existing in the trade, shipper needs, and the variety of transportation services available are equally valid criteria

in determining naturally tributary cargo. . . . By questioning the notion that certain ports have proprietary right to certain cargo, we are increasing the need for ports to compete for their traffic and . . . increasing their incentive to develop innovative services to attract enough cargo to remain profitable.[8]

A basic principle of traffic management is to find the most economical routing for a consignment of goods. In this context "economical routing" always has had a twofold meaning, applied both to the cost of transportation and to the time the goods must spend in transit. If using landbridge service would expedite delivery to an overseas market by two or three days, it must be assumed that the faster method will be selected. This would be true especially if the shortened transit time cost no more than the longer, all-water route.

Another problem encountered fairly early in the new era of containerization was the liability of the water carrier for the loss of a container or damage to its contents. Almost all containerships carry some of their boxes on deck and therefore subject them to the effects of storms and heavy seas, to say nothing of temperature changes on passages through different climatic zones. For many years, steamship practice held that the maximum amount for which the carrier would be liable in the event of loss of a package was five hundred dollars, unless a higher valuation had been declared at the time the bill of lading was issued. With the advent of the container, however, the question arose, "What is a 'package'?"

The answer was provided in the 1978 court decision which held that, in those instances where goods stowed in the container had been packaged in cartons or wrappings which clearly separated each item or each quantity contained within the package from similar items or quantities held in other cartons or wrappings, liability of the carrier was five hundred dollars for each and every one of the individual packages. If the goods were not segregated—as would be true for a container filled with bulk grain—and therefore no separate mark or number might be ascribed to each unit being transported, the liability of the carrier would be fixed at five hundred dollars for the entire container, which the court considered to be the "package."

FEEDER SERVICES

As the interests of the shipowner have been extended deep into the landmass behind the ports, two developments have occurred since the initial long-distance movement of containers in international commerce. The first was the reassertion, as a practical precept of containership management, of the old ideal that an oceangoing ship is economically most efficient when operated from one loading port to one discharging port. The costly and time-consuming practice of sending the ship after the cargo therefore had to be abandoned. This precept recognized that containerships depended upon shore facilities for loading and unloading, and consequently had to be routed to appropriately equipped ports. The enormous daily cost of the big ships required that turnaround time be as short as possible. A complete cargo of containers therefore should be assembled in the marshaling area before the ship arrived.

It was recognized, however, that all the containers needed to fill the ship might not be available at a single port. Quite often, several hundred boxes would be held at a marine terminal within a comparatively short distance from the main port, while additional containers would be offered at outlying points requiring at least a full day of steaming to reach. The question to be answered, quite literally on a port-to-port basis, was this: "Is it cheaper and more efficient to pay trucking costs to bring the containers from port Y to the ship's berth at port X, or to send the ship to port Y?" Clearly, the number of containers and the ocean freight rates payable on their contents would have much to do with the answer, but as a general rule it may be asserted that where the number of containers is small and the highway distance from Y to X is approximately one hundred miles, it would pay the owner to keep the ship at port X and to absorb the trucking costs. Where the quantity of containers is substantial and the road distance significant, as from Norfolk, Virginia, to Newark, New Jersey, or from Los Angeles to Oakland, California, the usual decision is to move the ship.

In shipping circles, the matter of "vessel cost" invariably is related to total performance, which means that the time required to make a coastwise voyage to deliver or pick up cargo often becomes the compelling factor, surpassing even the very measurable fuel and port fees. To send a ship from port A to port B may be approved because it involves only eight to ten hours of steaming time. To get from port B to port C, however, twenty-eight to thirty hours of steaming time are needed. The total cost in ship time must be determined because it affects the number of voyages completed in a year as well as many other aspects of efficient management of the vessel and the fleet. Every operator must balance the advisability of moving the ship against the cost of assembling the cargo at a single port. Where this results in a net reduction of expense to the shipowner, the idea of naturally tributary cargo vanishes in the harsh glare of realistic cost analysis.

Containers were built to be weatherproof and easy to handle mechanically. They were planned for easy shifting from one carrier to another—water, rail, or highway—in a matter of minutes at an acceptable level of cost. When it was proposed to take advantage of coastwise sea routes and inland waterways by using smaller craft (either barges or deep-sea vessels) to distribute and pick up cargo at outlying ports, the response was immediate and affirmative, as demonstrated by the actions of a towing company based in New York City. It set up a common carrier barge service linking New York with New Haven and Boston, departing every Tuesday from each terminus. Containers destined to these cities were transshipped to the barges, and a fixed fee was paid for their onward transportation. If no containers were offered to the feeder carrier, no payments were made. The success of these efforts was owed to the regularity of schedules. Shippers and consignees knew when their containers would be picked up or delivered, and the deep-sea carrier could determine in advance what their feeder service would cost.[9]

Because the big containerships were so expensive, owners desired insofar as practicable to restrict them to operation between a single port of origin and a single port of destination—what quickly came to be known as "load centers." The question of distributing and picking up containers in the western European area, including the United Kingdom and Ireland, demanded attention at the inauguration of service. "Was it feasible," asked the operators, "to send the ship from New York to Rotterdam only, and to bring to that port containers originating as far away as Bergen, Oslo, Stockholm, Glasgow, and Southampton?" The answer lay in the existence of a rather large fleet of "short-sea traders," smaller ships designed to run between Southampton and Dunkirk, for instance, or from Oslo to Bremen. There also were somewhat larger coastal vessels that were operated between Rotterdam, Le Havre, Marseilles, and points in the eastern Mediterranean. If these ships could be used , and their schedules synchronized with the arrivals and departures of the oceangoing containerships, the objective of load centers might be attained while still providing container service to an extensive area of Europe.

It became apparent that, while the existing short-sea traders and coastwise vessels could be used, they lacked the capability to handle containers rapidly, efficiently, and economically. This deficiency was remedied in some cases by modifying the little ships for the trade, and in other instances bold entrepreneurs designed, built, and offered for charter vessels intended expressly to serve as feeders for the transoceanic carriers. In the years since 1966, an increasing fleet of purpose-built feeder ships has been introduced into these waters and has accomplished two objectives: it has extended the network of container services over an enormous area without adding unreasonably to total transit time for import and export cargoes, and it has made possible the most efficient use of the big containerships, with resulting economies for all concerned.[10]

It was to be expected that the advantages of feeder service would be appreciated in other parts of the world, especially in the Orient. Because the ports in this area are separated by greater distances of open ocean, compared to either Europe or the United States, the feeder ships had to be significantly larger than the vessels employed in those two regions. A notable variation from the European experience was the number of ships owned by the transpacific carriers and assigned exclusively to feeder operations. A third distinction lay in the establishment not only of load center (or principal transshipment) ports, but in setting up major collecting ports along the feeder routes. From these collecting ports a moderate-sized support fleet was brought together to handle container traffic to the smaller ports ("outports") within the hinterland of the collecting ports.

A case history is provided by American President Lines. This company selected Yokohama, Japan, and Kaohsiung, Taiwan, as principal ports for its mainline transpacific container service. It assigned six smaller, but fully containerized, ships to run from Japan and Taiwan to major collecting points at Hong Kong, Singapore, Colombo, and Fujaira (a United Arab Emirate). Containers destined to, or originating in, either these ports or their outports were handled by the vessels of the support fleet which consisted of chartered ships and also common carriers working under contract with American President Lines. Transfers between ships were accomplished at the major collecting ports. When the company-owned containerships returned to Taiwan and Japan, the containers they had collected were loaded aboard the mainline ships for ultimate delivery to the United States. Although two transshipments were involved, the combination of rapid and dependable service, along with company insistence on meticulous care in the handling of the boxes resulted in customer satisfaction, and an enlarged territory in which American President Lines could seek business.

Generally speaking, there are two reasons why the deep-sea carriers charter feeder vessels rather than purchasing them. First, the investment in containerships is so great that little capital is available for acquiring the small craft. Second, by taking the feeder ships on time charter, the management of ships engaged in the highly specialized coastal trade is left in the hands of experts, with corresponding reduction in the responsibilities of the transocean carriers. Regardless of whether the feeder ships are owned or chartered, the shipper of goods receives a single bill of lading covering the entire movement from the moment the carrier accepts the container until it is delivered to the consignee.

LEASING *VERSUS* OWNING CONTAINERS

Again and again in these pages references has been made to containers, but there has been very little comment concerning their construction, maintenance, dimensions, or ownership. To appreciate fully the growth in the use of containers on the sea routes of the world, it is necessary at this point to return to the beginning of the era.

On that April day in 1956 when McLean's *Ideal X* sailed from Port Newark with the first load of containers, the boxes secured to the spar deck were modifications of the standard highway trailer used by truckers in the eastern and southern United States. They were 35 feet long, 8 feet wide, and 8 feet high and therefore fit on the generally available flatbed trailers as well as on the chassis provided by McLean. The containers were owned by the steamship company and furnished to the shipper. No other shipowners on the coast at that time carried containers; no thought was given to the possibility of interchanging with cooperating organizations.

Several years later, while still engaged in hauling railroad cars from New Jersey to Savannah, Texas City, and New Orleans, Seatrain Lines decided to compete for some of the truck cargo. It devised a container that had the same height and width as McLean's but was only 27 feet long. Its reason was that this length permitted two containers to be loaded on a standard 55-foot railroad flatcar, whereas only a single 35-foot box could be transported on that flatcar. When Matson Navigation Company introduced containers into its California-Hawaii trade, it had to choose a size that could be maneuvered around the narrow, winding Hawaiian roads. The approved length was 24 feet. Meanwhile, European shipowners, cautiously entering the container transportation business, selected boxes that, like all American units, were 8 feet high and 8 feet wide, but they varied in length. There were 10-foot, 20-foot, and 40-foot units. Explaining their rationale for such dimensions, they pointed out that this gave shippers great flexibility, while making certain that the 40-foot cells of the containerships would be used efficiently.

Inasmuch as each operator furnished containers to its customers and loaded only those containers, the issue of interchangeability did not arise immediately. It was only after the successful entry of several carriers into the transatlantic services and sudden expansion of demand for container-

ized transportation that any consideration was given to standardizing exterior dimensions. The International Standards Organization (ISO) urged
that the steamship business worldwide accept a uniform height and width
of 8 feet and lengths of 10, 20, and 40 feet. Unfortunately, American operators had invested many millions of dollars in their individualized boxes and
were adamant against change. Despite the fact that Sea-Land, the largest
single operator in the world, strongly advocated the 35-foot length and
refused to adapt its ships or its tariffs to the suggested ISO dimensions, the
trend was inexorably against individuality and toward standardization. The
width of 8 feet was accepted universally; the height was questioned as
early as 1967 and still is under discussion. The 20- and 40-foot lengths
have gained worldwide acceptance.

A major reason for approval of some of the ISO proposals was the
fact that steamship owners found it financially almost impossible to purchase the large number of containers needed to support the ships. Increasingly they turned to organizations that specialized in building and renting
containers. In the effort to meet the requirements of the maximum number
of deep-sea operators, these leasing companies concentrated upon those
boxes most in demand, the 20- and 40-foot units. These were rented for
whatever length of time suited the customer; it was possible to obtain the
use of a box for two weeks or eight years, or for any period in between.
Furthermore, these lessors maintained a number of depots around the
world where containers could be returned to owners at the end of the
agreed term of lease.

The development of the neutral pool idea depends upon the gradual
elimination of the present practice of steamship companies owning (or
leasing on a long-term basis) a sufficiently large number of containers to
meet the needs of their various trade routes. As has been pointed out earlier
in this chapter, there are significant and recurring difficulties in keeping
track of these boxes, and it has been necessary for shipowners to set up
expensive and highly sophisticated systems to protect their investment.

In broad outline, this is the plan for the neutral pool: Steamship lines
or shippers would obtain their boxes from the pools maintained by companies specializing in owning and renting containers. Each container would
be acquired by the carrier for a definite, individual movement, and when
the contents had been delivered to the ultimate consignee, the container
would be returned to the control of the pool. This would be accomplished
by the consignee notifying the representative that the container was empty
and requesting instructions as to the disposition of the box. If the consignee
needed a container for an outgoing shipment, and the just-emptied unit was

satisfactory for the contemplated load, it would be assigned immediately for that purpose. This would eliminate the present wasteful procedure of returning the empty box to the marine terminal. Many export traffic managers have complained of the time lost under the present system of releasing to the oceangoing carrier every container as soon as it is emptied.

The neutral pool would eliminate the miniature pools set up by two or more operators who agree to interchange their equipment. These smaller pools have limited resources and encounter problems in tracing, cleaning, repairing, and positioning the boxes. Operators of the neutral pools are experts in these areas and have the organization needed to handle them effectively and economically.

Neutral pools would supply standardized equipment that would be interchangeable among all ships and all modal carriers. Procedures for handling containers would become uniform in all parts of the world, to the benefit of shippers and receivers of goods. Local shortages would be ended; should there be an unforeseen demand for boxes, the neutral pool would have its huge resources on which to draw.

That the existing container-leasing companies already possess most of the capabilities required for the introduction of neutral pools is demonstrated by their growth and the continuing expansion of their inventories. As the use of containers increases and boxes are distributed more widely, the desirability of neutral pools becomes more explicit.

Finally, in analyzing the trends that support the growth of intermodalism, landbridge, and neutral equipment pools, it must be noted that the ocean carrier has come to depend increasingly upon supporting activities such as the leasing companies and the various third parties doing business in cities far inland. These important members of the import-export team provide rapid and accurate information on the progress of a shipment and make possible the effective intelligence network on which the structure of containerization has been erected. Until recently, the value of these support operations in forecasting demand for shipping capacity, both in terms of containers and ship spaces, was not appreciated. Lacking a scientific basis for estimating their needs, shipowners in the early days of conversion from break-bulk operations depended entirely too much on the anticipated economies of scale, and built more container-carrying capacity than could be justified. This produced the crisis of over-tonnaging which afflicted the major trade routes, especially the north Atlantic and the north Pacific. Inevitably, destructive freight rate wars occurred, and there were many allegations of unethical and illegal practices adopted in the scramble to find cargoes for the big, expensive, and unfortunately superfluous ships. As the crisis eased, everyone involved in the movement of containerized cargo became aware of the new interdependence of all concerned with the new procedures, an interdependence which could improve the whole business of liner shipping.

THE BENEFITS OF CONTAINERIZATION

When international traffic of containerized cargo was introduced in 1966, there were many statements about the great benefits that would redound to the shipper. There also were predictions of new prosperity for shipowners. That these anticipations were voiced in sincere optimism and hope cannot be denied, but in the light of subsequent events, it must be admitted that the reality fell short of the dream.

There were obvious benefits to the shipper. There was, for instance, a marked reduction in pilferage of valuable cargo, such as television sets. Heavy boxes and crates for goods were eliminated, with welcome savings in the cost of packing for export. In those cases where containers were stuffed properly, a substantial improvement in the percentage of goods delivered in perfect condition was noted. Ship speeds were raised and, until the fuel crisis of 1973, ocean passages at previously record-breaking levels became routine. Because containers were handled by machines, the time required to put them aboard ship or to unload them was cut to hours in place of the days formerly needed. Shippers who dispatched small lots (quantities sufficient to fill only a portion of a container) were encouraged to bring their consignments to the container freight stations at the marine terminal, where these lots were consolidated and stowed in the big containers. A wide variety of boxes was developed to meet the different needs of shippers. One company advertised that it had sixteen specialized containers available for its customers. Perhaps one of the greatest benefits resulting from the containerization of cargo was that containers opened up the vast opportunities to benefit from the use of a total transportation system that utilizes the strengths of each of the individual modes in order to provide the most efficient system of moving goods. The full benefits of this advantage are yet to be fully realized.

On the negative side, there were disappointments. Many containers were carried on the weather deck, and sustained damage from heavy seas washing over them. In some cases, whole containers were swept overboard. The broiling sun encountered in summer passages often caused condensation damage to the goods stowed inside the unventilated metal boxes. Insurance rates, which had been expected to decrease, remained relatively

A container is attached to the lifting frame of the massive shoreside crane. Photograph courtesy of North Carolina State Ports Authority.

stable as the underwriters evaluated their responsibilities under the new system of transportation. Ocean freight rates, which shippers expected would come down because of the lower stevedoring costs, were kept at the old levels, partly as a result of the enormous cost of the new ships. In a period of inflation, however, many rates were not changed, which was, in a sense, a saving to the shipper.

Many lessons have been learned in the years since 1966. Among the most important are these:

1. Container services are of maximum benefit to exporters and importers when there is a two-way movement of goods. Only when the greater proportion of boxes is filled in each direction may the promised advantages of containerization be enjoyed.

    A corollary of this principle is that the benefits of container service accrue only on trade routes joining areas ready and able to receive and ship goods in the big boxes. To use containers for one-way movements and to demand that the box be returned to the place of origin without additional charge is to invite the water carrier to establish a freight rate for the container which is high enough to compensate for the expense of the homebound trip. Some exporters have discovered that in these circumstances, it is cheaper to use established break-bulk transportation.

2. Maximum efficiency and hence greatest economy in transporting containers can be attained only by employing ships built and operated for that purpose.

    There is a pattern in some trades to employ ships designed with two-thirds of the cargo capacity devoted to cellularized stowage of containers and the remainder of the ship's space allotted to odd-sized or wheeled cargo. While a number of these combination types exists today, their productivity and profitability are under increasingly rigorous scrutiny.

3. Containers used in intermodal movements must be of uniform, standardized design and sizes which can be interchanged worldwide as the flow of commerce dictates.

4. Essential to realizing the potential of containerization is the growth of neutral pools. Because intermodal movements are economically of great benefit to the commercial world, the demand for a practical, inexpensive, and convenient arrangement for picking up or returning containers can be met most effectively by the establishment of these pools.

5. Computerized control of the entire container transportation system is mandatory. As the neutral pools become more common and use of their equipment grows more general, the need stands out for carriers to have not only the kind of data the computer can provide, but also to interchange information concerning the location, condition,

and employment of individual containers. Thus EDI and AEI must be developed and accepted.

6. Contributing to the effectiveness of this computer-based system are the elements of the infrastructure supporting container services: third parties, container depots, maintenance and repair units to keep the containers in good condition, and the other associated activities.

7. Intermodal transportation is demanded by importers and exporters who seek the fastest and least expensive means of getting their goods across the oceans. They want not only the convenience and the rapidity of the landbridge, but they also seek a standardized contract of carriage enunciating the responsibilities of both shipper and carrier at every stage of transportation.

In summary, it may be said that the idea underlying the use of the container in the transportation of goods over the world's sea routes has spread because it met a need and facilitated international commerce. At the same time, it must be acknowledged that it created many new and unforeseen challenges, not least of which was the enormous financial cost of the transformation of ships, ports, and techniques of business. The change has been as profound as that resulting from the development of efficient and economical steam engines for ships. Equally undeniable is that the concepts of handling cargo movements and patterns of sea-trade have been altered irreversibly, and in every sense a new era has dawned for all who use the sea as an avenue of commerce.

CHAPTER TWELVE

The Ocean Bill of Lading

It is much to be regretted
That your goods are slightly wetted
But our lack of liability is plain,
   For our latest Bill of Lading,
   Which is proof against evading,
Bears exceptions for sea water, rust and rain.
   Also sweat, contamination,
   Fire and all depreciation
That we've ever seen or heard of on a ship.
   And our due examination
Which we made at destination
   Shows your cargo much improved by the trip.
   . . . .
   It really is a crime
   That you're wasting all your time,
For our Bill of Lading clauses make it plain
   That from ullage, rust or seepage,
   Water, sweat or just plain leakage,
Act of God, restraint of princes, theft or war,
   Loss, damage, or detention,
   Lock out, strike or circumvention,
Blockade, interdict or loss twixt ship and shore,
   Quarantine or heavy weather,
   Fog and rain or both together,
We're protected from all these and many more,
   And it's very plain to see
   That our liability
   As regards your claim is absolutely nil,
   So try your underwriter,
He's a friendly sort of blighter,
   And is pretty sure to grin and foot the bill.*

---

*From "Them Damaged Cargo Blues," by James A. Quinby, as quoted by Daniel A. Tadros in "COGSA Section 4(5)'s 'Fair Opportunity' Requirement: U.S. Circuit Court Conflict and Lack of International Uniformity; Will the United States Supreme Court Ever Provide Guidance?" in *Tulane Maritime Law Journal,* Vol. 17, No. 1 (Fall 1992), pp. 17–18. Reprinted by permission of *Tulane Maritime Law Journal.*

As a device of commerce, the ocean bill of lading is of comparatively recent origin. During medieval times, the merchant accompanied his goods and selected his buyers on the spot, exchanging his property for gold or other considerations of value. In these simple circumstances, there was no need for documents that set forth the terms under which the merchandise was transported or would permit transfer of title from one person to another. Methods of dealing through agents, who took the place of the traveling merchant, developed during the heyday of the Hanseatic League (fourteenth and fifteenth centuries), and ways of making loans to finance the movement of goods were formulated by the banking families and cities.

The first document to be used was the receipt given by the carrier to the shipper in which possession of the goods was acknowledged, and it was agreed that delivery would be made only to the person (or agent) designated by the shipper. The most notable early example of a statute regulating these relations is the French Maritime Code of 1681, promulgated by Louis XIV.

The next step in the development of the bill of lading was to establish a contract of carriage. When the merchant dispatched his goods unaccompanied by his personal representative, he and the carrier had to agree upon the terms under which the cargo would be transported and delivered. At first, these terms were those of the trade, but gradually the conditions were written into the codes of commercial law. The English common law principle was that the carrier was liable for right and safe delivery unless he could show that he had been prevented from this by an act of God, an act of the king's enemies, or the inherent vice of the goods. Later it was argued that the contracting parties should be free to negotiate any terms they wished, and the freedom of contract developed in the second half of the nineteenth century to a point where the carrier accepted the goods to be transported when and how he liked.

Shippers became discontented with the continuing efforts of the carriers to avoid any culpability for damage or loss and agitated successfully for the enactment of legislation to protect themselves and their interests. Today, the laws of sea-carriage in most nations of the world are quite definite in their delineation of the responsibilities assumed by both carriers and shippers.

In tracing the gradual growth of the bill of lading in use today, it is appropriate to cite its importance as a document of title by which ownership of cargo can be transferred from party to party. Whereas the medieval merchant accompanied his goods and sold them in overseas markets, today the cargo often changes ownership several times while in transit. The bill of lading has become identified with the cargo, and because the document is negotiable, title may be transferred from one person to another with little difficulty. The significance of this was not fully appreciated until the advent of fast mail-carrying steamships made it possible for shipping documents to arrive at a market center well in advance of slow cargo carriers. Now that airmail has reduced transmission time to a matter of hours, the convenience of the negotiable bill of lading has greater value to traders. The right of possession of the cargo can be transferred from local seller to domestic buyer and from him to the overseas purchaser without the intermediary seeing the cargo. The clauses of the bill of lading, which affect the insurance coverage as well as the financial aspects of the transactions, therefore become especially important.

THE COMMON CARRIER

A common carrier holds itself out to the public as one which, for a reasonable price, is ready, willing, and able to transport goods for anyone, without discrimination. Essential to the understanding of the status of the common carrier by water are the following facts:

1. The common carrier is required to serve all shippers alike; the carrier may not choose its shippers and must accept, within the limits of the facilities and capabilities of its vessels, the legitimate business of all applicants.
2. The common carrier may limit its business to a certain type of goods to be transported; for instance, refrigerated cargo in a refrigerated ship.
3. The common carrier normally operates over a definite route in repetitious service between stated termini.
4. The common carrier under the general maritime law of the United States (prior to the enactment of the Harter Act of 1893 and the Carriage of Goods by Sea Act of 1936) was required to deliver the cargo at the stipulated destination in the same good condition in which it was received from the shipper unless the carrier could show that the damage or loss incurred by the cargo resulted from one of the following five exceptions: (a) The act of God; e.g., lightning, floods, storms; (b) The acts of public enemies; e.g., a bombing attack upon a ship by an enemy during a period of hostilities; (c) The acts of public authorities; e.g., the confiscation of tainted food by the health authorities of a nation; (d) The inherent nature of

the goods; e.g., the perishability of fruit like grapes or bananas; (e) The acts of the shippers; e.g., faulty packaging or improper marking of the shipment.

Even with these exceptions, which ordinarily serve to relieve the carrier of responsibility for loss or damage traceable to these causes, it would be incumbent upon the carrier to show that no negligence on its part had contributed directly to the loss or damage. For example, a consignment of grapes moving from Argentina to the United States in refrigerated stowage might spoil because of overripeness at the time of loading. So long as the carrier could prove that the refrigerator compartments in which the grapes were transported had been kept at the prescribed levels of temperature and humidity, and that adequate care had been given to the cargo, there would have been no negligence and the loss therefore would not be deemed to have resulted from any fault of the carrier. The general rule is that when customary stowage results in damage to the cargo, the burden of proof lies with the cargo interests which must demonstrate conclusively that the stowage and care given to the cargo by the carrier were inadequate.

It is noteworthy that the courts, in determining the liability of carriers for damage to or loss of cargo, have extended maximum consideration, under the law, to the welfare of shippers. For example, when cargo was damaged in a storm, the carrier was held responsible because the worst of the disturbance could have been avoided by a reasonable deviation from the ship's initial course. In a similar ruling, the court decided that the failure of a master to take adequate precautions to meet a weather emergency constituted negligence within the meaning of the statute. The carrier consequently was held liable for the loss sustained by the cargo.

THE PRIVATE CARRIER

The private carrier, as the name implies, transports the goods of a single person and is privately employed. It is neither ready nor willing to accept cargo from the general public. Some private carriers are owned by the corporation using the transportation; others are under charter or some other form of contract. A tramp vessel chartered to a steel manufacturing company, transporting iron ore to be used by a steel company in fabricating its metal products, is a private carrier. A barge line owned by a common stock corporation, but carrying only the output of a particular mill or refinery, is a private carrier. There is no legal reason why two or more shippers, by mutual consent, may not use the same ship to transport their goods under separate, privately negotiated contracts (or charters) and still have the vessel retain the classification of a private carrier.

The private carrier is not protected by the provisions of the Carriage of Goods by Sea Act, 1936. It is liable to the shipper only for that damage or loss attributable directly to the negligence of the vessel. The private carrier is, however, under obligation to furnish a seaworthy vessel, unless the charter or contract affirmatively lessens this requirement. These provisions of liability would apply only to chartered or contracted tonnage; they would have no significance if the carrier were owned by the same company that held title to the goods being shipped.

LIABILITY OF THE COMMON CARRIER
UNDER U.S. LAWS

The liability of the common carrier by water has been limited by two general federal statutes in the United States. The Harter Act of 1893 was passed to establish the responsibility of the common carrier to the shipper when the goods were transported under a uniform bill of lading. It applied to both the foreign and domestic commerce of the United States and was mandatory upon the "manager, agent, master, or owner of any vessel transporting merchandise from or between ports of the United States and foreign ports." The provisions of the law cover the movement of cargo from the beginning of the voyage (defined as the moment when the anchor breaks ground, or the last line is let go) until the goods are delivered to the consignee when the carrier-shipper relationship is dissolved.

In 1924, a convention was adopted at Brussels, Belgium, by the major maritime nations to serve as the basis for a uniform statute governing, on a worldwide basis, the relationship between shipper and carrier under the terms of the ocean bills of lading. To bring American law substantially into harmony with this convention, the Carriage of Goods by Sea Act was passed by the Congress in 1936.

The Carriage of Goods by Sea Act (often referred to as COGSA) did not fully supplant, nor did it repeal, the Harter Act of 1893. The older law applies, if the carrier does not elect the coverage of COGSA, to the American coastwise and inland waterways trades, and to the period during which the carrier has custody of the goods before they are loaded on the ship and after they are unloaded from the ship. The 1936 law applies to all shipments in the foreign trade of the United States, but only from the time the ship's cargo hook takes hold of the goods until discharge at the end of the ship's tackle in the port of destination ("hook to hook" coverage). Domestic operators in the coastwise service may place themselves under the protection of COGSA by stipulation to that effect in their bills of lading.

Other limitations to the liability of the carrier normally are included in the bill of lading by reference to the appropriate statutes. The principal restrictions are those stating that there is no responsibility for damage by fire, unless caused by the design or neglect of the carrier; the limitation of the liability of the shipowner to the value of his interest in the ship plus pending freight; and the provision that if the owner's interest is insufficient to meet all losses, the shippers will accept a proportionate settlement. It is significant that the operator of a vessel under bareboat charter is given all rights and privileges of a shipowner.

Both the Harter Act and COGSA hold the carrier responsible for loss or damage arising from negligence in proper loading, stowage, custody, keeping, care, and delivery of the goods if they have been packed adequately. Rough handling that causes damage is a fault of the carrier. Poor stowage resulting in the cargo shifting or coming into contact with other commodities that produce taint or odor is considered the shipowner's responsibility. Failure to deliver the stipulated quantity of cargo for which receipt was given becomes the basis for a collectible claim against the carrier.

Liner-service companies fill their vessels with miscellaneous cargo, and often find it advantageous to send ships into ports not on their advertised routes. COGSA permits a "reasonable" deviation to save human life or property at sea. The shipowner, however, must be able to prove that the change of routing for the purpose of loading or delivering cargo or passengers is not "unreasonable." For example, if a vessel were loaded partially at Norfolk and then called at Baltimore for additional cargo, without having included Baltimore in its advertised schedule, the delay of a day or two probably would be construed as reasonable. In one actual instance, a ship advertised to sail directly from Calcutta to North Atlantic ports called at an Indian outport to take on a cargo of castor beans. The loading of the beans required two weeks, thereby delaying by that length of time the ship's arrival in the United States. The court held this to be unreasonable deviation.

The law fixes the shipowner's limitation of liability for goods at the value of the vessel plus pending freight, regardless of the value of the cargo lost or damaged. Should the vessel be lost, liability is limited to the amount of the freight earnings. If it can be shown that the loss or damage occurred with the shipowner's knowledge of factors leading to that loss or damage, the carrier's petition to limit liability will not be granted by any court.

Pursuant to the provisions of the 1936 act, the carrier is responsible for the value of the individual package or other customary shipping unit up to a maximum of five hundred dollars, unless a higher valuation has been declared in the bill of lading, and correspondingly higher freight rates have been paid by the shipper. The claimant must be able to prove that the damage or loss occurred while the package was in the custody of the carrier. If the packages were shipped in apparent good order and condition and the contents were found to be broken or damaged upon opening the containers at destination, the claimant must prove that the goods actually were in sound condition when they were delivered to the carrier. If the carrier can show that the damage was not due to his negligence, he may be absolved of liability. Explosive and flammable cargo may be destroyed or landed short of destination without the carrier incurring any liability, if, in the opinion of the master, this action is necessary to assure the safety of the ship.

COGSA prohibits shipowners from phrasing their bills of lading to reduce liability under that act. The shipowner may not limit responsibility for the negligence of ship's personnel with regard to loading, stowage, custody, care for, or delivery of the cargo. A list of exonerations from liability, however, is included in both COGSA and the Harter Act, and these exonerations have been sustained by the U.S. courts. The net effect has been to change the status of the common carrier in American waterborne commerce. No longer is that carrier the absolute insurer of the goods, subject to certain specified exemptions set forth in the general maritime law. Instead, the carrier has been placed in the category of one who sells only careful transportation, governed by special and very definite laws of sea-carriage.

THE BILL OF LADING
AS A CONTRACT OF CARRIAGE

The bill of lading, as a contract of carriage, sets forth the terms of the agreement between carrier and shipper under which certain goods are accepted for transportation between named ports in a designated ship with a stipulated sailing date in exchange for a financial consideration. The contract becomes effective when it has been signed by the master (or his deputy) and accepted by the shipper.

Pursuant to the provisions of both the Harter Act and COGSA, the carrier is required to issue a bill of lading as a receipt for the goods, and the bill constitutes prima facie evidence of such receipt. The bill must contain information as to the marks and numbers of the packages, the quantity of packages or the weight or measurement of bulk cargo, and any exception to the basic statement that the goods were received "in apparent good order and condition." The carrier must provide a "shipped" or "on board" bill of lading (meaning that the cargo has been stowed aboard ship) on demand of the shipper.

In promulgating the terms of the contract, the carrier often includes many provisions not covered by existing statutes but recognized as valid contractual conditions. For example, in a clause describing the ways in which goods may be stowed in the vessel, the term "under-deck stowage" is extended to cover the use of poop, forecastle, deckhouse, shelter deck, or other covered space. Cargo will be given ordinary stowage unless the bill of lading stipulates that it be refrigerated or heated; failure of the shipper to demand this care exempts the carrier from liability for resultant damage.

The master is granted authority to discharge cargo short of the agreed port of destination when, in his judgment, there is the reasonable apprehension of danger to the ship or cargo. This apprehension cannot be based on rumors or imagined dangers; it must be founded on actual or substantial peril. Once cargo is discharged under this provision of the contract, the shipowner has no further responsibility. The shipper or consignee must accept delivery and assume any expense which may be incurred as a result of this delivery short of destination.

Another example of the clauses included in the contract is the reservation to the carrier of the right to effect transshipment to other carriers of cargo destined to ports not on the ship's route; this "on carriage" is to be executed pursuant to the terms of the connecting carrier's bill of lading, regardless of whether those terms are easier or more onerous than those of the originating carrier's contract.

Only a few of the clauses included in a bill of lading have been singled out for comment. They are sufficient to indicate the nature of the contract. While each carrier will write its own contract, there will be similarity in the basic provisions of those bills that are issued to shippers in the foreign commerce of the United States.[2]

It is important to observe that the information and statements contained in the bill of lading are accepted in these three particulars:

1. The accuracy (truth) of the loading tally; the statement that the cargo has been "shipped" in a named vessel; or the declaration that the cargo is "on board" a particular ship. There is no allowance for shortages. A deficiency (shortage) in one lot may not be made up by

a surplus (overage) in another lot of identical goods. The quantity of goods delivered to the consignee must correspond to the tally stated in the bill of lading.

2. The truth of the statement that, unless otherwise attested by the carrier's notation on the bill of lading, the cargo gives the external appearance of being in good order and condition.

3. The truth of the date of loading. A "shipped" or "on board" bill of lading issued by the carrier states that on the date of the bill of lading, the cargo actually was stowed aboard the vessel. This may be significant in proving that the seller complied with the terms of the contract of sale, which often stipulates that shipment must be made by a certain date.

THE BILL OF LADING AS A RECEIPT

Current shipping practice in the United States provides that, when the shipper delivers the goods to the terminal for loading aboard a vessel, he or she be given a certificate known as a "dock receipt" (in some trades this is called a "mate's receipt" or a "boat note") which acknowledges that the cargo has been received and is in the custody of the carrier. This receipt is furnished to the shipper after the individual packages making up the consignment have been examined by one of the carrier's inspectors (checkers) to detect external or superficial damage or shortages, or other exceptions to the statement of "apparent good order and condition." The shipper provides the description of the goods, the numbers of packages, and the weights. On the reverse side of the receipt, the checker inserts the measurements of the packages and the "exceptions" noted. The checker initials the bottom of this sheet, and then passes it to the designated official (usually the receiving clerk) for signature and return of the original to the shipper. The dock receipt is the carrier's permanent record of the exact quantity and condition of the shipment at the time it came into his custody. It serves as a temporary receipt until the freighted and signed bill of lading is obtained from the carrier; at that time, the original dock receipt is surrendered by the shipper and is filed with the other papers relating to the shipment.

The bill of lading is completed by the shipper on forms supplied by the carrier. COGSA requires that the shipper furnish in writing certain data concerning the goods, and current practice dictates that the shipper insert these specifications in that section of the bill of lading headed "Particulars Supplied by the Shipper of Goods":

1. The exact name of the commodity, i.e., granulated sugar, dried kidney beans, industrial refrigerator cabinets, etc.
2. The details of the shipment, showing the types of packages (bags, bales, boxes, crates, or whatever is appropriate), including the number and identification marks of the packages.
3. The gross weight of the goods.

The shipper "shall be deemed to have guaranteed to the carrier the accuracy at the time of shipment of the marks, number, quantity, and weight, as furnished by him; and the shipper shall indemnify the carrier against all loss, damages, and expenses arising or resulting from inaccuracies in such particulars." (COGSA, Section 3(5)).

Normally, the contents of each package are not examined by the carrier; the shipper is obligated by law to provide an accurate description. Most carriers, however, reserve the right to open the containers for verification should there be suspicion that the contents are not as described in the bill of lading. In accepting the goods in "apparent good order and condition," the carrier is bound to declare what is the external appearance of the cargo. Where bulk cargo weight is ascertained neither by carrier nor by shipper (as in the case of bulk grain loaded at a public grain elevator), the master may insert that fact in the bill of lading and so be freed of the obligation to discharge the weight stated in the bill of lading.

Since the shipper guarantees to the carrier the accuracy of the marks, number, quantity, and weight of the goods, in case of a claim for nondelivery of a part of the shipment, he must be able to prove among other details that the quantity stated on the bill of lading actually was shipped in good condition. One of the defenses open to the carrier is to show, in his behalf, that the packages were delivered in the same quantity and condition as shipped, and that there was no negligence on his part in the loading, handling, stowage, carriage, care for, and discharge of the goods. Under COGSA, the statute of limitations is fixed at one year; notice of loss or damage must be given not later than three days after the cargo has been delivered to the consignee, and suit for recovery of damages must be filed by the claimant within one year after delivery of the goods.

THE BILL OF LADING AS EVIDENCE OF OWNERSHIP

In medieval and early modern times, when the merchant accompanied his goods, he always could assert his ownership. As this arrangement yielded to a less direct contact with the cargo, some method of transferring title had to be devised. The simplest means of accomplishing this was to send the consignee a copy of the bill of lading which had been issued by the ship to the merchant. This might be done in a special envelope entrusted to the master, or it might be dispatched by a faster vessel so that the consignee would be awaiting arrival of the ship with the goods. If there were some desire to protect the goods against the possibility of an impecunious purchaser taking possession, the merchant's agent in the port might be the addressee of the bill of lading. The carrier agreed to transport the goods from port A to port B and there to deliver them to the shipper, or to the agent of the shipper, or to the person designated by the shipper to receive them, or to the order of the consignee.

The bill of lading in this manner came to represent the goods in respect to which it had been issued. The possessor of the bill of lading could pass authority to accept delivery to a third party by a statement written on the bill that he transferred his interest to that party. Endorsement and transfer by the owner of the bill of lading actually transferred legal ownership and the bill of lading became a document of title to the goods.

THE NEGOTIABLE OR ORDER BILL OF LADING

In foreign commerce today, the great bulk of bills of lading is issued by carriers to the order of the consignee which means that the carrier, shipowner, charterer, or master will deliver the goods at the port of destination not solely to the named consignee, but to any person designated by him. Through the use of the word "order," the bill of lading becomes more than a receipt from the ship for the goods, and more than the contract of carriage. The bill, by the insertion of this word "order," possesses a legal and commercially important characteristic in that it becomes a transferable document of title. The law governing bills of this type expressly rules, in Section 3, that:

> A bill in which it is stated that the goods are consigned or destined to the order of any person named in such a bill is an order bill.
>
> Any provision in such a bill, or any notice, contract, rule, regulation, or tariff that it is non-negotiable shall be null and void and shall not affect its negotiability within the meaning of this Act unless upon its face and in writing agreed to by the shipper.

The legal ownership (the property interest in the goods described in the bill of lading) can be transferred from the consignee named in the bill

Lykes Bros. Steamship Co., Inc.

has been informed that one or all of San Francisco Bills of Lading SFR. 1, SFR. 2, SFR. 3 issued in Mombasa for the S.S. Leslie Lykes, Voyage 94, have been stolen, and further it has been reported that attempts have been made to sell these negotiable documents in the Nairobi area. The public is hereby advised that the above indicated Bills of Lading stand null and void and therefore of no value.

Advertisement in New York *Journal of Commerce*, September 30, 1985, p. 1-B.

to any other persons, and by them to still other persons, without any of them seeing the goods or having physical possession thereof. This transfer of possession is accomplished initially by the consignee signing his name on the bill of lading, thereby converting the bill into a "bearer" document. A refinement of this is for the consignee to direct that the goods be delivered to a particular person, and then to affix his signature to the endorsement.

The bill of lading thus becomes in practice a negotiable instrument. The endorsees and holders of the bill are entitled legally to rely upon the tally and upon the statements in the bill of "apparent good order and condition." In the eyes of the U.S. courts, the bill has been fully negotiable since 1916 when the Federal Bills of Lading Act was passed.

There are advantages to the seller who uses the order bill of lading. For instance, the merchant who ships property under a negotiable bill of lading can insist on payment for the goods before endorsing and turning over the bill of lading to the purchaser. Similarly, by retaining possession of the bill, a bank which advanced money against goods represented by the order bill has security for its financial interest so long as it retains possession of the bill. Order bills of lading should be canceled or repossessed by the carrier at the time of delivery to avoid claims by those who might have purchased the bill of lading in good faith from an unscrupulous person.

THE STRAIGHT (NONNEGOTIABLE) BILL OF LADING

Markedly in contrast with the order bill of lading is the "straight" or non-negotiable bill, under which the carrier accepts cargo for delivery to the named consignee only. Transfer of title to the property cannot be effected. Possession of the goods can be obtained by the consignee on presentation of a copy of the bill together with satisfactory identification of the agent. It is preferable to have the original bill presented at the time delivery is requested.

Except for the fact that the words "or order," following the name of the consignee, are deleted, the physical appearance and the text of the two bills of lading are identical. Some steamship companies use a paper stock of different color for ready separation of the straight from the order bills. Not infrequently, a conspicuous heading on the straight bills will be imprinted to prevent confusion on the part of the user.

Because of the limitations on the use of the straight bill of lading, normally it is employed by shippers who likewise are the consignees (e.g., a manufacturing company sending components to its assembly plant overseas; or consignments dispatched to purchasers who have paid in advance for the goods).

THE BILL OF LADING IN FOREIGN TRADE FINANCING

Payment for goods shipped in export trade is more complicated than in domestic commercial arrangements and often requires the services of a financial agent like a bank. Without attempting to describe the intricacies of payment for goods moving in international commerce, the following sketch will indicate the role of the negotiable bill of lading in the financing of foreign trade transactions.

Assume that a consignment of ten typewriters, worth $250 each in New York, is sold to a purchaser in Lima, Peru. Shipping costs come to a total of $100 and the insurance premium on the whole transaction is $50. The amount of money involved in a "cost, insurance, and freight" quotation is $2,650. To assure prompt payment in American currency to the seller, especially on the part of buyers who reside in countries where collection in dollars may be difficult, it is customary for the buyer to arrange with the bank for a letter of credit to be issued in favor of the seller for the total value of the shipment (in this case, $2,650). The letter of credit is a certificate that the amount of money stipulated therein has been placed on deposit with an American bank and is available to meet the seller's charges.

To collect the value of the shipment, the seller prepares a "bank draft," a form of check against the deposit established for the use of the seller and witnessed by the letter of credit. He attaches this draft to the other documents needed to support the transaction: the three original bills of lading freighted and signed by the carrier attesting to the fact that the goods have been loaded in the designated ship prior to a specified date; the certificate of insurance, protecting the purchaser against loss in the event of disaster during transportation; the seller's invoice, showing the value of the merchandise ($2,500), the cost of insurance ($50), and the ocean freight ($100); and the letter of credit.

The order bill of lading, to simplify the process of collection for the seller and also to safeguard the ownership of the goods, would be made out so that the name of the seller would appear on the lines for both shipper and the person to whose order the shipment is consigned; the actual purchaser's name would appear on the line designating the person to be notified when the ship arrives at her destination. The seller would be required by the bank to endorse the three original bills of lading to the order of the bank, and thus to transfer title to the goods to that financial institution. All the documents necessary to support payment to the seller likewise are surrendered to the bank. The seller, on receipt of the money, drops out of the transaction and the bank assumes temporarily the role of owner of the goods.

The seller's bank in New York, after taking possession of the bills of lading, insurance certificate, invoice, and bank draft, would endorse the bills of lading to the order of the buyer's bank in Lima. All documents then would be sent to Peru, and the Lima bank would in turn assume the role of temporary owner of the goods. As a matter of routine, and to explain the existence of three original signed bills of lading, one copy is sent by airmail, one follows by steamship mail or a second airmail carrier, and one remains in the sender's file for use in the event that both bills should be lost in transit.

On the arrival in Lima of the documents from New York, the bank notifies the purchaser that he can come to the office and receive the bills of lading endorsed to the order. The Lima bank, having completed its role in the transaction, drops out of the picture, and the buyer is free to proceed to the carrier's office. Here he will exchange the original bill of lading for a delivery order and, on the strength of this last document, will present himself at the marine terminal to accept delivery of the property.

The carrier must insist that the original order bill of lading be surrendered at the time the goods are turned over to the consignee. The bill should be canceled, and filed along with the executed delivery order, as proof that the terms of the contract have been fulfilled by delivery. If either of the other two originals should be presented at a later date, the carrier properly can refuse to honor them and support its position by producing the canceled bill against which delivery was effected.

It is obvious that the nonnegotiable bill of lading, because it does not permit transfer of title, cannot be used in a transaction of the nature just described.

CHAPTER THIRTEEN

How Freight Rates Are Made

An amazing assortment of goods is moved over the world's ocean trade routes. Of necessity, the carriers charge for the service they render. These charges vary almost as widely as do the cargoes, for they mirror both the shipowner's costs and the special conditions prevailing on the trade routes traversed by the ships.

THE THEORY OF FREIGHT RATES

Ocean freight rates may be described as the prices charged for the services of water carriers. Each ship operator develops its own rates, usually without consultation with the shippers. The charges reflect the cost of providing the carriage, the value of this service to the owner of the goods, the ability of the merchandise to support the expense of transportation, and economic conditions in general.

There are no exact pricing formulae applied uniformly to the various items moving in transoceanic commerce. Little interference is experienced in the international movement of goods. To a noticeable extent, ocean freight rates truly reflect the working of the laws of supply and demand. In tramp shipping, particularly, it is possible to observe how these factors influence the rise or fall of freight rates from day to day and from cargo to cargo.

Tramp ships transport, in shipload (or "full cargo") lots, commodities which, like coal, grain, ore, and phosphate rock, can be moved in bulk. The fact that usually only one shipper and one commodity are involved simplifies the establishment of a freight rate for this particular movement. To the capital charges of ownership and the expense of administration and overhead must be added the costs of running the ship, handling the cargo, and paying port fees and harbor dues. Against this total is set the number of tons to be hauled, and the resultant figure is what the tramp must charge, per ton of cargo loaded, to break even on the contemplated voyage. If competitive conditions permit, a margin for profit will form part of the quoted

241

rate. If, however, the prevailing economic climate is unfavorable, the owner has the privilege of retiring the ship to a quiet backwater, there to wait until the financial skies are brighter.

To illustrate this mathematically, recall that total cost is the mathematical sum of the fixed costs and the variable costs of doing business:

Fixed Costs (FC) + Variable Costs (VC) = Total Cost (TC)

Further, the cost per ton to break even (B/E) is simply the total cost divided by the number of tons carried (expressed in whatever unit of tonnage is being used). Note that this does not take into account any of the intangibles such as desirability of the cargo, desirability of the route, or market conditions:

$$\frac{\text{Total Cost}}{\text{Tons Carried}} = \text{Break–Even (B/E) rate per ton}$$

Under favorable conditions, it is possible to include a profit in the formula as follows:

$$\frac{\text{Total Cost} + \text{Profit}}{\text{Tons Carried}} = \text{Quoted rate per ton}$$

The following calculations will demonstrate the theory. A producer of a bulk high-grade ore wishes to ship 75,000 tons from port A to port B. You, as owner of a vessel positioned in port A and suitable for this movement, wish to make an offer through your broker for this work. Your fixed costs for the entire voyage, which you estimate to take thirty days, total $135,000 (thirty days × $4,500 per day) the variable costs for the voyage total $324,000 (thirty days × $10,800), and ideally you would like to make $70,000 profit for the voyage. Therefore:

Fixed Costs (FC) + Variable Costs (VC) = Total Cost (TC)

$135,000 + $324,000 = $459,000

$$\frac{\text{Total Cost}}{\text{Tons Carried}} = \text{Break-Even (B/E) rate per ton}$$

$$\frac{\$459,000}{75,000\,\text{Tons}} = \$6.12 \text{ per ton}$$

Under favorable conditions, it is possible to include a profit into the formula as follows:

$$\frac{\text{Total Cost} + \text{Profit}}{\text{Tons Carried}} = \text{Quoted rate per ton}$$

$$\frac{\$459,000 + \$70,000}{75,000\,\text{Tons}} = \$7.05 \text{ per ton}$$

The tramp operator does not depend upon the long-term goodwill of the shippers, but is free to accept those offers which appear profitable at the moment. When adversity threatens, those charters are accepted which minimize anticipated losses. If there is a choice, the cost of temporary lay-up is contrasted with the loss which continued operation might produce, and the less expensive alternative is selected in a bow to the inevitable made with whatever grace can be mustered.

Liner-service companies, on the other hand, depend for financial prosperity upon the accumulated goodwill of shippers who, through the years, come to rely upon the regular and continued operation of the company's fleet. Temporary withdrawal from service whenever economic conditions are less than favorable is unthinkable.

The liner will sail on her regular run, whether full or not. She will carry a wide variety of commodities, each with its own peculiarities, in quantities which can be estimated in advance more or less accurately, but never with complete certainty. The ports of call are known far in advance of sailing, and the total expense of working the ship can be calculated with acceptable precision. Since, however, the exact distribution of tonnage, commodity by commodity, varies with every trip, it is not possible to establish a rate that reflects the cost of transporting a single ton of a particular commodity as closely as does the tramp owner's computation.

This is not to suggest that liner-service operators cannot compute to a nicety the costs of owning and operating their ships. They know to a fraction of a cent their daily costs for amortization and interest on borrowed capital, and what administrative expenses they must charge to individual voyages. In the same manner that their counterparts in the tramping trade are able to fix individual rates, liner owners can determine what they should charge per ton to carry a single commodity when it is offered in lots sufficient to fill one of their ships. The difficulty arises when the liner operator is forced to compile a list of charges for transporting hundreds of different commodities not in the ship sailing tomorrow, but in ships departing at weekly intervals during the next year or even over a longer period.

Because the ship is committed to sail on a fixed date, there may be a tendency among some shipowners to say, "It makes little difference what I charge for individual commodities, as long as the aggregate revenue is adequate to cover my expenses." The contrary view is, "Unless I know that each ton of cargo will pay its full cost and earn a profit, I will not accept that item."

Between these contrasting outlooks, there is an intermediate theory that deserves thoughtful scrutiny.

From experience, the liner-service operators know approximately what is going to move, voyage after voyage, and have a good idea of what tonnage to expect. They must estimate the overhead to be charged against each commodity and the out-of-pocket costs of handling them at ports of loading and discharge. An apportionment of revenue must be made to defray the administrative expense of vessel operation. Finally, a small profit should be added to compensate the owners for the risks they assume as well as for their skill and enterprise, for by providing transportation they enhance the value of the goods. They are justified in assigning a reasonable value to this real, albeit intangible, contribution.

Underlying these general principles are certain factors which influence, in one way or another, the establishment of freight rates for individual commodities moving in liner-service vessels.

The first of these factors is that freight rates should be reasonable to shipper and to carrier. The shippers must be satisfied that the money they pay for transportation will not drive the price of their goods above the competitive level of the markets where they trade. If the exporters or importers are trying to compete with goods from sources closer at hand, they will consider that the cost of transportation, no matter how low, is nothing less than a barrier to trade.

In determining what is reasonable as a charge for transportation, the shipper's complete indifference to the financial condition of the carrier must be remembered. The sales appeal of a given article often is set by the price which includes the expense of transportation. Should the margin between the seller's total costs and the market price be too narrow to leave a profit, the seller attempts to convince the carrier to reduce the prevailing freight rates. The argument always is, "If you don't come down, you will lose all my business. If you will help me to keep my price at the competitive level, you will benefit by my continued patronage. After all, your ship is going to sail on this route anyhow, so why not make this concession?"

The second factor which influences the establishment of freight rates is competition. If a carrier sets rates higher than those of its rivals, patrons may be lost to shipowners whose services are available at lower prices. If, however, a figure is quoted which nets no profit, the outreach may be too successful, and the carrier may be overwhelmed by the volume in which this commodity is offered. Whereas a few tons could be handled on each voyage, this nonprofit item cannot be allowed to crowd out other commodities on which the rate is remunerative.

Another type of competition is the rivalry between ports. In their never-ending search for cargoes to move through their facilities, the various ports of an area stress their modern piers and wharves, their intraport systems of roadways and railroads, and the frequency of sailings to all parts of the world. Ports also advertise their location with reference to major overseas destinations, as well as the excellent rail and highway networks feeding the port.

A good deal of cargo for overseas markets originates with shippers in inland cities who have the option of using one of several ports. The rail or truck routing that gives the lowest cost of transportation normally is preferred. A shipper may develop the habit of moving all goods from city X to seaport A because the inland freight rate is a few cents per hundred pounds cheaper than to seaport B. Rail or truck lines operating only between city X and seaport B must compete for the business by bringing their rates to the level of those applying to seaport A. This "port equalization rate" applies only on cargo with foreign destinations and actually represents a reduction in revenue on the part of the domestic carrier(s). Where the steamship line maintains service only from seaport B, it is possible that it may develop special "through rates" in conjunction with the inland carriers, under which each of the modes of transportation offers a reduction provided the business is routed through seaport B.

Some commodities are found naturally in widely separated geographic locations. The sellers of these commodities compete with each other on a worldwide basis. Buyers seek the lowest cost. If the combination of foreign price plus transportation produces a figure higher than the quotation from a rival area, the buying pattern may be changed to take advantage of the more favorable price. These examples make this clear:

Tin originates in Bolivia, Malaysia, Indonesia, and Zaire. When exporters of Bolivian tin raise their prices, or the carriers of tin from Bolivia to the consuming market establish a new freight rate, the users of tin com-parc the new total with that of the mineral from the other sources and place their orders accordingly.

Copper is imported to the United States from Chile, Canada, and Central America. The difference of a cent a pound in the landed price in New York often determines whether the movement will be from one area or another.

No factor of competition is more difficult to assess in the analysis of freight rates than that which results from the struggle of different geographic areas for the same market. This emerges when the trade from two widely separated manufacturing nations comes into direct conflict in a consuming market thousands of miles from both producers. For instance, the United States and Japan both send large quantities of the same kinds of machinery to Chile. The Chilean buyers consequently are in the position of pitting Americans and Japanese against each other and taking advantage of whatever bargains they can obtain. While ocean carriers serving the two supplying nations are not faced directly with a demand to meet a freight rate established by the purchasers, they are aware that they are in competition. The pressures are felt from both suppliers and importers, and therefore the carriers must establish (or maintain) a rate acceptable to the consignees. That the freight rate may not be profitable to the ship operator is of no concern to the buyer, who is interested only in obtaining goods at the lowest possible total cost.

Competition is keen between the operators of the big containerships. The two most important trade routes—transpacific, linking the Orient to the West Coast of the United States and Canada, and transatlantic, connecting Western Europe and the United Kingdom with ports of Canada and the United States on the Atlantic and Gulf coasts—have become very attractive, and in mid-1993 were suffering from the resulting excess of capacity compared to the quantity of cargo moving. A factor contributing to the problem was the fluctuating value of the U.S. dollar relative to other currencies. This meant that imports from abroad sometimes were comparatively cheap, and good sales were made easily; at other times, exports from the United States were expensive (in terms of the foreign buyers' currencies) and therefore not in great demand. The imbalance of trade was reflected in the number of empty containers which had to be transported at minimal freight rates or free of charge from the United States back to the overseas areas. It was a logical step, therefore, for carriers to add whatever they could to the freight rates for cargo destined to the United States in the hope of defraying some of the expense of repositioning the empty boxes.

On the long routes such as the round-the-world service, where all the cargo is in containers, the carriers selected a limited number of ports serving productive hinterlands, and restricted calls to those ports, denominated in the trade as "load centers." Containers filled with goods for export were brought to and assembled at these centers by rail, truck, and barge. Inbound containers were distributed by the same means to destinations within a specified radius of each load center. The cost of pickup and delivery within this territory was included in the ocean freight rate.

Certain commodities essential for many purposes in the world economy are always in demand. Very rarely do these commodities move in shipload lots. To put them into the hands of their users, they must be dispatched by liner-service ships, but their value is so low that they cannot be charged the actual cost of transportation. Facing this dilemma, the ratemaker has no choice but to set rates that permit their movement even though it means the carriage is performed at a financial loss to the shipowner. To offset this difficulty, the only solution is to set rates for items of high value which will absorb the loss incurred on the low value commodities.

"Charge what the traffic will bear" is a basic tenet of ratemaking, the significance of which may not be evident at first glance. A hypothetical example will make it clear. Imagine that electric washing machines were assessed $2.50 per cubic foot, and bagged cement was charged $1.00 per cubic foot for transportation from San Francisco to Valparaiso, Chile. Based on the value of the two items, the cost of sea-carriage would add about 12 percent to the landed price of the washing machine, but would double the price of the cement.

The comparatively small markup in the price of the washing machine will not affect its sale. The increase in the price of cement is the limit to which cost can rise without driving it off the market.

The shipowner knows that it costs $1.25 per cubic foot to operate the vessel. The revenue from the washing machine left a surplus from which the deficit incurred by the cement could be paid. Illogical and superficially indefensible as this system may appear to be, it is the only workable method of providing the transportation for those commodities which must move, but which cannot afford to pay the cost of liner service.

It follows (quite logically, in this case) that if cement is to move at all, it must be accompanied by a reasonable tonnage of washing machines, so that the total mix of cargo will produce a profitable load. Ideally, if there is an equal balance between the two commodities, there will be a profit of

$1.00 per cubic foot. When this balance is destroyed, and twice as much cement as washing machines is stowed in the ship, the shipowner loses substantially.

The following calculation will demonstrate the theory:

Ideal Mix of Washing Machines and Cement		
40 cubic feet @ $2.50 per foot	$100.00	
40 cubic feet @ $1.00 per foot	40.00	
Ship's revenue		$140.00
Cost for 80 cubic feet @ $1.25		
per cubic foot		100.00
Surplus		$ 40.00

Actual Mix of Washing Machines and Cement		
20 cubic feet @ $2.50 per foot	$50.00	
60 cubic feet @ $1.00 per foot	60.00	
Ship's revenue		$110.00
Cost for 80 cubic feet @ $1.25		
per cubic foot		100.00
Surplus		$ 10.00

Because exploitation of the shipper seems to be implied in the understanding of "charging what the traffic will bear," it is preferable, given the economic conditions existing in the last decade of the twentieth century, to think in terms of the value of transportation in the interchange of goods. This interchange, or trade, takes place only when the object traded commands a higher price at the market than it does at the point of production. A corollary of this is that the market price is fixed by the competition of similar goods from different sources. It follows, therefore, that in modern commercial practice transportation has become an integral part of the distribution process established by the manufacturer or exporter. An efficient process reflects cooperation and coordination in which every participant is aware of the impact of transportation upon the final demand for the object offered for sale.[1]

In recent years, as shipping capacity exceeded the requirements for cargo space, the ability of the carrier to assess rates on a unilateral basis was eroded. Shippers had more influence on associations of carriers, and became more insistent that their ability to pay freight rates be considered. An example of the impact of shipper demand was furnished in June 1985 when the Transpacific Westbound Rate Agreement carriers announced that they would raise the rate by one hundred dollars on 40-foot containers moving from the Orient to the United States. This was to be effective on July 1; on September 1, the rate would be increased again by another two hundred dollars. At a meeting held in Hong Kong, shippers protested so vigorously that the carriers first postponed action until a later date, and then canceled the proposal altogether.[2]

Shippers are concerned that their cargoes be delivered in good condition and on time. They have indicated by actions and in expressions of opinion that the price of transportation is of less significance than the quality of service. This was made known in a survey of several hundred shippers of high-value goods who evaluated these features of ocean transportation in this order of priority: (1) date of ship's sailing and scheduled arrival at port of discharge; (2) duration of the voyage from loading port to discharge port; (3) the reliance which shippers could place on the carriers' published schedules; (4) quality and availability of containers; (5) the reputation of the carrier, based on previous experience or history; and (6) the freight rate charged. Shippers of goods of low value understandably gave higher consideration to the freight rate, but placed it second to the date of sailing and the date of arrival, which were considered most important in the selection of a carrier. In third place was the reputation of the carrier, followed by the reliance which the shipper could place on published schedules being realized in the performance of the ships. Transit time was in fifth place, and the availability of containers was given lowest priority.[3]

The shipowner is faced with the necessity of earning maximum profit from the goods offered on its trade route, while interfering as little as possible in their flow. In theory, the ship operator seeks to carry a minimum of those cargoes which pay either noncompensatory or break-even rates, and looks always for those items on which there is assurance of good profits. Even in theory, however, all the unprofitable commodities cannot be excluded. Frequently the low-grade raw materials are essential to the manufacture of goods which, in their turn, offer handsome profits when later transported across the seas. Since the carrier depends for much of its profit on continued trade in their manufactured articles, the unprofitable item must be lifted at whatever rate the shipper of that commodity will pay.

Carriage by water is still the cheapest form of transportation ever devised by man. In terms of the cost per pound of most commodities moved across the seas, the charges assessed by the liner operator are insignificant in proportion to the sales price at the overseas market. It is substantially correct that carriers would be happy if profits from freight rates averaged one and a half to two cents a pound. For those commodities moved in tramp ships, the return to the ship, in terms of cents per pound, is almost ludicrously low. A sampling of charter rates during a period of comparatively good business showed that it was possible to send a pound of sugar a quarter of the way around the world for less than half a cent. One authority computed that to raise tramp rates on grain by $1.50 a ton, which might be welcomed by many owners, would increase the cost of the flour in a one-pound loaf of bread by approximately one-sixteenth of a cent.

When freight rates are considered for what they really are—the earning power of a ship engaged in hauling the vital commodities of the world—they are seen to be aids, rather than barriers, to international trade.

FACTORS IN OCEAN FREIGHT RATE MAKING

The ideal of the ocean carrier is to foster international trade and to build up the tonnage of cargo carried by the proprietary ships. Although more attention may appear to be given to the large-scale shippers of goods, the small businessman actually is not ignored because the rates quoted by liner companies are the same for all shippers, regardless of the quantity of cargo offered. In practice, the small-scale shipper benefits from the ability of the large-scale shipper to demand more favorable treatment—a demand which can be supported by the threat to transfer business to a competitor.

As was indicated above, liner-service operators may increase the cost of sea-carriage only with extreme caution. Although they may need more revenue, shipowners cannot take the risk of raising rates to levels which might throttle trade or invite new competition by making profits so attractive. The usual method is for the carrier to increase rates gradually, by increments of 5 to 10 percent, and to be guided step-by-step by the reaction of the shipping public.

Inasmuch as the shipowners must have cargo in sufficient quantity to provide adequate loads for their vessel, any commodity which moves in substantial and regular volume from a given port is important to their economic well-being. It is reasonable, therefore, that the rate on that commodity be somewhat lower than on items moving only occasionally and in small lots. For example, cotton is a major export cargo from a port on the Gulf Coast of the United States. Month after month, the flow of the "white staple" can be depended upon to provide nearly half of each ship's load. The rate, therefore, may be lower per ton than on wool, which occasionally moves through this same port, and in much smaller quantities.

A very significant factor in making a freight rate is the amount of ship space needed to stow a ton of the commodity. In theory, all rates are based on a weight ton (either the long ton of 2,240 pounds, the metric ton of 2,204 pounds, or the short ton of 2,000 pounds) occupying 40 cubic feet of ship space. It is pertinent to note that, as the metric system gains worldwide acceptance, the metric ton and the cubic meter, rather than the hundredweight and the cubic foot, are becoming the standards for freight rates.

Cargo which stows in less than 40 cubic feet is referred to as "deadweight cargo," and habitually is freighted by weight, usually at a certain charge per hundred pounds. Cargo requiring more than 40 cubic feet for stowage of a weight ton is known as "cubic cargo," and is freighted by volume, usually a a particular amount per cubic foot. Since packaging varies, the carrier in many instances will offer two rates, one per cubic foot and one per hundredweight, but reserves the right to charge "by weight or measurement, whichever yields the greater revenue."

A vessel loaded so that all cargo space is filled and the hull is immersed to the load line is said to be "full and down." A ship with 400,000 cubic feet of cargo space and a deadweight of 6,000 tons might be "down to her marks" with 6,000 tons of a heavy (dense, or deadweight) commodity stowing at 17 cubic feet per ton, and still have 298,000 cubic feet of unfilled space. If she carried cargo that occupied 40 cubic feet per weight ton, only 240,000 feet of space would be used for a full load of 6,000 tons. If, however, the cargo averaged 60 cubic feet per weight ton, the revenue tonnage would be 6,667, with all space filled.

In making rates, the handling and stowage characteristics of a commodity are taken into account. For example, an unboxed automobile requires ship space in excess of the actual measurement of the vehicle. The rate therefore includes a charge for this empty space. Fragile cargo must be protected; to do so may take cubic footage beyond the measurement of the package. Steel beams need little care and occupy a small amount of space in comparison to their weight. They may be used to offset electric light bulbs, which are exceedingly bulky and very fragile. The rates for these items are adjusted in accordance with their varying characteristics.

The perishability, fragility, bulkiness, odor, or dangerous nature of a commodity, and the resulting responsibility for its protection and care significantly influence freight rates. Since certain commodities are damaged easily, or may be especially attractive to pilferers, the losses sustained from these causes must be made good when the claim is settled. Freight rates on

items of this sort consequently include an allowance to cover the anticipated loss.

Some commodities can be loaded only at special berths to which the
ship may have to be moved at considerable expense. For example, explosives normally are loaded in a remote area of a harbor, and the ship must be
taken to this isolated spot before any of its cargo can be worked. No other
cargo is available at the explosives loading facilities. The very high rate for
this commodity reflects these facts.

Another vital factor in making rates is the actual cost of handling
cargo at the ports of origin and destination. The charges for stowing the
commodity in the ship and the expenses of receiving, checking, watching,
coopering, shifting around the terminals, and delivery vary with the items.
Refrigerated cargo, for example, is expensive because of the extra compensation demanded by the longshoremen who work in subfreezing temperatures. Coal and grain are loaded and unloaded mechanically, and therefore
the charge per ton is low. No uniform fee for handling can be assessed
against all cargo moving through a particular terminal because the cost
varies with the individual commodity.

In general, it is true that the possibility of obtaining return cargo influences freight rates. If the ship always returns to her home port in ballast,
the revenue from the outbound passage has to be sufficient to defray all
costs of the round voyage. Contrariwise, where cargoes are available in
both directions, the average rate per ton probably will be lower than in the
trade which offers business only in one direction.

Exceptionally heavy packages, defined in the break-bulk services as
those over 3 tons, traditionally have been freighted at the regular rate for
the particular commodity, with a scale of surcharges based on the actual
weight. This practice reflected the fact that, until relatively recently, ship's
cargo gear had a safe working load of only 3 tons, and to hoist anything
heavier required that the heavy-lift, or "jumbo," boom be used. Depending
upon how the ship was rigged, working the jumbo might entail using the
winches for four booms. This would idle one or more gangs of longshoremen for whatever time the jumbo might be in service. An alternative to
rigging the heavy-lift boom was to hire a truck-mounted or barge-mounted
crane of very great capacity. This saved much work and time on the part of
the longshoremen, but added noticeably to the cost of handling the overweight parcel. Unavoidably, the expense so incurred had to be charged to
the shipper. Even where modern ships have cranes or booms handling up to
10 or more tons without rerigging, there still is much arduous, time-con-

suming labor involved in stowage of a heavy piece of cargo, and compensation to the ship is justifiable. Extra-long pieces (timbers or steel beams, for instance) cannot be handled quickly and often interfere with the process of stowing other cargo. While there is no uniformity in the actual basis on which the charge is computed, many carriers have set a limit of 35 feet as the maximum to be accepted without assessing additional fees. It should be understood that the operator rarely derives a profit from handling these overweight or over-length items; usually the added charge offsets the out-of-pocket expenses incurred.

An important expense of a voyage is the premium paid for insurance of the vessel. Many considerations affect the underwriters' computations, not least of which is the geographical area in which the ship is to be operated. Some regions present greater dangers to ships than do others; seasons of the year also have a bearing. Insurance coverage will not be valid, except at a higher premium rate, if the ship is sent to regions not included in the description and limitations of risk. War risk and perils of navigation in ice-clogged waters are not part of normal coverage. When a carrier is offered a consignment of cargo that requires the ship to depart from the insured area to effect delivery, or will take the ship into a war zone, it is appropriate that the shipper pay the higher insurance fee. Sometimes this is accomplished by adding a surcharge (usually a fixed percentage) to the freight rate. In other cases, where the "off-limits" ports are visited only occasionally, the carrier will impose an arbitrary charge. From this procedure the shipping industry refers to these addenda as "arbitraries."

Arbitraries also may be assessed against cargo destined to ports where facilities are antiquated, primitive, or nonexistent, and where the ship will face the risk of delays in handling the cargo. Regardless of the words used to describe the extra charge, it is standard practice for carriers to compute, as an integral part of the rate, the expense of putting into ports which do not assure quick turnaround. An interesting variant on this was the imposition of a 25 percent surcharge on cargo carried by the transatlantic superliners. The explanation was the heavy expense of working cargo at the passenger ship terminal in Southampton.

Freight rates in international trade have to be quoted in the currency of some country. For many years, the U.S. dollar served this purpose. When the dollar lost its stability, shipowners were troubled because their freight tariffs were more rigid than the international money market. To protect carriers who accepted payments in a foreign currency and then converted to the national funds at a loss, a "currency adjustment factor" was adopted. This could be modified as often as needed to keep ship revenues approximately in balance with the prevailing rate of exchange.

Only after the foregoing items have been taken into account in setting freight rates does the steamship ratemaker consider costs of vessel operation. When fuel oil prices were increased drastically in 1973, shipowners had to devise a means by which to adjust their revenues quickly with the least possible impact on existing trading patterns. Two possibilities existed. One was to establish new rates whenever the cost of fuel oil escalated beyond an agreed level. This was rejected because of the extreme volatility of oil prices and the resultant instability of freight tariffs predicated upon these prices. The alternative was to continue existing tariffs, and to impose a "fuel oil surcharge" on every revenue ton of cargo. This surcharge could be varied upward or downward as oil prices fluctuated. Shippers agreed that, as a temporary measure, this scheme was probably the most nearly satisfactory arrangement that could be found.

Fuel oil prices, however, never returned to the pre-1973 level, and a new system which reflected the changed conditions had to be generated by the carriers. Rather than continuing the surcharges, freight rates were recomputed to encompass fuel oil costs on a given day, designated as a "base date." As fuel prices fluctuated from the level which prevailed on the base date, increases or decreases (in the form of percentage figures) were included in the carriers' bills. The merit of this plan was that the recomputed freight tariffs had some stability, and changes were made only after appropriate notice.

Other costs of ship operation do not exert so great an influence in making freight rates. Supplies, spare parts, repairs, maintenance, crew wages, and vessel time need to be calculated in addition to the dues exacted in ports of call, canal tolls, pilot fees, and other miscellaneous expenses of the voyage. While these are not negligible, it is not practicable to prorate them against individual commodities, for the reason that liner-service operators cannot predict infallibly what the composition of a ship's load will be on any single voyage.

A ship carrying 20,000 manifest tons of cargo on each fifteen-day leg of a round voyage lasting thirty days might have direct operating expenses, other than fuel, of $10,000 a day. Assessed against the total lift, this would mean that each ton of cargo should contribute 50 cents a day, or $7.50 per voyage. Divided by 40 cubic feet, this would equal 18.75 cents per foot; divided by 20 hundredweight, the charge would be 37.50 cents per unit. Given the size of this contribution, it is understandable that direct operating expense is the least significant of the criteria for setting freight rates.

TYPES OF OCEAN FREIGHT RATES

Ocean freight rates are divided into two categories, *class rates* and *commodity rates*. In general, the class rate may be described as that which is assigned to a large number of unrelated commodities which have been studied individually and found to require the same revenue for their transportation. The commodity rate is a charge for carrying a specified article such as, for example, granulated sugar in bags.

Class rates vary in number, but many water carriers establish from six to nine classes, depending upon the variety needed in the rate structure. The most expensive is Class D, assigned to dangerous cargo (explosives and corrosive acids). The next most expensive is Class 1, and the least expensive is Class 8. The higher the number of the class, the lower the rate—a standard pattern followed by liner service tariffs. There is no mathematical relationship between classes.

Examples of the classification of cargo are shown:

Article	Class
Flowers, artificial	1
Formaldehyde	2
Fuses, hazardous	D
Glass, sheets, frosted	7
Grilles, iron or steel	4
Graphite, not otherwise specified	3
Graphite, in bulk, in bags or barrels	6
Gypsum	8
Heaters, coal burning	5

The corresponding rates were:

	D	1	2	3	4	5	6	7	8
Per 100 lbs.	$4.45	$3.50	$2.90	$2.25	$2.20	$1.78	$1.65	$1.56	$1.35
Per cu. ft.	2.50	1.95	1.65	1.25	1.12	1.00	.92	.88	.75

Commodity rates are fixed by water carriers usually as a result of pressure from shippers who find it competitively impossible to pay the freight rate of the class to which the commodity otherwise would be assigned. In many cases, the difference between one class and the next lower class represents a reduction in freight revenue which is greater than the carrier is willing to grant. In that event, to avoid establishing a new class, a special rate will be assigned to the item. For example, frosted glass, in sheets, is placed in Class 7 and the rate is 88¢ per cubic foot, or $1.56 per hundred pounds. The carrier, in response to a request for special consideration, decides that an acceptable rate for frosted glass, in sheets, could be 80¢ per cubic foot or $1.45 per hundred pounds. This is a compromise between two classes. On the one hand, the shippers are convinced that they cannot pay the higher rate; on the other hand, the carriers are unwilling to come down to the next lower class rate. The result is a "commodity" rate that is mutually acceptable.

Commodity rates take precedence over class rates, so that if the same item were listed in both parts of the tariff, the commodity rate would be applied. There is no necessary relationship between commodity rates since they are made after special consideration of each item. The description of every listing is very definitive:

Commodities	*Freighted Per*
Citrus fruit, fresh, viz.: oranges, lemons, limes, tangelos, tangerines, and grapefruit, under refrigeration, in cartons or boxes not exceeding 42 lbs. each	Carton
Nails, iron or steel, plain, galvanized, or cement coated (except shoe or horseshoe)	100 lbs.
Paper, wrapping, not corrugated, other than cellulose film (cellophane), cloth-line, glassine, gummed, laminated, oil, parchment, tissue, transparent, or waxed	100 lbs.

Regardless of how an item is freighted, the carrier always incurs some expense in processing the papers related to the shipment. It is customary, therefore, for shipowners to require a minimum payment on every bill of lading issued.

"Through rates" are charged for shipments originating with one ocean carrier but transferred to connecting carriers at intermediate ports. By way of illustration, a consignment is sent from Hamburg (Germany) to Antofagasta (Chile). It goes in a German vessel from Hamburg to New York, and there is transshipped to a Chilean-flag steamer for the voyage to South America. The combined operation is handled under one bill of lading, and therefore is known as a "through route." The freight rate for cargo moving in this manner is designated as a "through rate." Usually the originating carrier issues the bill of lading, collects all charges, and subsequently divides the revenue with the other carrier(s) in the proportions established by the through rate agreement.

In many cases, the through rate is lower than the combination of rates of each of the participating carriers. For example, a ton of coffee may be sent from Buenaventura (Colombia) to New York in a Colombian-flag ship for $22.00. The freight rate for coffee carried from New York to Livorno (Italy) by an Italian-flag vessel is $36.80. The through rate from Buenaventura to Livorno, by agreement between the carriers, is $54.00. Each carrier has reduced its rate by $2.40 in order to meet the competition of a Greek operator whose ships sail directly from Colombia to Italy, and whose charge for the service is $54.50.

Not all through rates represent concessions in the rates charged by participating carriers. In some cases, two ship lines will offer the benefits of through service, but each will charge the full tariff rate for its portion of the total transit. This situation eventuates either from lack of direct sailings between countries of origin and destination or from significantly less desirable schedules by the only carrier linking the two ports. Some shippers will use the through service even though it is more expensive because they consider the time in transit to be worth the difference financially. There are other cases where no direct link exists between the exporting and importing countries. Lacking the pressure of competition, the through rate is the total of the connecting carriers' charges plus any accessorial fees. For example, when no line sailed directly between Australia and Chile, an Australian importer wishing to bring Chilean wine to Melbourne would have had it carried to San Francisco and there transshipped to a transpacific operator for the onward movement to Australia. The through rate would be constructed in this manner: From Valparaiso to San Francisco the rate was $32.00 per ton. Transfer costs in San Francisco from one marine terminal to the other were $11.00 per ton. The freight charge from San Francisco to Melbourne was $40.00, bringing the through rate to $83.00 per ton.

FREIGHT RATES FOR CARGO IN CONTAINERS

Although vast changes in shipping have been occasioned by the container revolution, there is no difference between the principles by which freight rates are made for cargo carried in containers and those by which rates are established for break-bulk cargo.

Certain facts must be accepted. Containers are of uniform size and are loaded and unloaded by mechanized and almost completely automated methods. Regardless of their contents, these big boxes are handled at the same speed, using the same number of longshoremen and the same equipment. To position and secure an empty container takes the same care as it does to stow a box filled with delicate precision instruments of high value. Certainly not to be overlooked is the fact that most containers are stuffed by the shippers, who thereby become responsible for the efficient and economical use of shipping space.

Among the time-honored factors influencing break-bulk freight rates are demands for high levels of stevedoring skills in handling and stowing various commodities and products. The susceptibility to damage and pilferage is another basis for computing cost. The amount of ship's space necessary to accommodate a revenue ton also is taken into account. When, however, goods are received at ship's side in huge weatherproof boxes that will be stowed in the vessel by people and machines that give all containers, regardless of what is inside, exactly the same care, the applicability of these justification for a freight rate become questionable. If it costs no more to put a filled container into its shipboard cell than it does to deposit an empty container in the adjoining cell, how can the shipowner defend a rate structure built on theories and practices displaced by technological developments?

The first argument in support of the existing system is that the possibility of sustaining a major loss is much greater in the container age than in the days of break-bulk shipping. A container loaded with washing machines might be swept overboard during a storm, and the claim would amount to many thousands of dollars. Loss of a single washing machine would cost the carrier a few hundred dollars. There is a modicum of truth in this argument; many containers have been carried off by boarding seas. The freight rate, which has been assessed against all the washing machines in the container, however, includes an allowance to cover this contingency. The argument loses much of its force in the face of fact.

The second point advanced in defense of existing freight rates is that the introduction of the container did not end the need to transport those low value commodities which move in small quantities, and therefore are dependent upon liner service. Some method is required to continue the subsidy of these commodities, but nothing better than the break-bulk principles has been brought forth. One school of thought advocates the adoption of a single rate for all containers, regardless of the commodities inside. This may be logical in view of the technology of container shipping, but it poses as many problems as it solves. If the rate favors the movement of cement, the revenue to the ship will be inadequate. If the rate is predicated on washing machines, this will stop the movement of cement. It also will reduce correspondingly the tonnage of cargo offered to the ship.[4]

Some years ago, an operator in the transatlantic trade instituted a "container rate," and illustrated the method by which it would freight cargo. A shipper of microwave ovens would be charged a gross figure of $1,500 for the container. Other merchandise could be mingled with the ovens so long as it had approximately the same value and was subject to the same freight rate. The shipper, of course, was responsible for stowing the packages within the container.

In this case, the ship operator substituted for the traditional commodity rate schedule a new listing for containers loaded at the shipper's option with one or more types of cargo which were "compatible" and therefore were charged the same freight rate. The shipper furnished the carrier with an accurate manifest showing exactly what had been placed in the container. Regardless of how much of the container's interior space was used by the shipper, the rate for the container remained the same.

A variant on the foregoing system was that adopted by a carrier plying between New York and South Africa which charged the same rate for all containers without regard to what might be in the boxes. This "freight all kinds" rate was set arbitrarily by the carrier: initially it was $4,150 for a 20-foot box and $7,300 for a 40-foot container.

Steamship ratemakers for years have been searching for a logical and simple system by which freight rates can be applied to cargo moving in preloaded containers. No entirely satisfactory substitute has been found for the existing (and frequently criticized) rate structure, which produces adequate revenue without unduly antagonizing shippers.

Several tentative suggestions have been propounded by both carriers and shippers as bases for discussion. Rates for containers would be established for designated groupings of goods. High value merchandise, typified by the washing machines mentioned earlier in this chapter, would be charged a fixed fee for a container load. Less highly valued merchandise would be assigned appropriately lower rates. The problem commodities typified by cement, which cannot pay fully compensatory liner rates, would be identified and a minimum charge fixed for their transportation.

Once the system became effective, shippers would be charged a single fee for the use of a container from origin to ultimate destination. The fee would be predicated upon the shipper's declaration of value of the goods that have been loaded into the container. To illustrate, a hypothetical steamship line running between New York and Rotterdam would set charges for completely filled containers according to this scale:

> Valuation under $200 per metric ton or cubic meter: $500
> Valuation of $201 to $500 per metric ton or cubic meter: $800
> Valuation of $501 to $750 per metric ton or cubic meter: $1,050
> Valuation exceeding $751 per metric ton or cubic meter: $1,400

The shipper would be free to load any number and variety of commodities in the container, so long as the value did not exceed that stipulated when the reservation was made with the carrier.

To protect against abuses, the carriers would have the right to open and examine containers and would enforce these rules:

1. Only one shipper is permitted to use a container.
2. A single bill of lading is issued to each container.
3. If the valuation of any of the merchandise loaded in the container exceeds the agreed dollar limitation, the rate for the whole container will be that which applies to the goods with the highest value.
4. All containers are considered as fully loaded; there is no prorating for less than container lots.

PROJECT RATES

From time to time, a major contractor will be engaged in an overseas project involving the movement of thousands of tons of many kinds of equipment and supplies. Rather than calculating each shipment by the tariff, the contractor and the carrier(s) on the route will negotiate a special "freight all kinds" rate per agreed ton. In this case, "agreed ton" means that everything will be freighted uniformly by one method (i.e., exclusively by weight, or exclusively by measurement). This project rate applies only to those shipments by the contractor which are part of the construction project, and expire automatically when the job is completed.

During the life of the project, shipments will be incremental, sometimes filling a ship and sometimes amounting to only a few hundred tons, and will be as varied as these sample listings: pressure vessels, tanks, catalytic cracking towers, and reactors for oil refineries; boilers, generators, transformers, and turbines for electric generating plants; kilns, plant components, machinery, and furnaces for mining operations. In one instance, an ammonia plant had individual lifts which ranged up to 420 tons, and some were over 40 feet long. The total movement for the project came to 20,863 tons.

The study of the development of ocean freight rates, and the application of those rates to the movement of cargo, is of major concern to those who are involved either in shipping goods or transporting those goods. As the use of computers becomes more and more widespread, it is predictable that shippers and carriers will engage in probing analyses and searching comparisons of different freight rates as a normal part of their business.

For a transoceanic transportation system to benefit both shippers and carriers, freight rates must be sufficiently lucrative to furnish the economic incentive to carriers to offer the needed or desired means of transportation, while still being low enough for shippers to profit financially by sending their goods to overseas markets. That there is—and very probably always will be—as much an art as there is a science in finding these nearly-magic points, is abundantly clear to users and providers of deep-sea shipping.

CHAPTER FOURTEEN

The Traffic Study

Among the responsibilities of the executives charged with developing sources of revenue for a steamship company, none is more exacting than preparing the *traffic study*. This is a systematic compilation of data related to one or more of the many problems related to selling the service the ships are intended to provide. It may be concerned with major aspects of traffic management, such as commencing service on a new trade route; it may be limited to a simple matter of determining the most attractive color scheme to be used in redecorating the passenger spaces. In either case, it is a methodical procedure by which to reach a decision affecting the earning capability of the ships.

The traffic study is a forecast of future trends of the business of the carrier, based upon present practices and past experience in the same field. It depends to a great extent upon the history of the steamship company, as reflected in its records. Equally important is the personal knowledge and expert opinion of the persons invited to participate in the study.

Three traffic studies conducted by American shipowners typify the extremes of disaster and success which can result from these efforts. The first shows how even the most careful examination of all aspects of a new idea may be upset by a single feature appreciated by none of the executives involved in the study. The second demonstrates how success is achieved when all participants share the vision of what can be attained. The third illustrates how factors altogether beyond the shipowner's control can negate the most punctiliously executed study and lead to bankruptcy.

The first study was conducted several years before Malcom McLean demonstrated the practicality of handling cargo in pre-loaded containers, rather than in the conventional manner used in break-bulk carriage. At the time the study was initiated, the project was of unusual complexity because it dealt with a wholly new, indeed a revolutionary, procedure involving the delivery in foreign ports of cargo encased in a large sealed box which could be placed directly on a waiting truck or trailer without being opened. Only enough longshoremen were needed to hook the hoisting gear to the box and to release it.

Among the elements which had to be taken into account were: the best size for the boxes, the feasibility of obtaining return cargoes that could be stowed in the boxes, the problem of recovering the boxes from the ports, the desirability of making the ship self-sustaining through the installation of very expensive gantry cranes as compared with developing special facilities to handle the containers at each port, the potential savings in stevedore costs which might be used to offset the expense of starting the program, and the reactions of waterfront labor groups to the new technique.

One of the critical items in the study was the size of the boxes, because local trucking capability in the foreign countries to be served had to be determined. After establishing the nature of the support that might be obtained abroad, the condition of the highways, especially the arc of road curves, had to be studied. The recommended solution was quite ingenious: it capitalized on the trucking industries of all the different nations involved. Three of the proposed boxes could be fitted on an American trailer; two could be loaded aboard a foreign trailer, or one box could be carried easily on the bed of a medium-performance truck in any area of the ship's proposed operation. Once these determinations were made, the traffic study, except for the labor aspects, was completed with relative ease.

Trouble was encountered in measuring the extent and strength of the reaction from foreign longshoremen. As it turned out, the best available advice from experts in the evaluation of labor attitudes appeared to be conservative and realistic, but in fact was colored by unwarranted optimism. In the light of the available data and conclusions, the costly project was approved, and millions of dollars were spent. Two ships were converted, containers were purchased, and much publicity was given to the new system. The ship was loaded with no labor problems in the American port, but at the first overseas point the longshoremen refused to work the ship except under terms and conditions which negated the whole idea. Eventually, arrangements were made to deliver that initial cargo, but the project had to be abandoned and the ships laid up.

The second traffic study was dedicated to an analysis of the characteristics to be built into new ships planned for a particular trade route. It was typical of the major effort required and epitomized the depth of specialized knowledge demanded of those directing the study.

The shipowner was developing a replacement program for its fleet of cargo ships. Major changes in cargo packaging procedures had occurred shortly before the study was begun. In addition, a substantial movement of refrigerated produce from the United States to two overseas ports had developed. Finally, the competing carriers on the route were replacing their ships with vessels of significantly greater speed. It therefore was imperative that the proposed vessels be both thoroughly modern and embody radically new ideas in ship design.

First consideration was given to speed. A canvass of both the sales staff and representative shippers proved that there was a strong demand for drastic reduction in transit time. Intensive study of port working schedules led to a finding that, given the cargo-handling techniques of the time, only a few hours could be saved by improving production on the part of the stevedores. Sustained sea speeds would have to be increased by about one-half, as compared to the existing fleet's normal cruising speed of 14 knots. Engineering computations by the naval architect indicated that it was operationally and economically feasible to build the new ships with that greater capability.

The next step in the process was to examine those characteristics of the ship which affected the rapidity, ease, and economy of emptying and refilling the cargo spaces. Ships' officers, stevedores, terminal superintendents, and operating executives were directed to carry out this aspect of the study. Exhaustive consideration resulted in the recommendation that the new ship have three hatches abreast over each hold, in effect opening the entire below decks area. Coupled with this improved access to stowage space was the need for flexible, high-speed cranes, rather than the conventional booms. To accommodate the large quantities of refrigerated cargo, insulated spaces would have to be cooled to 0° Fahrenheit. Special attention was to be given to assuring that this cargo would be moved rapidly to protect it from spoiling.

The naval architect took the results of these elaborate studies by the composite group of traffic specialists, cargo-handling experts, stevedores, ships' officers, cargo-gear riggers, and specialists in handling perishable foodstuffs, and converted them into plans for a fleet of large, high-speed, versatile, and economical ships that proved to be outstanding in their responsiveness to the requirements of the trade.

In this instance, the investment to be made as a result of the traffic study was so great that those in charge were justified in using every resource available, and in devoting thousands of man-hours to assure that every detail had been examined with painstaking thoroughness, and that every recommendation had been weighed in relation to all others before final decisions were reached.

It is appropriate also to describe one other traffic study which led to disaster because of circumstances totally beyond the shipowner's control or ability to anticipate.

The United States Lines proposed to build large containerships to operate in a round-the-world service. At the time, fuel oil prices were at their historic peak, and ship operators worldwide were taking every measure to reduce fuel consumption. The most reliable and apparently prescient forecasts indicated that if fuel oil prices changed at all, they would climb upward. The new ships, therefore, were designed for a very economical speed of 18.5 knots. By the time they were delivered by the builder, the picture had changed drastically and far beyond anyone's expectation. Fuel oil prices had dropped precipitately, and competing ships were entering the trade with speeds of up to 24 knots. The ultimate results of these changes drove the United States Lines into bankruptcy.

A traffic study is an essential tool of management. It systematizes thinking related to problems of every type of steamship traffic. It requires much imagination and complete freedom from preconceived notions on the part of those who direct the study. Finally, it places the responsibility for each step and each recommendation squarely on the shoulders of the individual participants.

Take, as an illustration, the action of a traffic manager who has heard many complaints that the ocean freight rate on stainless steel kitchen sinks is so high that American exporters of these items are priced out of the overseas markets to which the ships are sent. To become acquainted with the general economic situation relating to stainless steel sinks in these countries, the traffic manager requests information from the appropriate governmental agencies. The outbound manifest section will determine exactly how many tons of steel sinks moved during the past year. The terminal manager will supply data on the costs of loading and discharging, and any special problems that should be considered in analyzing the freight rates. From the shippers themselves will be obtained data relating to the sinks sold in overseas markets in direct competition with their products. When all the material has been assembled and is available for study, the traffic manager is in a position to review the entire matter intelligently and systematically, and to decide whether a reduction in the ocean freight rate is in order. Furthermore, the traffic manager will be able to determine whether the reduction would help the exporters to sell more sinks in the foreign markets, with the obvious benefit to the steamship carrier of obtaining more cargo.

As a normal routine of traffic management, it is customary for periodic analyses to be made of cargo manifests. These analyses often disclose changes in tonnage and revenue which suggest that a traffic study be undertaken to find answers to questions like these:

What are the most important commodities, in terms of tonnage and ship revenues, moving this year, and what changes are to be observed when compared with last year's cargo lift? What are the current freight rates? What were the freight rates a year ago? Have shippers made any formal applications for adjustments in freight rates, and if so, what disposition was made of those applications? Are there any obstacles to the movement of these important commodities which exist today but did not exist a year ago? Have any barriers been removed? What is the cost of stevedoring for each of the major commodities? What is the total cost to the company of transporting each of these commodities? What is the frequency of claims? How does the cost of claims settlement compare with freight revenues from each item? What is the true margin of profit? Are these items carried more as a convenience to shippers than as contributors to company profits? If there has been a loss of business this year as compared to last year, in the light of the information provided to answer the foregoing questions, is it worthwhile to make an effort to regain this tonnage?

Earlier in this chapter the story was recounted of a steamship company's successful fleet replacement program. With imagination, it is possible to visualize how so complex and critically important a study would be conducted.

The board of directors directed the vice president, traffic, to coordinate the study and to request information and assistance from all departments. When all the data had been gathered, the coordinator would make final recommendations as to the character of service needed, the special features deemed essential in the design of the ships, and the maximum acceptable cost of the vessels.

The first step in the traffic study was to evaluate the characteristics of the ship that would be most satisfactory as a replacement for the existing type of vessel. This involved not only determination of size, speed, capacity, and special features of the ships, but also the ports to be served, the approximate schedule each ship would have to follow to meet the demands of shippers, and the types and tonnages of cargo to be carried. The coordinator ordered the managers of the inbound and outbound freight traffic divisions to compile statistics showing the fluctuations in the amount of business during the previous decade. The operating department furnished the data on the facilities and limitation of the ports along the route, the comparative cost of operating newer and larger ships at substantially increased speeds, and the number of tons of cargo handled in an hour by longshoremen in each port visited. The accounting department supplied information concerning the average revenue from each of the various items carried, as well as the approximate net profit from a typical voyage.

As these data came to the desk of the coordinator, they were collated with information from shippers and consignees as to their ideas, desires, and anticipated needs for marine transportation during the next decade. Various governmental agencies meanwhile supplied more elaborate and extensive information, statistical and otherwise, than company records could provide. Forecasts and predictions as to the economic growth of the region where the ships would operate also had been solicited from international banking houses and foreign commerce associations.

When the accumulation of facts, figures, records, and statistics had been completed, the coordinator was able to determine with considerable accuracy what they signified in terms of ship speed, schedules, capacities, earnings, and the other details to support the final recommendations for a certain number of ships of a particular design to operate on a set frequency of sailings.

The needs of the service, the peculiarities of the cargoes, and the economic justification of the improved design were all recorded in systematic and convenient fashion. The completed traffic study filled hundreds of pages and represented a huge investment in the form of executives' time, clerical labor, and other costs.

There are no fixed limits to the subject matter of a traffic study. It is precisely what the words imply: a tool of management. It has only one purpose, and that is to provide a systematic method of analyzing a problem and giving to management the best possible answer. In form, therefore, the traffic study can be extremely varied. Depending upon its nature, it may take the shape of a learned researcher's written report, or it may be only an oral statement. It could take months of work on the part of practically the entire organization, or it might require only eight or ten hours of one person's time. Since it often contains many secrets of the company's operations, it is never released to the public, but its substance often is revealed in statements to government agencies, applications for route franchises, or announcements of new developments by the company.

The very nature of the traffic study requires that the person directing it have a wide knowledge of company operations. The more varied the experience, and the more comprehensive the understanding of company activities and problems, the more likely it is that the conclusions will be accepted. By the same token, the responsibilities placed upon the person who must make the final recommendations in the traffic study are tremendous. Almost any other duty in the traffic department becomes, by comparison, less significant. A traffic manager whose predictions have proved to be correct most of the time is of incalculable importance to the success of any steamship organization.

CHAPTER FIFTEEN

Steamship Conferences

From the early days of transoceanic shipping until the present, an international flavor has characterized the business of moving goods from one land to another. Merchants of many nations brought their wares to overseas markets, seeking the most profitable transactions. They cherished their own ideas of what constituted proper business practice, and resisted vigorously any effort of one sovereign power to impose its code of commercial morality upon the citizens of another country. This almost instinctive hostility toward regulation was absorbed early by steamship men who had inherited from their predecessors a sturdy independence and a willingness to assume great risks in exchange for great returns. Despite this attitude, however, there was a dim awareness among shipowners that uninhibited competition could be disastrous not only to them but to their customers. The alternative to government control had to be an industry-generated and industry-managed system of supervision and regulation.[1]

Awareness changed into concern about the time that improvements in steam engineering, particularly as they applied to marine installations, made it possible for powered vessels to undertake long voyages. Bitter rivalry between the steamers and the sailing ships became the normal condition of business and forced the growth of the idea that shipowners who faced the same problems on the same trade routes and scrambled for a share of the available business had much to gain by establishing some form of mutually acceptable regulation. By surrendering a fraction of their rights to independent action in exchange for protection from predatory competition, the shipowners hoped to benefit themselves as well as their clients.

The soundness of this idea was put to the test in 1875 when steamship owners in the London-Calcutta trade became involved in a freight rate "war" with the operators of sailing ships going between these two ports. In their search for a way to end this unhappy situation, the owners called a conference at which was advanced the idea of an industry association to police the trade. Approval of the idea resulted in the formation of the Calcutta Conference.[2] Although they were written in 1961, the following words from a report submitted to the U.S. Congress, after noting that the investment in an individual ship is larger than a corresponding invest- ment in the component units of land or inland waterways transportation, described the rationale of the conference:

> Because of the peculiar mobility of ships, it is entirely possible for a shipowner to place his vessel in a particular service on relatively short notice and without hindrance from any law or regulation of any nations. As a result, the only method that has proved practical to assure continuity of service on a particular route with a degree of stability of rates, in view of the very large investment required in the establishment of a regular service, is by providing specific in- ducements to shippers to utilize the services of the particular line or lines regularly serving that route. The conference system, with an appropriate tying device, has proven to be the most effective method, both from the point of view of the carrier and the shipper.[3]

The significant events in the development of the Calcutta Conference are of interest.

Just at the time the Suez Canal was opened in 1869, steamships were becoming not only more numerous and more efficient, but they were replacing sailing ships on one route after another. Because they did not depend upon the wind, the powered vessels could take advantage of the shorter distance to India made possible by the canal, whereas the sailing ships were thwarted by adverse wind conditions in the Red Sea and had to use the route around the Cape of Good Hope, almost 4,000 nautical miles longer. The steamers not only made the voyage more quickly, but they could predict with reasonable accuracy the day of arrival at their des- tination. To offset these disadvantages, the sailing ship owners reduced freight rates, a move met by even greater concessions from the steam- ship operators. The destructive nature of this struggle immediately be- came apparent.

The major steamship operators (Peninsular and Oriental Steam Navi- gation Company, British India Company, and T. & J. Harrison) and some of the smaller carriers met in the 1875 conference and jointly agreed to end concessions to shippers, to adopt uniform freight rates, and to offer identi- cal terms of carriage. It was expected that these arrangements would stabi- lize shipping practice and assure more regularity in schedules, less frequent adjustments of rates, and greater convenience for shippers. The importers and exporters, however, resented the loss of concessions, and threatened to transfer a larger proportion of their business to the sailing ships, which were offering more favorable terms. The prospect of losing cargoes prompted the conference to develop the "exclusive patronage" contract, which would commit the shipper to give his business only to carriers belonging to the conference. The shippers rejected the proffered contract, demanding some guarantee of preferential treatment before they would bind themselves to the conference. Responding to this demand, the conference proposed in 1877 to establish the "deferred rebate," which would be paid after a designated period during which loyalty to the conference had been demonstrated.

The arrangement required that shippers desiring to receive the rebate agree to give their business only to the lines that were members of the Calcutta Conference. In return for this exclusive patronage contract, the conference members bound themselves to return one-tenth of all freights paid during a six-month period contingent upon the continuing exclusive patronage of the conference carriers during a further period of six months. Failure to live up to the terms of the contract automatically canceled both the earned refund and the credits being established toward a second refund.

The penalty for "disloyalty" was set forth in the following words, taken from a circular issued in 1885 by the England-China Conference:

> Shipments for London by non-Conference steamers, at any of the ports of China or Hong Kong, will exclude the firm making such shipments from participation in the return, during the whole six-monthly period within which they have been made, of any portion of the freight charged, even though the firm elsewhere may have given exclusive support to the Conference lines.[4]

The working of the new system was described very clearly in this quotation from the report of the Royal Commission on Shipping Rings submitted to Parliament in 1909:

> . . . if at the end of a certain period (usually four or six months) they have not shipped goods by any vessel other than those despatched by members of the Conference, shippers will be credited with a sum equivalent to a certain part (usually 10%) of the aggregate freights paid on their shipments during that period, and the sum will be paid over to them if, at the end of a further period, usually 4 to 6

months, they have continued to confine their shipments to vessels
belonging to members of the conference. The sum so paid is known
as a "deferred rebate." . . . If, during any period, a shipper sends
any quantity of goods, however small, by a vessel other than those
despatched by the Conference lines, he becomes disentitled to rebates on any of his shipments by conference vessels during that period and the preceding one.[5]

Acceptance of the exclusive patronage contract was a voluntary act
on the part of the individual shipper. The alternative was to pay the rate
quoted in the tariff without expectation of receiving a partial refund. Inevitably, this meant that the landed cost of the goods at destination would
be greater for the noncontract signer than for its competitor. This economic pressure brought many shippers under the contract; by the close of
the century the deferred rebate scheme prevailed in practically all the conferences of carriers operating out of the United Kingdom. In many of
these trade routes, the conference system with its rigid hold on shippers
produced the closest approach to a monopoly that is possible in ocean
shipping.

The Royal Commission found that deferred rebates had proven effective in gaining and holding the loyalty of shippers, as evidenced by the
large sums the carriers owed to individual shippers. To control this limited
monopoly, the commission recommended that conferences be directed to
deposit with the Board of Trade copies of all conference agreements, rebate
circulars and claim forms, all understandings with lines outside the conference, and all agreements with shippers' associations which had been recognized by the Board of Trade. To satisfy complaints that customers did not
have ready access to tariffs of conference carriers, it was further recommended that tariffs be published and at least one copy be filed with the
Board of Trade.[6]

In 1923, the British Imperial Shipping Committee concluded a further study of steamship conferences and found that, to some extent, deferred rebates were necessary in most trades. The system, however, did
deprive the shipper of much of his freedom of choice and removed the
corrective effect of free competition.

The contention is valid that the deferred rebate is an effective shield
from the competition of both independent liner operators and tramps. Few
shippers will risk the loss of benefits accrued under the deferred rebate
system to take advantage of the comparatively small savings to be gained

by employing either the independents or, when the volume of cargo justifies movement in shipload lots, by chartering a tramp. As a useful tool in building up dependable patronage, the value of the deferred rebate was acknowledged in both the English and the American investigations.

American attitudes toward monopolies and competition are quite different from those of both Western Europe and Japan, where monopolies and agreements in restraint of trade are acceptable business practices. In the United States, these arrangements among commercial firms are outlawed and discouraged by the stringent provisions of the antitrust laws. Aware of the restrictive nature of steamship conferences, and consistent with the antitrust sentiment prevailing in the United States, a committee of the House of Representatives was appointed in 1912 to investigate the conference system and its effect upon American foreign commerce.

Under the chairmanship of Representative Joshua W. Alexander of Missouri, a subcommittee of the Committee on Merchant Marine and Fisheries conducted the investigation and held hearings over a two-year period. In 1914, it published its four-volume report, and made a number of recommendations for legislative action. Chief among them was that the conference system be exempted from the provisions of the antitrust law, but made subject to continuous scrutiny by a regulatory agency. Two practices of European conferences were condemned: the deferred rebate and the use of the "fighting ship."

The Alexander Committee considered that the deferred rebate was intended to establish a near-monopoly of ocean transportation on the trade route in which the carriers operated. The fighting ship, defined as a vessel used on a sea-lane by a group of operators (for example, a conference) for the express purpose of excluding, preventing, or reducing competition by driving a nonmember carrier off that route, was viewed as the weapon of monopoly. Evidence had been presented proving that this practice had been followed, particularly in the North Atlantic, to the detriment of nonconference carriers.

A flagrant example occurred in 1908. German passenger ship operators reacted to competition for immigrant passengers on the Hamburg-New York run by using fighting ships to destroy this rivalry. Suitable steamers were chosen from the conference members' fleets and were sailed on the same days and between the same ports as the independents' ships. Fares were reduced enough to attract most of the passengers to the fighting ship. When more passengers bought tickets than the fighting ship could accommodate, they were transferred to the conference members' ships at the same low fares. Losses resulting from this activity were prorated among the conference members in proportion to the number of their ships. The committee summarized the situation in these words:

> It was thus a case of all the lines, united in conference, opposing every sailing of a single opposition line. By distributing the loss over the several members of the conference, each constituent line would suffer proportionately much less than the one line which was fighting the entire group, and which would inevitably soon exhaust its resources in the conflict with the combined power of the large lines with their superior speed and better third class accommodations.

This type of predatory competition also existed in cargo service, as the committee took pains to illustrate. The case in point was that of a German "fighting corporation" formed in 1905 by six cargo liner companies. This corporation had as its sole purpose the destruction of rivals on its members' routes. Four ships were owned and others were chartered. These vessels sought the bulk cargoes normally transported by the independents, at freight rates which were intended to bankrupt the independent carriers.

The Alexander Committee's recommendations furnished the solid basis for what became the Shipping Act of 1916. Steamship conferences organized in the United States were to be exempted from the provisions of the Sherman antitrust law, on condition that all joint actions be subject to some form of government supervision. The tools of monopoly—deferred rebates, fighting ships, and discriminatory practices—were disapproved. To support its recommendations, the committee declared that trade with foreign nations required that uniform rates be available to any and all shippers, that they be comparatively stable, and that they take into consideration all the elements of transportation. Those carriers which elected to operate outside of the conference framework were not subject to government control unless discrimination were charged by a shipper.

It is important to note that the attitude and thinking of the Alexander Committee, which opposed cartels and other restrictions on trade but recognized that international shipping required special consideration and treatment, have been accepted and supported by the Congress. In a report written in 1961 from the House Committee on Merchant Marine and Fisheries, the need for a carefully controlled exemption from antitrust legislation was set forth in these words:

The conference, fixing as it does rates and practices, is permitted to exist only as an exception to the antitrust laws of the United States, and such exception is granted only because of the peculiar nature of ocean transportation, and provided certain conditions are met. In order to secure the benefits of such immunity from the antitrust acts, the conferences are required by Section 15 of the Shipping Act of 1916 to file all their agreements with the appropriate regulatory body, which at present is the Federal Maritime Board, and obtain approval of that body. The Board has considerable jurisdiction under the terms of that act to regulate the conferences and see that they observe the restrictions upon which their immunity from the operation of the antitrust acts is predicated.[7]

GENERAL RATE INCREASE
EFFECTIVE FEBRUARY 1, 1986

The Member Lines of the United States and Gulf Ports/Eastern Mediterranean and North African Freight Conference, announce that spiraling operational expenditures necessitates the implementation of a General Rate Increase, for both Port to Port and Intermodal Rates, effective February 1, 1986, as follows:

Five percent (5%) on rates up to $165.00 W/M or M

Five percent (5%) on all weight rated commodities

Five percent (5%) on all container rates, rounded up to the highest $25.00.

Minimum Bills of Lading and Optional Bills of Lading will also be increased by $10.00

Any questions you may have relative to this announcement, should be directed to the Member Lines, their Agents or the Conference Office.

Constellation Line   Prudential Lines, Inc.
Farrell Lines, Inc.   Waterman Steamship Corp.
Lykes Lines

                              R. H. Cabrera
                              Chairman

Perusal of the various laws enacted by the Congress of the United States to regulate steamship conferences reveals the persistence of the nineteenth century hostility toward monopolies of any sort. This attitude may be discerned in the provisions of the Shipping Act of 1984, even though by this date the influence of these associations of carriers had been curtailed very sharply. Intra-conference competition, for example, was evident in the frequent announcements to the shipping public that rates on certain commodities were "open"—that is, each carrier in the conference was free to set rates at any level that seemed appropriate. Significant and unilateral improvements in the quality of service also demonstrated the rivalry between conference members. In combination, these actions signaled that conferences did not pose the threat of monopoly.

An analysis of the liner services of nine major maritime nations was conducted in 1957, and pointed out that the fleets of the individual carriers were small. Forty percent of the operators owned twenty or fewer ships each; an equal percentage claimed ten or fewer vessels. The largest single-owner fleet embraced only 2 percent of the total number of ships assigned to liner service. From these facts the conclusion was drawn that no single operator, nor any combination of two or more operators, attempted to dominate a trade route through control of the largest fleet. The conferences, consequently, could be described as having neither the capacity nor the intention to establish a monopoly.[8]

As the conference system evolved after 1875, the exclusive patronage contract (also called the loyalty contract) and the accompanying dual freight rate structure were considered indispensable to the existence of the associations. The purpose of the contract was to provide the members of each conference with a steady flow of cargo from shippers whose support would be forthcoming over a reasonably long period of time. In exchange, the members of the conference agreed to reduce the nominal (or "tariff") freight rate by a stipulated percentage—a benefit granted only to those shippers who signed the contract.

In the United States, from the effective date of the Shipping Act of 1916 until 1948, the regulatory authority exercised only the most cursory type of supervision over the contracts on the premise that the basic agreement having been approved, issuance of the contract by the conference automatically was approved. In 1948, the Maritime Commission carefully examined the details of the dual rate system, and prescribed modifications to be made by one conference. A major attack on the dual rate system was initiated in 1949 and culminated in 1952 in a decision by the U.S. Supreme Court that the differential between contract and noncontract rates was arbi-

THE "8900" RATE AGREEMENT
WISHES TO ANNOUNCE:

DUE TO STEADILY INCREASING OPERATIONAL COSTS, THE "8900" RATE AGREEMENT HAS FOUND IT NECESSARY TO INCREASE RATES AND CHARGES IN F.M.C. NO. 9, 10 & 11 FREIGHT TARIFFS. EFFECTIVE MAY 1, 1985, AN INCREASE OF FIVE PER CENT WILL BECOME EFFECTIVE WITH THE DATE THE VESSEL SAILS FROM THE PORT OF LOADING OR THE DATE THE CARGO IS RECEIVED BY THE CARRIER, WHICHEVER BENEFITS THE CARGO.

THE "8900" RATE AGREEMENT COVERS TRADE FROM POINTS IN THE UNITED STATES MOVING THROUGH U.S. ATLANTIC AND GULF PORTS AT INTER-CHANGE TO MIDDLE EAST PORTS, WEST OF KARACHI AND NORTH EAST OF ADEN, BUT EXCLUDING ADEN AND KARACHI AND TO INLAND POINTS IN BAHRAIN, IRAN, IRAQ, KUWAIT, OMAN, QATAR, SAUDI ARABIA AND THE UNITED ARAB EMIRATES.

Very truly yours,

THE "8900" LINES
ANTHONY A. DE GIGLIO
VICE CHAIRMAN

trary and consequently unlawfully discriminatory. The use of the dual rate structure by two North Atlantic conferences therefore was permanently enjoined. Further legal action culminated in the Supreme Court's ruling, announced on 19 May 1958, in the case of *Federal Maritime Board et al.* vs. *Isbrandtsen Company, Inc., United States of America, and Secretary of Agriculture,* which held that the use of contract/noncontract rates proposed by the Japan-Atlantic and Gulf Freight Conference violated that provision of the Shipping Act of 1916 prohibiting restrictions to trade and unjust discrimination (in this case, setting up a retaliatory device to stifle competition). The dual rate system was declared illegal.[9]

Congressional hearings conducted between 1958 and 1961 examined all aspects of the conference system. Testimony offered by both carriers and shippers led to the conclusion that conferences were essential in the foreign trade of the United States. The loyalty contracts, with the associated dual rate structure, were given general approval. As the conferences existed at that time, these factors supported their continued operation:

1. The "ease of market entry"—any ship on the ocean may stop at any port and discharge or load cargo. It costs a great deal to establish a liner service, but nothing beyond the investment in a single ship for a tramp owner to participate, as opportunity affords, in a specific trade.
2. The rigid fixed and operating cost structure of the steamship industry. It costs almost as much to sail a ship one-quarter full as completely loaded. This may encourage the independent to cut rates as a means of obtaining cargo.
3. No governmental control over the level of ocean freight rates.
4. A marked difference in the operating costs of similar ships flying diverse flags.
5. Usually an imbalance between inbound and outbound cargo. For example, on Trade Route 21 (from U.S. ports on the Gulf of Mexico to the United Kingdom and European continent) the disparity was 4 to 1 in favor of outbound loadings in 1959. This places enormous pressure on the carrier to find homeward cargoes.
6. Overtonnaging of ocean trade routes, which tends to accentuate the already severe competition existing among ocean carriers.[10]

Conferences were intended to provide, through the carriers' own efforts, the stability demanded by international trade but not furnished by national governments. The dependence of liner companies upon regular and repeated patronage is well known and is corroborated by the findings of a recent study of a trade route originating in the United Kingdom. Of the 3,900 different clients of the liner services on that route, only three shippers accounted for 25 percent of the total tonnage carried. The next 25 percent was generated by fourteen customers, and the third 25 percent came from eighty-two patrons. Only 2.53 percent of the shippers using these liners contributed 75 percent of the cargoes. Another line's experience was similar. On the route between northwest England and the Middle East, between 25 percent and 40 percent of the business originated with twelve shippers.[11]

It is significant that the Senate Committee on Commerce, in its report written in 1961 on the proposed amendment to the Shipping Act of 1916, quoted with approbation the comments of the Alexander Committee in 1914:

COMPANIA PERUANA DE VAPORES (CPV)
(Peruvian State Line)

We regret the decision by members of The West Coast of South America Conference to put into effect 7/8/85 a general rate increase of 8%, both north and southbound to and from Peru and Chile.

CPV considers this increase inopportune at this time and hereby wishes to notify its customers, shippers and freight forwarders that we have already notified the Conference we intend to take "independent action" to and from Peru and Chile with current rates.

We hope this action will induce members of the Conference to reconsider their position and decline the general rate increase.

A member takes independent action against an increase in conference freight rates (New York *Journal of Commerce,* June 18, 1985, p. 18-A).

It is the view of the committee that open competition cannot be assured for any length of time by ordering existing agreements terminated. The entire history of steamship agreements shows that in ocean commerce there is no happy medium between war and peace when several lines engage in the same trade. Most of the numerous agreements and conference arrangements discussed in the foregoing report were the outcome of rate wars, and represent a truce between the contending lines. To terminate existing agreements would necessarily bring about one of two results: the lines would either engage in rate wars which would mean elimination of the weak and the survival of the strong, or to avoid a costly struggle, they would consolidate through common ownership. Neither result can be prevented by legislation and either would mean a monopoly fully as effective [as], and it is believed more so than, can exist by virtue of an agreement.[12]

Three types of steamship conferences exist in the world today; closed conferences which apportion the capacity of their members' ships to the volume of cargo offered (rationalization); closed conferences which do not practice rationalization; and open conferences which do not limit capacity of member fleets. Only the United States requires as a matter of law that conferences admit to membership any common carriers prepared to serve the trade routes covered by the associations.

Proponents of the closed conferences with rationalization argue that it is only by limiting competition between carriers for the available business to a few dependable performers that the standards insisted upon by shippers will be maintained. Restricting membership in the conference to that number of carriers which will provide transportation for the proffered cargo is efficient and economical. Although conferences offer lower rates to those shippers who sign loyalty contracts, most of the cargo actually is controlled by a small number of shippers who are more concerned over the service they receive than with the relatively small saving afforded by the loyalty contracts. (In this connection, it is noteworthy that the Shipping Act of 1984 prohibits the use of loyalty contracts and dual freight rates.)

Records of two closed conferences which practiced rationalization and offered loyalty contracts supported these comments. Over a twenty-year period, marked by times of political instability and operational difficulties, load factors for these conference members came to almost 90 percent of capacity.

More common than the above-described conferences are the associations which have closed memberships, but do not attempt to rationalize tonnage. While freight rates and other matters governing transportation of goods are agreed upon jointly, conference members continue to compete with each other for the available cargo. From time to time, because of economic conditions, some restrictions may be imposed, such as sharing cargo tonnage, allocating ports to be served, and arranging schedules to enhance the efficiency of ship employment. These coordinated efforts, even without rationalization, have been beneficial. One conference, for instance, reported that over a span of five years its load factors ranged between 75 percent and 90 percent in one direction and between 85 percent and 92 percent in the other direction.[13]

Advocates of the closed conference recognize the desirability of having the concerns of the shippers given full consideration, and therefore recommend that so-called shippers' councils be formed to negotiate with the associated carriers. In support of their recommendation, these advocates point to the success of the Australian Meat Shippers' Council, which forced the conference covering the trade between Australia and the United States to lower its rates. A parallel case was that of the Australian wool-shipping interests which formed the Joint Wool Commodity Group, and exerted sufficient pressure on the Australian Northbound Shipping Conference to bring freight rates between Australia and Japan down by approximately 10 percent.[14]

The Australian Overseas Transportation Association is a major council whose functions are: (1) to obtain economies in shipping by rationalizing tonnage; (2) to approve freight rates; and (3) to approve agreements between shippers and shipowners. Loyalty contracts and rebates, discounts, and the like are permitted. Founded in 1929, the association includes producers and exporters. Boards having significant influence on conference matters are the Dairy Products Control Board, the Wine Overseas Marketing Board, and the Meat Board. The goal of the association when it was established was rationalization through cooperation, which left considerable strength in the hands of the shippers. The closed Australian conferences, based on strong loyalty contracts and rationalization with pooling of cargoes, have not led to the monopolistic abuses feared by some theorists.[15]

Under the closed conference system, internal pressure upon members is exerted to operate only that number of ships required to satisfy the demands of the trade. To maintain a certain frequency of service without putting additional ships on the berth, a number of conference members in recent years contracted for space in each other's vessels. Company Alfa, to cite a hypothetical case, sails on alternate Fridays, company Kappa schedules its departures on the same route for the intervening Fridays. Alfa has built up a strong clientele of loyal shippers who control a weekly total of 250 containers which they insist upon dispatching every Friday, but want the Alfa bill of lading and Alfa service at the port of discharge. To keep this business, Alfa contracts with Kappa for 250 container spaces on each sailing. (The transaction is known in the trade as "space chartering.") Alfa and Kappa retain their individuality. They do not merge any of their activities, nor do they reveal any carrier-shipper relationships. There is no reduction in intercompany and intraconference rivalry. The number of ships serving the trade route is maintained at the level which gives reasonable assurance of survival for conference members and forestalls disastrous freight rate wars. A significant, and certainly not coincidental, benefit is that the load factor of the conference members' ships is kept at satisfactory levels.

A British report on conferences contained these observations on the relative merits of open and closed conferences:

> ... the "open" conference appears least likely to serve the interests of shippers. It is also least likely to serve that of shipowners; in their evidence to us they agreed that such a conference arrangement typically resulted in low load factors, low profits, and rising freight rates. ...
>
> The "closed" conference with fully rationalized sailings therefore appears to us most likely to serve the best interests of both

shippers and shipowners. We appreciate that we have here come to
a different conclusion from those reached by some others who have
studied conference arrangements; we believe that they may have
given too little weight to the full range of the needs of shippers and
to the practical results of unrestricted competition in all fields other
than price. We identify the opportunity for providing a planned
systematic series of sailings as the feature of shipping conferences
which is potentially most beneficial. The full exploitation of that
opportunity requires a "closed" conference.[16]

Conferences which may be joined by any common carriers serving
the trade routes are precluded from setting up any restrictions on the number of ships or the total carrying capacity of vessels operated by conference
members. Agreement is reached on a common tariff of freight rates, and
some adjustments may be acceptable for sailing schedules. Competition
within the ranks of the conferences, however, remains keen, often manifesting itself in unilateral revocation of published freight rates for particular commodities.

Advocates of the open conference assert that competition between
carriers, held within the framework of the association, results in the lowest
cost of transportation and the highest levels of service. In theory, this may
be true, but in the harsh realm of ship management the theory loses vitality.
It is axiomatic that when too many ships seek too few cargoes, two results
are inevitable: the revenue to the ship will be reduced to the unprofitable
level, and the quality of service will suffer. Shippers have no institutional
loyalties, and use those vessels which meet their needs most effectively
without regard to previous performance. As has been noted repeatedly in
this volume, owners of cargo are concerned only that what they send across
the oceans shall arrive in good condition and on schedule. Whether the
carrier makes a profit or sustains a loss is not a matter of interest to either
shipper or consignee.

Conferences, especially those which are governed by the U.S. law
requiring open membership, have been losing their economic power for
decades, and no longer pose any threats to monopolize a trade. In 1953,
Daniel Marx, Jr., identified six factors which restricted the monopoly pow-
ers of the conference:

1. Intraconference competition.
2. Actual or potential competition from other lines which may or may
   not intend to join the conference.

3. Alternate sources of supply or markets.
4. Actual or potential competition from tramps.
5. The bargaining strength of shippers.
6. Government regulation or intervention.[17]

These factors still exert powerful constraints on the conferences. An important addition to Marx's list could be made in 1985. This was the significant competition from airlines, which have siphoned off a very large percentage of the highest paying cargo. The economic effect on the water-borne carriers has been to distort the time-honored rate structure under which the revenue from commodities that paid high freight rates actually subsidized the movement of those items which could not afford to pay the full cost of sea carriage. It is not an exaggeration to assert that this competition from the airlines has undermined permanently the financial stability of many steamship companies.

The Shipping Act of 1984 directed that all agreements of conferences domiciled in the United States contain these provisions: (1) a statement of the purpose of the association; (2) specific assurance that any common carrier serving the trade route would be admitted (or readmitted) to membership upon application; (3) permission for members to withdraw, upon reasonable notice to the conference, without penalty; (4) establishment of an independent neutral body to police the obligations of the conference and its members; (5) a mechanism for consultations to resolve intercarrier disputes other than by judicial process, and to cooperate with shippers to prevent and eliminate malpractice; (6) procedures to consider promptly shippers' requests and complaints; and (7) authorization for any conference member, upon advance notice of not more than ten days, to take independent action on any rate or service stipulated in the tariff filed with the Federal Maritime Commission.

In addition, the law specified that conferences might not issue loyalty contracts nor set up dual rate structures; that they could not make any refunds not provided for in the published tariffs, nor deny cargo space to any shipper who had filed a complaint or had patronized a competing carrier; and that they might not employ fighting ships or offer deferred rebates. Discrimination between shippers or ports also was categorically forbidden.

A change from established procedure ended the role of the Federal Maritime Commission in enforcing the law against conferences. Instead, the commission shall investigate reports of alleged malpractice, and if sufficient evidence is uncovered, shall refer the matter to the United States District Court of the District of Columbia for action. If the allegations are sustained, the district court could enjoin the conference(s) permanently against the questioned conduct. A carrier found in violation of the law or an order of the commission could be fined $5,000 per day for each violation. If the court determined that the violation(s) had taken place "willfully and knowingly," the penalty could be increased up to $25,000 per day per violation.

Experience with self-policing of the conference system by means of a neutral body had been favorable since the system was established on January 1, 1979, pursuant to a directive from the Federal Maritime Commission, with included these stipulations:

1. The basic agreement forming the conference must show how complaints against conference members are to be handled.
2. The self-policing body must have no relationship to the conference members, and must be able to examine, and to acquire, whatever information and documents it needs by making appropriate demands upon the carriers concerned.
3. There must be provision for adjudicating disputes and for levying penalties. Accused parties must be afforded the opportunity to rebut charges made against them.
4. The self-policing agency must file two reports each year with the Federal Maritime Commission.
5. The self-policing bodies may not limit the carriers they police from producing documents and information demanded by the Federal Maritime Commission, nor must the self-policing agency deny access by the commission to any data it may have accumulated in connection with an investigation.

In a clarifying statement, the commission announced that these "neutral bodies" would be expected to make "self-initiated, on-site investigations . . . regularly . . . into the activities of each member line." These investigations were to be handled

> with reasonable discretion, and did not have to be identical in nature. As a matter of normal routine, the agencies were to reveal the identities of complaining parties, but this would be waived in those circumstances that might encourage retaliation by or against members or . . . when it would unfairly prejudice the member's ability to rebut any material allegation made against it.

An example of the authority which was granted to a neutral body was set forth in a report published by the New York *Journal of Commerce* on September 15, 1983. A conference had contracted with a neutral body for policing service, and included in the agreement the power to assess fines. Acting on complaints, the neutral body determined that a carrier member had been guilty of malpractice (although the offense was not described, it was said to have involved rebates from the published freight tariffs), and assessed a fine of over $9 million.

Historically, there has been criticism that the conferences do not prevent disastrous freight rate wars. This charge is true. Numerous wars have occurred on all trade routes. One of the more interesting (and one of the longest) was the war between the United States/South and East Africa Conference and the Seas Shipping Company (operating under the trade name of Robin Line) from 1935 to 1937. This war started in June 1935 when Robin Line announced its entry into the South and East African trade, and applied for membership in the conference. The application was denied on the grounds that there already was sufficient conference tonnage available to meet the needs of the American shipping public. Robin persisted in its plans and announced sailings to South Africa. The conference replied by reducing rates, and in the course of the war, rates fell to $4 a ton, regardless of commodity. By 1937, all exclusive patronage contracts between shippers and the conference had expired. A major American automobile manufacturer was asked to renew its contract with the conference but was given no assurance concerning the level to which the rates would go at the end of the war. The manufacturer refused to sign the contract, and the conference retaliated by refusing to allot space to the automobiles of this shipper. The manufacturer appealed to the Robin Line for assistance, and an agreement was reached to transport the vehicles to South Africa for $8 a measurement ton. Robin Line also promised that after the war ended, the freight rate would be no higher than it had been in 1935. This had the effect of stifling further gains from the war, which came to an abrupt end on July 1, 1937. It was characterized throughout by bitterness on both sides. It is noteworthy that from the end of the war until the sale of Robin Line to other owners in 1955, there was no dual rate system in the South African conference.[18]

The introduction in 1969 and thereafter of new, very large, and extremely fast containerships on the routes from Japan, Hong Kong, and Taiwan to both Pacific and Atlantic coasts of the United States precipitated new rivalries which very nearly destroyed the entire conference structure in the Pacific. Containerships were placed in service as quickly as individual owners could take delivery, and in a short time a major problem of overtonnaging existed. The fierce struggle for available cargoes was characterized by rate cutting, secret rebating, and wholesale resignations from the conferences followed by recisions of the resignations when a modicum of agreement was established. As the volume of cargo dropped substantially during the worldwide business recession that began in 1971, turmoil on the route increased significantly, but under pressure from numerous governments a period of relative calm was reached in 1975. The transpacific trade has been plagued intermittently since then by a series of skirmishes between the carriers, precipitated again by adverse economic conditions in the entire Pacific basin. Several carriers were forced into bankruptcy, conference memberships were reduced, and sailing frequencies were curtailed. In mid-1985, some semblance of peace prevailed, but the basic difficulty of too many ships looking for too few cargoes persisted.

An insight into the actions and reactions involved in a freight rate war was granted by the extensive hearings conducted by the Federal Maritime Commission into the friction between the American-flag Grace Line and the foreign-flag Viking Line during 1960 and 1961. The commission's findings were not made public until November 1962. The following excerpt is revealing:

> When Conference rates were opened, it was the policy of Grace not merely to meet Viking's rate, but to go down immediately to the minimum rate which Grace considered it could charge. Thus when rates were opened, Grace's rates were not decreased by stages but generally in one big cut.
>
> The Conference rate, effective on and after December 14, 1955, on agricultural implements, was $27 per ton. It was opened March 7, 1960 and Grace made its rate $12 on that date. Viking's rate prior to the rate war was $24 except for one shipment at $20.25 early in 1960. On household washing machines, the normal Conference rate of $20 was opened with a minimum of $15, effective February 22, 1960, which was the rate Grace made effective on that date. The Conference opened the rate without any minimum effective March 7, 1960, and Grace's rate on that date became $11. Viking's rate prior to that date was $18. On toys, with a value of less than $350 a freight ton, Viking normally charged $31.50 and the Conference charged $35. During August 1960, both Viking and Grace charged $13.50. Grace intended to go as low as Viking's breakeven point in setting its rates, but even such low rates were

met, and Grace went to even lower rates. On individual rates, both Grace and Viking undoubtedly reached noncompensatory levels.

When the rate war ended, although many rates went up to normal, others, while raised, did not rise to their previous levels. Commitments to shippers kept some rates from returning all the way up to their normal levels. Viking's policy during the rate war was to cut its rates, so long as it obtained enough revenue to cover loading, discharging, and commissions, plus "something for the ship," such as $1 or $2 a ton.[19]

The rate war lasted throughout 1960, in which year there was a major decline in trade with Venezuela. The war gradually ended early in 1961, and all rates slowly increased during that year.

Every discussion of conferences stresses that they give stable rates to the shipping public. This beneficial result is obtained in part from the conferences' practice of making rates which all members are able to accept. Reaching agreements on rates often is a tedious process, and during these discussions the shipping public gains from the status quo being maintained. Furthermore, proposed rate changes must be filed with the Federal Maritime Commission, and advance notice of intended increases in rates must be given to concerned parties.

As a normal function, conferences from time to time initiate reviews of their rate structures, usually as a result of developments which necessitate earning greater revenues. Typical of this situation was the drastic rise in the cost of bunker fuel oil in 1973, which most conferences countered by adding a surcharge to the rates. Shippers do not have to wait for this kind of conference action to have rates examined; they may submit applications for adjustments in freight rates at any time. These requests are handled by the rate committee, composed of a small group of traffic experts appointed by the conference chairman from the membership. The shipper furnishes data relating to the value of the commodity, its selling price at point of importation, the price of competing articles offered on the same market, the number of tons of the commodity that the shipper exports (or imports) in a year, and the freight rate suggested by the shipper as fair and reasonable. Comparison of this information with similar data supplied by the statistical section of the conference staff leads to a recommendation from the committee to the whole conference. If the recommendation is approved the change must be forwarded to the Federal Maritime Commission for filing. Eventually, new pages showing the revised rates are published and distributed to holders of the conference tariff.

Conferences have sustained a number of misfortunes in recent years in addition to pressures from shipper organizations such as those in Australia. The overtonnaging of trade routes is a worldwide problem, and as already mentioned has resulted in the withdrawals from membership of several carriers. Freight rate wars have become almost cyclical in the more important trade routes, a situation not ameliorated by the growing use of intermodal routings, especially those overland movements competing with the all-water transportation of goods to or from the Orient to the Atlantic and Gulf coasts of the United States, as well as to European destinations.

Whereas it may have been true earlier in the twentieth century that conference carriers dominated, but did not monopolize, the major trade routes of the world, the situation has changed significantly. Economic pressures caused by the prolonged recession which has afflicted the shipping of all nations since 1973 have forced many carriers either to suspend operations or to sell out to larger and stronger organizations. The enormous increase in the cost of building and operating containerships encouraged the formation of consortia of carriers. Space chartering between carriers which otherwise are intense rivals proved to be another way for individual carriers to maintain frequency of service without the necessity of operating ships carrying only partial loads. Rerouting vessels to one or two ports at each end of the route, and increasing use of feeder ships, has made possible reductions in fleet sizes. International balances of payments and overvalued currencies created unbalanced movements in which vessel revenue was derived disproportionately from one direction, rather than from the round voyage. None of these actions and problems, it should be noted, was exclusive to conference members.

It remains true, however, that conferences serve a useful purpose. They still attract members from the stable group of carriers, and they continue to set and to maintain standards of service which are desired by shippers. If they ever posed a threat to monopolize the movement of cargo on trade routes, that day has passed into history, and conferences today are more likely to be seeking ways to assure that their members will survive the difficult period which has overtaken them. That they can and do perform a useful role has been demonstrated in the past, and it seems that, as they march into the second century of their existence, they will continue to provide certain standards of conduct and service which will be welcomed by those who use the seas.

CHAPTER SIXTEEN

The Logic of Steamship Scheduling

To those who frequent the waterfront of any major port city, a special thrill is to see one of the huge containerships come into her berth precisely on time. Equally exciting is to watch the departure of the proud queen of the seas exactly at the advertised hour. What appears to be a simple, almost routine process involving a minor amount of calculation actually is a complex exercise in coordinated management. To pierce the veil normally masking the details of this activity is essential if this phase of ship operation is to be appreciated.

Drawing up a schedule for a steamship service is much more than establishing the time at sea between ports by dividing the number of miles to be traveled by the speed of the ship, and then adding enough hours to unload and reload the vessel. The determination of the basic rules to be followed in a liner-service schedule requires a combination of empirical knowledge and interpretive ability. Managers experienced in the ways of ships and ports and the vagaries of the sea collaborate with those who are wise in the ways of traffic and can convert the demands of shippers into the practicalities of ship operation. Their common goal is to meet the needs of shippers while achieving efficient and profitable employment of the fleet.

Schedules are inseparable from the idea of liner service. One or more ships plying a fixed route and making port calls at regular intervals provide the transportation essential to the commercial enterprise of the region. In time, if the ship movements have been dependable over a protracted period, shippers come to expect that vessels always will be available according to the established pattern, and any disruption in that pattern upsets their business practices. Merchants are especially concerned that the ships sail on the advertised day because many international trade transactions are financed by letters of credit stipulating that the goods be dispatched no later than a certain date. Failure to meet this requirement can interfere with the financing of the deal.

In particular, therefore, the more frequently a fleet can offer a sailing, the more likely it will be to gain the good will of shippers and prosper from their patronage. This premise is valid so long as there is no question concerning the time the goods spend in transit.

The Blue Seas Line, for a hypothetical example, owns a number of 20-knot ships. One of the routes it serves is between Landport and Seahaven, which are separated by 4,800 miles of ocean. The vessels traverse the distance in ten days, and require four days in each port to discharge and reload. The aggregate of these times is exactly four weeks. A fortnightly service is maintained, using two cargo liners. If a shipper is exceedingly fortunate in timing the movement of the cargo, it is possible for the goods to arrive at the loading berth only a few hours before the ship sails, and to be discharged at Seahaven on arrival day, so that the transit time of the goods is ten days. Another shipper, however, misses the sailing from Landport by a matter of hours, and the goods must wait two weeks for the next departure. This consignment is the first loaded aboard the ship, and the last to be discharged. Not only must the goods wait fourteen days, but at Seahaven they will not be released until the end of the two days needed to empty the ship. Total transit time for this lot of cargo is twenty-six days (fourteen days of waiting, ten days of steaming, and two days for discharge). Blue Seas Line's customers must be prepared to accept a maximum transit time of twenty-six days, but can obtain a minimum of ten days. If no objections are voiced by shippers, management would be correct in assuming that the service offered within these limits is adequate.

As cargo offerings improve, Blue Seas Line assigns a total of four ships to the route, making possible weekly departures from both termini. Maximum transit time is reduced to nineteen days (seven days of waiting, ten days of steaming, and two days for discharging) while the minimum transit time is maintained at ten days. Although each ship earns a small profit, there is space available for additional cargo. Calls therefore are ordered at Harborside and Transitown, which lie on the direct route to Seahaven and require no increase in steaming time. At Harborside, a day and a half are used to handle the cargo, while at Transitown working the cargo takes two full days. The duration of the round trip has been lengthened to thirty-five days. To continue to provide weekly sailings, Blue Seas must place a fifth ship on the route.

The new schedule challenges management with two significant problems. The first is the complaint of the shippers that, although weekly departures are available, transit time has been increased by the calls at Harborside and Transitown. The minimum now is $13\frac{1}{2}$ days, compared to ten formerly, and maximum transit time has been extended from nineteen to $24\frac{1}{2}$ days. For those exporters who are paid on delivery of their goods to the importers, the additional time represents a significant economic burden. Management concedes that the service offered by Blue Seas Line between Landport and Seahaven is no longer adequate for the needs of the shippers.

The second problem is comparable in magnitude. The tonnage of cargo offered on the route did not increase despite the fact that to maintain weekly departures on the route by way of Harborside and Transitown, it was necessary to assign a fifth ship to what economically is a four-ship service. If freight rates are raised to the point where all ships earn a profit, there is great likelihood that the higher charges will force some shippers to withdraw from the market. If ship revenues are not augmented, however, the company will be pushed into a money-losing operation.

The requirement originally presented by the shippers for a weekly service was justified by the additional cargo revenue that resulted. Attempting to enhance ship earning power by adding the calls at Harborside and Transitown undermined the adequacy of the service and imposed heavy financial burdens on the carrier. While it was technically possible to have the ships call at the two intermediate ports, the decision proved to be faulty because it did not adequately consider the impact on the shippers of the longer transit time.

The first step in making a schedule is to convert the broad statements of what is desired by the traffic department into: the particulars of how many tons of cargo must be handled in terminal ports and in primary and secondary ports of call, the physical characteristics of the ports of call which affect the movements of ships into and out of their water, the hours during which these ports provide cargo working arrangements, and critical times of arrival of the ships at certain intermediate primary ports. As these details are assembled and appropriately related to the expressed desires of the traffic department, the outline of the schedule begins to emerge. Many suggestions will be put forward as the various versions of tentative schedules are examined. Of major importance to the operating department is the designation by the traffic experts of the primary ports along the route which will be visited on every trip outbound and homebound, and what ports will be considered as secondary, to be served only when sufficient cargo is offered to justify the expense of the call.

Secondary ports present a problem to the liner service that is operated with little spare time in its schedules. If, for example, calls are made at three primary ports en route, and turnaround time at the outbound terminus is to be accomplished in forty-eight hours, a six-hour call at a secondary port can be troublesome. One solution lies in the operational and traffic histories of the line. If calls at one or more secondary ports have been included on every voyage, it is good management to provide sufficient time for those visits. This arrangement will eliminate the unavoidable disruption to schedules which must follow unprogrammed demands on ship time. Another solution is to develop the schedule at a cruising speed that can be increased as necessary to compensate for the time required to make the calls at the secondary ports. In either instance, the value of close coordination between the operating and traffic departments is evident.

Cargo ships are designed to operate at a certain speed, and barring unusual events beyond the control of the owner or of the master, will be run at that speed. No allowance is made for the possibility of unfavorable weather interfering with the completion of the appointed voyage, unless there are reliable data showing that at certain seasons of the year it is impossible to maintain maximum speed. This is true for those vessels assigned to year-round service on the North Atlantic, where winter storms reach fantastic dimensions, and require significant reductions in speed. In other regions, for example along the southeastern coast of South Africa, winter storms make slow speeds necessary if major damage to vessels is to be avoided. In still other areas, such as the Caribbean Sea and the Gulf of Mexico, weather is usually excellent but the threat of hurricanes is known to all who voyage in those waters. They are, however, unpredictable in every way: when they will occur, where they will reach dangerous dimensions, what course they will follow, and how long they will menace the sea-lanes. Operators sending ships into those areas have found over the decades that they can meet the problem best by alertness and flexibility at the time the storm approaches. If a hurricane delays a voyage for several days, this is an isolated phenomenon that does not justify altering schedules for the duration of the hurricane season.

A basic rule in making schedules, therefore, is that the ships will be operated at designated speeds, and from sea buoy at the port of departure to sea buoy at the port of arrival, the performance of the ship will be up to standard.

Next in order of consideration, and complicated by their variability, are the type and tonnage of cargo to be transported over the entire length of the intended voyage. Not all items moving by sea can be handled with the same rapidity (computed in tons per hour): cotton bales are stowed aboard ship at one speed, while agricultural machinery is placed in the hold at a markedly different pace. Similarly, elevators in New Orleans deliver grain to ships at a very great number of tons per hour, but in India the laborers shovel it out at an agonizingly slow tempo. The variety of commodities, the

Automobiles, palletized break-bulk cargo, heavy equipment, and roll-on/roll-off cargo move in two directions over this huge ramp of a modern multipurpose cargo liner. Photograph courtesy of Barber Blue Sea.

quantity of each, the skill and rapidity with which the stevedore performs, and the ability of a designated berth to handle the flow of break-bulk cargo are vital pieces of information on which to base the forecast of time needed in each port of call. The accurate determination of what will be carried, and in what quantity, is a factor in developing the schedule. Study of current and past manifests of actual loads carried in the ships assigned to the route provide much of this essential information. Supplementing these data will be the traffic department's estimates of anticipated trends in cargo movement, by commodities and ports of loading and discharge, and often by seasons of the year.

The transformation of these data into a proposed sailing schedule is accomplished by the combination of the accrued experience and pragmatic wisdom of shipmasters, terminal superintendents, and stevedores who have worked with these goods, ships, and ports, and know what can be accomplished at every point where the ship calls. The importance of accuracy in fixing the number of hours needed to unload the inbound cargo and to take aboard the outbound tonnage cannot be overestimated in the break-bulk trades, where performance of longshoremen varies greatly from port to port. Errors in the estimate of time needed to turn the ship around are cumulative and can disrupt the regularity that is the essence of liner service.

To establish a workable schedule that will assure maximum performance for the big, fast, and very expensive containerships now operated on major trade routes between industrialized countries is at least as crucial to ultimate profitability of the steamship enterprise as it is in the break-bulk trades. The aggregate hourly costs of these huge carriers come to hundreds of dollars and delays, other than those occasionally and unpredictably arising from causes beyond human control, are intolerable.

Few, if any, of these vessels are what the trade calls "self-sustaining," meaning equipped with cranes to handle the containers in which their cargo is loaded. The critical element in setting up the port working schedule is the availability of dockside cranes to lift the containers off and on the ships. This is especially true for those ships that transport upwards of four thousand 20-foot boxes and require from two to five cranes for optimum dispatch. To bring two ships into a berthing area where there is space for only one, or where insufficient cranes are available, is economically unacceptable practice, and every effort must be made to assure that this type of mistake does not occur.

Schedule makers for containerships may be free from concern about the capability of individual gangs of longshoremen and the difficulties of stowing certain commodities in a break-bulk ship, but in exchange they must assume the burden of coordinating the port time of the ships with the complex operation of the container terminal. Weather plays little part in the planning, inasmuch as the containers themselves are weatherproofed. Responsibility for the multiplicity of detail relating to terminal operation belongs to the terminal superintendent, who must inform the schedule makers of every factor which must be given particular attention in setting the final timetable.

An aspect of scheduling which affects the operations of containerships is the trend toward intermodal transportation. In addition to the constraints encountered as a routine part of schedule making by other types of marine carriers, schedules for ships that carry hundreds of containers destined for intermodal connections in mini-landbridge or landbridge services must be planned in conjunction with those of rail and motor carriers. This means that the containership schedule makers must communicate and develop relationships with their counterparts in the other modes of transportation. It is axiomatic that scheduling by all concerned with transporting cargo routed as an intermodal movement is complicated manyfold by the requirement that each of the connecting modes must coordinate their arrivals and departures and that all carriers must be on time.

The structure and equipment of break-bulk carriers require special consideration from the scheduling team. Few fleets in the merchant service consist of identical vessels; far more likely is the heterogeneous collection of ships built in different yards to different plans, and often intended for trades different from those in which they are now employed. The individual characteristics of these ships have profound influence upon the rapidity with which longshoremen can handle the cargo, whether they are loading or unloading.

In the hypothetical Blue Seas Line, the common characteristic of the ships was their 20-knot speed. It would be realistic to imagine that two of the five ships assigned to sail between Landport and Seahaven had six hatches, each rigged with two sets of cargo booms, and equipped with high-speed winches. The other three ships had seven hatches, five of which had individual fast-acting cranes, while the No. 1 and No. 7 hatches each had one conventional mast and boom assembly. At first glance it would appear that the rapidity with which cargo could be handled would differ significantly between the types of ships. Experience brought out the fact that all worked cargo at about the same speed. This important information would facilitate greatly the development of the timetable for the fleet.

Despite the remarkable success of naval architects in giving a balance of cargo-handling capability to all hatches in a break-bulk ship, the age-old problem of the "limiting hatch" or "long hatch" has not been eliminated. To some extent, the difficulty of having more cargo in one hold than in any other is structural, and to some extent it is the result of the quantity or characteristics of the cargo stowed in a hatch. The Liberty ships had one disproportionately large hatch, and if the whole load were to be taken off in one port, the working schedule for the ship had to be keyed to the big hatch. The time in port was determined by that one hatch. Those who plan the loading of ships attempt to distribute cargo throughout the ship to mitigate the impact of the limiting hatch. Their efforts are an outgrowth of the number of hours allotted to each port.

Containerships affcct timetables through the complexity of the terminal operation that must support them. When a number of ports of call must be considered by the schedule makers, the actual experience of the ships becomes of paramount importance in seeking the most efficient employment of the vessel's time. Ideally, all terminal operations are standardized, and only minor deviation from approved activities should occur. In practice, many variances from the ideal are encountered for a large number of reasons. Routine analyses of terminals along the route are supplied to the schedule makers in order that adequate, but not excessive, time be assigned to each port. Although it is economically imperative that the ship get to sea as quickly as good management and proper care of the cargo will permit, it is equally important to control the movement of the containership to assure that there will be a berth at the next port, and that the terminal will be ready in every respect to service the ship on her arrival.

Despite the mechanization of the terminal which has accompanied the introduction of containerships on the principal trade routes, local labor customs and working hours must be respected by schedule makers in precisely the same way that they are for the break-bulk ships. For example, in the port of New York, work may be continued through the meal hour, provided the longshoremen are paid penalty overtime wages. In the observance of Labor Day, however, the holiday is complete, and only in the direst of emergencies will people report for work. Longshoremen in certain foreign ports will not work during the meal hour regardless of the financial inducement, but will violate holidays for premium compensation.

Calculating the length of time the ship must spend in port to work her cargo is a major challenge in making liner-service schedules. The ship earns no revenue for her owners while in port, and therefore every effort must be made to reduce this unproductive period. The rapidity with which cargo is worked by longshoremen varies from port to port, and often from terminal to terminal within a port. The more the schedule makers know about the cargo and the workers, the more closely can they estimate the hours required to unload or load the ship. Other time factors that must be considered are related to the movements of the ship: Is tide significant in assuring that the ship can use the channels? When do pilots work? What restrictions apply after dark?

Underlying the idea of liner service, whether by break-bulk or container-carrying ships, is regularity—the dependable arrivals and departures of ships at the ports listed in the itinerary and the timetables. To assure this regularity, many expedients are practiced. The amount of cargo accepted for a port may be limited to the quantity which can be handled in the time allotted for the call. For example, the break-bulk ship works cargo at the rate of 50 tons per hour and is scheduled to spend only fourteen hours in port. To maintain the schedule, a maximum of 700 tons will be booked into and out of that port. Again, the ship may be worked around the clock on the theory that overtime wages are less costly than ship time. Improving port turnaround means more voyages per year for the ship, and hence greater revenue will be earned. Intimately related to this is the fact that in many instances two fast ships can do the work of three slower vessels. The economy to the shipowner is obvious.

Certain assumptions must be made as the plan for steamship service is converted into the reality of the schedule. These assumptions are predicated upon the experience of the shipowner in operation of seagoing vessels, and are intended to achieve the dependability that is implicit in liner service.

First, it is assumed that the vessels in the schedule will be operated at designated speeds and their performance will be up to standard. It is incumbent, therefore, that the company provide the ship with all the necessary parts and materials to maintain the vessel properly.

Then, it is assumed that the cargo liner will be loaded with a representative variety of goods, stowed according to the line's approved stevedoring practices. This representative load will be based upon analysis of cargo manifests of enough voyages to define the trends in commodity movements.

Next, it is assumed that ports of call, and the sequence in which they are visited, will remain unaltered during the projected lifetime of the timetable. Working conditions in each of these ports are considered to be stable and not subject to significant change.

Then, it is assumed that port operations will not be disrupted by strikes, riots, or civil commotion, and that there will be no major breakdowns of cargo-handling equipment in the ports.

Finally, no allowance is made for unfavorable weather because of the unpredictability of storms and their intensity, or the effect they might have on port cargo operations.

It is important to note that ship schedules reflect those facts which affect the practicality of the ship's movements. Pertinent, therefore, is the analysis of harbor depths and the range of the tides. If a port of call can be navigated only at high tide, the schedule must be sufficiently flexible to accept the unavoidable variations in arrival and departure times. The flexibility may be assured by including an adequate number of unprogrammed hours, and authorizing the master to adjust speeds to assure arrival at high tide. This same device may be used in connection with sailing times, depending upon the problems that may be confronted at the next port. If several ports of call are affected in this manner by the tides, failure to make appropriate allowance for the changes in the hours of high tide can lead to total disarray of schedules.

Some ports have strict rules about the hours when ships may move within the limits of the harbor. In Capetown, for instance, pilotage from the sea buoy into the ship's berth is compulsory and is available only during daylight hours. Pilots take the ships from the sea buoy in strict observance of their times of arrival—first come, first served. Some shipowners, in the effort to avoid long delays, plan arrivals well before dawn, even if this means an excessive consumption of fuel oil because of the high speed required.

Longshoremen observe different working hours from port to port. These idiosyncracies must be taken into account in preparing the schedule, so that adequate time will be allowed to handle the cargo. Some of these local peculiarities involve no night work, no work on Saturdays after five o'clock in the evening, lunch hours extending from eleven o'clock in the morning until one o'clock in the afternoon, and no work during certain religious holidays.

Holiday work, when local custom permits it, offers some problems for ship operators. Much of the commercial activity of the port is suspended; consequently no cargo is delivered to the terminal or taken away. Supporting services (tugs, heavy-lift cranes, shifting of lighters) must be arranged in advance and are very expensive. Many longshoremen, often the best workers, elect not to report for work, and overall efficiency is reduced. It is, therefore, routine for schedule makers to adjust schedules for individual voyages to avoid having ships in port over holidays.

Break-bulk cargo liner service, concerned as it is with handling thousands of tons of hundreds of commodities, requires somewhat flexible schedules. It is not unusual for a ship to be considered as being on time if she arrives during working hours on the scheduled day, regardless of what time had been set in the schedule for her docking. This is accepted practice during those seasons of the year when the final two or three days of the voyage may be spent fighting storms which slow the ship. A realistic schedule will include an allowance of time to assure departure at approximately the advertised hour. If these liner-service vessels sail at intervals of two or three weeks, no serious difficulties result from these unavoidable delays. Shorter intervals call for managerial attention to prevent port congestion of the company's fleet.

Delays in themselves may not be especially serious, particularly when they are only of two or three hours' duration. In their cumulative effect on fleet operations, however, they may cause numerous difficulties, not least of which is the overlapping of schedules. This overlapping, known as "bunching," is the obvious and cumulative result of a number of delays (or "slips") along the route. Ships of a single fleet which have bunched up in a port overtax the facilities available to the operator and may cause at least one ship to miss her next outward sailing from the home port.

To prevent bunching is one of the major objectives of schedule makers. Depending upon the relative importance to the carrier of the outbound and homeward trades, and the cargo commitments made, it may be possible to compensate for lost time by omitting ports on one leg of the voyage. Speeding up cargo operations is practical only to a certain extent, especially if port time already has been figured at approximately the maximum capability of ship and port. It is not always possible to transship cargo to avoid the necessity of calling at smaller ports.

Throughout this discussion of schedule making, there has been no mention of the effect on the schedule of the operational necessity to make repairs and to put ships into drydock at periodic intervals. Routine voyage repairs are accomplished while the ship is in port on her regular schedule. The proper performance of this work within the allotted port time is supervised by the staff of the superintendents of the deck, engineering, and catering departments. Drydockings for normal hull inspection and repainting are set months in advance, and adjustments are made to permit the ship to be withdrawn from what otherwise would be normal port activity for the relatively short period required in drydock. As the vessel gets older, and the magnitude of repairs increases, it may become mandatory to set aside several successive days for the required work. This presents no insurmountable problem so long as it can be foreseen and appropriately scheduled. Emergency repairs are effected on an emergency basis, and any changes brought about as a result are made in the most satisfactory manner possible.

Schedules for voyages of tramp ships in the dry-cargo trades are predicated upon the same considerations that govern schedule making for cargo liners. The major difference is that no repetitious trips have to be taken into account for vessels on single-voyage charters. Time chartered vessels, if employed on the same route for the duration of the charter, are handled as though they were cargo liners. If they are assigned to different voyages during the life of the charter, the planning would be the same as that for single-voyage chartered ships.

Tanker schedules follow much the same routine as do those of cargo liners, except that often the ship does not repeat a voyage immediately. The schedule may be made for a number of single voyages within the framework of employment over a period of several months. Since tanker cargoes are liquid and are pumped rather than handled by longshoremen, that aspect of scheduling is eliminated. In its stead are substituted several problems peculiar to tankers: the location of the tanks into which the cargo is to be pumped (i.e., the distance and gradient of the pipeline through which the oil must be pumped by the force of the ship's equipment); the diameter of the pipes (i.e., the quantity of oil which can be moved in a given period); and the season of the year, because heat or cold affects the speed with which the liquid flows through the pipes. Port time for tankers always is set in terms of hours, and much effort is expended to turn the ships around within the limited time.

When one considers the extent of the sea routes, the variations in winds and currents, the almost complete lack of uniformity in the methods of handling ships in different ports of the world, and the amazing amount of detail that must be taken into account in making up the schedule, it is remarkable, and a credit to the schedule makers, that the ships come into port and depart as near to the predicted hour as they do.

CHAPTER SEVENTEEN

Scheduling and Bunkering

Once the owner decides on the employment of a ship, it is necessary immediately to develop a sailing schedule which shows the date of departure, the ports of call and the dates and times when those calls will be made, and the anticipated time of arrival at the destination. In direct support of this schedule is a "bunkering plan," which must be formulated to show where the ship will replenish her fuel supplies and the quantities to be taken aboard from the suppliers named in the plan. The bunkering plan is the result of studying the fuel needs of the vessel, her earning capability, the availability and cost of fuel in ports along the route, and the cost in ship time to take on fuel in the selected outport(s). The planning studies also take into account the requirements for the safety of the ship imposed by international treaties, the regulations imposed by a number of quasi-official bodies, and the insistence of the owner that the voyage return a profit (or, in bad times, that the losses be kept to a minimum).

For the operator or charterer of tramp ships, preparing the bunkering plan is basic to the computations preceding every proposed voyage, and is related directly to the earning power of the vessel. This is especially noticeable when the commodity to be transported is heavy (dense), and every ton of fuel means one less ton of revenue cargo.

In stabilized liner service, in which the needs of the ship can be predicted accurately, the bunkering plan becomes a standard routine to be followed voyage after voyage.

The sailing schedule reflects the owner's decisions about where the ship is to go and becomes the foundation of the voyage. Until these decisions are converted into definite movements over a selected route, with certain ports to be visited for a predetermined number of hours, no estimates can be made as to the fuel needs of the ship, and no recommendations can be offered as to the most desirable refueling points. The bunkering plan (which automatically becomes the bunkering schedule when it is approved) supports the voyage program by specifying where refueling is to be effected.

If economic considerations justify the action, and the sailing schedule can be adjusted to allow the time for the call, the ship may be sent to a port for the sole purpose of taking on fuel. If, however, the schedule is rigid, and adherence to the advertised timetable is of paramount importance, the choice of fueling points must be limited to those ports to which the ship already is committed to accomplish the purpose of the voyage. Whatever the circumstances, every voyage of a powered vessel depends upon both the sailing and the bunkering schedules. Coordination is essential between the traffic department, which must please the customers, the operating department, which seeks optimum performance from the ships, and the treasurer's department, which looks for a profit from the ship's employment.

Speed is a tangible asset to steamship operators, but there are definite limits to the amount of speed that can be offered to shippers. To increase service speed, not only must the power plant be enlarged (to double the speed requires eight times the horsepower), but the entire hull design has to be changed to permit the vessel to move efficiently through the water. When to these considerations is added the necessity to find space for the larger engine installation and tankage to carry the greater quantity of fuel oil, some of the complexities of speed become apparent.

Schedules, whether for a new service or to modify an existing ship operation, are the product of coordinated activity often involving the highest levels of management. When a tentative schedule is submitted for approval, affirmative answers must be forthcoming to these questions:

1. Does the proposed schedule meet existing or anticipated competition? Have the demands of shippers for minimum transit time been measured against the capabilities and performance of competing carriers?
2. Does the proposed schedule reflect improvement (or correct deficiencies) in cargo-working capabilities of the ports along the route? As part of the inquiry, cognizance must be taken of the status of programs to install labor- and time-saving equipment, and to negotiate better working hours (from the viewpoint of saving ship time) with labor groups.
3. Does the proposed schedule take into consideration those factors adversely affecting efficient operation? Is there congestion from too many ships attempting to work cargo at the same time through inadequate port facilities? Are alternative ports available?
4. Does the proposed schedule make the best use of the ship's speed and cargo-working characteristics? The cost of speed must be con-

The ore-bulk-oil carrier *Eric R. Fernstrom* (built 1971), 101,850 tons deadweight, receives diesel fuel from two barges. Photographs by Jeff Blinn, courtesy of Moran Towing Co.

sidered in the schedule, but at the same time the earning power of the ship cannot be overlooked. The cardinal rule is that every aspect of the proposed employment of the ship must contribute positively to her revenue-earning potential. The application of this rule is exemplified by this hypothetical situation. Dawn arrival will assure no delay in working cargo. To achieve this arrival, it is necessary to set a speed exceeding that which results in most economical operation. The final decision therefore involves consideration of the cost of ship's time, the convenience of shippers and consignees, the competitive advantage, and the impact on the whole voyage.

5. Is the maximum economy, consistent with the requirements of the service, achieved by the cruising speeds necessary to maintain the schedule? Has the earning potential of the vessel been measured against the proposed procurement plan for fuel to be taken aboard during the voyage?

Formulating the bunkering plan after the tentative sailing schedule has been approved includes consideration of these rules:

1. Every bunkering plan must comply in all respects with international load-line treaties and also with the requirements of marine insurance underwriters concerning reserves of fuel oil.
2. The bunkering plan must assure the maximum earning power of the ship. (This applies with particular force to tramp shipping and to the full shipload transportation of any commodity which, per ton, weighs as much as, or more than, the fuel.)
3. The ship may not deviate significantly from her assigned route solely to acquire fuel at a low price. (Deviation usually involves actually departing from the prescribed course.) Fuel normally is procured in the most satisfactory ports along the established route.
4. Before the ship is ordered to a specific port to take on fuel, the provider must give assurance that supplies are adequate to meet the needs of the ship.

Compliance with load-line requirements is basic to any bunkering plan, under penalty of having the ship declared unseaworthy. Without attempting to trace the history of the load-line agreements in detail, suffice it to recall that in 1875 Samuel Plimsoll, a member of the British Parliament, led a successful campaign to require ships to bear markings on their sides showing the depth to which they could be loaded safely in various areas of the world and seasons of the year. These rules in time became international conventions and the world now is divided into zones designated by the self-explanatory terms of tropical, seasonal tropical, summer, and seasonal winter. There is a further marking to allow for the difference in the buoyancy of fresh and salt water. These markings are determined to give greater freeboard to vessels facing the increasing hazards of the sea as the seasons change. (Ships of not more than 100 meters (328 feet) in length are required to have a special load line for voyages into the North Atlantic in winter. This line appears on the sides of these small vessels with the distinguishing letters WNA, for Winter North Atlantic.)

American shipowners were placed under the obligations of the International Load Line Convention of 1930 when the Congress ratified the agreement in 1931. The actual load lines are determined by the classification societies when the designs are submitted for their approval. Enforcement of load line regulations in the United States has been assigned to the U.S. Coast Guard. Courts of law have held repeatedly that overloading makes a ship unseaworthy. The owner is deprived of any legal protection for loss or damage sustained by an unseaworthy vessel. Marine underwriters have resisted successfully any claims for restitution of loss when a ship

> # IMPORTANT NOTICE TO
> # CONTRACT SIGNATORIES
> ## BUNKER SURCHARGE
>
> The Member Lines of the U.S. Atlantic & Gulf/Australia-New Zealand Conference wish to advise the shipping public that the previously announced Bunker Surcharge of 20% per revenue ton due to become effective December 15, 1981 has been reduced to 18%.
>
> The Conference has also published further precautionary increases which will be subject to review and adjustment based on actual cost experience.
>
> Schedule of Surcharges follows:
>
> | | |
> |---|---|
> | January 15, 1981 | 20% Per Revenue Ton |
> | February 15, 1982 | 22% Per Revenue Ton |
> | March 15, 1982 | 25% Per Revenue Ton |

has been loaded deeper than the assigned marks and thereby has been rendered unseaworthy.

When a vessel crosses from one zone to another, as in the case of a ship going from New Orleans to Liverpool in December, she must be loaded so that when she crosses the winter zone line, she will meet the prescribed limits. Arrival in Liverpool with a draft exactly at the winter load line would be prima facie evidence that she had less than the mandatory freeboard when she entered the zone. The most scrupulous observance of applicable load lines and zone areas is required of all those involved in determining how much cargo is to be put into a ship.

For example, a tanker is assigned to a voyage from Bahrain Island, in the Arabian Gulf, to Galway, Ireland, sailing on December 15. Bahrain Island is in the tropical summer zone; the Mediterranean is in the seasonal summer zone; and the Atlantic, from Gibraltar to Galway, lies in the seasonal winter zone. Because fuel prices are lowest in Bahrain Island, the ship is to bunker there for the entire voyage. The tanker's load therefore must be adjusted so that when she clears Port Said for Gibraltar, she will be at the summer load line. If fuel consumption between Port Said and Gibraltar does not lighten the ship sufficiently to meet the winter load line, then the cargo load must be reduced by the difference between the allowed deadweight and the actual deadweight. The voyage planners have constructed the bunkering schedule so that as each load-line zone is entered, the ship will comply with the international rules.

Another aspect of the demands for safety of life at sea is the underwriters' mandate that all ships carry a reserve supply of fuel equal to not less than approximately one-quarter of the fuel to be burned between scheduled ports of call. This means that a vessel proceeding from New York to Panama cannot carry just enough fuel to reach her destination plus 25 percent of the amount needed from New York to some intermediate, but unscheduled, port where fuel is obtainable. The ship must take on 125 percent of what will be consumed on the passage to Panama. If she is fueled in New York for the round trip voyage, she would carry enough oil for the trip plus 25 percent of the amount needed from Panama back to New York.

The second rule in drawing up the bunkering plan is to assure the maximum earning power of the ship. This requires not only a knowledge of the ship's routing, the possible ports where oil may be purchased, and the load-line restrictions, but also awareness of the freight rate payable per ton of cargo loaded, the daily costs of the ship in addition to fuel, and the characteristics of the cargo being transported. In liner service, it is generally true that what is carried is bulky and fills the ship's holds before the vessel is down to her load line. Bunkering in this type of operation involves selection of the ports along the route where fuel can be obtained in adequate quantity at a good price without delaying the ship. Tramp ships often carry commodities which, per ton, weigh at least as much as fuel oil. Every ton of fuel put aboard the ship which exceeds the anticipated requirements therefore reduces the potential profit by the revenue from one ton of cargo.

When the great expense of owning and operating a ship is appreciated, the reason for the third rule in preparing the bunkering plan becomes clear. Just because a fueling point distant by two days of steaming from the shortest course between origin and destination is selling oil at a reduced price does not justify diversion of the ship from her routing. Not only must the intent of the contract of carriage be met, and all reasonable speed be made to traverse the sea distance, but the cost to the owner in ship time cannot be overlooked. If the ship is in liner service, the ripple effect may extend through the entire company fleet. If the ship is a tramp, the effect of this diversion could have serious consequences on her next employment.

As a result of the fuel crisis of 1973, which increased the price of crude oil from $2.70 a barrel to a maximum of $38.00 a barrel before it settled to the 1993 level of about $18.00 a barrel, the refiners improved their techniques to extract higher percentages of the lighter portion of the crude oil. The new methods left a heavier residue than did the superseded methods. This residue was sold as marine fuel oil, and was burned in ship's boilers and used in diesel engines adapted to this fuel.

Shipowners noted that the quality of the marine fuels they were buying was lower than in pre-crisis days, and that the impurities in what was furnished were causing damage to the diesel engines. To meet the demands of these owners for more satisfactory and dependable supplies, the purveyors of marine fuels in Singapore, the world's busiest bunkering port, set up the so-called Singapore Bunkering Procedure, the elements of which have been copied by other bunkering points. Three sets of documents are required by this procedure: a pre-delivery note, specifying the quantity, grade, and basic specifications of the supplies ordered by the purchaser; a receipt from the ship, showing not only the quantity of oil pumped into the vessel's tanks but also the gauging of the tanks and the temperature readings of the oil; and a post-delivery document which verifies the receipt and gives the results of the simple test made by the ship to determine the quality of the oil.

To improve the situation, new and faster methods of analyzing fuel in a properly equipped laboratory were devised by the British ship classification society, Lloyd's Register, and its Norwegian counterpart, Det Norske Veritas. Lloyd's Register established a Fuel Oil Bunker Analysis Service, with laboratories in the United Kingdom, Singapore, and Houston, Texas. Samples taken during the actual process of delivery to the ship were sent to the nearest laboratory, and the results of the analysis were brought to the ship, or transmitted by radio if the ship had proceeded to sea. A similar activity under the name of DNV Petroleum Services, was set up by Det Norske Veritas, which opened laboratories in Oslo, Fujaira (United Arab Emirates), Singapore, and Rotterdam. To encourage use of these facilities, costs were kept low, averaging about 45¢ per metric ton of oil delivered.

A further step was taken in 1991 when the Norwegian Bunkering Forum was created by ten major shipowners in Norway. This group presented a united front in dealing with suppliers, and sought to obtain more favorable terms of sale and conditions of delivery from the purveyors.

The suppliers, apparently concerned over the complaints being made against them, formed the International Bunker Industry Association in May

1993. This group, composed initially of twenty-five suppliers, was intended to become a forum through which to address matters of concern to the worldwide bunkering industry.

Some of the difficulty may be explained by the fact that marine fuel very rarely comes directly from the refinery process. Usually, to meet ships' specifications, fuels must be blended. If this can be accomplished at the refinery, the delivered oil should meet all requirements. More frequently, the blending takes place on the delivery barge while it is being moved to the ship's side, a voyage which takes no more than three hours on the average, and therefore gives little time for proper blending. Representative samples of what is being furnished, taken at the bunker manifold, are sent in special containers, carefully labeled with the name of the ship, supplier, date and hour of delivery, and any other pertinent information requested by the testing laboratory. From these samples, it is possible to determine if the fuel is fit for use.

The most common reasons that fuel may not be fit for use are:

1. The fuel is unstable, and therefore unusable.
2. The flashpoint is low, and is unsafe.
3. Contamination exists from waste materials, such as chemical waste or discarded automobile lubricating oil.
4. The residual fuel contains excessive amounts of catalytic "fines," which may cause damage to diesel motors. (This is the result of intense cracking during the refining process.)
5. The fuel is hard to burn.[1]

Bunkering a ship is not an office procedure alone; rather it requires coordination between ship and office. The office selects the port and the suppliers; the ship accepts and uses the fuel. Good bunkering management therefore entails close relationship with the vessel and her engineering staff, and adherence to these rules by both shipboard and shore personnel:

1. Fuel requirements must be specified exactly, and the buyer must make certain that the supplier has a complete copy of the requirements.
2. The supplier's paperwork must be examined for agreement with the stated specifications.
3. The water content of the fuel must be determined, and the acceptability established of fuel oil with that percentage of water.

4. The bunkering line and hose connections must be secure, and the ship and the supplier must agree on the rate of flow and the pressure to be maintained in the lines.
5. All readings of the flowmeter and dips of oil taken before delivery starts and after delivery is completed must be witnessed.
6. A relatively simple shipboard test of the compatibility of the fuel oil is essential.
7. Following delivery, standard tests should be conducted for water content, density, viscosity, and flash point of the fuel.
8. If a laboratory is to conduct the analysis of the bunkers, the samples supplied must represent the total quantity of the oil received. Containers must be properly, accurately, and completely labeled.
9. Complaints, or notice of intention to complain, should be filed with the supplier at the time of bunkering, or as soon thereafter as possible.[2]

To appreciate the principles of bunkering, the following example of how a bunkering plan is prepared will be helpful.

A modern bulk carrier of 63,500 tons deadweight has a speed of 15 knots. She consumes 37 tons of oil per day at sea and 10 tons per day when in port. With all tanks filled, she can carry 2,870 tons of fuel and 250 tons of water. Stores normally weigh an additional 100 tons. The minimum cargo capacity therefore is 60,380 tons. Vessel earnings can be increased by reducing the fuel load to that which is needed for the planned voyage.

Assume, for the purposes of this illustration, that the ship is assigned to trade for a year between two ports approximately 6,300 miles apart. Routed nonstop from loading point to place of discharge, the voyage requires 17.5 days at sea plus four days to work cargo. On each voyage the engines consume 648 tons of oil at sea and 40 tons in port. The reserve requirement comes to 162 tons, and water and stores amount to 350 tons. The cargo lift is 62,300 tons. The alternative routing is to go by way of three fueling points, which would lengthen the voyage by three days. The longest leg between fueling points is nine days, requiring 333 tons of oil. Adding the reserve of 84 tons and the 40 tons of fuel to satisfy port needs, the total weight of oil comes to 457 tons. Together with the 350 tons of water and stores, the reduction from the ship's deadweight leaves a cargo lift of 62,693 tons. The shorter voyage, however, makes possible the completion of 9.36 round trips delivering 583,128 tons in one year, while the longer passages leave time only for 8.3 deliveries totaling 520,352 tons.

The ship must always have on board sufficient fuel to make the prescribed voyage, regardless of how much cargo may have to be sacrificed. Once the minimum fuel requirement has been determined, the question of whether to load additional oil or more cargo will be answered only after studying the prevailing freight rates, the costs of fuel along the route, and the potentials for profit (or reductions in cost) which may exist.

Ships in liner service, repeating their voyages, usually take on the same quantities of fuel, water, and stores in the same ports on every trip. A pattern is thus established which makes bunkering a matter of procurement rather than of planning. For example, a vessel operating from New York to Valparaiso (Chile) via several South American ports might find that Cristobal (Panama Canal) is the cheapest point at which to buy oil. The bunkering pattern would call for the ship to sail from New York with sufficient fuel, plus reserve, for the voyage to Cristobal. At that port, oil would be taken aboard for the voyage from Cristobal to Valparaiso and return. The reserve requirement would be computed on the basis of the fuel needed for the last leg of the northbound passage. At Cristobal, homeward bound, the ship would be supplied with enough oil, including reserve, for the passage to New York and then back to Cristobal, where the procedure would be repeated.

As soon as the ship has been assigned to a voyage, the bunkering staff must determine what ports are available or desirable as possible fueling points. These are some of the questions which must be answered for each port as the bunkering plan is developed:

1. Are supplies of fuel in this port plentiful?
2. Is the fuel of the desired type and quality, and is it available in the quantity required?
3. What is the price of the fuel? Does this price include delivery, if barging is involved?
4. What are the physical arrangements for bringing oil to the ship (i.e., pipeline, barge, harbor tanker)?
5. Can the ship take on fuel while working cargo at her berth?
6. If a barge is used for delivery, will it be brought to the ship after dark? How many tons of oil can the barge carry, and what is the pumping rate per hour from the barge into the ship's tanks?
7. If fueling must be accomplished only at a special fuel pier, what fees are involved? How much time is needed to shift to this facility, and how fast is fuel loaded aboard ship?

8. What regulations govern the fueling of a ship at anchor in the harbor?

As soon as possible after a fueling port has been designated, the local agent must be notified. The information, at the minimum, must include the name of the ship, the estimated time of arrival, the estimated quantity and grade of fuel oil required, the length of time the ship is scheduled to be in the port, and the amount of cargo, if any, which will be handled during the port call. Two days before the scheduled arrival, the master must send a radiogram (or telephone or fax message) giving the time of arrival of the vessel and the approximate number of barrels of oil the ship will require. This notification permits the agent to make appropriate arrangements to receive and service the vessel. A confirming message usually is sent by the master twenty-four hours before arrival to assure that the vessel will be accorded the treatment desired. It comes as no surprise to anyone that the agent is waiting at the berth when the ship is being moored.

Oil companies, particularly major organizations with many foreign affiliates and bunkering stations, offer contracts to shipowners on a year-long, worldwide basis. Should there be no contract, the operator must purchase fuel at the local (spot) price, which is subject to daily fluctuations as a result of changes in the cost of crude oil, tanker charter rates, and the workings of the laws of supply and demand. The contract price is normally increased only after advance notice to the purchasers. Reductions in price are always made effective immediately since they are advantageous to purchasers and serve to retain goodwill. By signing a contract, the shipowner obtains a degree of stability in fuel oil costs. This permits computation of voyage expenses to be made, with acceptable accuracy, at the beginning of the voyage.

Because no single oil supplier has sales outlets in every port of the world, shipowners trading in several geographical areas usually sign contracts with more than one provider. When this is done, the different suppliers are responsible for certain ports or for definite geographic regions. For instance, a liner-service company operating in a number of different regions might contract with M company for ports in the United States and the east coast of South America, N company for West African ports, O company for ports in southern and eastern Africa, and P Company for the Mediterranean. By spreading the business among the various suppliers, the shipowner is assured that all vessels will obtain fuel of acceptable quality at the published contract price. When supplies of oil are plentiful, ships usually are bunkered on a first come, first served basis, without regard to whether the vessels are covered by contracts. In the event of shortages, however, priority would be given to vessels under contract.

Into the bunkering schedule are written the names of each port on the ship's itinerary, the places where she will take on fuel oil, the estimated quantity to be loaded, and the amount of oil the ship is expected to consume between bunkerings. If the vessel is engaged in conventional liner service, and her refueling points remain practically unchanged voyage after voyage, the responsibility of preparing the bunkering schedule may be assigned to a junior member of the operating department, usually in the office of the superintendent engineer. Should the ship be assigned to tramping operations, especially under voyage charters, the senior executives may either prepare the bunkering plan themselves, or insist on approving it before it becomes effective. This results from the fact that the earning power of the ship is affected directly by the ports selected and the quantities and prices of the oil purchased.

In the tanker trades, a basic fact is that the quantity of fuel taken aboard invariably reduces the payload. Furthermore, the ship delivers her cargo to ports where oil is not naturally available. To make the tanker as useful as possible, therefore, the proposed bunkering plan should not envision taking any fuel out of the destination port except in special circumstances. If, for example, a steam-driven tanker is delivering a cargo of aviation gasoline, and maximum tonnage is needed for airline operations, the shipowner would be justified in buying ship fuel at this port of discharge. If, however, the cargo were the crude oil from which ship fuel is derived, purchase of bunkers would have the effect of reducing the quantity of oil delivered to that port.

One of the reasons for using very large crude oil carriers (200,000 tons deadweight or larger) in preference to ships of about 70,000 tons deadweight, is that the big ships deliver twenty-eight barrels of cargo for every barrel of fuel they burn, whereas the smaller ships deliver only eleven barrels of cargo for each barrel consumed. The same reasoning applies in comparing diesel engines and steam turbines; diesels use less oil per horsepower output than any other form of seagoing power.

In making the bunkering plan for a tanker, therefore, the ideal is to deliver the greatest possible quantity of cargo, in order to earn maximum revenue, while removing from the discharge port the minimum amount of fuel oil. Achievement of this ideal may be facilitated if an intermediate and low-priced bunkering port can be visited without significant deviation from the shortest sea distance, and the time spent in taking on the required fuel is offset by the increased earnings of the ship.

Making the schedule for a tanker follows the same processes used for dry-cargo carriers, except that the tanker is self-sufficient in her ability to discharge her cargo. Regardless of the hour of the day or night when she arrives at the receiving terminal's facility, a tanker commences cargo operations immediately. If she is to load at this port, the delivery of cargo begins as soon as the hoses from shoreside tanks are connected. If the vessel is to discharge, her pumps are started when all hoses have been matched with shore piping systems. No large crews of longshoremen or cargo checkers are needed; usually permanently assigned terminal personnel handle all details. Hardly ever does a tanker deliver a cargo and then take on an outgoing load, simplifying the problem of port turnaround time to that extent.

The dry-cargo tramp trade is governed in its bunkering and scheduling practices by the same principles that apply to the liner and tanker operations. There is still the need to load cargo as quickly as possible. In the negotiations for a voyage charter, the number of days allotted for loading and discharge is fixed, with corresponding bonus and penalty for reducing or exceeding these limits. The master must supervise operations and keep an accurate record of time used and activities pursued. Bunkering for a trip under a voyage charter entails the same considerations as in the liner trade: if the cargo is bulky, then the port where the appropriate fuel can be obtained at least cost is chosen, while for dense cargoes the revenue from each ton of cargo carried is compared with the price of fuel oil to determine where and in what quantity the fuel is to be acquired. To illustrate the process, the imaginary voyage of the *Lucky Lady* will be followed.

The *Lucky Lady*, a diesel-powered vessel of 18,150 tons deadweight, has been chartered for a voyage from Hampton Roads to San Antonio, Chile, carrying coal at a rate which barely meets operational expenses. The terms of the charter permit the owner to load not less than 15,000 tons and not more than 17,000 tons of coal. Northbound, the *Lucky Lady* has been fixed for a part load of 6,000 tons of slab copper from San Antonio to Baltimore, and all the bagged sugar the ship can accommodate from Callao, Peru, to New York City. The freight rate on the copper is at the break-even level, but the rate on sugar is very profitable.

The essential facts influencing the decisions required for the bunkering plan were: (1) the ship consumed 21 tons of fuel per day at sea, and 7 tons per day when working cargo in port; (2) there was no diesel fuel available in San Antonio; (3) fuel could be purchased in Callao, but at a high price; and (4) the lowest priced fuel was sold in Panama.

To reduce the cost of the voyage, it was determined to buy only enough fuel in Hampton Roads to reach Panama. There, fuel for the voyage from Panama to San Antonio and return would be purchased. When the *Lucky Lady* came through Panama enroute to Baltimore and New York, she would be supplied with oil for that passage.

Steaming time from Hampton Roads to Panama was 4.75 days; from Panama to San Antonio, 7 days; from San Antonio to Callao, 3.5 days. The passage from Panama to Baltimore would require 5.2 days, and from that city to New York approximately a half-day. Total fuel consumption at sea was calculated to be 565 tons; the ship's tanks had a capacity of 800 tons.

The quantity of revenue cargo was established by the tonnage of fuel, stores, and water that had to be aboard when the ship departed Panama southbound, and from Callao northbound with the combined loads of copper slabs and bagged sugar. Fuel needs were 415 tons for steaming, 56 tons for reserve fuel, and 19 tons for cargo work, for a total of 490 tons; water and stores added another 350 tons to the ship requirements, and left 17,310 tons for cargo. Pursuant to terms of the charter, 17,000 tons of coal were loaded in Hampton Roads. Northbound from Callao, the ship had to allow 109 tons for the trip to Baltimore, plus 28 tons reserve; four days of cargo work required 28 tons of oil, and the short distance from Baltimore to New York needed only 11 tons. Stores and water remained at the constant figure of 350 tons, so the maximum tonnage of sugar that could be loaded came to 11,624 tons.

The bunkering plan and schedule were developed with all aspects of the ship's employment in mind. Full advantage was taken of the flexibility granted by the charters for both the coal and the sugar cargoes, and fuel was purchased at the least expensive point. By these devices, the greatest revenue was earned from the ship's employment.

In summary, the economic success of any ship depends upon the skill with which the schedule is developed, the manner in which advantage is taken of the characteristics and capabilities of the ship, and the nature of the cargo as well as the prevailing freight rates. Customer desires for the shortest possible transit time and the requirements by the owner that the ship be used effectively and efficiently usually may be combined to satisfy all parties concerned. In the tanker and many dry-cargo tramping trades, it is deadweight cargo that is carried. Because only cargo produces revenue, the accurate determination of how and when to fuel the ship is vital to owner and operator. That the intricacies and possible pitfalls of planning the scheduling and fueling of the ship have been mastered is one of the signs of professionalism in ship management.

CHAPTER EIGHTEEN

Planning for a New Ship

It is almost axiomatic in the steamship business that the best ship for any trade is one which has been designed expressly to meet the particular needs of the route to which the ship is assigned. This belief is not vitiated by the fact that many ships are superficially almost identical, and have been used successfully in widely different services. Standardized ships are accepted because planning, designing, and building ships intended particularly for certain trades is an extremely costly undertaking. Shipowners cherish the dream of the perfect ship to fit the needs of their operations, and every ship built to individual specifications embodies as much of that dream as the vision and skill of the naval architect can translate into reality.

Dreams, however, shatter on contact with reality. They must yield to the newest developments not only in marine engineering and naval architecture but also in the techniques of packaging and handling of cargo. Dreams also bow to the requirement that the ship must earn her way and pay a profit. The new ship therefore represents the combined inspiration and professional experience of owner, marine engineer, traffic manager, operations chief, and naval architect.

Planning for a break-bulk ship brings to the surface many details, both structural and economic, which are present, but less clearly seen, in the planning for a containership. The methodical, step-by-step process described in the following paragraphs may be applied to any type of ship. While the process, as delineated, refers to break-bulk ships, the modifications to fit other ships are readily apparent.

The process starts with an examination of the trade route to be served: present and anticipated cargo movement, existing and anticipated competition, and efficiency of the ships now in the owner's fleet. The purpose of this study is to ascertain how the new ship will fit into the company's scheme of operation, and thus to define with precision her specific mission. Competition must be evaluated both from the standpoint of increasing market share and the possibility (even if it seems remote) of cooperation with these rivals to assure mutual survival in times of severe international economic difficulties. Estimates of the flow of cargo—the different types and tonnages of goods offered for transportation, and the capability of the ship to accept this "mix"—during the predicted life of the ship demand careful scrutiny. The wrong decision, as, for example, building a ship with two deep 'tween decks rather than three or four shallow decks to accommodate the wide variety of incompatible commodities characterizing the trade, might doom the vessel economically even before she sails on her first voyage.

The following list designates the areas of concern and the depths of inquiry necessary to define the mission and to give promise that the break-bulk ship will fulfill her mission:

Basic Data
1. Anticipated years of operational life of the ship.
2. Ports of call, length in miles and duration in days of each voyage, and number of voyages planned for each year.
3. Estimated average tonnage of cargo to be loaded on outbound and homeward passages of each voyage. Types and quantity and the maximum weights of extra-heavy-lift items must be indicated separately.

Traffic
4. Total deadweight tonnage and cubic capacity required in the ship. If refrigerated cargo is to be carried, the tons of this kind of cargo, and the number of cubic feet of refrigerated space needed, must be stipulated separately.
5. Liquid cargo capacity (i.e., number and characteristics of deep tanks and other liquid cargo spaces) essential in this trade.
6. Cubic capacity for dry bulk cargo and the various types of this cargo to be transported (special features of below decks spaces allocated to dry bulk cargo, or usable for this kind of cargo).
7. Cubic capacity and deadweight tonnage of special cargo lockers. If special features are required, they must be identified.
8. Provision for stowage of containers (sizes of boxes which must be accommodated, the number and weights of the boxes, stowage plan to include below decks stowage and on-deck stacking of containers).
9. Provisions for handling wheeled vehicles (square footage needed, by decks; access arrangements; stowage and securing of vehicles).
10. Provisions for handling heavy-lift items.

Operations

11. Location of bunkering ports on the trade route(s) to which the ship normally will be assigned. Quantity of fuel to be carried by the ship when on her assigned route. Provision for carrying additional quantities of fuel if the ship is diverted to other routes.
12. Propulsion equipment and other engineering requirements imposed by the nature of cargoes carried.
13. Harbor and port restrictions (depth of channel at low tide in the port with the least depth of water; berthing arrangements; depth of water at the berth; canal locks, including dimensions of lock chambers; dock entrance widths, and depth of water on the sills; tide ranges).

Port Cargo Handling Facilities

14. Equipment in ports of call: number, type, and location within the port of fixed dockside equipment to unload and load bulk cargoes; number, capacity, and availability of dockside cranes; container-handling facilities; type, capacity, and availability of heavy-lift equipment.
15. Supporting facilities: provision for storage of dry and liquid bulk cargoes; access to ship's side of highway and railroad vehicles.

Regulatory Agency Requirements

16. Government regulations affecting ship construction.
17. Classification society requirements.
18. Load line rules.
19. Requirements relating to subdivisions of the hull.
20. Limitations affecting hull admeasurements.[1]

Other Considerations: For specialized ships, such as refrigerated carriers, heavy-lift vessels, bulk liquid chemical carriers, and liquefied natural and petroleum gas transporters, the need is overwhelming for a very accurate assessment of the peculiar requirements of these individual trades and the current and long-term demand for this type of ship. The considerations noted in items 14 and 15, above, are of particular significance for these types of ships.

Once the mission has been determined, the owner can translate it into proposals on which the naval architect can base suggestions for a preliminary design, and can commence a series of technical studies leading to specifications of length, beam, depth of hull, draft, speed of the ship and resultant shape of the underwater body, and horsepower. As these ideas take on more substance, it becomes feasible to prepare outlines on which to base an initial estimate of construction costs. When these materials are assembled and available, the financial and traffic managers are in a position to evaluate the revenue-producing capability of the ship in comparison to the cost.

To ascertain the maximum price which the prospective owner can afford, it is satisfactory to make *pro forma* calculations which show what the vessel must earn per ton of cargo carried if she is to pay operating expenses, construction cost, and interest. Because a ship carrying only one type of cargo presents a much simpler example of this calculation than would a break-bulk vessel, the following example has been chosen to illustrate this point:

The estimated cost of a tanker of 30,000 tons deadweight is approximately $42,400,000. She is to be operated between Texas and New York and her normal load will be 28,200 revenue tons. To determine what she must earn, these hypothetical calculations are made:

Operating days per year	350.0
Length of voyage, in days	10.1
Number of voyages to be completed in a year	34.7
Cargo delivered in one year, in tons	978,840.0
Crew wages for 26 persons, per year	$1,470,000.00
Subsistence of crew	50,000.00
Stores, supplies, and equipment	95,000.00
Maintenance and repair	350,000.00
Insurance	190,000.00
Other expenses	35,000.00
Port fees and charges	682,000.00
Fuel costs	1,980,000.00
Capital cost (construction amortized over twenty years; interest payable at 16 percent per year)	4,980,000.00
Total annual costs	9,843,000.00[2]

The freight rate required to meet these costs is $10.04 per ton. This figure is derived by dividing the total annual cost by the number of tons of cargo carried in a year. The senior traffic executive must determine whether the freight rate which can be charged (given the present and predicted state of the market) will equal or exceed the required freight rate.

The 500-ton capacity traveling gantry crane of a lighter-carrying ship (LASH) is prepared to hoist a lighter aboard the *Bilderdyk*. Photograph courtesy of LASH Systems, Inc.

Transporting a single commodity such as oil permits the comparatively simple computation shown above. In the general cargo trades, the wide variety of goods carried and the significant differences in their value per ton complicate the calculation of vessel earnings. Regardless of whether the goods are moved in a break-bulk carrier or a containership, however, the structure of freight rates remains essentially the same, as these two examples make clear:

1. A container filled with washing machines is charged a higher freight rate than one filled with paper napkins and paper tablecloths.
2. Containers of fresh, refrigerated fruits and vegetables are assessed higher charges than containers loaded with canned goods.

As the planning process moves ahead, and specific questions arise concerning the configuration of the ship, the most careful scrutiny is required of past records of cargo movements and also of predictions of future trends on this route. Will the proposed speed meet the demands of the shippers for expedited service? What will be the proportion of items paying high freight charges (high rated) compared to items paying low rates (low rated)? How many containers will be of standard 20 and 40 foot lengths? How many different sizes and types of containers are used by shippers on this trade route? How many plugs (electricity outlets and connections to refrigerant resupplies) are needed for refrigerated containers?

Notwithstanding the mass of statistical, mathematical, and economical information generated in the decision-making process, it remains true that there is no substitute for the experience and accumulated wisdom of the senior executives, and final decisions concerning the new ship should represent the best judgment of the group. The vice president, traffic, draws upon experience and knowledge of the vagaries and vicissitudes of the trade, its peaks and valleys, and the nature and intensity of competition to determine if the proposed ship will be satisfactory in all respects. The chief financial officer evaluates the costs and profit forecasts. The vice president, operations, scrutinizes the design to be certain that the ship embodies the latest developments in naval architecture and marine engineering, and gives promise of performing efficiently and economically.

At about this point, a tentative decision to build may be reached. The architect prepares a sketch embodying the principal recommendations of the studies, including specific dimensions, characteristics, and special features needed for the trade. This sketch is examined and criticized rigorously. Appropriate modifications or major changes are made. When final agreement has been reached on the design, the architect can begin the arduous, and very costly, process of drawing the plans and writing the specifications to be used by shipbuilders in submitting their proposals for construction.

A survey of dry-cargo ships constructed during the half century from 1910 to 1960 revealed that there was a striking similarity in vessels throughout the period. There were significant advances in engineering and shipbuilding which made it feasible to increase ship speeds from an average of approximately 10 knots to about 15, and welding replaced riveting in the fabrication of hulls. The basic techniques of cargo handling, however, remained substantially unchanged, and although the capacity of the cargo carriers was expanded almost threefold during this half century, the pattern of ship design did not have to be altered to any great extent. Because the variations that did occur were evolutionary, it was possible for shipowners to plan new vessels which represented genuine improvements on the past but showed no radical changes. Based on past experience and on what, in retrospect, seems to have been only elementary economic analysis, new ships were ordered from builders who competed for the business by submitting bids; the lowest was deemed the most satisfactory. The idea had yet to be appreciated that combining purchase price and full-life operating cost as part of the design process would lead to the determination that a certain kind of ship was, or was not, economically desirable.

From 1919 to approximately 1960, the dry bulk cargoes of world commerce were transported, with rare exceptions, in ships of not more than 15,000 tons deadweight capacity. The decade beginning in 1960 marked the start of the sudden growth in the size of dry cargo carriers. In the bulk trades, especially in the movement of iron ore, this trend became evident as ships of 40,000 to 50,000 tons deadweight were introduced. This growth continued as ever-larger vessels were ordered. In February 1993, 142 dry-bulk carriers exceeding 150,000 tons deadweight were in existence worldwide.[3]

Break-bulk ships in liner service during this same period were increased in size to about 25,000 tons deadweight and speeds of 20 knots, while containerships were made bigger and bigger as demand soared. In 1993, many ships had capacity for 4,000 or more containers of 20-foot length, and the Peninsular & Oriental Steam Navigation Company (P & O Line) was reported to be designing a ship to carry 6,000 20-foot equivalent units.[4]

In the dry-cargo trades, ships are employed in one of two modes: tramping or liner service. Tramp ships in nonspecialized operation (general traders) transport almost any cargo offered. The nature of this form of shipping has permitted owners to make evolutionary improvements in design, rather than radical changes. They are still bound by the fact that the least well-equipped port with the shallowest draft determines the size and outfit of the ship. Modern tramp steamers are intended to enter almost any commercial port.

The opportunities for success in tramping sometimes seem more rewarding if the carrier specializes in the transportation of two or three commodities of somewhat similar characteristics. Because iron ore, grain, and coal move in vast quantities, it is economically feasible to put very large carriers into service transporting only these three cargoes. At the end of 1992, there were 1,496 ships between 30,000 and 50,000 tons deadweight, and 222 carriers in the 100,000 to 150,000 tons deadweight category.[5] A few of the smaller ships had cargo gear; the larger vessels depended entirely upon shore facilities to load and discharge their cargoes.

Liner service implies repeated voyages over the same sea route, with calls at specified ports. If replacement of one or more ships on a route is required, experience will dictate whatever is desired to modernize or improve the design. If the intent is to enter a new trade route, before any specifications for ships can be laid down, the owners must engage in an exhaustive study of that route.

Sea-Land Service commenced transatlantic operations in 1966 with fully equipped (self-sustaining) ships. It soon proved to be more efficient and profitable to construct dockside cranes and to design ships with no cargo-handling capability. So long as the ships plied only between equipped ports, there were no handicaps to trade. In 1980, however, Sea-Land opened a new service to Middle Eastern ports which had no container-handling cranes at dockside. To meet the demands of the shippers for container transportation, the company equipped four ships with the requisite gantry cranes, having calculated that the cost of procuring, installing, and maintaining the shipboard cranes, as well as the loss in cargo deadweight incurred by the presence of the heavy cranes, would be more than offset by the increased freight earnings.

On some transoceanic routes, ships combining the features of the containership and the roll-on/roll-off carrier filled a need. They transported very heavy and often oversized items which could not be fitted into containers and presented problems in loading and stowing aboard break-bulk ships. The designers of these ships paid particular attention to the height of the vehicular decks, the capacity of the stern ramp, and the possibility of a movable intermediate deck on which smaller and lighter wheeled units could be carried. Because the demand for this type of transportation never was very great, the number of these combination ships was small.

The 160-ton capacity centerline cargo ramp of the *Hellenic Innovator* can be positioned to port or starboard to work cargo. Photograph by Jeff Blinn, courtesy of Moran Towing Co.

In considering how to adapt the break-bulk ship to carry cargo, it is essential to take into account the nature and quantity of whatever is offered for transportation. There is so much variety in the normal load that emphasis is placed primarily on the ease and efficiency with which cargo can be worked. As was pointed out in a treatise on naval architecture:

It is well to agree on the fact that what constitutes an efficient layout from the point of view of cargo carrying and cargo handling is greatly dependent upon the special requirements of each trade. It is obvious that if a great preponderance of the cargo moving in a given trade route consists of long rails, piling, pipes, etc., the optimum ship for that trade should have pillars, special rig to facilitate handling extra long drafts of cargo in and out of the holds, etc.

The versatility of a roll-on/roll-off ship was proven by this walk-on/walk-off cargo. Photograph courtesy of Atlantic Container Line.

Extra long holds result in very large bale cubic per cargo gear; extra long hatches result in a smaller number of hatches, and a smaller amount of cargo handling gear, per ship. A ship designed with the object of being optimum for handling and stowing long pieces of cargo would not be an optimum ship to carry general cargoes. The ability of the ship to survive damage involving flooding also may be lessened.

An operator who wants to move general cargoes in and out of a number of ports, on the other hand, has no interest in extra long holds and hatches. He will prefer to have as many hatches, and cargo handling gears, as he can get satisfactorily in the ship, in order to facilitate reaching and moving the cargo he must handle in each port, with a minimum of interference. The requirements of the majority of long trade routes will average somewhere between these extremes.[6]

Containerships, despite their superficial similarity, are tailored to suit the requirements of their assigned routes. This is apparent in the provision of plugs for power for refrigerated containers, the length of containers accommodated in the cells, the number of containers which can be stacked below and above decks, the location of the deckhouse or other protective structures near the bow, and the methods of securing containers in their cells. These features are seen very clearly in the *Jervis Bay,* a 24-knot vessel with space for 4,000 20-foot equivalent units,[7] and by way of contrast, the *Cape Hatteras,*[8] which can accommodate containers of any length from 20 to 49 feet.

If speed is crucial to successful competition, the cost of providing record-breaking speed must be determined to the nearest dollar. Speed is not just adding horsepower to the engines; it entails many refinements in hull design which affect significantly (and often adversely) the cargo stowage capabilities of a ship. The plodding Liberty ship of World War II had one enormous advantage: her hull was almost rectangular, which made possible efficient use of all the space in the holds. By way of contrast, a postwar break-bulk cargo liner with twice the Liberty's speed had hull lines so fine that the forward end of the hatchway in No. 1 hold was almost useless for cargo stowage. The full effect of increased speed must be determined before any decision is reached; failure to consider the less obvious aspects can be economically disastrous.

Since the days of the clipper ships, the users of sea transportation have demanded speed. The ultimate answer, for containerships, was given in 1972 when Sea-Land Service placed its huge 33-knot vessels in service. On all the sea routes to which these carriers were assigned, new records for cargo ship passages were established, and in some instances the records held by the fastest passenger liners were eclipsed. Following the oil crisis of 1973, when the price of fuel oil suddenly became the major item of operating expense, the cruising speed of these turbine-driven vessels was reduced drastically. In 1981-82, they were withdrawn from commercial service and sold to the U.S. Navy, which converted them into support ships for military operations overseas.

Whereas in 1945 an aspiring shipowner could choose between reciprocating steam engines, geared turbines using high-pressure steam, and moderately powered diesel motors, the choice by 1990 had been narrowed to a range of diesels. There still was variety as to the type of power plant which might be installed: medium or slow speed motors, single or multiple engine propulsion, direct or diesel-electric drive. Motors with output of 30,000 to 50,000 brake horsepower were available from a number of builders. The economy of the diesel compared to steam turbines was sufficient to induce the owners of the *Queen Elizabeth 2,* originally a geared turbine steamer, to remove the turbines and to replace them with nine diesels totaling 130,000 brake horsepower coupled to generators which in turn powered the two electric driving motors. The *Berge Sigval,* a 16-knot supertanker of 306,430 tons deadweight, is propelled by a single motor of 35,000 brake horsepower.[9]

Liner service worldwide has turned increasingly to the use of containers, evidenced by the introduction on many trade routes of fleets of large, fast, and extremely costly carriers. As has been noted earlier in this volume, one of these ships can do the work of three to five break-bulk vessels by reason of greater size, high speed (with, consequently, voyages of shorter duration), and minimal port turnaround time. Owners, however, are ever on the alert to obtain greater productivity from their ships, both to meet competition from other carriers and to satisfy the demands of the shippers. Sea speed is a function of design, and not much can be done to increase it once the ship is in service. Cutting down the hours spent in port therefore has commanded increasing attention in recent years. A radical approach to achieving this goal was seen in these three ships:

On December 10, 1991, the *Nedlloyd Asia* attracted attention when she sailed from Kobe, Japan, for Singapore. A containership built to carry 3,562 20-foot units, she had no hatch covers to protect the holds from invading seas, and the cell guides extended to the heights of four containers above the weather deck. By careful design of the cells, clearance was reduced to the minimum, so that an almost unbroken surface was exposed to the elements. Unusually large bilge pumps were installed to cope with the volume of water predicted to enter during the worst storms at sea as well as during the most severe tropical disturbances. By building the cell guides above the weather deck, containers could be emplaced without the need of special tie-down devices, which saved time both in loading and unloading. Eliminating the hatch covers permitted continuous stacking, without interruptions to close the hatch, thereby further reducing the hours devoted to handling containers.[10]

Container sizes vary noticeably for any number of reasons. Shipowners seeking to increase their loads have grappled with the problem of transporting boxes of assorted sizes with only moderate success. The *Cape Hatteras* represented a new approach to the problem. Technically designated as a "multi-measurement containership" (MMC), the vessel was built to accept all sizes of containers in use in 1993. Movable guides were

Energy Independence was the first seagoing coal-burning steamship built in the United States since 1921. She loaded her first cargo, 32,366 long tons of coal, at Hampton Roads on August 8, 1983. Photograph courtesy of General Dynamics.

fitted to the cells, and could be adjusted to accommodate containers be-tween 20 and 40 feet in length. With a nominal capacity of 923 20-foot boxes, she offered 204 plugs for refrigerated containers. Her 9,000 brake horsepower motor gave her a speed of 18 knots.[11]

The *Atlantic Lady,* owned by Oost Atlantic Lijn, of Rotterdam, was also a "hatch cover-less" carrier. As was true of the *Nedlloyd Asia,* the clearance between vertical tiers of containers was minimal, but the possi-bility of boarding seas was mitigated by placing the bridge-house at the forward end of the ship. In a winter crossing of the North Atlantic, she cruised at 18 knots into headwinds of near-gale force, and "nothing ever [came] in except rainwater," according to one reporter. In port, the absence of hatch covers cut the turnaround time by one-half, compared to a ship of similar size equipped with hatch covers.

An unusual feature of the *Atlantic Lady* was the provision of two internally recessed bow and stern "spud poles." These pointed, bottom-holding vertical poles are similar to those used in dredges, and serve to prevent all movement relative to the wharf when containers are being discharged or loaded. The ship, with a capacity of 1,643 20-foot units, was said to be the most advanced containership available for charter at the time she was built.

By skillful use of the computer, it becomes feasible, during the planning stage, to postulate any number of contingencies in which the ship may be involved, and which might have a major impact upon the profitability of the vessel.

For instance, if the ship is to be used as a general-purpose tramp, the projected cost of construction can be made the basis for determining the minimum revenue (freight rate or charter hire) which must be earned if operating costs are to be met, and the bank loans repaid. As part of the calculation, a "best case scenario" can be assumed: each year the ship will make six revenue-producing voyages, will require only two weeks of shipyard time, will be forced to travel in ballast a total of twenty days, and will be idle between charters not more than ten days. Just as important would be the "worst case scenario": the ship would make six revenue-producing voyages, but would lose four weeks to shipyard repairs, would spend forty-five days in ballast voyages, and would have to tarry another thirty days waiting for charters. Many other possibilities may be programmed into the computer to obtain a realistic conception of the ship's value over the full term of her working life.

These economic considerations precede the final decision to acquire the new ship. Contributing to the discussions must be not only the senior executives of the owning corporation, but also the naval architect, whose suggestions can have very significant bearing on the outcome of the deliberations. This was brought out in an earlier chapter in describing how Malcom McLean's architect came to the conclusion that the projected roll-on/roll-off ship for the Atlantic coastwise trade was not economically justifiable.

Ship management, regardless of the types of ships involved, must take into account the factors which influence decisions. In the following paragraphs, the questions set forth are as pertinent to the operators of break-bulk ships as to the owners of containerships in liner service and to the owner of a single-deck tramp steamer which is to find employment anywhere in the world.

1. *Trading pattern*. Does the design meet the needs of the established pattern of operation, including the ability of the ship to serve all the ports on the route, to carry the quantity and variety of cargo offered

The 22-knot "lighter aboard ship" (LASH) *Benjamin Harrison* was built in 1980 to carry 80 lighters and 119 containers. Photograph courtesy of McAllister Bros.

(or anticipated for the future), and to provide rapidity of transit satisfactory to the shippers?

2. *Speed of the ship.* Does the ship have sufficient speed at least to equal or surpass the competition on the route? Is the proposed speed economically sustainable, given existing freight rates and predicted prices for fuel?

3. *Dimensions of the ship.* Is the proposed size correct for the ports the ship is to enter, and the type and quantity of cargo she is to carry?

4. *Hull form and displacement.* Does the design incorporate the best hydrodynamic qualities possible within the limitations imposed by the requirements of the intended employment of the ship? Do the hull lines produce cargo stowage spaces which are acceptable and economical to work?

5. *General arrangement of the ship.* Does the design result in optimum usage of the interior layout of the ship with reference to cargo loading and discharge, but not discounting in any way the need to stow cargo efficiently and safely? Are cargo-handling devices correctly assigned to satisfy the requirements of the ship's employment?

6. *Cubic measurements within the hull.* Are the capacities of the cargo holds distributed appropriately, with due appreciation of the need to

balance working times for each compartment? Is cargo handling facilitated by the internal arrangements of space?

7. *Choice of machinery.* Has the most effective and reliable system of propulsion been selected, in view of the projected employment of the ship? Is the recommended installation the most economical, in terms of sustained performance in circumstances of maximum strain as well as in ideal situations? Does the study evaluate the problems which can arise from using fuel which barely meets the specifications of the engine builder?

8. *Outfit of the ship.* Are the weight and cost of different types of cargo gear and supporting equipment proportionate to the capabilities of the ship? What is the difference in cost between the optimum installation and one that meets minimum capabilities and specifications? What effects can be predicted from the decision to accept less than optimum outfit?

9. *Cargo capacity and ship's total deadweight tonnage.* What is the net revenue-producing capability of the ship after fuel, water, and stores have been placed aboard?

The answers to each of these questions can be found only by careful examination of every suggestion or proposal, not only for its immediate applicability and practicality but also for the "second order" effects of these ideas. For instance, if a containership is to be built, the proposal to install gantry cranes to make the vessel independent of port facilities must be analyzed to establish "first order" effects like increased costs of building, reduced cargo tonnage, and more expensive ship maintenance. At the same time, second order effects like greater flexibility in scheduling ports of call and elimination of crane-hire expense must be given due consideration. Only by the systematic evaluation of both first and second order effects can correct decisions be reached; the utility of the computer in this evaluation is self-evident.

By coincidence, the computer became a tool of steamship management at approximately the same time that major changes in transoceanic transportation were taking place. The astounding rapidity with which containerization invaded the trade routes was perhaps the most conspicuous example, but was not the only significant variation from traditional shipping practice. Ship capacities and cruising speeds were increased, and many improved cargo-handling systems became available. Simultaneously, shipbuilding costs escalated noticeably. The old procedure of enhancing the capabilities of ships, without any radical departures from the customs of the times, no longer was satisfactory. By linking the computer and the ship managers' need for better bases for decisions, it became possible to project the profit-making potential of a ship over an extended period of time. That previously elusive figure, the freight rate (or charter hire) required to break even, was given substance, as previously pointed out.

Steamship owners, despite the incursion of the "thinking machine," still must make decisions affecting the future welfare of their organizations. They continue to consult with the naval architect and the marine engineer as they seek the proper interpretation of the data supplied by the computer. Owners and managers must be wary of the possibility of becoming so engrossed in the financial aspects of the business that they think of the ships only as cogs in the mechanism called waterborne trade. It remains true that it is the ships that must do battle with the elemental forces of nature, or lie in remote and perchance exotic harbors while being loaded or discharged, and do the bidding of the skillful and dedicated people who make up their complements. Managers ashore must always remember that the ship is the only vehicle of transportation in which a number of human beings live, work, and play for protracted periods of time as they exercise final control over the actual performance of that admirable creation.

CHAPTER NINETEEN

Passenger Cruises

Vacation cruises, defined as the transportation of pleasure seeking travelers on ocean voyages offering one or more ports of call, are the survivors of the once flourishing passenger steamship business. Its economic importance may be gauged by the fact that in the United States alone, more than 60,000 persons are employed in the cruise industry, and in 1993 in ports of that nation almost five million persons were embarked. Dozens of ships, representing an investment of billions of dollars, serve these trades, which flourish in many parts of the world.

The cruise business, as it exists today, began in 1946, and has been growing through the years. Although the great majority of cruise passengers originates in the United States, the demand for these seagoing vacations is found in continental European nations, the British Isles, Australia, and Japan. Norwegian owners dominate the scene, both in the size of their fleets and the number of beds offered for sale. The vessels themselves have become floating resort hotels, equipped with elaborate facilities for passenger recreation, and offering well-publicized professional entertainment for the pleasure of the voyagers.

Of comparatively recent origin, the roots of the cruise business in the United States may be traced back to 1867, when Mark Twain and a number of other Americans voyaged to the Mediterranean in the paddle wheel steamer *Quaker City*. Exactly when cruising began in western Europe is not readily determinable. A "special Mediterranean tour" was operated by the Peninsular & Oriental Steam Navigation Company for British clients in 1844, but repetitious offerings of pleasure voyages were not made by this company until 1889, when the *Chimborazo* was sent to the Mediterranean.[1] In 1891, Albert Ballin, the guiding genius of the Hamburg-American Line, sent the *Augusta Victoria* on a cruise around the Mediterranean rather than sail her half-empty during the winter on the Hamburg-New York route.[2]

Until the disappearance of regular passenger liner service in the late 1960s and early 1970s, almost all the ships that engaged in cruising out of

U.S. ports were assigned for the major portion of the year to shuttle operations between fixed ports. During the winter months, when the volume of passenger traffic dropped to very low levels, it was common practice to divert all but the very largest liner service vessels to cruise operation, even though only a portion of their accommodations could be considered acceptable for warm weather travel. In the years antedating World War II, as many as ninety ships were engaged in cruising during the colder months. Year-round cruising was not feasible until air-conditioning was installed on ships, and passengers could be assured of comfortable quarters regardless of outdoor temperatures.[3]

Cunard Line introduced the *Caronia* in 1949 as a ship intended primarily for cruising, but adaptable to liner service whenever there was sufficient demand. This dual purpose design proved satisfactory, and other steamship owners followed Cunard's lead. Interchanging ships between liner and cruise service ended when jet-propelled aircraft began carrying passengers across the oceans. International steamship shuttle service was overwhelmed by the competition, and gradually faded away during the years between 1960 and 1972.

Driven off their regular routes by the airplane, many passenger liners were placed in year-round cruise service. Newer ships like the *Caronia* had been planned for this employment, and were fitted with the amenities demanded by the cruising public: outdoor swimming pools, broad decks for strolling and playing games, large public rooms with good views to seaward, complete air-conditioning, and private baths for every cabin. These vessels made the transition to their new employment with considerable success. The older ships were sent to the breakers.

An outstanding example of the transition from scheduled liner operation to year-round cruising is found in the history of Holland America's *Rotterdam,* which had been built in 1959 for the dual service in the same pattern as Cunard's *Caronia.* For the liner phase, she had two classes, which were similar and complementary. All first-class cabins were provided with private facilities, as were most of the tourist-class accommodations. The cabins were all well outfitted. Public rooms were comparable. It was planned that the ship would have only one class when she was assigned to cruising. Those tourist-class cabins which did not have private facilities were not envisioned for sale for the cruises.

The ship had space for five hundred passengers in first class and for one thousand in tourist class. There was little to choose between the public spaces of the two classes, so the premium paid by first class travelers was for the privilege of sharing the lounges and other common areas with fewer occupants. When the ship was assigned permanently to cruise operation, all separations between the two classes were removed. The ship remains largely unchanged from her configuration when delivered by her builders.[4]

As work weeks have been shortened, and vacations (or holidays) have become universal in the industrialized nations, the demand for recreation has intensified. As early as 1954, Greek shipowners sensed this, and began to offer short (three to seven day) voyages from Piraeus on the Greek mainland to the nearby islands of the Aegean Sea. These proved immensely popular, and afforded employment to two dozen ships.[5] In 1972, short cruises from Florida to Caribbean destinations became available, and have become among the most popular offerings on the travel market.

Essential to the explosive growth of holiday voyages from many ports was the extension of scheduled airline services to distant points. Often including the cost of air travel in the price of the cruise, shipowners have found it profitable to base ships in the Mediterranean, Australia, Indonesia, and Singapore, as well as islands of the Caribbean, while seeking patronage in the United States and western Europe.

The decision to build a new ship for the cruise service is of first magnitude. At least two years must elapse between signing the contract with the shipyard and delivery to the owners. Since 1990, the cost of the large cruise ships has risen to $200 million or more.[6] The owner therefore must be optimistic that there will be thousands of persons willing and anxious to pay (in the aggregate) millions of dollars or marks or francs to gratify their desires for a vacation voyage. Although this is an enormous gamble, the odds have favored the shipowners since 1945.

An unusual story of ship design and outfitting came to its end on May 4, 1984, when the *Fairsky* arrived in Los Angeles on her delivery voyage from the shipyard at La Seyne-sur-Mer, France, bringing to a climax three years of construction and ten years of planning. The owners of the $150 million vessel hired four interior design firms—from England, Finland, Italy, and the United States—to plan different areas of the ship. While coordination and consultation among these four were necessary, each one carried out individual schemes for their assigned sections. The American designer, Joszi Meskan, commented in an interview that her awareness of the larger physical dimensions of Americans had influenced the design of seats throughout the ship. She also remembered that many American women habitually use hair dryers, and therefore had the lamps on every dressing table equipped with outlets for 120-volt electrical equipment.[7]

The alternative to building a new ship is to convert an existing vessel to meet the specific needs of the operator. One of the most thoroughgoing conversions in recent years was that of Costa Lines' *Costa Allegra*. Launched in 1969 as a containership, the *Annie Johnson* was transformed, at a cost of $160 million, into a deluxe cruise ship with a capacity of 800 passengers accommodated in 405 cabins. In the process, the hull was lengthened, the main machinery was replaced, a new midbody section (13.5 meters [45.4 feet] long and 25.75 meters [86.5 feet] wide) was inserted, and the upper two decks of the new superstructure were fashioned of aluminum to enhance vessel stability. The result was described in the owner's booklet distributed in 1992 when the *Costa Allegra* entered the Caribbean trade:

> Surprises await you at every turn. On the pool deck, you'll splash in a stream that flows across the transparent ceiling of the Murano Bar, one deck below. Hallways, public rooms and unexpected corners are enlivened with vivid paintings, infused with the energy and spirit of Europe's great artists. Glass elevators glide past a towering wall mural in the sky-lit lobby atrium. The designer's generous use of glass has given *Costa Allegra* a refreshing sense of spaciousness—and views of the Caribbean that no ship can surpass. . . .
>
> *Costa Allegra* staterooms are designed for spaciousness and comfort. Each is equipped with television, radio, in-room movies, a hair dryer, telephone and safe deposit box, in an impeccably tasteful setting highlighted by teak Scandinavian cabinetwork. Suites add the luxury of private verandahs and whirlpool baths. And the superb Grand Suites offer separate living rooms, dinettes, and wet bars.[8]

As operators gained experience in year-round cruise service, they had to adapt to the perceived desires of their patrons. In 1988, a design consultant observed that the new generation of cruise ships was being built from the inside out, to satisfy the requirement that the vessel be a floating pleasure palace. This was more important than to create a ship which was esthetically acceptable when viewed from shore. This consultant also noted prophetically that the seven-deck high "atrium" built into the *Sovereign of the Seas,* which came into service in 1987, would be a benchmark in future ship design. This feature, which in this ship was called the "centrum," was designed into the Carnival Cruise Lines' sister ships, *Fantasy, Ecstasy,* and *Sensation,* built in 1990, 1991, and 1993, respectively, as the "grand atrium plaza." Reportedly the largest and most spectacular incorporated in any ship, this "plaza" is topped by a domed glass skylight and surrounded by computer-controlled luminous neon strips the color patterns of which can be "subtly changed and blended to suit the mood or the time of day." The central feature of the "plaza" is a kinetic sculpture 6 meters high which has brilliant geometric designs rotating on cylinders to create a moving, flashing, colorful effect.[9]

The size of cruise ships catering to the U.S. market increased greatly over the years. Whereas the *Norway,* accommodating 2,400 passengers, was the exception when she was commissioned in 1980, the *Fantasy* class of 1990 had a routinely accepted maximum capacity of 2,604. A significant number of ships provided beds for at least two thousand travelers. The length and draft of these ships, while limiting the choice of ports of call, do not seem to have affected their popularity with vacationers.

Part of the operating overhead expense of a cruise is the cost of providing the entertainment demanded by the passengers. Actors, singers, and performers of all sorts must be hired in competition with shore-side theatres and hotels. Cruise directors who organize and direct social activities aboard ship usually have rather large staffs whose sole occupation is to assure that passengers are kept happy. The cruise director of a Royal Viking Line ship in 1993 had a staff of seventy people: an assistant cruise director, an administrative assistant, a cruise hostess, a fitness director, a stage manager and two assistants, a TV director/producer, a bandmaster, and ten or twelve musicians and a cocktail pianist, plus enrichment lecturers and star performers.[10]

As the passenger liners were phased out of scheduled shuttle operations and cruising became a year-round activity, shipowners settled into fixed patterns of operation. Some restricted their business to a specified area, such as the Caribbean or the Mediterranean, varying their schedules with the seasons and desires of passengers. Other companies established a routine of three, four, or seven-day voyages from the home port to fixed points. The great bulk of cruise business in 1993 was in these short cruises.

Selection of a base port from which cruise ships will operate is conditioned primarily on the convenience with which passengers may be transported to that point. For decades, almost all cruises from the U.S. Atlantic coast originated in New York, in large measure because of the network of railroads which fed that metropolis. The obvious drawback to New York was that a winter voyage to the Caribbean began and ended with at least twenty-four hours of steaming through cold weather and often stormy seas. When high-speed jet-propelled aircraft put all cities east of the

The 32,396 gross tons *Royal Majesty* was built in 1992, and typified the medium-sized cruise ships of that period. Photograph courtesy of Kvaerner-Masa Shipyards Inc.

Mississippi River within two to four hours' flying time from Miami, the picture changed dramatically. Most of the ships serving the Caribbean area now are assigned to the Florida ports of Miami, Port Everglades, Port Canaveral, and Fort Lauderdale. An incidental benefit to the shipowners was that the airplane widened enormously the region from which cruise patronage might be obtained. It is no longer remarkable that residents of California are among those embarking on one- or two-week cruises from Florida.

For the long cruises, defined here as twenty days or more, the operators must draw on the comparatively small pool of retired or semiretired persons. That these long voyages are difficult to sell is borne out by the facts of operational history. Hapag-Lloyd offered a 155-day, 30,000-mile voyage around the world in 1984. About two thousand persons traveled in the ship, but only forty-two made the entire cruise.[11] In 1992, the *Queen Elizabeth 2* started her world cruise with seven hundred embarked passengers. When she returned to her home port 128 days later, only two hundred persons could boast of having made the entire circuit. Similarly, of the 410 passengers embarked on the *Sagafjord* at the start of a 96-day voyage, only 160 were booked for the whole cruise.

The explanation for this apparent loss of patronage lay in the willingness of the shipowners to subdivide the long cruises into a series of "segments" of varying lengths. Travelers who for any reason did not wish to make the whole cruise elected to join the ships at ports where scheduled airline connections could be made conveniently, and to spend a number of days voyaging to a preselected port of debarkation. In this way, the cruises became profitable enterprises for the operators. Recently, for example, a round-the-world cruise was subdivided into segments typified by a sixteen-day trip from Hong Kong to Bombay via Bangkok, Singapore, and Cochin (India). Another ship had a fourteen-day unit from Rio de Janeiro to Argentina, the Falkland Islands, the Straits of Magellan, and Callao, Peru.

Longer cruises, exemplified by those from the Atlantic coast of the United States to the eastern Mediterranean or around the world, represent a challenge to the managerial skill of the operator while facing a gamble. To win the favor of a notoriously fickle and highly selective public, the traffic managers must devise itineraries to allure those looking for shipboard vacations. They must determine how many hours ashore will satisfy the desires of the passengers for sightseeing and shopping, how many days should be spent at sea between ports so that the travelers will not become too fatigued, and how long the cruise should last from start to finish. Their goal is to come as close as possible to the ideal set forth in this quotation from a column by Georgia Hess in the travel section of the *San Francisco Examiner and Chronicle* on September 21, 1980:

> Where does Supership sail? When I'm aboard, it will be in waters where there are fascinating ports of call for two or three days running, then a day at sea, then more ports, then another rest day, etc. Others might prefer the vastness of mid-ocean where day follows day at sea, allowing adaptation to the rhythm of nature and the leisure to do nothing but sleep.
>
> When Supership is in port, no other ships are there to disgorge their hundreds of shop-seekers. Taxis are available as well as tour buses, but of course Supership always docks within walking distance of midtown, like on the Grand Canal in Venice.
> Supership calls at a judicious combination of tried-and-true destinations and rarely visited ports: in the Greek Islands, for instance, she never skips Santorini, but might add Samothrace.

To meet the expectations of people like the newspaper columnist quoted above, the experts begin their planning by canvassing by mail, by telephone, and in person the travel agents who are the best producers of cruise business, have the greatest contact with the travelers, and therefore know what their current desires may be. From these analyses of the travel trade and the reactions of their patrons to experiences on cruises, surprisingly accurate data may be obtained. Additional information may be procured from resort hotels and conventions of business and professional associations where wealthy travelers congregate. Assessing all these bits and pieces of knowledge, the cruise manager can determine rather definitely what will be acceptable to the public.

Occasionally, these experts are frustrated by events altogether beyond the control of shipowners. Incidents from the not-too-distant past illustrate the variety of these circumstances.

In late 1973, the Greek Line proposed to use its *Olympia* for a series of week-long voyages from Piraeus to eastern Mediterranean ports. The first trip was scheduled for early March 1974. As the new year dawned, friction between Israel and its Arab neighbors was so threatening that the cruise program had to be canceled, and for want of other employment, the *Olympia* was laid up.[12]

Eastern Steamship Lines, operators of the *Bahama Star* in cruises between Florida and the Bahama Islands, announced in January 1975 that it was terminating the service because of the extremely high cost of fuel oil and foodstuffs. Whereas in 1973 only 150 passengers were needed to pay expenses of the voyage, by the end of 1974 it was necessary to carry at least 350 to break even. The ship was laid up following the owners' determination that the required quota of travelers could not be found every week.[13]

The *Oriental Empress,* owned by C. Y. Tung, of Hong Kong, left Los Angeles on December 7, 1973, on a projected one-hundred-day cruise around the world. The international crisis resulting from fuel shortages caused abrupt cancellation of the voyage when the ship reached Hong Kong on January 8, 1974. The ship had exhausted her supply of oil, all efforts made en route to obtain fuel having been unsuccessful. Her passengers were flown back to the United States, and the unused portion of their ticket money was refunded.[14]

With the number of companies and the need for many passengers to defray the cost of operation and to liquidate the enormous investment in the ships, competition within the industry is intense. Traffic managers constantly seek new ways to bring patronage: more interesting itineraries, voyages timed to suit schedules of employed persons, "exciting" shipboard activities, high-class entertainment, and special-interest cruises, to name only a few. Perhaps the greatest stimulus to the cruise industry was the introduction of the short cruise of three, four, or seven days. This brought cruising within the reach of those who either had limited holiday periods or could not afford the longer voyages.

The demand for cruise service was greatest in the United States, but was not limited to this nation. Clients in England, western Europe, and Japan showed noticeable eagerness for these seaborne vacations. German, French, English, Scandinavian, and Japanese owners built ships to participate both in the U.S. trade and to satisfy local customers. Patronage was greatest in the United States, where more than 3.2 million passengers paid over $5 billion to take cruises lasting at least two days. The average length of cruises was 6.2 days. The forecast for the decade of the 1990s was for steady growth to a minimum of six million and a maximum of ten million travelers disbursing between $12 billion and $18 billion each year. The analysis also showed that eight carriers provided 67 percent of the cruise ship beds offered on the American market and 47 percent of the world supply.[15]

An adventurous innovation in cruise incentives was to invite persons to take part in the first passenger ship voyage through the Northwest Passage. Sailing from St. John's, Newfoundland, Canada, on August 20, 1984, the *Lindblad Explorer* completed the voyage through these northern waters on September 12. Only thirty-five ships had traversed this route across the northern rim of Canada since 1906. Capitalizing upon the successful outcome of the 1984 venture, a larger ship, the *World Discoverer,* carrying 140 passengers, sailed on August 23, 1985, from Nome, Alaska, to Halifax, Nova Scotia, on what was said to be the first eastbound crossing of the Northwest Passage. The trip was completed successfully on September 14.[16]

Shore excursions are made available, usually at extra cost, to passengers on almost all cruises. Normally, the shipowner specifically and categorically disavows any connection with or responsibility for these sightseeing trips, and all its promotional literature contains carefully worded statements to that effect. It is true, however, that the disavowal is somewhat technical, in that the shipowner nearly always has selected a single concessionaire at each port of call to provide the tours, tickets for which are sold on board the cruise vessel . The alternative is to hire a travel agency with a worldwide organization and have it responsible for all shore trips. The shipowner, in either case, must assure that the contractor or concessionaire performs to specification. Obviously, it does the shipowner's reputation no good if passengers are displeased by their experiences ashore. After all, they do not have the opportunity to choose among the competing excursion operators. In realization of this ultimate managerial burden, steamship companies exercise great care in the selection and appointment of concessionaires.

An interesting exception to the general rule that shore excursions are optional at extra cost was observed during 1980 in the voyages of the motorship *Aquamarine*, which sailed fortnightly from Hong Kong or Kobe on cruises to China. Because of restrictions imposed by the government of China, only those passengers who had made reservations for shore trips were allowed to leave the ship for any purpose. Shore excursions therefore were made an integral part of the cruise "package."

Sun Line, advertising the *Stella Maris*'s two projected fourteen-day "grand gala" cruises in the Mediterranean during the fall of 1985, announced that the voyage would offer thirty-five ancient sights "with all land arrangements complimentary." Pearl Cruises of Scandinavia, as did the *Aquamarine*, included the cost of "nonoptional" shore excursions in China.

Just as ships engaged in liner service were designed expressly to meet the needs of a particular route and clientele, so vessels intended for cruise operation must be planned to meet the demands of this specialized employment. Whether an existing ship is to be purchased, or a new ship is to be built, the prospective owners must fix definitely the trade to which the ship will be assigned, and the special features needed to fit her for this assignment. The Norwegian Caribbean Line (since 1988 known as Norwegian Cruise Line) for instance, established to its satisfaction that there was a good opportunity to operate a very large ship in short cruises from Florida to the Virgin Islands. The superliner *France* was available for purchase and seemed to meet the ideas of the potential buyers. Exhaustive studies were conducted to determine the cruising speed desirable on this route, the adaptations and modifications essential if the passenger accommodations were to be acceptable in the subtropical environment, and the earning capability of the ship. The computations indicated that the proposal to acquire the *France* and put her into the seven-day cruise service was economically sound. In June 1979, ownership was transferred from the Compagnie Générale Maritime of Paris to the Norwegian Caribbean Line. A multimillion dollar conversion, which included changing the ship's name to *Norway*, preceded her entry in May 1980 into year-round cruise operation. The wisdom of the decision to acquire what was then the largest cruise ship in the world has been borne out by the owners' experience.[17]

When named in 1980, the *Norway* was the world's largest cruise ship, accommodating 2,400 passengers. Her crew numbered 800. Photograph by Jeff Blinn, courtesy of Moran Towing Co.

Built and operated to cater to very wealthy passengers who demand (and will pay for) the utmost in luxury and personal service, the *Sea Goddess I* and *Sea Goddess II* carried 116 passengers on seven- and fourteen-day cruises from base ports to off-the-beaten-track and relatively unknown harbors in the Mediterranean and Caribbean seas, along the Atlantic coast of South America, and to many Pacific Ocean ports. Delivered by Finnish shipbuilders in 1984 and 1985, the ships had fifty-eight two-room suites, each complete with full bath, remote control television, radio, stereo, videocassette recorder, refrigerator, and bar stocked with liquor chosen by the occupants. A uniform rate was charged for the suites, and no additional expenses were incurred for personal services or beverages at the bar. Tipping was discouraged. Meals were served at the convenience of the passengers, and every dish was prepared to order.[18]

One of the owners' advertisements offered these inducements to those who could afford to indulge their tastes:

> A cruise ship that takes exception to all the clichés and regimented activity of traditional cruises, she has the ambiance of a regal yacht, the amenities of a stable liner. . . .
>
> Long before you sail, the Captain will write to ask your preferences in every detail, from the competitive sports you want in your visits ashore to the complimentary spirits you wish in your personal bar.
>
> And the moment you come aboard, you will sense that a *Sea Goddess* is indeed a different world. The Persian carpets warm your welcome. The European staff knows your name. . . .
>
> Come live the *Sea Goddess* life.

In 1988, the *Seabourn Pride* was introduced, to be followed the next year by the identical *Seabourn Spirit*. Both were designed to cater to the super-luxury trade. Differing from the *Sea Goddess* pattern, the newer ships were somewhat larger, accommodating 204 passengers. Eighty standard suites measuring 277 square feet, two suites of 400 square feet, twelve "regal suites" of 554 square feet, two "owner's suites" of 530 square feet, and a pair of larger "owner's suites" of 575 square feet make up the passenger quarters. Each size of suite has its own price range, which is all-inclusive. The 140-person crew is not permitted to accept tips.[19]

The booklet describing these ships contains these paragraphs:

> You'll see a lot more world for your money. In fact, the "must-see" ports as well as the "seldom-seen." The ships' shallow draft and exceptional navigability allows [sic] them to go where many ships cannot. Enchanting coves. Hidden harbors. Even upriver to the heart of such fascinating cities as London, Seville, Manaus, Bangkok, Bordeaux, and more.
>
> You are invited to a nightly epicurean adventure. Yet choice is always part of the menu. Not in the mood for sea scallops, saffron bisque, Barbadian flying fish and homemade fig ice cream? Fine.

The 133-meter (439 feet) long, super-deluxe cruise ship *Seabourn Spirit* was designed to enter shallow and compact harbors. Here she is passing under London's Tower Bridge. Photograph courtesy of Seabourn Lines.

Choose from the "Simplicity" listings instead: Roasted game hen. Traditional Irish stew. Or ask for a special order, we will accommodate.

Selecting the ports of call for the cruise requires the exercise of the most careful judgment. Unless the cruise is aimed at the small coterie of travelers who seek exotic places seldom visited, the itinerary must include a few of those cities which have earned and retained popularity with the public. If a judicious mixture of well-known tourist attractions and "unexploited" spots can be attained, the cruise planners may be reasonably certain that their public will react affirmatively. For short voyages from the Atlantic coast of the United States, favorite destinations have been the islands of the Caribbean. Longer cruises include both famous attractions such as Hong Kong, Honolulu, Nice, London, Singapore, and Stockholm, and out-of-the-way places such as Bali, Spitsbergen, and the Straits of Magellan.

One of the eighty identical suites in the super-deluxe cruise ship *Seabourn Spirit*. The ship was built in 1988, and had a maximum capacity of 204 passengers in 104 suites. Photograph courtesy of Seabourn Lines.

A significant trend in the sales management of cruises emerged about 1975 and has become more prominent in the years since then. Instead of stressing the glamourous nature of the ports of call, increased emphasis was given to the luxury and comfort of the ships, the pleasures to be enjoyed in passage from one harbor to another, the professional entertainment provided each evening at sea, the varied nature of shipboard activities available to passengers, and the elegance of the meals served in the dining rooms. The unique feature of the cruises—a vacation afloat while living in a deluxe hotel—became a major selling point, and if the number of persons embarking on cruise ships each year were the criterion, it was what the traveling public wanted.

To emphasize this sales point, and to offer a new and unusual vessel in which to enjoy this vacation afloat, a four-masted bark, built originally as a millionaire's yacht, was modernized and converted to carry eighty-eight passengers in great luxury. The *Sea Cloud* came into service in 1979, and was so well-received that within a decade several wind-powered (but

The *Wind Spirit* and her two identical sister ships were built in Finland in 1986 and 1987 to carry 148 passengers in luxurious accommodations. The ships were 110 meters (360 feet) long on the waterline, 15.8 meters (64 feet) in beam, and had 21,500 square feet of computer-operated sails. Photograph courtesy of Windstar Cruises.

auxiliary-engine equipped) ships of a completely new design were built and assigned to trade in the Mediterranean, Caribbean, and South Pacific areas.

The first of these innovative ships to be offered to the public was about 600 feet long, and had five masts supporting triangular (schooner-type) sails unfurled and furled by computer-controlled machinery. Accommodation for approximately four hundred passengers was provided, not quite to the level of luxury of the *Sea Cloud,* but very competitive in service and fare structure with conventional power-driven cruise vessels.

Later versions of sail-powered cruise ships were smaller, barkentine-rigged ships which relied more on manpower than machinery for sail handling. The newest of these "sailing ship resorts" are the *Star Clipper* and *Star Flyer,* built in Belgium at a cost of $40 million each, which carry 180 passengers and a crew of seventy. Deployed to the Mediterranean, Caribbean, and South Pacific, this fleet of wind-driven ships attracted favorable response from the traveling public.[20]

Peak demand for cruises, both in the United States and in western Europe, occurs during the winter months when those who can arrange vacations seek respite from the rigors of cold weather and its attendant discomforts. In recent years, shipowners serving the U.S. cruise market have found it advantageous to base their ships in southern ports; Miami and Los Angeles are the most popular. Several operators run their ships out of San Juan, Puerto Rico, and other Caribbean points.

To counter the keen competition between operators of the longer cruises, very careful attention is given to advertising and promoting these voyages. The special features of the ship which make her desirable are stressed, as well as the glamourous and unusual aspects of the ports of call. Cunard Line's folder describing a world cruise contained these words:

> Discover new parts of the world on the most talked about ship of our time—*Queen Elizabeth 2*.
>
> You'll experience a round-the-world voyage never before accomplished—in the true spirit of the great adventurers. The *QE2* will visit 32 enchanting ports on 4 continents, including 9 maiden arrivals. Sail . . . to the tip of South America, transit the Strait of Magellan (a world cruise first), and explore the coasts of Africa, Asia, and the Indian subcontinent.
>
> And all in the unparalleled splendor of the *QE2*.

In the case of ships which, like Carnival Cruise Lines' fleet, sail repetitively on fixed routes, the emphasis is placed upon the ships and the activities offered on board, as set forth in this quotation from the company's catalog of cruises:

> On every Carnival cruise you'll relax on a floating resort created just for your vacation pleasure. That's because we specialize in serving you, pampering you, and making sure your "Fun Ship" cruise is your most memorable vacation ever.
>
> Days of sparkling ocean visits . . . nights of thrilling entertainment . . . tropical ports of call . . . tempting cuisine—pampering service . . . an endless variety of activities . . . it's clear that a Carnival cruise offers you more of everything compared to ordinary resort vacations.

Longer cruises represent a special effort on the part of the operator, and in most cases are planned for a selected ship and a particular time. The names of the ships and their owners serve to attract patrons; either these travelers are "repeaters," who have made previous cruises with the ship or the company, or they are persons who have been impressed with the reputation of the operator. Often the reservation books are opened twelve to

The *Queen Elizabeth 2* is the only large passenger ship operated in both liner and cruise service. Photograph by F.J. Duffy.

fifteen months before the departure date; there is always as much publicity and advertising as can be arranged to attract attention and to provide impetus to the sales campaign.

To establish some rules and thereby to forestall cutthroat competition, thirteen cruise ship operators came together in 1979 to form the Caribbean Cruise Association. As was true of the conferences established in other trades, the aim of this group was to adopt a code of ethics concerning promotion and sale of cruise services, and to fix certain areas of responsibility for the welfare of the traveling public. Five years later, after an interim merger in 1972 into the International Passenger Ship Association, the Cruise Lines International Association came into existence with administrative offices in New York and San Francisco. This body consisted of the twenty-five major cruise ship operators catering to the tourist trade from the United States, functioned in a manner similar to other steamship conferences, and was subject to surveillance by the Federal Maritime Commission by reason of its relation to American foreign commerce.

A fundamental principle upon which all these carriers agreed was that the more desirable the accommodation aboard ship, the higher the cost to the person taking the cruise. The most modern ships feature cabins which, by categories, are almost identical in size, decor, facilities, and amenities. About three-quarters of all rooms are designated as "outside," with portholes looking out to sea. Suites and oversize rooms, which could be combined to form a suite, are in the best locations. Inside rooms cost less than outside, and double rooms are priced lower than single-bedded quarters. Showers are provided as standard; tubs are available only in the more high-priced cabins.

From the tariff of a high-class cruise ship, these per-person fares have been selected to demonstrate the variations in price depending upon location of the room, size, and amenities:

Navigation (top) Deck	Deluxe stateroom: King-size bed, sitting area, bathtub and shower, outside	$3,095
Navigation Deck	Deluxe cabin: 2 lower beds, sitting area, bathtub and shower, outside	2,575
Main Deck	Large cabin: 2 lower beds, shower, outside	2,095
"A" Deck	Large cabin: 2 lower beds, shower, outside	2,010
"A" Deck	Large cabin: 2 lower beds, shower, inside	1,595
"C" (lowest) Deck	Standard cabin: 2 lower beds, shower, outside	1,870
"C" Deck	Standard cabin: 2 lower beds, shower, inside	1,295

Seating in the dining room of the ships with large passenger capacity frequently is limited, and two "sittings" may be required to handle all the embarked passengers. There is a perennial argument about the relative desirability of "first sitting" and "second sitting." Travelers with children and those who follow early schedules usually elect the earlier hour; those who consider that dining at later hours reflects a more elegant standard of life, or who normally lead lives starting later in the day, choose the second sitting. The food is identical; sometimes it may be a bit fresher at the first sitting. Unavoidably, diners at the first sitting are aware of subtle pressure to vacate the dining room to permit it to be prepared for the second sitting.

The *Queen Elizabeth 2* spends part of each year in shuttle service between New York and Southampton. When so assigned, she is operated as a multiclass ship. On her transfer to cruise operation, the barriers between classes are removed, and the less desirable rooms are closed off. Passenger accommodations are allocated between the Columbia and the Mauretania dining rooms, with the higher-priced cabins keyed to the Columbia dining room. On one cruise, for instance, fares for cabins using the Columbia room ranged from $5,928 to $6,641, whereas for those keyed to the Mauretania room, the range was between $4,118 and $4,800.

In addition to the revenue from the sale of tickets, cruise operators look to the ship's bar (or bars, in many cases) and shops for significant contributions to voyage profits. On short trips, bar profits can make the difference between a break-even operation and a profitable voyage. On long trips, where there is a great deal of social activity and many private parties, the bar profits can be substantial. Shops of all sorts are more and more prominent aboard cruise ships. The "International Promenade" on the *Norway* had shops offering luxury goods at prices rivaling those in the most exclusive stores ashore. Jewelry, porcelain, watches, clothing, sportswear, and children's clothes and toys were features. Passengers were lured into these places by their presence and also by the fact that on the high seas there are no duties on imported goods. (Whatever is purchased at sea must be declared to customs officials, and may be subject to duty when brought into the United States if the value exceeds the "free allowance" accorded to returning residents.)

Some ship operators have elected to contract with specialists to handle all details connected with the shops. If this is done, the concessionaire procures the merchandise, hires the necessary sales personnel, maintains the required inventories, and assures that stocks are replenished before the commencement of each voyage. Usually the contract stipulates that seagoing salespersons be quartered and subsisted with the cruise staff or at the same level as junior licensed officers.

To reduce the operational responsibility of the shipowner while making certain that qualified personnel are assigned to those duties, some shipowners contract with food-service organizations to take over the entire catering activity of the cruise ship. When this is done, the contractor usually assigns to each ship under contract a supervisor selected for competence and experience. The contracting firm purchases, delivers, and stows aboard ship all food supplies. It plans the food service for each ship, and hires, trains, and supervises the kitchen and dining room staff. The crew's galley, which follows an entirely different menu from that of the passenger-service kitchen, also is the responsibility of the food service contractor.

The shipowner must bear the ultimate burden of proper care of the passengers. To assure their satisfaction, one shipowner placed on each of its vessels a highly qualified specialist designated as the "hotel manager." Discharging exactly the functions implied by the title, the hotel manager reported directly to the master who traditionally is the official responsible for the safety and happiness of the passengers. This relationship between hotel manager and master was somewhat unusual, inasmuch as it is customary for the purser to be designated to supervise the contract and contractor personnel. The novel arrangement, however, was satisfactory to all parties: the purser concentrated upon the manifold duties of that office, and the master controlled the standards to which the ship was held.

The practice of having concessionaires or contractors operate the dining rooms and bars has not met with universal approval by passengers. Many complaints have been filed against poorly trained, inefficient, and ungracious service personnel. Maritime labor unions have alleged that workers are procured for the least possible expenditure of money, and with no regard for the qualifications of these persons. The unions also have charged that the contractor's workers are exploited and poorly housed.

Whatever the truth may be, using concessionaires does place the reputation of the shipowner in serious jeopardy. In the first place, passengers assume that everyone working aboard ship is employed directly by the steamship operator, and therefore condemn the company for the shortcomings and mistakes of contractor personnel. In the second place, the concessionaire may have been the lowest bidder for the contract, and could be inexperienced in shipboard operations. In the third place, the contractor does the purchasing and inspection of foodstuffs, and the quality of what is procured may not be known to the ship's representatives and contract supervisors until it is offered to the passengers. If the quality of foodstuffs is inferior, this could have serious effects upon the popularity of the ship with the traveling public.

Many cruise operators have capitalized on the popularity of casino gambling by installing full-scale casinos aboard their ships. To avoid conflict with territorial laws governing gambling, seagoing casinos usually are open only when the vessel is in international waters. Professional personnel to staff the casinos in some cases are recruited from shore-side casinos; in other instances, the whole operation is placed under contract with a reputable casino management organization. Regardless of who is in charge of gambling activities, the reputation of the shipowner is always in jeopardy. Complaints reflecting upon the honesty and integrity of the casino staff could become very serious, and ultimately be detrimental to the carrier's reputation. It is noteworthy that there have been no publicized scandals since casinos have become commonplace on cruise ships.

For those operators who send their ships on a variety of voyages, some long and some short, some repeating earlier experiences and some new in many respects, the normal procedure is for the traffic department to conjure up the itinerary that will be most attractive to the public, and then to have the marine operations department determine what is feasible, given the characteristics and capabilities of the ship. Of major importance is the depth of water available in the suggested ports of call; unless it exceeds the draft of the ship, it will be necessary to bring passengers ashore in tenders. If tenders are required, local conditions of wind, surf, height of waves, and landing area must be scrutinized, as well as the tenders themselves. If the ship must rely on its own boats, or the tenders available in port are small, the possibility that passengers may be injured in getting into the tenders at the ship's anchorage must weigh heavily in the decision to call at, or to eliminate, that port.

Each proposed port of call is given systematic and methodical study, and only those which are acceptable from the viewpoint of the navigators and shiphandlers are approved. The traffic department must adapt its plans to the conditions discovered by the operating department. Once the ports of call are set, the engineering department works out the schedule of the ship's movements to achieve maximum economy and efficiency. Speed is of relatively minor importance to cruise passengers, but is of great significance to management. Slower speeds require very much less fuel than the maximum speed of which the vessel is capable. Whenever speed can be reduced without thereby increasing the duration of the voyage to an uneconomical point, it is standard practice to slow the ship. While most of the purpose-built ships have speeds of approximately 23 to 24 knots; these maximum levels are reached only occasionally. One itinerary for a round-the-world cruise of a 23-knot ship required only a single leg of sixty-two hours' duration when the speed was 21.7 knots. All other legs were accomplished at lower (and hence at more economical) speeds which ranged between 15 and 20 knots.

Certain basic principles apply to making cruise schedules. The ship should arrive either at the anchorage, if tenders are to be used, or at the berth, if wharf or pier is available, not earlier than eight o'clock in the morning. Time for the passengers to enjoy the attractions ashore must be proportioned to the physical size of the place being visited and the interest it may have for tourists. Generally speaking, an average stay of four hours for an island like Saipan has been found satisfactory; for a well-known city with numerous attractions like Honolulu or Copenhagen, a call of at least sixteen hours is proper. In a place where shopping is the great lure, as is the case in St. Thomas (Virgin Islands), a full business day must be allowed for the pleasure of the passengers.

Departure time poses something of a problem because of the possibility of stragglers. Standard procedure is to notify all members of the cruise party that the ship will sail at the appointed hour, and anyone not on board will have to find his or her way to the next port of call at personal expense. This notice is widely disseminated by every possible means of communication aboard ship. It is accepted practice to fix the departure hour to accommodate the ship's arrival at her next scheduled stop. If the distance to be covered is short, as from San Juan, Puerto Rico, to Christiansted, St. Croix (Virgin Islands)—104 miles—departure time might be as late as 2:00 A.M. and cruising speed would be set at 17 knots to assure arrival at eight o'clock that same morning.

Only rarely is a cruise ship operated at maximum speed. Instead, the lowest speed that will meet requirements is chosen. For instance, from Barcelona, Spain, to New York, is 3,728 miles. At 22 knots, this distance can be traversed in seven days and two hours; at 20 knots, in seven days and nineteen hours; and at 19 knots, in eight days and five hours. Very likely, the decision would favor twenty knots, which would permit departure at 7:00 P.M. and arrival at 2:00 P.M., a good hour for the end of the cruise.

Ideally, arrival at every port of call would be in the early morning and departure would be effected after dark, so that passengers might spend the entire day ashore. In the real world of winds, tides, and distances, however, the schedule must be made to fit the circumstances encountered in the port at the time of the proposed call. If tides regulate the hours of entry and departure, or pilots take ships strictly in the order in which they arrive at the pilot station, the schedule must take these facts into account.

Once the itinerary and schedule for the cruise have been determined, the supply division of the shipowner organization begins its work. The deck and engineering departments of the ship must requisition enough material and spare parts for every reasonable and foreseeable need, and must make sure that delivery schedules can and will be met. This is particularly critical where the ship is completing one fairly long cruise and is to start on another of equal duration within a maximum of twenty-four hours after arrival.

The catering (or hotel) department must order the foodstuffs that will be required for the cruise, based upon the menus which have been prepared. Some appreciation of the quantities involved may be gleaned from this list of purchases made for a 1,200 passenger ship assigned to a ten-day cruise from Los Angeles to the "Mexican Riviera":

15,186 pounds of meat
 3,547 pounds of lobster
 2,720 pounds of assorted size prawns
 1,150 pounds of crabmeat
 4,242 pounds of assorted fish
18,600 pounds of fresh vegetables
 4,850 pounds of frozen vegetables
 7,900 pounds of potatoes
22,200 pounds of assorted fresh fruit
 9,500 pounds of flour
 2,700 pounds of assorted pasta
  960 gallons of fresh milk
 1,960 cans of assorted fruits
 7,900 pounds of poultry
 1,800 pounds of coffee
 1,460 pounds of sugar

Bar supplies were of the same magnitude, as evidenced by this list:

286 bottles of French champagne
690 bottles of American wine
215 bottles of French wine
585 bottles of Italian wine
 40 bottles of cognac
 60 bottles of whiskey
 38 bottles of gin

55 bottles of bourbon
   and rye whiskies
27 bottles of rum
155 bottles of vodka
 95 bottles of assorted liqueurs
3,940 bottles of assorted beers
5,976 bottles of soft drinks

When the *France* made a round-the-world cruise lasting ninety-one days (from January 10 to April 10, 1972), her executive chef carried out his promise that there would be no repetition of the same recipe. Fresh vegetables, fresh meat, and fish were procured at various ports of call, and advance notice of what would be required had to be furnished to the local purveyors so that they could assemble the designated quantity of each item. Wines and spirits of all types and vintages also were stocked against the demands of the passengers.

Although it is an extreme case because of the length of the cruise and the approximately 1,200 passengers carried, the manner in which laundry was handled for the *France* is very instructive.

It was impractical to put aboard the ship the estimated million pieces of linen (tablecloths, bedspreads, sheets, towels, and smaller items) which would be used during the ninety-one days of the voyage. Good housekeeping practice militated against accumulating the soiled linen in bags which would have to be stored in closets until the end of the cruise. The solution was ingenious. Quantities of clean linen were shipped ahead to selected ports of call. When the *France* arrived at those ports, the soiled linen—as many as 150,000 pieces—was exchanged for the pre-shipped clean items. This collection of dirty linen was sent back to France in a connecting cargo ship. Even these preparations were inadequate to meet all requirements, so laundries in Rio de Janeiro, Valparaiso (Chile), Bombay, and Capetown were placed under contract to do the well-nigh impossible: to wash, dry, iron, and return to the ship within twenty-four hours almost ninety thousand pieces of linen.[21]

Whether the cruise be for three days, four days, or seven days—the categories of cruises most popular in the United States—the pattern of operation has become standardized; depart in the early evening, and return to the home port no later than mid-morning. Only eight to twelve hours therefore are available to take on stores and supplies for the next sailing. It takes little imagination to comprehend the coordination required between the management staff ashore, the suppliers, the service agencies located in or near the port city, and shipboard personnel. A careful schedule of deliveries must be set up, and rigidly adhered to; qualified inspectors must be on duty to assure that what is being put aboard the ship is what the purchase contract called for, meets specifications, and is in the quantity ordered. The operation is complicated by the fact that after several months, some key personnel from the ship's company will be rotated every time the ship comes to port. It is the responsibility of shore management to adjust to this circumstance. The resupply routine is somewhat more difficult in those instances where the turnaround day is Sunday, when everyone is on the overtime payroll, and some emergency procurement may be impeded because a supplier has closed for the weekend.

Every cruise ship sooner or later must be refueled. Some ships carry enough oil for two or more consecutive short voyages; others, especially those assigned to longer cruises, may require fuel at the start of every trip. Depending upon the power plant of the vessel, certain types of oil must be provided. A steamer like the *Norway* burns heavy oil (bunker "C"), whereas a vessel with medium speed diesel motors operates on marine diesel oil. The newest ships may have slow-speed diesels, some of which have been adapted to use bunker "C" while others work only on marine diesel oil. Depending upon the type, quality, and quantity of oil available in the ports of call, one or more refueling points will be selected, and the schedule will include the time needed to refill the tanks.

An important function of the operating department is to arrange to bring the ship into port and to care for her until she departs. That means a pilot must be waiting to direct the cruise ship without delay to a waiting berth, for passengers do not accept apologies when they are delayed in getting ashore. Tugs must be available (if required) at the specified times. (Many of the newer vessels have bow thrusters, which permit maneuvering without assistance—a great asset in berthing and unberthing the ship.) Launches or tenders, when needed to ferry passengers to and from shore, have to be at the ship's side when the anchor splashes into the water. Cruise vessels normally are accorded "yacht privileges" in ports of call, so formalities of entrance and clearance are reduced to the minimum. Ship's officers must be informed of any local regulations which might be troublesome to passengers, and directed to disseminate that information. Since the operating department is domiciled in the home port, it must rely on the ship's agent, who is selected before the start of the cruise and is known to be experienced, dependable, and resourceful as well as reasonable in charges for services rendered.

It is axiomatic that the ship's agent must be furnished with complete information concerning the ship's movements, and that the agent in turn assure that the ship's personnel are instructed in how to communicate with it. The names of the agents in the different ports of call are published for the benefit of passengers.

Employment aboard a cruise ship is very exacting, especially for members of the hotel staff who are in direct and constant contact with the passengers. The master, purser, chief steward, hotel manager (if there is one aboard), head waiter, and senior wine steward are chosen not only on the basis of technical competence but also for their tact, diplomacy, suavity, and patience. Especially on the longer cruises, these people are subjected to almost unending demands for special attention and the resolution of difficulties, real and imaginary, experienced by the travelers. Room stewards, bellmen, bartenders, and table waiters are under constant pressure to render prompt and courteous service regardless of the circumstances in which their day's work must be performed. The senior medical officer of a large cruise ship found that many members of the steward's department suffered from ulcers, hypertension, anxiety, and insomnia. He admitted that these health problems resulted in part from the sheer length of the voyage, but was convinced that the predominant cause was the pressure always to please everyone, even the most arbitrary and unreasonable passengers.

This same pressure to perform is experienced in the ships assigned to short voyages. When the vessel arrives in the forenoon and sails in the evening, the time in port is barely sufficient to accomplish the work required to prepare the ship for the next trip. Typically, in those few hours, the ship must be cleaned thoroughly, and every cabin must be stripped, wiped down, refitted, and made to look as though it had never been occupied. Damaged fittings and scarred bulkheads must be repaired. Stores must be taken aboard and stowed properly. To achieve what is necessary, the practice is growing, especially for the very large cruise ships, of sending teams of shore-side craftsmen and workers to assist the ship's company, especially in the repair and major cleaning work. The contribution of the ship's company is restricted by the obligation to release bedroom stewards and stewardesses, bellmen, and receptionists from their cleaning chores about two hours before sailing time in order for them to change to clean uniforms and take their stations to greet oncoming passengers.

Although not a licensed or certificated seafarer, and not in the shipboard chain of command, the cruise director is a major contributor to the success of every cruise. This person—there is no tradition that the director be a man or woman; both sexes have been used with marked success—is responsible for running all the shipboard games and entertainments. The basic reason for having the director (and on the large ships, the assistants to the director) is to encourage the passengers to take part in those games, sports, meetings. sessions, or other forms of amusement or instruction that take place on a typical day at sea. Every activity therefore is scheduled through the director's office; there can be no conflicts in the use of space or equipment. Events involving passengers are scheduled in this office, and published in the ship's daily news sheet.[22]

Cruises are gaining in popularity not only because they carry people to overseas points, but also because they offer a completely different style of life for the duration of the cruise. As floating vacations, cruises demand specialized management, and to meet this demand corporations are formed to design, build, own, and operate ships to cater to those who would make of an ocean voyage the "thrill of a lifetime."[23]

CHAPTER TWENTY

Industrial and Special Carriers

Included in the thousands of vessels which collectively compose the merchant marine of the world are many fleets which are neither common carriers nor tramps, and because of their restricted employment or very specialized design, belong to one of the two divisions of a different category of shipping. That division known as the *industrial carrier* serves the needs of particular industrial enterprises, while the other, called the *special carrier,* meets the demands peculiar to certain types of cargo.

Industrial carriers are those ships which exist as part of the plant and transportation properties of large industrial organizations and are operated exclusively for them. The "Great White Fleet" of refrigerated ships ("reefers") operated by Chiquita Brands, the world's largest banana supplier, typifies this category. The predominant purpose of this collection of ships is to provide the transoceanic transportation essential to the life of the parent concern. There are no other users to be considered by the owners, and no obligations to be met except those laid down by Chiquita Brands, which has full responsibility and control.

Other ships, such as newsprint transporters or automobile carriers, are owned by steamship companies which are not affiliated with any industrial activity, and have been built to carry a certain cargo with greatest efficiency and economy. These ships are the special carriers; they are made available, either under charter or in regular berth service, to those users who must send their goods across the oceans. For their own reasons, these users choose not to become owners and operators of ships; instead they benefit from the distinctive capabilities of the specialized vessels when the need for their services arises.

It is apparent that many ships correctly designated as industrial carriers are designed to transport a single commodity and therefore may be considered as both special and industrial carriers. There is nothing contradictory in this finding, so long as the principles underlying the reasons for the existence of these ships are understood.

INDUSTRIAL CARRIERS

The industrial carrier is defined as the marine transportation link in the process of manufacture or distribution (or both) of the materials used or produced by an industrial organization. Some carriers handle nothing but raw materials; others transport only the finished goods, while still others will be used interchangeably.

Some industrial carriers serve a one-way trade, and as a consequence the parent concern may place the ship in berth service for the return trip. The economic reason for this action is to reduce the cost of ship operation, and to eliminate, insofar as possible, the need to sail ships in ballast on nonrevenue producing voyages.

Exxon Corporation, the world's largest oil company, at the end of 1992 managed a fleet of fifty tankers of its own and a constantly changing number of time and voyage chartered vessels. To supervise this large, world-girdling activity, a complete vessel operating department exists within the Exxon corporate structure.

Chiquita Brands, the banana-growing and distributing company domiciled in the United States, owns a fleet of thirteen reefers dedicated to providing the transportation required to serve its markets.

The principal purposes of the industrial carrier are:

1. To control delivery schedules of raw materials or finished products (or both) handled by the parent concern.
2. To reduce the cost of ocean transportation by elimination of the middleman.
3. To provide efficient and economical transportation for the type of cargo of particular interest to the parent concern.

A heavy burden of expense and responsibility is inherent in owning and operating a fleet of oceangoing vessels. Only those corporations which have a demonstrated need for large-scale transportation of goods in shipload lots, or between ports not adequately served by commercial carriers, have found it profitable to acquire and manage one or more ships. The alternative to the heavy investment in ships and supporting activities is to rely on short and long-term chartered tonnage. In either case, the transportation so supplied is correctly defined as industrial carriage. It is the use to which the ship is put, rather than the design or ownership, which determines that a vessel is an industrial carrier.

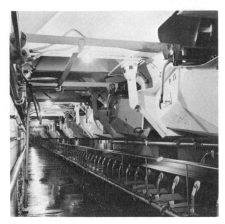

Top left: Melvin H. Baker, a self-unloading bulk carrier. The port for the conveyor is at the stern. *Top right:* Discharging conveyor extended through stern port. *Bottom left:* Discharging coal to inland waterways barges. *Bottom right:* Conveyor systems below cargo compartments. Photographs courtesy of Nordstroms Marine Systems.

Stolt-Nielsen, the world's largest operator of transoceanic liquid chemical carriers, for example, is able to provide either full shipload (i.e., chartered) service on a long- or short-term basis or small lot carriage, as the needs of the shipper direct. By using this company, the shipper is relieved of the burden of ship management, while still having the advantage of industrial carriage.

As already noted, the industrial carrier is controlled by the parent corporation, which sets its own schedules. Vessels, both owned and chartered, are dispatched strictly in accordance with the needs of the industry; no customers have to be informed of sudden changes in sailing times or space allocations within the ships. For companies like Exxon and Chiquita Brands, which depend upon ships to transport materials required in their operations, this factor alone justifies the maintenance of controlled fleets. The oil company moves its tankers to support its refining and distribution operations; the fruit company routes its ships to those ports where the demand for bananas is at the maximum.

Ownership of an industrial carrier is justified economically if the normal pattern of transportation exceeds the capabilities of established operators on the sea routes of interest to the organization, and the investment in ships and the expense of management are less than using chartered tonnage. The industrial carrier brings to its proprietary corporation the benefit of dependable, efficient, careful, and economical transportation of its cargoes. So long as control of the fleet is vested in the parent enterprise, it is immaterial whether the ships are owned or chartered.

SPECIALIZED CARRIERS

One of the more interesting, and certainly more significant, trends in commercial shipping during the twentieth century was the emergence of shipowning companies which restricted themselves to transporting specialized cargoes. These companies usually were owned by corporations entirely independent of their customers, and tailored their operations to meet the perceived needs of the shippers.

The specialized ship is one designed for the express purpose of carrying, usually in shipload lots, a particular type of cargo, either in bulk or in packages of stipulated size and nature. Among the many varieties of specialized carriers are ships built to transport cargoes such as automobiles and trucks, bulk cement, chemicals in liquid form, coal, iron ore, liquefied natural and petroleum gases, newsprint and other paper products, petroleum and its by-products, refrigerated fruits and meats, and wood chips.

Although transportation by water is the most economical means of movement ever devised by man, there is no single commodity for which the individual cost of carriage does not constitute, in some measure, a barrier to its ready sale in the markets of the world. The carriers are entitled to be compensated for their services, but the shippers expect that this compensation will be as low as possible. To meet this expectation has called for the exercise of amazing ingenuity on the part of shipowners, naval architects, and shipbuilders. In the second half of the twentieth century the fruits of these endeavors have become particularly important in a wide range of shipping operations, as one specialized design after another has been created to meet specific needs for sea transport. Extraordinarily complex ships have been built to provide safe and efficient, as well as economical, trans-

To assure uncontaminated handling of many different types of chemicals at one time, an intricate web of cargo pipes is essential. Photograph courtesy of Moss-Rosenberg Shipbuilders.

portation. Paralleling these achievements have been successful attacks upon that age-old problem of the shipowner: to reduce the time required to work the ship in port and get her back to sea.

Designed to transport most efficiently a single commodity in shipload lots, the specialized carrier often performs well in areas where the conventional ship could not function. An example of specialized carriers meeting a demonstrated need is seen in the transoceanic movement of liquefied natural and petroleum gas. Once the practicality of transportation had been proven, many ships were built expressly for these trades. By the end of 1992, liquefied natural gas carriers of over 20,000 cubic meters' capacity numbered 72. A fleet of 201 liquefied petroleum gas carriers of over 10,000 cubic meters' capacity also was in existence.[1]

Huge tonnages of newsprint move over the sea routes. The rolls of paper are very heavy and are easily damaged by careless handling and improper stowage aboard ship. Two hazards especially must be guarded against: projections from bulkheads which gouge into the rolls, and water

The chemical tanker has a complex piping system, double bottom, double skin, and cofferdams separating the numerous cargo tanks. Photograph courtesy of Stolt-Nielsen, Inc.

damage from leaking pipes. To assure perfect delivery of the cargo voyage after voyage therefore requires special attention from the naval architect.

A Danish-Norwegian partnership in 1989 saw an opportunity to capitalize on a need by meeting these challenges, and designed a vessel which incorporated several features which set the ship apart. The *Trans Dania,* first of three identical units constructed by a German shipyard, had two cargo decks, each completely sheathed in plywood painstakingly installed with no projections from the surface. The heavy rolls of newsprint were handled by a complete system devised through the combined efforts of the owners and an engineering firm. The heart of the system was a hydraulically operated side door, 13.7 meters (46 feet) high and 8 meters (26.8 feet) wide. Two cargo elevators, each of 16 tons capacity and equipped with a 2.9 meter (8.75 feet) square platform, lifted the reels of newsprint from the wharf to the level of the cargo decks. An essential and permanent part of the ship's cargo-handling equipment were electric forklift trucks equipped with special clamps to handle the newsprint without damage. Three of these units were allocated to the upper deck, and two trucks were assigned to the lower deck. Completely mechanized, the system had a potential handling rate of 1,640 metric tons per hour, but the figure reached in routine operations was between 500 and 600 metric tons per hour.

Further to assure that the newsprint would be delivered in perfect condition, no water delivery lines or discharge pipes were to be installed above the cargo. A pipe and cable canal accordingly was provided on the weather deck between the engine room, at the after end of the ship, and the forward superstructure.

Normally operated in the Baltic sea, the *Trans Dania* was driven by a 4,080 brake horsepower motor turning a single screw, and had a speed of 15 knots. She was 113.6 meters (381.7 feet) long overall, had a beam of 17.5 meters (58.8 feet) and fully loaded drew 6.7 meters (22.5 feet) of water. Twenty-eight ballast tanks were installed as a concession to occasional homebound but non-revenue producing voyages.[2]

In many parts of the world, there is a continuing demand for cement in very large quantities. For decades, it was impossible to ship this commodity in bulk and to discharge it with the self-unloading equipment installed in coal and ore carriers. Cement is extremely fine and powdery in its composition, packs easily, and has a very high angle of repose. Mechanical discharge required that the cement flow to the conveyors, a movement eventually achieved by pumping compressed air into the mass. Using this principle, engineers developed several self-unloading mechanisms by which ships carrying cement in bulk could discharge their cargoes efficiently and economically.

When she was delivered in 1981 to her owners, Empresa Nacional de Elcano, the *Castillo de Javier* was the largest self-unloading bulk cement carrier in the world. She was a vessel of 44,612 tons deadweight, and was 189 meters (635.9 feet) long, 31.37 meters (105.4 feet) wide, and when fully loaded had a draft of 11.91 meters (40 feet). Two oil engines with a combined output of 12,300 brake horsepower gave her a speed of 14 knots. The big bulker had six holds, two of which were exceptionally large and were intended for the cement cargoes. Transverse screw conveyors moved the cargo to each side of the hold, where the cement fell through a valve-operated trap door into pipeways laid in the double bottoms. Vacuum pumps sucked the cement out of the ship in two cycles, one from the hold to a reloader chamber, and the other from that chamber to the shoreside silo. By means of this system, the ship could be emptied at the rate of 600 tons an hour. The builders, Astilleros Españoles, of Bilbao, Spain, claimed that the mechanism they had devised made it possible to carry not only bulk cement but also low density commodities like flour or any granular or pulverized material. A further advantage of the pipeway system was that the tank tops were flat and easy to clean, thereby making it feasible to carry different types of cargo on the return voyage. The ship's utility was enhanced by the three 20-ton cranes so mounted that they served all six hatches.[3]

As earlier noted, specialized carriers often are steamship operators who devote themselves to handling only these selected items. They therefore must be fully aware of the economic factors which influence the seasonal flow of the commerce, the hazards involved in the production cycle, and the competition from other areas. With experience, they become experts in predicting the peaks and valleys affecting the trades they serve.

An analyst examining the fresh food trade between Central America and Europe noted that the principal offerings were bananas, citrus and deciduous fruits, other fruits and vegetables, meat, fish, and dairy products. The prospects of substantial cargoes being available depended upon climatic conditions during the growing season, which influenced the size and quality of the harvests. Consumer tastes varied unaccountably, and unfortunately political developments often intruded on purely commercial activities. All these factors, together with the seasonal nature of the trade, combined to tax the commercial skill and experience of the operators of refrigerated tonnage, who also had to master the techniques of stowage, care, and preservation of their cargoes. A final complication was the volatile and largely unpredictable nature of the market, which rose and fell for a wide variety of reasons. If the established operators found the economics of the refrigerated cargo trade challenging, it was even more exacting for the owner of tramp reefers, who might be engaged in a particular phase of this trade only intermittently. Fortunately, these bold entrepreneurs always have found ways to survive.

Responding to the steady expansion of the worldwide demand for fresh fruits and vegetables, a large fleet of reefers was built in recent decades to provide the requisite transportation. The fleet, on March 31, 1992, numbered 981 ships with an average size of 326,000 cubic feet. Only seventy of this fleet had refrigerated capacity of 600,000 cubic feet or more.[6] The largest reefers were used by those purveyors of perishable foodstuffs who used highly mechanized loading and discharging terminals, and had in existence the comprehensive distribution system needed to deliver the goods to the retail stores. Some of these ships were operated by corporations which produced, processed, transported, and marketed their fruits and vegetables, and thus created a complete system to which every component part made a specific and vital contribution.

The refrigerated-cargo ship *Hansa Bremen,* of 19,461 tons deadweight, was built in 1992 and had a speed of 21 knots. Her four hatches were served by the two sets of twin cranes, which could be operated singly or doubled-up for extra-heavy loads.

Typical of these vessels was the German-built *Chiquita Deutschland,* a 22.25-knot banana carrier with 645,586 cubic feet of insulated and temperature controlled cargo space, which was put into service in 1991. Chiquita Brands also marketed a variety of other perishable goods, and provided in this ship seven groups of compartments in which the temperatures could be separately controlled. Because the trend in shipping refrigerated cargo was to use pallets rather than big containers, this vessel had five deck levels in each of three large holds, and three levels in the smaller forward hold. The uniform clearance (deck to overhead) was 2.2 meters (7.4 feet). In addition, there was space for containers, with plugs to provide power for their refrigeration equipment.[7]

Geest Line is a British carrier which for many years has served the trade between the United Kingdom, the islands of the Caribbean, and Central American. Although the primary business of the line is to transport bananas to England and the Netherlands, it also brings to the United Kingdom quantities of fresh vegetables and exotic produce such as nutmeg and

Cargo space in a 1993-built refrigerator ship, showing raised flooring for circulation of cooled air. The uniform height between decks is 2.2 meters (7 feet 3 inches). Photograph courtesy of Danyard A/S.

red pepper sauce. Outbound from England, Geest Line ships carry the products of the United Kingdom and the European continent and thus participate in a substantial two-way commerce. Geest Line furnishes an outstanding example of a common carrier operating a fleet of specialized ships.

In 1993, the *Geest St. Lucia,* first of two identical, fast vessels built to replace obsolescent tonnage, was introduced into the company's Caribbean trade. She was built by Danyard, of Frederikshavn, Denmark, and was one of the largest ships of her type in the world, with 640,000 cubic feet of refrigerated space and accommodation for 439 20-foot containers. On a draft of 10 meters (33.6 feet) her deadweight was 13,981 tons, and her 16,520 brake horsepower engine gave her a speed on trials of 21.4 knots. She was 158.1 meters (531.2 feet) long, and 24.4 meters (81.9 feet) wide. Temperatures in the seven separate temperature zones had a range between –29° Celsius for frozen goods and +13° Celsius for bananas. Separate air coolers and fans circulated air in sufficient volume to assure adequate ventilation for all fresh produce.[8]

One of the world's largest reefers, the *Geest St. Lucia* had a speed of 21.4 knots. In addition to her refrigerated cargo, she carried 439 containers. Photograph courtesy of Danyard, Denmark.

The third category of refrigerated ships is that of the tramp, employed usually on long-term charter. J. Lauritzen, the Danish shipowner, put the *Ditlev Lauritzen,* the first of four identical vessels, into service in 1991. At that time, her capacity of 765,000 cubic feet of belowdecks controlled temperature space made her the largest refrigerated ship in the world. She also had space for 422 20-foot containers. As a specialized tramp, the ship was designed with flexibility to handle all types of refrigerated cargo as well as to load back-haul cargoes such as containers and automobiles exported from Japan. The ship was 160.4 meters (539 feet) long, 23.5 meters (79 feet) wide, and had a draft of 9.8 meters (33 feet). Her 15,300 brake horsepower engine gave her a cruising speed of 19 knots.

Lauritzen's experience in this form of specialized transportation began shortly after World War I. The *Gunderson,* of 1920, was the first "pure" reefer in the fleet. From then on, Lauritzen operated, always under charter to fruit importers, a small number of well-designed, relatively high-speed reefers. As the demand for fresh fruits and vegetables increased, the company progressively built more and larger ships until the *Ditlev Lauritzen* class was acquired.

When built in 1990, the 19-knot refrigerator ship *Ditlev Lauritzen* was the world's largest. She was equipped for operation by a crew of six. Her belowdecks capacity was 21,684 cubic meters (765,650 cubic feet). Photograph courtesy of J. Lauritzen A/S.

This $50 million ship had five holds, all with five levels, and clearance of 2.2 meters (7.4 feet). The belowdeck area was divided into nine zones comprising 23 cargo spaces, and temperatures could be set from a low of –29° Celsius for deep-frozen cargo to +13° Celsius for bananas. Fans circulated air through the coolers and thence downward and longitudinally through the gratings, assuring maximum ventilation for perishable items such as fruits and vegetables.

Facing the stiff competition of the time, the *Ditlev Lauritzen* was equipped with all the automatic and computer-controlled machinery and labor-saving devices available when she was launched. This elaborate outfit made it possible for the ship to be operated by a crew of six; she entered service with a master, two navigating officers, a chief engineer, a second engineer, two experienced deckhands, and a cook/steward.[8]

Transoceanic movement of extremely heavy items—railroad locomotives, electric generators, and mining equipment, for example—has been part of overseas shipping operations for decades. In the years immediately following the end of World War II, the Norwegian firm trading under the name of Belships specialized in handling these offerings. With

The *Wakagiku Maru* was designed and built to carry very large and very heavy pieces. The massive cargo gear serves forward and after cargo holds. Photograph courtesy of NYK Lines.

carefully designed and strengthened booms, multi-sheave blocks, powerful winches, and reinforced decks, these ships often joined two booms to lift a unit weighing 500 to 600 tons. A great deal of skill was required not only to handle these colossal weights in the loading and unloading phases, but also in the securing procedures. As Belships proved the validity of the market, other carriers entered the trade, using vessels ranging from about 2,500 tons deadweight to 15,000 tons deadweight.

The advent of the containership was accompanied by the development of the very large and exceedingly heavy container-handling cranes which were manufactured in one country and shipped to an overseas destination to be installed in a port. These massive structures at first were transported in pieces and assembled on the final site, but it was not long before the crane buyers began to demand that the units be transported in one piece, ready to be emplaced on the wharf.

These very large and cumbersome structures could not be handled in the conventional heavy-lift ships. Three Dutch operators quickly came to dominate the scene. Wijsmuller Ship Management BV, of Ijmuiden, Mammoet Shipping BV, of Amsterdam, and Dock Express, of Rotterdam, individually designed and built a new type of ship which was given the generic title of "semi-submersible heavy transportation vessel." The ships were all planned to sink the hull to the level of the loading platform or, alternatively, deep enough in the water for the cargo to be floated into position over the deck of the ship, after which the ship was raised to proper height for the sea voyage. Exceptionally large modules of major construction projects, and big, awkward (and therefore sometimes relatively fragile) pieces of equipment—drilling rigs, offshore platforms, harbor cranes—were carried. All three operators found numerous customers, and the performance of their unusual ships justified their bold solutions.

Transporting unboxed automobiles across the oceans has been a regular feature of ship operation since the middle 1920s. Vehicles with empty gasoline tanks and disconnected batteries were hoisted aboard by cranes or derricks, and lowered to the designated deck where they were individually chocked and secured in a time-consuming and expensive process. Various ideas were advanced for improving the technique, but it was not until the middle 1950s that any major breakthrough was achieved. The American-designed and built *Comet* was one of the first ships constructed to carry unboxed vehicles which were driven on and off the ship, and had full gasoline tanks and connected batteries. The cars and trucks were secured by patented, fast-working, and reusable devices. A stern ramp and interior ramps between decks, as well as a powerful ventilating system, were the special features which revolutionized unboxed automobile transportation. Following the success of this experiment, several generations of car carriers were built and put into service, especially in Japan and Sweden.[11]

Wallenius Lines, of Gothenburg, Sweden, after trying a combination ship which could carry automobiles outbound and bulk cargoes homeward, abandoned that idea, and concentrated upon what came to be called the "pure car and truck carrier." This company operated a twenty-five-ship fleet worldwide in 1993, and was known not only for the efficiency and dependability of its vessels, but also for the fact that they were named for famous operas.

The *Aida* was put into service in 1991, and was followed by her sister, the *Otello*, in 1992. These 20-knot ships were designed for functional efficiency rather than for esthetic beauty. Like other purpose-built car carriers, their square superstructure, which extended the full length of the hull, was about 26.8 meters (90 feet) high. A distinctive feature of the Wallenius

Otello, Wallenius Lines' 1992-built pure car and truck carrier, has twelve vehicle decks. Vehicles are loaded over the stern and side ramps. The many ventilators seen on the weather deck are part of the system installed to assure safe air conditions when loading and unloading vehicles. Photograph courtesy of Wallenius Lines, Stockholm.

ships was the massive stern ramp, mounted at an angle of 25° to the center-line to permit drive-on/drive-off vehicle movements. The interior design featured twelve decks, four of which could be raised to accept loads as tall as 6.5 meters (21.8 feet). The fixed decks were strengthened to carry weights up to 2.5 metric tons per square meter. The high clearance and massive weight tolerance made possible the transportation of tractors, cranes, heavy earth-moving equipment, buses, helicopters, railroad loco-motives, and marine engines. As carriers of vehicles only, these ships had space for 6,118 automobiles or 3,208 cars and 531 heavy trucks. The total weight of the cargo was less than that needed to bring the ship down to her load line, and therefore water ballast tanks were installed to add 4,000 tons of weight as needed for the safety of the ship and cargo.

To simplify the handling of large vehicles, the 17,000 horsepower propulsion plant was offset to the starboard side, thereby creating a single unobstructed passage through the main hold area. Elaborate safety meas-ures, including a system to flood the cargo spaces with carbon dioxide, were provided. The ventilation system, used at maximum capacity during vehicle loading and unloading operations, effected twenty-five changes of air per hour.[12]

Vehicle carriers were owned almost exclusively by established ship operating companies, and were made available to automobile producing and exporting organizations under either charter or contract of affreightment. Regardless of the contractual relationship, the vessel operator supplied the experience and expert technique required to deliver cargoes on time and in perfect condition.

It must be repeated that ships of specialized design often are used by industrial organizations, and the line between the two categories may be very faint. It is the use to which the ship is put which determines whether she is an industrial carrier; it is the design and the principal cargoes which the vessel carries which fix the definition of special carrier.

CHAPTER TWENTY-ONE

Tanker Management

Ranging in size from enormous to almost tiny, transporting more tons of cargo of direct concern to more people in more parts of the world than any other type of ship afloat, tankers have become indispensable to the modern international industrial economy. As vital components of the merchant marine, tankers require many of the same managerial skills needed by any other type of ships engaged in moving cargoes across the seas. Dedicated to the movement of liquid commodities in bulk, however, these vessels demand specialized knowledge and techniques both from the personnel who take them to sea and those on shore who supervise their activities.

In the age-old history of shipping, transporting oil in bulk is a relatively new enterprise. The first steamship designed and built to carry petroleum in bulk, rather than in wooden barrels or metal drums, was put into service in 1886.[1] This was the *Glückauf* ("Good Luck"), built in England to the order of Wilhelm A. Riedemann, a merchant of Hamburg, to serve the German-American Petroleum Company.[2] She was a small ship, 300 feet long with a deadweight of 3,000 tons—hardly noticeable alongside today's gigantic crude oil carriers. Her place in history, however, derives from the fact that she was the prototype of the world's tankers, with steam-driven pumps segregated from the cargo tanks by steel bulkheads, and the engine room at the after end, separated from the cargo tank area by a cofferdam formed by twin bulkheads. This pattern of construction, it is appropriate to note, has not altered significantly over the years.

Since the *Glückauf* was launched, bulk oil carriers have multiplied in numbers, increased in speed and, most conspicuously, grown enormously in size. Change was slow at first; as late as 1920, the standard tanker had a deadweight of only some 12,000 tons, although there were a few vessels of about 20,000 tons.[3] In 1939, a small group of 16,000-tonners was in operation, but the majority of tanker-owning companies still leaned toward the "handy-sized" ships of 12,000 tons. It is a minor footnote to history that the average speed of all these ships was about 11 knots, compared to the *Glückauf*'s 10.

The demands for transportation of petroleum during World War II greatly exceeded the capability of the prewar fleet and called forth new standards for tankers. Bigger and faster ships were essential, and the United States built 532 oil carriers of the T-2 class. With a deadweight of about 16,750 tons and a speed of 14.5 knots, these ships proved conclusively that large, fast oil carriers were economical, efficient, and as versatile as the handy-sized tankers of 12,000 tons.[4]

Once the utility of the T-2 had been demonstrated, growth became characteristic of the tanker-operating industry. In 1947, the first of the really big ships were built. These "colossal" vessels of 25,000 to 27,000 tons deadweight were relegated quickly to lesser positions by the advent of tankers of 32,000 tons and, very shortly thereafter, of 45,000 tons. The peak was reached in 1979 with the completion of the *Seawise Giant,* a crude oil carrier of 569,783 tons deadweight owned by the C. Y. Tung interests of Hong Kong.[5] Owing to a worldwide reduction in consumption of oil a few years later, the demand for the very large crude carriers decreased markedly, and no new ships as large as the *Seawise Giant* have been built.

Paralleling the growth in the size of the ships was the proliferation of tankers in the world's merchant fleets. On December 31, 1992, there were in existence 3,016 commercial oil tankers, 288 combined carriers (designed to transport in shipload lots oil or dry bulk commodities, or iron ore), and 273 liquefied gas transporters.[6]

The big carriers (generally those of 200,000 tons deadweight or larger) are used exclusively to move crude (or raw) petroleum from the oil fields to the refineries. Distribution of refined products traditionally was the province of smaller, lighter draft vessels. These "delivery ships" were limited in size by the depths of harbor channels and berthing areas, and the capacities of storage facilities ashore. For many years, therefore, a fleet of tankers of 3,500 to 12,000 tons deadweight was employed in the U.S. coastwise trade. By the mid-1980s, a product carrier of approximately 50,000 tons deadweight had been designed to serve the majority of American ports. These newer and more efficient ships gradually displaced the older and smaller vessels.

During the years that the number and size of tankers in the world fleet was increasing, a concurrent change in the pattern of ownership became evident. Shortly after the end of World War II in 1945, half of the world's tanker tonnage belonged to, and was operated by, the oil companies. In 1991, operators not affiliated with the petroleum-producing and refining corporations (and therefore usually designated as the "independents") con-

Top: The 14.5-knot, 16,650-tons deadweight T-2 tanker proved her worth in war and peace. *Bottom:* First of the American-flag supertankers, *Esso Zurich* (built 1949) had a deadweight of 26,555 tons, and was 628 feet long. Photograph courtesy of Standard Oil Co.

trolled 72 percent of the world fleet.[7] This shift in transportation capability was deliberate, as the producers allocated to different purposes the funds which would have been invested in tankers and, at the same time, sought to divest themselves of the burdens of fleet ownership.

While it is true that the management of tankers has become more complex through the years, the transportation of liquid petroleum and its derivatives is not a unique type of shipping. It is specialized, but in fact it is only one aspect of the whole business of moving goods across the seas.

This elaborately equipped ship conversion and repair yard in Bremerhaven, Germany, has one of the largest graving docks in Europe, and can service any type or size of vessel. Photograph by Wolfhard Scheer, courtesy of Lloyd Werft Bremerhaven.

Tankers, like other ships, must be built, maintained, and repaired. Seamen must be obtained from the ranks of available seafarers, also sought after by other ships which may offer more attractive inducements. Sailing, bunkering, and drydocking schedules are based on the same fundamentals as for any other types of merchant vessels. As tankers have become larger and faster and have been equipped with more complicated machines and control devices, there has been a corresponding increase in the demand for highly-trained seamen. Dry cargo ships, especially container carriers, have been built with many of the same types of complex mechanical installations, and they have just as much need for the best and most competent mariners. Shipyards, especially those with repair docks able to accommodate the enormous tankers of today, are available only in a small number of ports, and are equally in demand by huge dry bulk carriers and very large containerships.[8] Time is money to the owner of any ship, regardless of size. Any delay to a ship is very nearly intolerable, and the complaints of tanker managers on this account are no more heartfelt than are those of other members of the shipowning fraternity.

It cannot be denied, however, that there are some aspects of ship management which are peculiar to the tanker business. Among these distinctive characteristics may be cited the nature and inherent properties of petroleum and its derivatives, the specialized terminals required for loading and discharging the ships, the normally one-directional flow of traffic, and the integration of the schedules of operation of refineries, distribution centers, and tankers.

The fact that petroleum traffic flows only in one direction is of major economic importance in analyzing the operation of tankers. Except in unusual circumstances, the ships are engaged for a significant portion of their lives in expensive and genuinely nonproductive voyages in ballast back to their loading ports. Various expedients have been examined in the search for ways and means in which to enhance the usefulness of the ship. In 1964, for example, Erling Naess, a very successful independent ship operator, ordered the first ship designed to transport full cargoes of oil, or dry bulk commodities, or ore (hence OBO), depending upon the demand for transportation of each of these commodities.[9] The theory was that, by judicious scheduling, after delivery of a cargo of oil the ship might be chartered to lift a cargo of grain or iron ore to a port not too far from the oil loading point, thereby virtually eliminating the ballast leg. A modification of this idea produced a ship which could carry only oil or ore cargoes (hence O/O).

The *San Juan Pioneer* was one of the first ships to be employed in this alternating trade. A typical voyage involved carrying oil from Sumatra to Los Angeles; sailing in ballast to San Juan, Peru, to pick up a full load of iron ore for Japan; and then proceeding in ballast to Sumatra to start the cycle over again. The passages from Los Angeles to San Juan and from Japan to Sumatra were relatively short, and the revenue from the ore cargoes measurably improved the ship's profit-making ability.[10]

This theory of combining trades did not produce the anticipated results. In 1966, when the OBO and O/O vessels appeared in the record books for the first time, there were 109 ships in the "combined" (or as it soon came to be called, the "combi") fleet, and the average deadweight of the ships was 37,587 tons. The number of ships reached its peak in 1976, when the registers listed 410 ships with an average deadweight of 111,413 tons. In 1992, the size of the fleet had declined to 282, with an average deadweight of 116,660 tons. Almost two-thirds of this fleet was over fifteen years old. The older ships were assigned to dry-bulk carriage, with

The integrated tug-barge *Belcher Port Everglades-Belcher Barge #102* was built in 1981 to carry 55,000 tons of oil. The 15,000-horsepower tug fits into a 35-meter notch at the stern of the 195-meter-long barge. Photograph by Aurora Photography, courtesy of Belcher Oil Co.

very little likelihood of ever being returned to transporting liquid cargoes. Twenty-five of the "combis" of more than 40,000 tons and an average age of thirteen years, were hauling oil exclusively. No new vessels of this type were under construction.[11]

As previously noted, oil companies look to the independents to augment the capabilities of their proprietary fleets. Sound economic justification exists for this position. The demands for capital to support activities related directly to the production of oil have become so great that little money is available for either construction or purchase of ships. If there is need for one or more ships of a design especially well adapted to meet the oil company's requirements, a long-term time charter for the anticipated life of the tanker may be negotiated with an independent. The charter party serves as collateral for the independent to borrow the funds with which to build the ship. This financial arrangement, devised shortly after World War II, has been used effectively in a number of instances.

Chartered tankers are integrated into the operation of the proprietary fleet, and their movements are controlled by the marine traffic department. Short-term, single-voyage, or consecutive voyage charters are used to meet immediate requirements which exceed the capability of the ships either owned or on long-term contracts. "Spot" coverage is a vital, but marginal, activity arising out of the need for additional ships for a voyage or two to meet unscheduled transportation demanded by the production or marketing divisions. "Unscheduled," in this case, means an unexpected contingency arising, for example, from a mishap withdrawing a ship from service, a sudden surge in demand for petroleum products, or the breakdown of a refinery. Should a temporary surplus of cargo exist, or a shortage of company-controlled ships develop, the prompt chartering of one or more tankers would be appropriate to ease the crisis without taking on the obligation to employ the ship once the pressing need had been met. Even though the price of the spot chartered ship may be comparatively high when measured against the company's average charter rate, the convenience of having a tanker at the time required, and only for that period, may be worth a great deal to the charterer.

Tankers generally are engaged in one of two distinctive types of service, distinguished as "clean" and "black" (sometimes also called "dark oil" or "dirty") trades. Ships in the latter trade carry only crude, residual, and darker oils up to diesel grade. Many of the heavy crudes require heating to reduce viscosity before they can be pumped ashore.

The clean trade, as the name implies, demands that the ship be very carefully prepared before any cargo oil is pumped into the tanks. Certain jet engine fuels, for example, must be carried only in tanks coated with inorganic, nonferrous compounds to eliminate contamination through corrosion of the tank walls. Lubricating oil may be emulsified if water is left on the tank walls; therefore, extra care must be exercised to assure that no trace of moisture remains to pollute the cargo. It is customary to fill ("press up") the tanks to capacity so that there is no void space in which condensation can form. In those instances where several grades of lubricating oil, varying in color from grade to grade, must be pumped through the same piping system, the lightest colored oil is pumped first. This assures against contamination from any residue encountered in the pipes.

Black (or crude) oils, which are transported only from oil-field terminals to refineries or prepared storage facilities, are markedly heavier than the refinery products. The characteristic high viscosity of the crudes, which usually must be heated to render them sufficiently fluid to move through the ship's pumping system, requires that each of the cargo tanks be equipped with coils through which superheated water is circulated. This heated oil is transferred ashore by the ship's pumps. As the carrying capacity of the tankers grew, so did the capacity of the pumps, measured in tons per hour. In the very large crude carriers (VLCC)—a designation applied to ships of 200,000 tons deadweight or larger—the pumps move at least 10,000 tons of petroleum every hour.[12]

As a consequence of a number of tanker casualties in which the cargo tanks were ruptured and millions of gallons of crude oil were spilled on

The double-hull crude oil carrier *Berge Sigval,* 306,430 metric tons deadweight, was built in 1993. She was 332 meters (1,115.5 feet) long, 58 meters (192.6 feet) wide, and had a draft of 22.8 meters (74.9 feet). Her speed was 15.4 knots. Photograph courtesy of Bergesen d.y. AS.

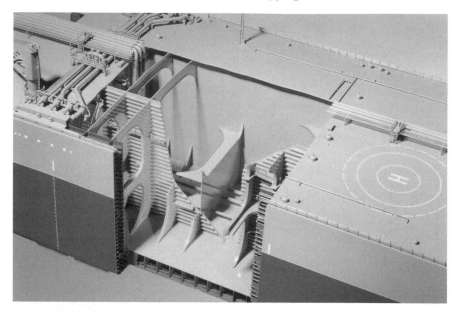

This cut-away drawing shows structural details of a double-hull tanker. Two of the three thwartships tanks are depicted. Drawing courtesy of Bergesen d.y. AS.

coastal beaches and in estuarine waters, the need to safeguard the environment became a major consideration of legislative bodies, marine insurance underwriters, and the petroleum industry. To prevent such disasters, the so-called double-hulled tanker was designed. This ship had a complete inner hull, separated from the outer by approximately 10 feet. The theory was that a grounding would pierce only the outer skin, and would not imperil the integrity of the cargo tanks. The first such ship was delivered by the builders in 1975. This was the *Chevron Oregon,* of 39,218 tons deadweight. In 1991, following new governmental regulations and greater public concern regarding pollution, the first of a number of large double-hulled tankers was put into service. This was the *Olympic Serenity,* of 96,777 deadweight tons.[13]

Although there was some debate among tanker operators over the factor of safety built into the double-hulled tanker, the trend in that direction was very strong. The first very large crude carriers built to these principles were the *Eleo Maersk,* of 299,381 tons deadweight, owned by Maersk Tankers, of Denmark; the *Arosa,* of 291,381 tons deadweight, owned by Arosa Maritime, Inc., of Greece; and the *Berge Sigval,* of 306,430 deadweight tons, belonging to Bergesen A/S, of Norway, which was the world's largest double-hulled tanker when commissioned in early 1993.[14]

Safety is a managerial responsibility of paramount importance not only on board ship but also around the terminals where tankers load and discharge. At sea, in the approaches to ports, at anchorage, at berth when pumping cargo as well as when awaiting orders, and throughout the normal routines of cleaning tanks, performing maintenance work, and standing watches, the utmost vigilance must be exercised constantly by all personnel if accidents are to be prevented. Clearly related are the provisions for the navigation of the vessel: selection of routings, use of pilots, proper communication procedures, supervision of electronic aids to navigation, and selection of adequate berths. Fire, obviously, is the ever-present hazard, and elaborate precautions are taken to reduce this danger. Management must assure that safety rules and procedures for shipboard and shoreside activities are consistent and mutually understood and respected.

To reduce the possibility of explosions set off by static electricity in the cargo tanks, tankers of 20,000 tons deadweight and larger must have installed onboard inert gas systems. The inert gas, with an oxygen content of not over 5 percent by volume, may consist of treated flue gas from main or auxiliary boilers, gas from a gas turbine's exhaust, or gas from a separate inert gas generator. This system pipes an inert gas into the tanks as the cargo is pumped out, thereby preventing the mixture of air and petroleum vapor which can become critical and subject to explosion from a single spark.

Following the development of the inert gas system has come the technique of crude oil washing of cargo tanks, which is safer than the time-honored method of washing tank walls with streams of hot water under high pressure. One of the benefits of the crude oil washing system is that cargoes are delivered with less contamination, at the same time that ballast water is clean and nonpolluting. These new methods, combined with the rapid strides made in electronic aids to navigation and in remote control of machines, have stimulated tanker managers to set up elaborate training programs based on simulators using computers and realistic scenic effects. Seafarers are able to hone their skills in every aspect of their profession, and to learn in advance of meeting them how to react to a wide variety of situations which might be encountered in the course of a voyage. As installations increase of newer, more versatile, and more comprehensive electronic systems which integrate control of shipboard functions, and only one watchkeeper is in charge of the ship, the need for frequent retraining becomes more insistent.

The centralized, computer-oriented, one-man operated engine control station is installed in a sound-proof room. Photograph courtesy of Merlin Gerin.

Victualing, storing, scheduling, repairing, and bunkering a fleet of tankers in worldwide service are other aspects of management responsibility. Few tankers are employed in repetitive voyages between designated ports, and therefore long absences from the home port often occur. To provide adequate supplies of food and stores of good quality, and to procure these at reasonable prices for scores of ships in oil-handling ports around the world, is an activity of impressive dimensions. The constant application of the principles of bunkering is mandatory for management of a globe-girdling fleet of tankers. Management never becomes routine when voyages are subject to unforeseen deviations, reroutings on short notice, and unexpected delays beyond control of either the ship's personnel or her owners.

One solution to the problems just described is for the owner to contract with an organization which specializes in managing ships. For a price, these firms will assume any or all responsibilities in connection with the operation of the ships. They will, for instance, provide crews; requisition all supplies, stores, and bunkers for each voyage; supervise repairs; designate agents to husband the ships in ports of call; and arrange for cargo and hull surveyors as needed. Contracting with these outside specialists relieves the owner of many of the burdens of management, but it interposes an additional bureaucratic level between the shoreside and the seagoing enterprise. Should the vessel be time chartered for a protracted period to operate in an area remote from the shipowner's domicile, the desirability and feasibility of turning over to a local management specialist the full responsibility for handling the ship are readily apparent. Substituting a contract for the owner's staff when the ship is frequently in nearby waters is an action which could be justified only by the actual experience and competence of the legal owner.

Regardless of their geographic location with reference to each other, the attitude of owner and contractor toward shipboard labor is of critical importance. If seafarers are regarded collectively as a depersonalized community rather than a valued component of the operating team, the efficiency and safety of the ship is in jeopardy. The pressure to reduce expenses in order to survive in a period of economic uncertainty unavoidably brings about careful scrutiny of every item of ship operating expense. Payroll is a major element. All too often, because effects are seen immediately and dramatically, the decision is made to hire seafarers who have no relationship to the nationality of the ship or the owner, and whose principal qualification is willingness to accept substandard wages and working conditions. Money is saved, but the decision has the potential for disaster. A low-cost, multinational and therefore multilingual crew may work harmoniously in normal circumstances, but in time of emergencies may become a disorganized mob. The problem is heightened by the commonly followed routine of replacing the crew at intervals of six to eight months with a new group of similarly recruited seafarers who predictably need time to absorb the procedures to make the ship safe, efficient, and comfortable. The lessons of recent ship operating history should be recalled, and owners and managers would be wise to accept the truth of the axiom that ultimately the success or failure of a voyage depends upon the men and women who take the ship across the seas and bring her home. They are the precious and irreplaceable element in ship management, be that ship tanker, bulker, general-purpose tramp, specialized carrier, or luxurious cruise ship.

No ports in the United States have sufficient depth of water to accommodate tankers of more than about 300,000 tons deadweight. To obtain the benefits of the lower unit cost of transportation afforded by the very large crude carriers, oil refiners devised a procedure by which ships of not over 75,000 tons deadweight met the supertankers in coastal waters, where the cargo was transshipped into these shallower-draft vessels.

A more economical and more permanent method of using very large crude carriers was put into operation off the Louisiana coast in 1981. A huge buoy was anchored in water over 100 feet deep to serve as the mooring point for the ship as well as the offshore terminal of a submarine pipeline connected to the storage facilities ashore. Located about 18 miles offshore, this unit, known as the Louisiana Offshore Oil Point (LOOP), can process over one million barrels of petroleum per day. The tanker is moored by a cable over the bow ("single point mooring"), which permits her always to face into the prevailing wind and sea. Her cargo is pumped through a floating hose to the buoy, where it flows into the submarine pipeline. The LOOP is one of a number of these offshore moorings in use around the world.

In 1993, there were 464 tankers of 175,000 tons deadweight or larger.[15] They gave to charterers the benefits of the economy of scale, and offered to shipowners these advantages compared to ships of about 75,000 tons deadweight or smaller: per ton of cargo carried, they were cheaper to build; crews were of about the same size; fuel consumption per ton of cargo delivered was less; and fewer hulls were needed to transport a given quantity of petroleum. One measure of the economy of the large ship is seen in the report that a 275,000 ton tanker delivers twenty-eight barrels of oil for each barrel of fuel oil burned.

These very large crude carriers have to overcome major problems in actual operation. Their great draft, ranging from 18.29 meters (61.46 feet) for a 200,000 tonner to the 24.61 meters (82.7 feet) of the 564,650-ton *Seawise Giant* (sold in 1991 to new owners and renamed *Jahre Viking*) restricts them to trade between a comparatively small number of ports. Ships with a draft exceeding 22.80 meters (76.6 feet) which are routed to Japan from the Arabian Gulf must use the deep Straits of Lombok rather than the thousand-mile shorter passage through the shallower Straits of Malacca. Tank cleaning is more hazardous than in smaller ships because of the vast size of the cargo tanks and the greater possibility of generating static electricity which could cause an explosion. Only a few ship repair facilities, especially dry docks, are large enough to accommodate these giants. It is, therefore, not surprising that the world fleet included only eighty-six tankers exceeding 300,000 tons deadweight at the beginning of 1993.

The largest tanker in the world, the *Jahre Viking* was 458.5 meters (1,540.4 feet) long, 68.4 meters (229.8 feet) in beam, and on a draft of 24.61 meters (82.7 feet) had a deadweight of 564,650 tons. Her 50,000 shaft horsepower steam turbines gave her a speed of 13 knots. Photograph courtesy of Jorgen Jahre Shipping A/S.

LIQUEFIED GAS CARRIERS

Closely related in many respects to the movement of petroleum and its derivatives is the carriage of liquefied natural gas and liquefied petroleum gas. These gases belong to two unrelated categories: those of which the vapors are flammable when mixed with air, and those of which the vapors are both flammable and toxic. In the first category are hydrocarbons, butane, butadiene, propane, propylene, ethylene, and liquefied natural gas. The chemical gases, vinyl chloride monomer, methyl chloride, ammonia, and propylene oxide, are members of the second category. The principal hazards associated with the first group are fire and possible explosion, while the second group may explode, catch on fire, or have toxic effects on personnel, possibly causing asphyxiation.

Routinely, liquefied natural gas is transported under pressure, but three different methods are used: (1) fully pressurized, i.e., under pressure but at the ambient temperature; (2) refrigerated and semi-pressurized, i. e., under pressure but cooled well below the ambient temperature; and (3) fully refrigerated, which hints at the process by which the gas is cooled to its boiling point at slightly above atmospheric pressure, and transported at that pressure. Liquefied gas is bulky; one ton of the gas occupies about four times the space of an equivalent weight of petroleum.

The first shipment of liquefied gas took place in 1928, when the *Megara,* a conventional oil tanker converted for the purpose, transported liquefied petroleum gas at a temperature of 0° Celsius and a pressure of 250 pounds per square inch. Although this movement was successful, it was not exploited. In 1958, the *Methane Pioneer* was introduced. A small dry-cargo carrier, she had been converted into a carrier of liquefied gas. Her pressure vessels were insulated by a "wool" made from balsa wood, and proved entirely satisfactory. Two years later, the *Bridgestone Maru,* a vessel of 25,626 tons deadweight, was designed and built specifically to haul liquefied gas from Indonesia to Japan. Her performance validated many theories relating to the techniques of shipping this new commodity.[16]

Ships carrying liquefied petroleum range in capacity from 5,000 cubic meters to over 100,000 cubic meters, most in the categories up to 10,000 cubic meters. They are suitable for the transportation of first category gases, and can be equipped to load ammonia or vinyl chloride. Cargo is carried at nearly atmospheric pressure and the temperature goes down only to −50° Celsius. Consequently, the tanks may be of the free-standing, prismatic type. These are internally stiffened, heavily insulated externally, and fabricated from special steels which will not crack in the low tempera-

The *Lake Charles* (built 1980) carried 125,000 cubic meters of liquefied natural gas in her five spherical tanks. Photograph by Eckstein, courtesy of Moore-McCormack Resources.

tures. All cargo tanks are installed a minimum of 760 millimeters from the outer hull.

Liquefied natural gas carriers vary in capacity from 25,000 cubic meters to 135,000 cubic meters. Most of the ships are able to carry at least 100,000 cubic meters of gas. Although many different systems for handling this commodity have been proposed since 1959, only two have gained widespread acceptance. One pattern is that developed by Moss, a Norwegian shipbuilder, in which free standing, spherical vessels are anchored to the inner hull. The other was created by Gaz Transport and Technigaz, of France. This system features free standing, prismatic pressure vessels, also secured to the inner hull. In both methods, the pressure vessels are wrapped in thermal insulation.

All carriers of liquefied natural gas are built with a watertight inner hull; those with the prismatic tanks are required to have a secondary containment system which will hold any cargo leakage for at least fifteen days.[17]

Transportation of these liquefied gases has become a major economic activity. The principal exporting nations are Indonesia, Algeria, Malaysia, Brunei, and Australia. Japan alone absorbs about two-thirds of the export trade. The main European markets are Spain and Belgium. In 1990, 54 million metric tons of liquefied natural gas and 33 million metric tons of liquefied petroleum gas were moved, giving employment to 849 ships ranging in capacities from less than 2,000 cubic meters to the 137,000 cubic meters of the largest carrier.

Liquefied natural gas is delivered to public utilities with large storage tanks, while liquefied petroleum gas is distributed to vendors with much more limited storage facilities. Consequently, the ships which transport "butane" are likely to be small. Even granting that butane at −51° Celsius presents less of a problem in handling than does liquefied natural gas at −160° Celsius, the burdens imposed upon management to assure that every voyage is completed without incident are almost identical. It is a tribute to the skill and vigilance of the ship operators that hundreds of voyages are made each years; for example, in 1991, there were 1,466 deliveries of liquefied natural gas, 400 of which went to Tokyo Bay.[18]

Liquefied gas carriers must be designed and constructed not only to meet the needs of the service for which intended, but also in accordance with the requirements of the ship classification society, of which Lloyd's Register of Shipping is probably the best known. A ship used for transportation of liquefied gases in bulk and built with membrane tanks would be given Lloyd's Register classification of "+100 A-1 liquefied gas tanker." Should the vessel be constructed with independent spherical tanks, the classification would be "+100 A-1 liquefied gas carrier."

Refrigerated gas cargo inevitably suffers some evaporation, which is know in the trade as "boil off gas," or BOG. This is not wasted; it is transferred by an electrically powered gas compressor to the boilers, where it supplements the fuel used to generate steam for the turbines. This gas, however, represents a loss to the shipper, and much attention has been given to reducing the BOG. A building program involving seven identical ships was initiated in 1989, and stipulated four independent spherical tanks, rather than the more conventional five. Among the advantages claimed for this arrangement of 125,000 cubic meter ships were ease of operation, maintenance, and repair, low initial cost, and reduction of the "boil off rate" (BOR) from 0.25 percent per day to 0.15 percent per day. In part, this improvement was attributed to the very heavy insulation applied to the four tanks, which was 210 millimeters thick, and consisted of two layers of phenolic resin and polyurethane foam, protected with aluminum alloy sheets and fastened to the tank with stud bolts. Stainless steel "thermal brakes" also were inserted between the skirts, which were of aluminum alloy and steel.

In July 1992, the world's largest liquefied natural gas tanker was the 137,000 cubic meter *Ekaputra,* built by Mitsubishi's Nagasaki yard in 1990 and assigned to transport gas from Indonesia to Taiwan. The 18.5-knot, turbine-driven ship had five highly insulated, Moss-designed spherical tanks from which the BOR was reported to be 0.10 percent per day.

It is significant that in 1992, most liquefied natural gas carriers were employed in stabilized routes, as in the case of the *Ekaputra.* They thus were shielded from the unpredictable and mercurial charter market for ships of this type.

CHEMICAL TANKERS

Liquid chemicals have been transported in bulk across the seas since about 1950. At that time, shippers of large quantities of animal fats, tallow, and vegetable oils were in quest of lower transportation charges, and began to charter oil tankers. As the advantage of bulk shipment of nonpetroleum commodities became apparent, additional liquids, including a variety of chemicals, were offered. As could have been expected, it was found rather quickly that some of the chemicals possessed characteristics which demanded more sophisticated techniques for bulk transportation than the standard oil tanker could offer. A number of tankers were modified to the extent necessary to meet the new requirements. Multiple piping and pumping systems were installed. Cargo tanks were coated to present a smooth, uniform surface which would resist corrosion and also prevent contamination of the cargoes.

While a number of chemicals are no more dangerous to transport in bulk than is liquefied petroleum, other chemicals are genuine "high risk" cargoes, and present management, both ashore and afloat, with peculiar problems, of which the following have special significance:

1. The danger of fire may be enhanced by the nature and characteristics of the chemical. Carbon disulphide, for example, has a low
   flash point and a wide range of flammability; phosphorus ignites
   spontaneously when exposed to air; adiponitrile gives off poison
   gases when it burns.
2. Vapors from chemicals may irritate personnel, thereby necessitating
   that vents exhausting to the atmosphere be elevated above any crew
   passageways. The exact height varies with the chemical(s) being
   transported. Additionally, vents must be at least 40 feet distant from
   any opening to the crew's living spaces.
3. Vapors from, or contact with, certain chemicals cause health risks.
   Protective clothing, including face masks, must be available for the
   ship's company, and therefore have to be part of the vessel's
   original outfit.
4. Some chemicals react when mixed with other chemicals. Very definite regulations have been promulgated concerning the compatibility of these liquids, and must be obeyed precisely. The operator of
   the ship and her master must be fully informed whenever a mixed
   load is to be carried. Appropriate steps then must be taken by those
   in charge of loading and by the master to assure that parcels loaded
   in adjacent tanks separated by a single bulkhead do not cause dangerous results if a leak should develop in that bulkhead.
5. Certain chemicals have the propensity to react violently when con-
   taminated by water. The master must be notified of any chemicals
   the ship may be carrying which react this way, and every precaution
   must be exercised to assure that no water of any sort reaches the
   tank(s) containing these chemicals. This "family" of chemicals
   should be transported only in tankers that have double bottoms and
   non-water ballast tanks adjacent to the spaces in which these liquids
   are contained.
6. Many chemicals are capable of polluting human and marine envi-
   ronments if they are spilled. Heavy penalties may be incurred if a
   spill occurs. The most stringent precautions, therefore, must be observed to prevent any accidental discharge.

Over the years, the offerings of chemicals to be shipped in bulk increased sufficiently to justify building ships which had been designed expressly to transport a wide variety of these liquids, including the exotic as
well as the extremely dangerous substances. A primary requirement was

that a tanker of this type have a double bottom for the entire length of the hull. To isolate the different chemical cargoes one from another, inner skins in at least some of the tank areas had to be installed. Pumping and piping systems were planned not only to prevent contamination of the cargo, but also to minimize the possibility that violent reactions could occur from mixing noncompatible chemicals. Although not an integral part of the safety features of the chemical tanker, the multiple piping and pumping arrangements do contribute significantly to the efficiency of ship operations in the rapid loading and unloading of the assorted cargoes.[19]

All these matters were studied by the International Maritime Organization before it promulgated its "Code for Construction and Equipment of Ships Carrying Dangerous Chemicals in Bulk." Concurrently, this organization prepared a list of hazardous chemicals for which specialized care was mandatory, as well as designating which chemical liquids were not hazardous. In agreement with a proposal by delegates from the United States, the organization directed that chemicals be carried only in tankers which belonged to one of these categories:

Type I. The most hazardous chemicals shall be limited to ships designed with double bottoms in way of the cargo tanks. The cargo tanks shall not be closer to the side of the ship than a distance equal to one-fifth of the vessel's beam.
Type II. Moderately dangerous chemicals shall be carried only in vessels with double bottoms and side cofferdams at least 760 millimeters inboard from the exterior plating of the hull.
Type III. Nonhazardous chemicals may be moved in ordinary tankers provided that precautions are taken to prevent loss of the ship when carrying high density cargoes. Normally this would result in selected tanks being left empty to distribute the weight evenly throughout the ship's structure.[20]

Ships dedicated to the transportation of "parcels" (i.e., less than shipload lots) of liquid chemicals have to be designed in full awareness of the problems peculiar to this trade. No single vessel can handle every type of liquid chemical; over 1,300 different chemical products have been identified as potential candidates for bulk transportation across the seas. Many of the chemicals now moving by ship have characteristics which must be considered in the selection of the steel for the bulkheads of cargo tanks. Progressive operators of parcel tankers seem to agree that most chemicals can be stowed satisfactorily in stainless steel tanks; a qualified number can be loaded in tanks fabricated of mild steel and finished with layers of organic and zinc coatings.[21]

On April 1, 1992, a fleet of 235 chemical/parcel carriers, aggregating 6,100,000 deadweight tons, was engaged in transporting over two hundred different types of liquid cargoes. The main product groups included organic chemicals and petrochemicals, inorganic chemicals and acids, vegetable and animal oils and fats, molasses, and special cargoes such as fuel additives and naphtha.

An assortment of rules, international conventions, and local ordinances affected this trade. The International Maritime Organization, stimulated by the rapid increase in the overseas movement of noxious liquids in bulk, adopted Annex II of the Marine Pollution (MARPOL) Convention. Among other directives, this convention stipulated the way in which chemicals must be discharged into receiving tanks ashore and dumped into the sea as residual waste. Super-efficient methods of stripping tanks were prescribed and stringent regulations written to cover pre-wash procedures when the more hazardous substances were transported.

Operating tankers in this highly specialized trade, conforming to strict rules, safeguarding personnel, and meeting competition is a demanding occupation in which experience, good judgment, and wide technical knowledge are vital essentials. Drawing on more than four decades of participation in the transoceanic movement of chemicals in bulk, Stolt-Nielsen S. A. was able to build a company with worldwide subsidiaries, and in the late 1970s emerged as the dominant operator. In 1992, this organization owned 94 ships ranging in size from 1,500 tons deadweight to 40,000 tons deadweight, plying routes in the Pacific, Indian, and Atlantic oceans as well as offering a dedicated vegetable oil service from Southeast Asia and the Far East to Europe, the Mediterranean, and the United States. In addition, the company was engaged in a worldwide trade hauling full cargoes of clean petroleum products, crude vegetable oils, molasses, and caustic soda.

Stolt-Nielsen took delivery in early 1991 of the *Stolt Helluland,* built by Kvaerner Kleven at Fløro, Norway. This 29,999 tons deadweight chemical/oil parcel tanker was intended for worldwide operations and was built to carry up to forty-one different chemicals or a full deadweight of sulphuric acid, phosphoric acid, or methanol.

Cargo segregations were totally independent, based on twenty-three center tanks and two tanks on deck, all fabricated completely of stainless steel. The sixteen wing tanks were coated with zinc silicate paint. All tanks

Stolt-Nielsen's *Stolt Markland,* a chemical tanker of 29,999 tons deadweight, was delivered to her owners in 1991. The ship's system of stainless steel piping and pumps permitted 41 grades of cargo to be loaded simultaneously in 23 center tanks, 16 wing tanks, and 2 deck-mounted tanks set aside for highly sophisticated cargoes. Photograph courtesy of Stolt-Nielsen Inc.

were protected by an inert gas generating system, and had individual hydraulic pumps. Tank capacities ranged from 317 cubic meters to 2,199 cubic meters.

Washing tanks between cargoes can be of critical importance in this trade. To facilitate cleaning, the *Stolt Helluland*'s center (largest) tanks were designed with a minimum of structural members and obstructions, and each tank was equipped with a fixed multistage, multinozzle cleaning machine, supported by a drying system employing two dehumidifiers.

Protection from overfilling a tank during the loading process was assured by the installation of a radar-based automatic level gauging system and by alarm devices activated when the tank was 95 percent full and sounding again at the 98 percent level. Cargo temperatures were monitored by sensors so placed that they indicated top, middle, and bottom temperatures in each tank.

Powered by a diesel engine of 12,840 brake horsepower using heavy fuel oil, the *Stolt Helluland* had a speed of 15.5 knots. She was 174.4 meters (585.9 feet) long, 29.5 meters (99.12 feet) in breadth, and had a draft, at summer load line, of 9.85 meters (33 feet).

Transporting bulk liquids of many kinds from and to all parts of the world, tankers have become the largest category of ships in the merchant fleet. Their utility and importance are beyond measure. The management of tankers, therefore, is one of the great challenges of the shipping business.

CHAPTER TWENTY-TWO

The American Shipping Subsidy System

International shipping involves not only the normal rivalry among carriers for the available cargo, but also the more subtle competition between nations with disparate standards of living. Often the pattern of trade between two countries reflects the significant differences in their economic status. Nation A, for instance, has a well-developed industrial economy with a high standard of living for its citizens. It exports manufactured goods to all parts of the world, and imports great quantities of raw materials. Nation B, in contrast, has an agricultural economy, and depends upon the products of its fields to provide the funds to pay for the manufactured items it requires. Its standard of living, compared to that of Nation A, is significantly lower, as evidenced by the differences in wages and prices prevailing in that country.

For many sound reasons, Nation A has encouraged its citizens to own and operate ships to serve its foreign trade, here typified by the interchange of goods between A and B. The costs of building, maintaining, and running ships under its registry are well above those of Nation B, which also has a merchant fleet plying from B to A and back again. If the principles of pure competition applied perfectly to this trade, the level of freight rates would be fixed by what the ships of Nation B must earn to assure an adequate profit. To remain in business and to obtain any of the cargo, the owner of Nation A's fleet cannot charge more than do their rivals.

There are valid reasons why each of the trading partners should have merchant fleets. One is that money paid to national-flag operators is retained almost entirely in the local economy, in much the same way that the proceeds of sales of domestic goods to citizens stay inside national boundaries. Another reason is that the earnings of the fleet from freights paid by foreign shippers are equivalent to exports of goods; in fact, they often are referred to as "invisible exports." Sweden, for instance, considered shipping as a major export industry which brought in about 8 percent of its revenue from external sources.[1] *Per contra,* money paid to carriers of other nationalities affects negatively the country's trade balance.

It can be argued that Nation B has greater justification for a national-flag fleet than does Nation A. With its limited ability to earn foreign exchange, it must find ways to augment the revenue from sale of its agricultural produce. A merchant marine participating in world trade offers a means to increase national income. The money so realized is essential to help pay for the imports needed by Nation B. In particular, the freight derived from carrying goods bought from Nation A reduces the net disbursement from Nation B's treasury, while the freight collected from Nation A for transporting its imports from Nation B represents positive credits. Carried to its logical conclusion, this argument would seem to justify the elimination of Nation A's merchant fleet in order to strengthen that country's export sales. The counter to this conclusion is that Nation A experiences the same difficulties with its international balance of payments, and therefore its invisible exports are vital to its economy.

Another purpose of national ownership of a merchant fleet is to provide service on those trade routes which are of greatest economic importance to the nation. By their presence on a particular route, the ships of Nation A attract vessels from other countries which are seeking gainful employment. It is a fact of shipping that no trade route is so insignificant that there is not at least one competitor of the principal carrier. Even a small fleet from Nation A will attract ships from other nations, thereby providing adequate transportation to meet the needs of importer and exporter.

Finally, a corollary to the ability of ships to earn foreign exchange with which to pay for imports is the employment of vessels in the "cross trades." That is to say, ships of Nation A may sail regularly between Nations M and P, rarely returning to a port in Nation A. Money earned in this manner is a direct and positive addition to the financial strength of the shipowning nation.

These arguments touch upon the basic rationale for national-flag merchant fleets. They gloss over the problems of disparity of cost and difficulties of competition which arise out of that inequality. This has been suggested earlier in this chapter in the commentary upon differences in national living standards.

A comparison of the costs of operating ships under the registries of these two countries shows that Nation B, with its lower standard of living, enjoys a significant advantage over Nation A. The freight rates charged by the shipowners of Nation B reflect this; what produces a satisfactory profit for them is less than the minimum required for survival of the ships flying the flag of Nation A. It is a harsh fact of shipping, set forth repeatedly in this volume, that cost of transportation influences the shipper's decision as to which carrier will be favored with the cargo. If service and schedule are substantially equal, it is almost certain that the lower cost carrier, regardless of nationality, will receive the business.

The dilemma facing the owner of ships registered under the flag of high cost Nation A is, to put it very simply, "Where can I obtain the money I need to bridge the gap between my costs and the revenue I can earn from carrying cargo at the rates set by my lower cost competitor?"

There is only so much that efficient and economical management can do to reduce costs. Once these possibilities have been exhausted, the most obvious source of the indispensable supplementary income is the national treasury. Commercial interests will not pay higher freight rates simply to maintain a national-flag fleet. There is no patriotism among shippers anywhere; they give their business universally to the carrier who provides the best service at the lowest cost, without regard to the flag under which the ship sails. Philanthropists show no interest in assisting a commercial enterprise in which some corporation is seeking to make a profit. With no other avenue open, maritime activities around the world have turned to their governments for financial help.

In 1978, the Maritime Administration of the U.S. Department of Commerce conducted a survey of the types of aid available to shipping and shipbuilding companies in fifty-eight maritime nations, and learned that the principal forms of direct aid offered to their merchant fleets were these:

Operating subsidies for ships.
Subsidies applied to ship construction.
Trade-in allowances for ships.
Low interest loans.
Subsidies on payments of interest on loans.
Government guarantees of loans to shipowners.
Accelerated depreciation of assets for purposes of taxation.
Tax free reserve funds.
Duty free imports of materials needed for ship construction.
Cargo preference schemes.
Restrictions on foreign-flag shipping in domestic trade
    (cabotage protection).
Maritime research programs.[2]

No single nation offered all the forms of assistance listed above, nor was any standardized pattern disclosed which emphasized one or another of these features. Instead, each nation adopted whatever schemes seemed most likely to assure the survival of their merchant fleets. In many instances, the survey brought out that a variety of indirect aid programs, the exact financial value of which was impossible to measure accurately, also had been established in one or more of the maritime nations studied. Among the less obvious forms of assistance were:

> Schools for merchant seamen.
> Hospital and medical care for merchant seamen.
> Social security payments to families of merchant seamen.
> Laws directing that ships engaged in both the domestic and foreign trades of a nation be built in that nation's shipyards.
> Laws dictating that domestically produced materials be used in construction and repair of national-flag ships.
> Laws requiring that purchases of food, stores, and vessel supplies be confined to domestic markets.[3]

Of the maritime nations, the United States has the most comprehensive, most widely publicized, and most openly administered subsidy program. It evolved over generations of experience, starting in 1847 when the postmaster-general was authorized to enter into contracts with steamship operators to transport mail destined to foreign countries. The underlying purpose of this legislation was to encourage American investment in, and operation of, steam-powered vessels in direct competition with foreign-flag carriers. In 1840, with support from the British government, Samuel Cunard had inaugurated regular passenger and mail service between England and the United States. To compete with Cunard, some method had to be devised to offset the higher costs of building ships in the United States and operating them under American registry. The mail contract appeared to be a satisfactory method. It called for lump sum payments for each voyage without regard to the amount of mail actually carried. A major deficiency in the law was the absence of a stipulation that the contractor set aside adequate funds to construct replacement tonnage.

In 1817, the Congress enacted a law which restricted the waterborne trade between the states to ships built and owned in the United States, and manned by citizens of the United States. Because California was admitted to the United States in 1850, the well-publicized Gold Rush voyages of the clipper ships from Atlantic coast ports around Cape Horn to San Francisco were legally interstate commerce, and therefore limited to ships meeting the criteria set forth in the 1817 law. Subsequently, an extensive coastwise trade, especially along the Atlantic and Gulf coasts, developed under this protective legislation and flourished until the advent of World War II. When the Panama Canal was opened to commercial traffic on August 15, 1914, it made possible an active intercoastal trade which prospered for the next quarter century. Aside from protecting the ships engaged in these trades against foreign competition, however, there was no government assistance.

This cabotage restriction described above applies today in the coastwise and intercoastal trade, and in the movement of cargo and passengers between the forty-eight contiguous states and Alaska, Hawaii, and the offshore commonwealths and possessions. An exception exists in the waterborne commerce between the mainland and the Virgin Islands, which were purchased from Denmark in 1917. Vessels of foreign registry are permitted to transport goods on this route despite the fact that both origin and terminus are on U.S. soil.

To assure an additional source of revenue to American-flag ships, which were experiencing difficulty in meeting foreign competition, the Congress enacted a law in 1904 which required that all cargo belonging to the U.S. military, or consigned to its overseas installations, be carried in ships either owned by the government or registered in the United States. In 1954, the "Fifty-Fifty Law" was passed. This legislation directed that at least one half of all cargoes financed by the U.S. government and destined to foreign nations (primarily economic aid to less developed nations, as well as shipments of agricultural products to relieve hunger or to initiate self-help programs) be transported in ships registered in and operated under the laws of the United States for not less than three years.[4]

Direct subsidy of U.S. ships was not adopted until the Merchant Marine Act, 1936, was signed into law by President Franklin D. Roosevelt. This legislation terminated the ninety-year-old mail contract program, and for the first time established a systematic method by which government aid could be granted to the merchant fleet. Until the act was amended in 1970, the provisions of the law applied only to ships engaged in liner services. Dry bulk carriers and vessels working in the tramp trades had been excluded, largely because in 1936 the fleet did not include any ships of this type which were engaged in the foreign trade.

As part of the Reagan administration's policy to reduce the role of government in commercial affairs, the provisions of the Merchant Marine Act, 1936, relating to ship construction subsidy have been suspended since

October 1, 1983. While no new operating differential subsidy contracts have been approved, none of the contracts in effect has been altered or canceled. Despite the practical abandonment of that portion of the law which was designed to support an active American shipbuilding industry, and the lack of any encouragement to new organizations to seek operating differential subsidies, the law retains its vitality and can become once again an important factor in American shipping at any time.

Of all the methods by which governments worldwide make funds available to assist in the support of their national flag merchant fleets, the U.S. law is probably the most complete and most openly administered legislation of this type. It is worthy of careful study. The analysis which follows is directed only toward those sections establishing the construction and operating differential subsidy system. The analysis is intended to provide information: it does not pass judgment on either the fundamental premise of government assistance to shipping or on the manner in which the purposes of the Merchant Marine Act, 1936, have been carried out.

Section 101 of the law contains the declaration of national policy concerning the U.S. merchant marine. Although this declaration was hailed in 1936 as the "Magna Carta" of the merchant marine, in reality it was a repetition, with only minor modifications, of the statement of purpose contained in the 1920 Shipping Act, and later "confirmed" by the 1928 Shipping Act. In its entirety, this declaration of policy, which has not been amended in the decades since adoption, reads:

> It is necessary for the national defense and development of its foreign and domestic commerce that the United States shall have a merchant marine (a) sufficient to carry its domestic water-borne commerce and a substantial portion of the water-borne export and import foreign commerce of the United States and to provide shipping service essential for maintaining the flow of such domestic and foreign water-borne commerce at all times, (b) capable of serving as a naval and military auxiliary in time of war or national emergency, (c) owned and operated under the United States flag by citizens of the United States insofar as may be practicable, (d) composed of the best-equipped, safest and most suitable types of vessels, constructed in the United States and manned with a trained and efficient citizen personnel, and (e) supplemented by efficient facilities for shipbuilding and ship repair. It is hereby declared to be the policy of the United States to foster the development and encourage the maintenance of such a merchant marine.

Proceeding logically, the act prescribes the basic responsibilities of the United States Maritime Commission, which was established to administer the law. An independent agency which reported directly to the president, the commission was assigned the dual role of promoting the merchant fleet and handling the details of subsidy agreements and also of regulating the water-borne commerce of the United States. In 1951, the independent status of the commission was terminated when the agency was placed under the Secretary of Commerce, and the regulatory functions were assigned to the independent Federal Maritime Board, of which the chairperson was the maritime administrator. The agency was reorganized again in 1961, when the independent Federal Maritime Commission was set up for the sole purpose of regulating ocean transportation and enforcing the provisions of existing legislation (at that time, primarily the Shipping Act of 1916). The Maritime Administration remained in the Department of Commerce, and administered the subsidy programs and promoted the American merchant marine pursuant to the provisions of the 1936 act. In 1981, the Maritime Administration became a component of the Department of Transportation, and the Secretary of Transportation was named as the official spokesman on all matters relating to maritime policy. (In the following paragraphs, all references to the secretary will be directed to the Secretary of Transportation.)

Pursuant to the requirements of Section 211 of the 1936 act, the secretary is empowered to "investigate, determine, and keep current records of" certain types of activity:

(a) The ocean services, routes, and lines from ports in the United States, or in a Territory, district, or possession thereof, to foreign markets, which are, or may be, determined by the Secretary to be essential for the promotion, development, expansion, and maintenance of the foreign commerce of the United States, and in reaching his determination the Secretary shall consider and give due weight to the cost of maintaining each of such steamship lines, the probability that any such line cannot be maintained except at a heavy loss disproportionate to the benefit accruing to foreign trade, the number of sailings and types of vessels that should be employed in such lines, and any other facts and conditions that a prudent businessman would consider when dealing with his own business, with the added consideration, however, of the intangible benefit the maintenance of any such line may afford to the foreign commerce of the United States, to the national defense, and to other national requirements;

(b) The bulk cargo carrying services that should, for the promotion, development, expansion, and maintenance of the foreign commerce of the United States and for the national defense or other national requirements be provided by United States-flag vessels whether or not operating on particular services, routes, or lines;

(c) The type, size, speed, method of propulsion, and other requirements of the vessels, including express-liner or super-liner vessels, which should be employed in such services or on such routes or lines, and the frequency and regularity of the sailings of such vessels, with a view to furnishing adequate, regular, certain, and permanent service, or which should be employed to provide the bulk cargo carrying services necessary to the promotion, maintenance, and expansion of the foreign commerce of the United States and its national defense or other national requirements whether or not such vessels operate on a particular service, route, or line;

(d) The relative cost of construction of comparable vessels in the United States and in foreign countries;

(e) The relative cost of marine insurance, maintenance, repairs, wages and subsistence of officers and crews, and all other items of expense, in the operation of comparable vessels under the laws, rules, and regulations of the United States and under those of the foreign countries whose vessels are substantial competitors of any such American vessel;

(f) The extent and character of the governmental aid and subsidies granted by foreign governments to their merchant marine;

(g) The number, location, and efficiency of the shipyards existing on the date of the enactment of this Act or thereafter built in the United States; . . .

(j) New designs, new methods of construction, and new types of equipment for vessels; the possibilities of promoting the carrying of American foreign trade in American vessels; and intercoastal and inland water transportation, including their relation to transportation by land and air.

Pursuant to the mandate of Section 212 (c), the secretary is directed:

To collaborate with vessel owners and shipbuilders in developing plans for the economical construction of vessels and their propelling machinery, of most modern economical types, giving thorough consideration to all well-recognized means of propulsion and taking into account the benefits accruing from standardized production where practicable and desirable.

The authority so conferred was used initially to design the ships which served so well during World War II: the famous C-2, C-3, C-4, Liberty, and Victory dry-cargo ships and the T-2 tanker. After the war, the Maritime Commission's (later the Maritime Administration's) staff of naval architects designed and supervised the construction of the Mariner class, the world's first large high-speed cargo ships built on a mass production basis. In the years since 1960, the administration has worked closely with designers of new ships to achieve significant advances in naval architecture.

To carry out the intent of the Declaration of Policy that ships of U.S. registry be manned by "trained and efficient citizen personnel, the U.S. Maritime Service was created as a "voluntary training organization for the training of citizens of the United States to serve as licensed and unlicensed personnel on American merchant vessels." This uniformed, federal service trained thousands of seamen during World War II. Section 216 (b) established the U.S. Merchant Marine Academy as the federal agency charged with educating citizens of the United States to serve as licensed officers of the national merchant marine.

CONSTRUCTION-DIFFERENTIAL SUBSIDY

During the colonial epoch of its national history, ships were built along the Atlantic coast of what was to become the United States at prices substantially lower than those prevailing in the traditional shipbuilding centers of western Europe. This economic advantage gradually diminished as stands of virgin oak were depleted and raw materials became more expensive. One of the factors influencing the enactment in 1847 of the ocean mail contract legislation was the disparity in American and foreign shipyard prices. Unfortunately, there was no provision in this or subsequent laws to assure that aging ships would be replaced.

The Merchant Marine Act, 1936, embodied a bold new approach, continued and reinforced by the 1970 act, which systematized the building of ships under subsidy. In Title V are found the terms and conditions under which government funds will be made available to defray a portion of the cost of building ships in American yards. Section 501 (a) states that

Any proposed ship purchaser who is a citizen of the United States or any shipyard of the United States may make application to the Secretary for a construction-differential subsidy to aid in the construction of a new vessel to be used in the foreign commerce of the United States. No such application shall be approved by the Secretary unless he determines that (1) the plans and specifications call for a new vessel which will meet the requirements of the foreign commerce of the United States, will aid in the promotion and development of such commerce, and be suitable for use by the United States for national defense or military purposes in time of war or national emergency; (2) if the applicant is the proposed ship purchaser, the applicant possesses the ability, experience, financial resources, and other qualifications necessary for the operation and maintenance of the proposed new vessel, and (3) the granting of the aid applied for is reasonably calculated to carry out effectively the purposes and policy of this Act. The contract of sale, and the mortgage given to secure the payment of the unpaid balance of the purchase price shall not restrict the lawful or proper use or operation of the vessel except to the extent expressly required by law. The Secretary shall give preferred consideration to applications that will tend to reduce construction-differential subsidies and that propose the construction of ships of high transport capability and productivity.

Recognizing that from time to time it may be necessary or desirable to reconstruct or modify vessels used in the foreign trade of the United States, Section 501 (c) provides that any citizen of the United States may apply to the Secretary of Transportation for subsidy assistance. Pursuant to this authority, many ships were enlarged and adapted to carry containers following the worldwide shift to that mode of ocean transportation. The funds to defray the costs of this type of financial help are derived from the annual appropriations for ship construction.

The prospective purchaser of the ship (or the shipyard) must submit an application for construction subsidy, together with complete plans and specifications, to the secretary. The plans are analyzed to ascertain that approved engineering and construction standards have been met. Concurrently, a determination must be made by the secretary that the proposed ship will be satisfactory in all respects for the trade for which she is intended, and that she is competitive with the foreign-flag ships employed on that trade route. Assuming that the plans and specifications are approved by the Secretary of Transportation, they are forwarded, in accordance with the terms of Section 501 (b), to the Secretary of the Navy for approval of the ship as a potential military auxiliary. The Navy's examination permits recommendations concerning the additional features which would make the ship more adaptable to service as a military auxiliary in time of war or national emergency. Typical of these "national defense features" would be increased shaft horsepower, enlarged generator capacity, greater lifting power for cargo booms and winches, limited refueling-at-sea capability, and provision for washdown after experiencing radioactive fallout. The applicant must approve the changes proposed by the Navy, as they affect the economic value of his ship. When the prospective owner has signified acceptance of the recommended modifications or additions, the Maritime Administration must determine which of these national defense features has commercial utility and which has only military value. Those items of strictly military value are paid for by the Maritime Administration and are deducted from the cost of the ship when the calculations are initiated to establish the amount of the construction-differential subsidy.

This provision has not achieved the results envisioned by the framers of the legislation. Although the cost of installing the military features is paid by the government, no arrangement exists to subsidize the added expense of operation, maintenance, and repair of the unit installed at the request of the Navy. Because of this deficiency in the law, shipowners have been reluctant to accept the recommendations of the Navy, and have convinced the Maritime Administration of the validity of their complaints. Although national defense features have been built into all ships constructed under subsidy, they are minimal.

A theoretical example will illustrate the problem.

The operator of a ship stipulated that an electrical generator have a capacity of 100 kilowatts, but the Navy requested that this be increased to 500 kilowatts. The Maritime Administration paid for the difference between the price of the 100-kilowatt unit and the 500-kilowatt unit. In service, the operation of the generator proved to be inefficient and expensive because its capacity was greatly in excess of demand. There was more need for attention and repair, which added to the cost of operating the ship, but there was no assistance from government funds to defray these added expenses.

Once procedures relating to the national defense features have been concluded, and the Secretary of the Navy has certified that the ship will be acceptable as a military auxiliary, the shipbuilders enter the picture. The owner invites interested yards to submit proposals, and is obligated to accept the lowest responsive and responsible bid. The government, through the Maritime Administration, may pay the fair and reasonable differential between the cost of construction in the United States and building in a qualified foreign shipyard, but is limited by law to one-half the American price.

The Secretary of Transportation is directed by the law to estimate annually the cost to build in foreign shipyards each of the different types of ships included in the construction program for that year. In making these estimates, the secretary uses American specifications. That is to say, the specifications on which the estimate is based are those called for by American practice, regardless of whether these specifications exceed those customarily followed by foreign builders. For instance, until very recently American shipowners ordered steam turbine propulsion plants, whereas foreign operators favored diesel motors. The comparison of costs between the two ships was a very complex matter, and inevitably ended up in a highly theoretical computation which the owners claimed did not give them the parity in costs which the act intended that they receive.

An example of how construction subsidy for a containership ordered in 1979 would have been computed is presented:

American shipyard cost (lowest responsive and responsible bid received)	$90,660,000
National defense features, of no commercial utility (to be paid by Maritime Administration)	850,000
Net cost of commercial ship	89,810,000
Estimated cost of building this type ship in a foreign yard	44,922,962
Dollar difference between United States and foreign construction costs	44,887,038
Foreign construction price as a percentage of U.S. construction price	50.02%
Construction-differential subsidy payable	49.98%

To assist prospective purchasers of ships to obtain money from conservative lending institutions, Title XI of the law authorizes the government to guarantee these loans, or to guarantee bonds issued by steamship companies for sale to the investing public. The fee for this guarantee on obligations incurred for construction or reconstruction of ships is fixed at a maximum of one-half of 1 percent per annum on the outstanding principal.

Vessels built under subsidy must be constructed in American shipyards, using American components insofar as practicable, and must remain under U.S. registry for twenty-five years or until paid for, whichever is the longer period. They must be operated (1) exclusively in the foreign trade of the United States, or (2) on a round-the-world voyage, or (3) from the Pacific coast of the United States to European ports on a round voyage which includes intercoastal ports of the United States, or (4) from the Atlantic coast of the United States to the Orient on a round voyage which includes intercoastal ports of the United States, or (5) in the foreign trade on a voyage including a call at Hawaii or an island possession or territory of the United States.

Section 506 provides that those owners of ships built under subsidy who operate these vessels in the coastwise or intercoastal service as a part of their foreign voyages shall return to the U.S. treasury a proportion of the construction differential. This proportion is based on the relation which earnings in the domestic (i.e., coastwise or intercoastal) trade bear to the total earnings of the vessel during the preceding operating year. This limitation was included by the Congress in the Merchant Marine Act, 1936, to protect American carriers serving the domestic routes exclusively, and was consistent with legislation dating back to 1817 restricting the waterborne commerce between the states to American-built and American-registered ships. Because they were free from competition with lower cost foreign operators, there was no need to grant subsidies to ships in the interstate trade. It was appropriate, however, that these same ships be safeguarded from incursions by subsidized carriers whose costs were reduced to foreign levels.

The application of this theory may be observed by referring to the calculations incidental to granting a construction-differential subsidy. The government's portion was $44,887,038, and the purchase price was $44,922,962. In theory, both the government and the shipowner would set aside annually an amount equal to 4 percent of their respective contributions toward the total cost of the vessel. The government therefore would allocate $1,795,481, while the owner would deposit $1,796,918 to meet the amortization payments. The ship was assigned to the round-the-world trade, and in making her regular voyages carried intercoastal cargo. Her freight earnings in the domestic route came to $750,000 for the year, while her total revenues aggregated $7,500,000. The ratio of domestic to total earnings was one to ten. Under the terms of the law, the owner would have to deposit not only his normal amortization of $1,796,918 but also would pay to the Department of Transportation an additional 10 percent of that amount or a total of $1,976,609. In other words, the amortization would be increased to the point where domestic operators suffered no harm from a less expensive ship being placed on their route.

As an incentive to owners of subsidized ships to replace them when they became economically obsolete even while mechanically still service-able, the Secretary of Transportation was authorized to purchase old vessels when their owners contract to build new tonnage. These "traded-in" ships had to be at least twelve years old, employed in the foreign trade, and considered in need of replacement because they were obsolete or non-competitive on the trade routes to which they were assigned. The value of these ships, when sold to the government, in the words of the law, "shall not exceed the cost to the owner . . . plus the actual cost previously ex-pended thereon for reconditioning." A reasonable depreciation based upon a twenty-five-year life expectancy was to be calculated in fixing the mone-tary value of the ship. The purchase price realized had to be applied by the seller to the construction cost of the new ship.

No appropriations have been made by the Congress for construction differential subsidy since October 1, 1983. The need to replace obsolescent tonnage was satisfied by granting authority for two fiscal years to a limited number of steamship operators to build their ships abroad. Those owners who took advantage of this opportunity were required to make all financing arrangements through private channels. Permission also was given to buy existing ships from foreign owners or builders, with the stipulation that any work required to bring these vessels up to American standards would be divided equally between American and foreign shipyards. Despite many protests from the American shipbuilding industry, this modification of the intent of the Merchant Marine Act, 1936, was effective at least through September 1985.

Ships intended for operation in the domestic routes are not eligible for subsidy, but the mortgages given by the owners to lending institu-tions can be guaranteed by the Maritime Administration, pursuant to Title XI of the merchant marine law. The limit on any single ship is fixed at $87\frac{1}{2}$ percent of the building price. Supported by this assurance, a number of tankers and bulkers have been built since 1970. Several ship operators have encountered overwhelming difficulties, and the Mari-time Administration has had to pay off the creditors. In May 1985, for instance, the Phoenix Companies of Houston and New York defaulted on debt service payments of $128,395,000, and the indentured trustee for the bondholders demanded and received full payment by the guarantors of the loan.[5]

OPERATING-DIFFERENTIAL SUBSIDY

Entirely separated from the program to assist in meeting the cost of building American ships in American yards is the system by which government financial aid is extended to ships registered in the United States and engaged in the nation's foreign trade. This separation was made necessary, if for no other reason, because of the complexity of the problem faced by the American operator. So long as the philosophy of government support is directed toward assuring that funds will be used only for designated purposes, the detailed specifications of the Merchant Marine Act, 1936, as amended by the act of 1970, are necessary. In the paragraphs that follow, an examination is made of some of the most significant principles by which American ship operating costs are subsidized.

Ships seeking to obtain financial assistance through subsidy contracts must be operated in the nation's foreign trade in an essential service. Deliberately, the definition of an "essential service" has not been set forth with finality; the intent of the Congress was to permit ships engaged in liner service as well as bulk carriers (primarily engaged in hauling dry commodities, but the movement of liquid bulk cargoes by tankers is not positively excluded) to obtain subsidies. The phrasing of the law permits assistance to tramp ships when they are operated in the foreign trade of the nation.

The details of the system are set forth in Title VI of the Merchant Marine Act, 1936, as amended and rewritten by the 1970 law. It is significant that the principles enunciated in the earlier legislation, which were unique and trailblazing, have not been overturned. Some of the details of administration have been changed but the essential elements laid down in 1936 remain intact.

Any American citizen is eligible to apply for an operating-differential subsidy contract. In submitting an application, the citizen must show, in compliance with Section 601, that

(1) The operation of such vessel or vessels in an essential service is required to meet foreign-flag competition and to promote the foreign commerce of the United States . . . , and that such vessel or vessels were built in the United States . . . ;

(2) The applicant owns or leases, or can and will build or purchase or lease, a vessel or vessels of the size, type, speed, and number, and with the proper equipment required to enable him to operate in an essential service in such manner as may be necessary to meet competitive conditions, and to promote foreign commerce;

(3) The applicant possesses the ability, experience, financial resources, and other qualifications necessary to enable him [so] to conduct the proposed operations of the vessel or vessels as to meet competitive conditions and to promote foreign commerce;

(4) The granting of the aid applied for is necessary to place the proposed operations of the vessel or vessels on a parity with those of foreign competitors, and is reasonably calculated to carry out effectively the purposes and policies of this Act.

The contract between the government and the shipowner for an operating-differential subsidy may be for a period as long as twenty years. Before the contract is approved, the Maritime Subsidy Board must conduct an investigation, as required by Section 602, to establish the necessity for this form of assistance. The board, by law, must find that a subsidy is needed to meet the competition of foreign-flag vessels in the essential service the applicant proposes to provide.

Section 603 (b) sets forth the terms of the operating-differential subsidy contract in these words:

Such contract shall provide, except as the parties should agree upon a lesser amount, that the amount of the operating-differential subsidy for the operation of vessels in an essential service shall equal the excess of the subsidizable wage costs of the United States officers and crews, the fair and reasonable cost of insurance, subsistence of officers and crews on passenger vessels, as defined in Section 613 of this Act, maintenance, and repairs not compensated by insurance incurred in the operation under United States registry of the vessel or vessels covered by the contract, over the estimated fair and reasonable cost of the same items of expense (after deducting therefrom any estimated increase in such items necessitated by features incorporated pursuant to the provisions of Section 501 (b) if such vessel or vessels were operated under the registry of a foreign country whose vessels are substantial competitors of the vessel or vessels covered by the contract: *Provided, however,* that the

Secretary of Transportation may, with respect to any vessel in an essential bulk cargo carrying service as described in Section 211 (b), pay, in lieu of the operating-differential subsidy provided by this subsection (b), such sums as he shall determine to be necessary to make the cost of operating such vessel competitive with the cost of operating similar vessels under the registry of a foreign country. . . .

In other words, compensation under the operating-differential subsidy equals the percentage by which the "fair and reasonable cost" to an American shipowner of operating a U.S. registered vessel with an American crew exceeds the estimated fair and reasonable costs to a foreign owner operating the same ship with a foreign crew.[6] The amount to be paid under the subsidy contract is determined by agreement between the applicant and the Secretary of Transportation, and consists of a percentage of the various items of expense enumerated in the passage quoted above. The applicant must agree that, throughout the life of the contract, the ships will be manned according to American practice, and that American living and working standards will be observed.

The whole philosophy of the subsidy system is epitomized in the calculations of the fair and reasonable difference in costs between U.S. and foreign operators. To show exactly how this works out in practice, a sample computation determining the percentage of wage costs to be paid by the government to the American shipowner is presented below. This sample reflects the provisions of the 1970 law, and illustrates the method of measuring the competition and identifying the components of wage expense that must be borne by the employer. To recognize the variations in cost among different nations as well as the impact of the competition experienced on the route from non-American operators, the participation of these foreign carriers in the trade was established in terms of percentage. This percentage figure then was applied as the "competition weight factor." In the calculation, shown below, the share of the Netherlands in the trade was determined to be 19.1 percent, that of Belgium was fixed at 22.1 percent, and Norway's proportion was calculated to be 39.2 percent. The percentage of American to foreign wages was multiplied by the competition weight factor to establish the weighted percentage. By combining the weighted percentages, the composite weighted percentage was derived, and this figure was subtracted from 100 percent (the American wage level) to establish the actual percentage of the seamen's wages to be subsidized. The table below demonstrates these steps in the computation.

	(a) United States	(b) Netherlands	(c) Belgium	(d) Norway
1. Number in ship's crew	39	26	39	32
2. Base wages	$ 53,687	$ 23,127	$ 24,779	$ 27,257
3. Allowances	1,074	3,097	4,584	289
4. Vacation pay	35,681	9,499	13,009	11,976
5. Pension and welfare	33,407	3,923	2,065	124
6. Social security	6,608	4,584	7,227	10,118
7. Overtime and other variable costs	48,732	7,021	10,944	12,389
8. Repatriation	—	—	—	413
9. Total wage costs	184,189	51,251	62,608	62,566
10. Unweighted percentage, United States to foreign wage costs	—	27.82%	33.99%	33.96%
11. Competition weight factor	—	19.1%	22.1%	39.2%
12. Weighted percentage	—	5.31%	7.51%	13.31%
13. Composite weighted percentage (sum of b, c, and d) is 26.13%				
14. Percentage of wage costs subject to subsidy is 73.62%[7]				

Similar calculations are performed for the other items of operating cost to which subsidy assistance is applicable.

The operating-differential subsidy contract requires that the operators maintain a designated frequency of sailings with a specified type of ship, that they operate their ships only in the essential service to which they are assigned, that they not operate any foreign-flag shipping, and that they meet certain requirements as to procedures of management. Ships under subsidy must be less than twenty-five years old, unless the Secretary of Transportation finds it in the public interest to waive this stipulation.

Operating-differential subsidy contracts ordinarily are granted only to one American operator in each essential liner service. Under the terms of Section 605 (c), however, if it can be shown that the subsidized American operator is not adequately meeting the needs of the American shipping public, and the Secretary of Transportation finds it is in the public interest to provide increased American-flag operations in the essential service, subsidy for one or more additional carriers may be authorized. In practice, the onus of showing that service is inadequate has rested upon the applicant.

Very few approvals of this "double-tracking" of subsidized service have been granted.

Operators who fail to meet contract requirements are subject to cancellation of their contracts, or to substantial reductions in the level of subsidy payments. Those operators, however, who can demonstrate conclusively that it is economically impossible to maintain the essential services to which they are assigned, even with the subsidy, may be relieved of the contract. There are no cases on record of cancellation of contracts because the carriers did not meet requirements; release from their contracts was requested during the 1970s by several carriers serving routes including Great Lakes ports.

Mindful of the abuses of government supports under the ocean mail contract system, the Congress directed that operators holding subsidy contracts provide for the acquisition of replacement and additional ships needed to keep their services competitive with those of foreign carriers. Section 607 (a) stipulates that any citizen of the United States who owns or charters one or more eligible ships may enter into an agreement with the Secretary of Transportation to establish a capital construction fund to finance the replacement or reconstruction of existing ships, or to acquire additional tonnage. All these ships must be built in the United States, and documented under the laws of this country. They must be used in the foreign, Great Lakes, or noncontiguous domestic trade or in the fisheries of the United States. The incentive to set up and maintain the capital construction fund lies in the fact that deposits are not taxed as part of a corporation's income, and if these deposits are used to construct ships, lighters, barges, or containers, the tax liability is waived.

The American steamship company which enters into an operating-differential subsidy contract with the Secretary of Transportation must assume these obligations:

1. The contractors must man their ships under wage scales and working conditions, and provide living quarters, as prescribed by the government. They must carry, in addition to the regular complement, those cadets and apprentices assigned by authority of the Secretary of Transportation.
2. All financial accounting must be in accordance with rules of practice laid down by the government. In actuality, the Maritime Administration issues the rules and prescribes the accounting practices to be followed. Reports on any phase of a contractor's busi-

ness must be submitted to the Secretary of Transportation whenever he directs. All financial records are subject to periodic audit by government officials.

3. The contractors may not, except with written approval of the Secretary of Transportation:

   a. Operate any vessel over twenty-five years of age;

   b. Engage in any auxiliary services directly or indirectly connected with the operation of the subsidized ships, such as stevedoring, ship repairing, ship chandlery, towboat, or other allied activities;

   c. Engage in the intercoastal or coastwise (protected) trades of the United States;

   d. Effect any merger or consolidation, or directly or indirectly embark upon any new enterprise not connected with the business of shipping;

   e. Own, charter, or act as agent or broker for, or operate, any foreign-flag ship that competes with an American-flag service determined by the Secretary of Transportation to be essential;

   f. Dispose of any interest in the subsidy agreement.

From the foregoing commentary upon the Merchant Marine Act, 1936, and the important amendments made thereto by the Merchant Marine Act of 1970, some understanding may be obtained of the procedures by which government aid is extended to American shipping. Tight control is evident in many aspects. Experience has shown that this supervision is required for the protection of the public interest as well as to assure that the U.S.-flag operator will be assisted in meeting the objectives of the law. It appears significant in the evaluation of these two laws that few changes were made in the basic principles of federal support of the U.S. merchant marine through construction- and operating-differential subsidies.[8]

CHAPTER TWENTY-THREE

The Business of Shipping

In acquainting the reader with the intricate story of the management of a modern steamship company, as has been attempted in the preceding pages, some of the fascination and the deeply personal aspects of the business of shipping have received short shrift. The fascination exists, however much it has been covered over with operational detail. The rewards of the enterprise are understood by some, appreciated by others, and shared by those fortunate ones of all ranks who lift their eyes above their desks and seek the far horizons beyond which sail the ships.

To show how the manifold activities and responsibilities of management actually can be combined in one individual's experience, the career of an imaginary steamship company president is outlined below, together with this fictional executive's reactions to the challenges, changes, and rewards of shipping as a career. Except that no single individual is the subject of the sketch, the career delineated is typical of that of many steamship company executives. The philosophical musings also are based more on memories of comments by friends and associates than on imagination.

It is a fall evening in a large seaport city. Outside the city lights are coming on one by one. Inside the big office the jangle of telephones has subsided, and the clatter of business machines has been stilled. A few men and women linger at their desks as they finish up some small task before leaving for the day.

In the president's office, a man sits at the desk beside a window commanding a view of the harbor. He looks down at the unending activity on the water, and his eyes dwell upon the shape of a ship standing out to sea. The president muses about what has gone into the ship's sailing, and his musings take him back over a lifetime of service in the transportation of goods and people across the oceans.

He looks around his office. There, in a special place of sentiment and honor, is his certificate of graduation from a maritime academy. He had been well-trained there; he had come to know something of the hard yet fascinating life he had chosen for himself when only a boy. He also had had the veil of management and its challenges lifted just a bit. It had been a good experience, learning to be a seaman and finding out why many things were done in a certain way, some of which are engraved in the traditions of the sea.

Just above the diploma was another framed document, this one written in an engraver's script and ornamented with pictures of two ships. This was a license authorizing the person named thereon to command any size U.S. flag ship on any ocean. His master mariner's "ticket"! What years of work and aspiration had preceded the wonderful day when he had been presented with that precious proof of qualification for that post of distinction and almost immeasurable responsibility! A year as an able-bodied seaman, four months as a quartermaster, a year as junior mate, followed by two years in tramp steamers plodding all over the world with cargoes of coal, grain, ores, fertilizer, and lumber had given him a firm knowledge of the vicissitudes of the seaman's life and a competence in his chosen profession that no amount of theoretical study could have produced. He had a good time on the tramp; the ports were both familiar and exotic, the hazards of navigation with pilots who spoke no English and seemed to understand no sign language, had added a gray hair or two. He made some good friends, too, real seamen who had no other ambition than to command ships sailing in international commerce.

Tramping was all right, but promotion required a variety of experience. So he transferred to a liner company, even though it meant starting over again as a third mate. He learned at first hand about precise schedules, difficult loadings of odd cargoes, round-the-clock operations in one port after another, endless paperwork, and always the need to keep the agents informed systematically of progress so that the tugs, pilots, lines-handlers, and supply people could be scheduled to avoid delays to the ship. It had been good duty. Promotions were swift, and soon he was chief mate. Chief mate! Memories of the never-ending demands upon his time, skill, and knowledge crowded in upon the president. Responsibility for safety of the ship's cargo, for proper loading of the ship to assure seaworthiness, for efficient supervision of longshoremen, seamen, cadets, and shoreside workers who swarmed over the ship, as well as meeting senior company executives who came down to the ship—all this had been his. He learned to be everywhere at once, to carry a hundred details in his head without becoming confused or excited. He had to concentrate upon his daily duties, and he took real pleasure in knowing that each job had been done well.

Three years sped by for the chief mate, and after a total of only six years with that company he was transferred ashore to be cargo superintendent in a small foreign port. The high-sounding title covered a hundred routine chores from arranging for lines-handlers to tie up the ship when she arrived to explaining for the hundredth time to unresponsive longshoremen how to sling up certain types of cargo. Six months of that, and he was moved to a major foreign port as assistant terminal superintendent. That had been a challenging job! He had his first contact with the financial aspects of shipping, and began to relate ship time to money, efficiency on board to coordinated and systematic support from the shore staff, and the flow of cargo to economical employment of resources of the cargo terminal. This experience was intimidating, initially overwhelming, and finally appreciated.

Two years ashore, although crowded with interest and real accomplishment, still had not brought him to the pinnacle of his youthful ambition. He requested, and received, return to sea duty and rejoiced once again to feel a ship's deck underfoot. Six months as chief mate preceded that wonderful day when the vice president, operations, had informed him that the company had decided to recognize his outstanding performance by giving him a command of his own. How thrilling it had been to walk aboard *his* ship, and to realize that he had the final responsibility for the safety of the ship and all the people on board. He also knew that much pressure would be placed upon him to hold to schedules in spite of fog and storm, and how little understanding his problems would receive from landlubbers who thought of ships only as money producers.

He enjoyed his responsibility as master, and watched the results of his efforts as he slowly shaped the ship to his own ideals of a well-run vessel. To his pleasant surprise, he received a letter—there it was, yellowed and creased, hanging alongside his license—from the company's board of directors expressing appreciation of his unceasing and exemplary devotion to duty. That letter was precious—rescuing a dozen men from a foundering fishing boat in a frightful North Atlantic storm, winning the annual award two years running for the safest ship in the fleet, earning commendations for having the finest and cleanest ship in the company's service. He always had a good crew, and they had worked together with pride and with a sense of purpose.

The president's eyes moved on, to stop for a moment in front of the naval reserve commission. What a wrench assignment to active duty had been, as he changed from master of his own ship to lieutenant, navigator in a destroyer! Responsibility sought him out, however, and before many months he had been promoted, assigned first as executive officer of a large ship and then commander of a small cargo ship. From that job he had moved up to command of a large transport and then a major shore station. In those years of naval service he had come to understand the reasons why merchant shipping was a vital component of a nation's seapower. He never forgot those lessons, for they influenced his life and his thinking when he returned to commercial pursuits.

When he was returned to civilian status, he found that significant changes in management ashore had come about. More emphasis now was placed on the art of management, and financial considerations loomed larger than ever before. To bring himself up to date, and to meet the evolving standards of ship owning and management, the president attended graduate school, qualifying for the degree of master of business administration. Equipped with this testimonial to his intellectual acuity, the president found employment as chief mate with the company he now headed.

Two trips as mate were followed by assignment to a command of his own. The policy of the company was changing, and more attention was being given to capitalizing on sea experience. As an experimental move, he was brought ashore as a member of the sales staff in the outbound cargo department. *That* had been a change! "Pounding pavements and ringing doorbells, working up a good sales promotion talk, and never being downhearted" were the maxims he learned to follow. He enjoyed those contacts with the shippers. For years, he had served them impersonally when he was loading and transporting their goods, but now he was meeting them face to face. It gave a new dimension to his work at sea. He understood what the formerly anonymous "shippers" thought, and he was better able to meet their requirements. From sales representative, he was transferred to the manifesting department for a few weeks, more for experience than for the value of his contribution to that type of work. That wasn't his "cup of tea," since he had been an active seaman, and he disliked the routine of checking figures and cargo descriptions all day long. He realized how important it was that he know this part of the business, even though it lacked glamour. A transfer soon came to the inbound traffic department, where he met the consignees, the men and women who were waiting for the goods his ships were bringing to the port. He came to know many people, many government officials, and much about the business of keeping customers happy. He enjoyed this human contact, and he liked the idea of helping to generate patronage for the line through giving good service.

A new world was opened to him when he was promoted to general freight agent. He became intimately familiar with the manner in which freight rates were made. He spent uncounted hours in sessions with executives of other companies, both carriers and shippers, discussing and making policies and seeking solutions to problems. He attended those all-important meetings of the Conferences (he always spelled the word with a capital, to distinguish those associations of carriers on the trade routes from just routine face-to-face talks with his colleagues). He was very happy when the chairman, acting on behalf of the membership of the Conference, presented him with a letter expressing appreciation for his substantial contributions to the work of the Conference, based on his extensive seafaring experience.

It was during those months when he was general freight agent that he found himself an active participant in the greatest change in shipping practice since the initiation of liner service in 1818. Suddenly, it seemed that the skills acquired in handling break-bulk shipments had been made superfluous, as huge boxes were placed aboard ship by enormous machines. Appearances, however, masked the fact that care still was demanded in placing containers in the ship, assuring safe delivery, preventing accidents to personnel and containers, and making certain that terminal areas were secure from theft. He drew upon those years of sea experience, and he found that he was the more competent executive because of his background.

Traffic and all it meant were fine and a wonderful education, but operating ships was the president's real love, for he was a seaman first and last. He welcomed, therefore, the assignment overseas as operations manager. It was good to get back to having direct contact with the ships and the seamen, the terminal personnel and the faithful watchmen, coopers, and tradesmen and women who worked so well and so anonymously! Long hours had been spent at his desk, and even longer hours in the terminal and around the ships, but they had been rewarding, instructive, constructive, and, above all, companionable hours.

Those happy two years passed all too quickly. Then came the cable summoning him back to the home office to take over the duties of vice president, operations. What a tremendous thrill that was, and how proud he felt! From cadet to vice president in charge of all the ships! It had been quite a climb, and he had enjoyed every step of the way. He recalled those discussions of company policy on the proper operation of the fleet which he had with the former president, the positions he had taken and for which he fought vigorously because he believed them to be right even though they had not been popular.

Although the president had spent his shipboard years as a deck officer and ship master, and had been a successful terminal operator, he had schooled himself in marine engineering practice. He followed with intelligent and informed interest the rapid replacement of steam turbines by diesel engines of previously undreamed of horsepower and astonishing reliability and economy. His company, always a leader in technology, had adopted a fleet replacement program which made great demands upon the engineering staffs afloat and ashore, equivalent to the changes in freight traffic management and cargo handling impelled by the container revolution.

Two years as vice president, and one day the directors called him into their meeting room. Everyone rose as he entered. The chairman greeted him and escorted him to the only empty chair in the room. He noted, as he walked toward the table, that a handsome card beautifully lettered with the word, "President," had been affixed to that chair. It didn't seem possible, but he was led to that chair, and when the directors burst into applause, he came out of the daze.

The president's gaze shifted to a frame in which were a photograph of himself, in the uniform of a quartermaster, standing beside the master of his first ship, and that red-lined page from an old desk calendar, with the notation in pencil: "I was elected president today."

Thirty-odd years of his life were shown on the walls of his office, mused the president, as he scanned the room quickly: Cadet, seaman, quartermaster, mate, lieutenant, captain, master, pier superintendent, sales representative, general freight agent, operations manager, vice president, and president. It had been a good life.

As the president reached for his hat, he glanced out of the window again. Another ship was standing out to sea, and her light shone brightly in the gloom. He walked out of his office and noted, from force of habit, the board showing locations of all the company ships—*his* ships, their next ports of call, and their dates of arrival and departure. He always looked at that board each evening as he left the office; he liked to identify himself with the ships and the men and women on board. He remained a seaman, was proud to call himself by that term, and he loved the ships.

Outside the building, he walked briskly to the ferry landing and boarded the ferry. He went swiftly to his usual place up forward, where he could see the ships and their lights. Another big steamer was standing in from sea. In his mind, he envisioned the preparations being made even at that hour to receive the ship. The hoarse whistle of an outbound ship turned his thoughts to the people who had toiled over manifests and crew lists, cargo plans and repair specifications, stores lists and bills of lading, and to the men and women who stowed the boxes and bales and assorted commodities, and secured the huge containers, in their appointed places in the ship.

The big vessel slipped down the harbor and was lost in the dark. She was outward bound, and she carried with her not only the work of hundreds of men and women but the fortunes of dozens and dozens of shippers and consignees, the dreams of countless people who would use the great piles of goods that she carried, to say nothing of the lives of the fortunate men and women who were taking her to sea.

As he watched the moving ships he could not help but reflect on how, just as he had grown and changed, so had the maritime industry. It had been, and would continue to be, a dynamic and energetic industry. What was once a world fleet of small break-bulk vessels had evolved into a fleet of very large specialty carriers along with a much smaller fleet of traditional break-bulk ships. On certain routes around the world, tramp vessels had given way to large, fast, liner service vessels. Through the years, technology changed virtually every aspect of the industry from ship design to satellite navigation equipment and electronic charts, to electronic tagging of equipment, to the omnipresent computers. Government regulation had become more comprehensive in its concern for the environment and in new attitudes toward supervision of the industry. The industry had progressed from merely operating ships to the integration of services into intermodal transportation systems with the long-sought single bills of lading. Most conspicuous had been the changing nature of the work force. It was no longer surprising to go aboard ships or around terminals and find women working alongside men as equals in their jobs. The work force was much more diverse ethnically and in gender than when he had started his career. Workers of today had to possess skills in interpersonal relationships, communications, and computers. Where would it end? One thing was certain— the dynamism of shipping would carry it forward.

The echo of the big ship's whistle sounded through the night. It was lonely, brave, challenging, competent, cheerful. The president looked down the harbor, and said to himself, "It has been a wonderful career. I wouldn't exchange a minute of it for all the wealth of the Indies. It has been rewarding, exacting, exciting, dynamic, important, and, above all, necessary. What an honor to be able to say, 'My business is shipping!'"

Notes

Chapter 2. Tramp Shipping

1. Drewry Shipping Consultants. *Trading Prospects for the Dry Cargo Bulk Carrier Fleet* (London, 1992), p. 11.

2. Ibid., p. 89.

3. Department of Transportation, Maritime Administration, *Merchant Fleets of the World . . . as of January 1, 1992* (Washington, D.C., 1992), p. 8.

4. "Bulkers and Tankers Have Same Concerns," in *Fairplay,* April 22, 1993, p. 17.

5. William McFee, *Watch Below: A Reconstruction in Narrative Form of the Golden Age when Coal Took the Place of Wind and the Tramp Steamer's Smoke Covered the Seven Seas* (New York: Random House, 1940), pp. 48-53. Much of the material presented in this book is drawn from the author's service as an engineer officer on British tramps prior to 1914.

6. The Liberty ship hull was 134.12 meters (441.5 feet) long, 17.37 meters (57 feet) in the beam, and had a summer load line draft of 8.45 meters (27.75 feet). Her deadweight was 10,400 tons. There were five hatches, each served by one set of cargo booms. The oil-fired boilers generated steam at 220 pounds per square inch to actuate a three-cylinder, triple-expansion steam engine of 2,500-shaft horsepower. In calm seas, the ship had a cruising speed of $10\frac{1}{2}$ knots.

7. The "S.D. 14" was 140.87 meters (462.5 feet) long, 20.42 meters (67 feet) in the beam, and on a draft of 8.84 meters (29 feet) had a deadweight of 14,910 tons. She had five hatches and five holds, each served by cargo derricks of five tons' capacity. Her grain cubic capacity was 22,920 cubic meters (784,280 cubic feet). Speed in service under average fair weather conditions was 14.9 knots. She had a five-cylinder diesel engine, nominally rated at 7,500 brake horsepower, which used only 6,750 horsepower for cruising speed. The main engine consumed about $25\frac{1}{2}$ tons of heavy oil per day. In 1968, the price of the ship was £900,000. Ships of this type were built as late as 1983, with the last delivery in 1988. "The Austin & Pickersgill 'S.D.14' Liberty-Ship Replacement," a special supplement to *The Motor Ship,* May 1967.

8. Drewry Shipping Consultants, *Shipping Statistics and Economics,* March 1993, p. 45.

9. "Cunard's Growing Bulk Carrier Fleet: Two Further Ships Named in Seville," in *The Motor Ship,* October 1973, p. 320.

10. Drewry Shipping Consultants, *Trading Prospects,* p. 113.

11. Ibid., p. 89.

12. *Fairplay,* January 21, 1988, p. 11.

13. McFee's *Watch Below* is a semiautobiographical account of the working and living conditions aboard British-flag tramps in the period from about 1905 to 1914.

14. Roland Hobhouse Thornton, *British Shipping* (Cambridge University Press, 1939), pp. 139-40. A brief history of the origins of the Baltic Exchange is included in these pages.

15. Ibid., pp. 130-31.

16. The term "lay days" is used, with different meanings, for both circumstances described in these paragraphs. The content usually indicates which meaning is intended.

17. A charter party embodying these stipulations sometimes is described as a "liner terms" or "berth terms" agreement. Generally speaking, this terminology implies that loading and discharging expenses are included in the charter hire, and are for the shipowner's account.

18. For a detailed analysis of both voyage and time charter parties, see Lars Gorton, Rolf Ihre, and Arne Sandevarn, *Shipbroking and Chartering Practice* (London: Lloyd's of London Press, 1980). The authors are, respectively, a professor of maritime and commercial law; a legal advisor to a major Swedish steamship company; and the marketing manager of that company.

Per Gram, *Chartering Documents* (London: Lloyd's of London Press, 1981) provides a "running commentary" upon specimens of standardized charter parties. The analyses of the three types of charter parties clarifies many aspects of these documents. A clause-by-clause examination of a typical "contract of affreightment" also is provided in this volume.

19. This simplified and abbreviated version of a time charter party is based on the standardized time charter party issued by the Baltic and International Maritime Council under the code name of Baltime 1939. It is used by permission of BIMCO.

Chapter 3. The Management of Tramp Shipping

1. In 1991, the worldwide movement of major bulk commodities was: coal, 367.2 million tons; iron ore, 357.5 million tons; grains, 219.4 million tons; bauxite/alumina, 55 million tons; and phosphate rock, 31.8 million tons, for a total of 1.031 billion tons. (Drewry Shipping Consultants, *Dry Bulk Carrier Trading Prospects* (London, 1992), p. 12.

2. A study of patronage of British liner trade revealed that one carrier had 3,900 clients, but 75 percent of the tonnage carried was offered by only ninety-nine shippers. Roy Pearson, *Containerline Performance and Service Quality* (University of Liverpool, Marine Transport Centre [1981]). p. 23. (Hereafter cited as Pearson.)

3. The Baltic and International Maritime Council was organized in 1905 under the name of Baltic and White Sea Conference. Its original purpose was to end the fierce rate war in those two areas, and for that purpose shipowners from the United Kingdom, Denmark, France, Germany, the Netherlands, Belgium, Spain, Norway, Sweden, Finland, and Russia assembled in Copenhagen. At the first meeting in November 1905, 102 owners from ten countries, controlling 1,056 ships, were present. Sailing shipowners were admitted in 1917; four years later, 157 owners of 450 wind-driven ships belonged to the conference.

Growth continued, and in 1927, owners from twenty countries and their fleets represented almost 14 percent of the world merchant fleet. In that year, the name was changed to Baltic and International Maritime Conference.

The organization held its first meeting outside of Europe in 1985. At this convocation in San Francisco, the name was changed once again to Baltic and International Maritime

Council (BIMCO), to avoid confusion with the somewhat better known steamship conferences. At the end of 1992, more than 950 owners controlling about 11,800 ships of over 365 million gross registered tons belonged to the council. In addition to the owner members, there were 1,600 brokers and 60 persons from marine insurance and other ancillary maritime enterprises who belonged to BIMCO.

A fundamental activity is the development of charter parties, bills of lading, individual clauses, and several other documents related to shipping. The council also provides its members with up-to-date information on port conditions, tariffs and charges, cargo regulations, labor situations, working hours, and samples of cost. Seasonal ice conditions are reported as circumstances warrant. (*Fairplay,* March 25, 1993: BIMCO Supplement, p. 7.)

4. Drewry's Shipping Associates, *Shipping Statistics and Economics,* March 1993, p. 32.

5. Bulkers of less than 50,000 tons deadweight comprised 47 percent of the dry bulk carrier fleet. The main divisions of cargo were grain, coal, and iron ore; cargoes related in some way to steel encompassed half of the seaborne bulk trade. The "minor bulks" were salt, sugar, timber, and tapioca, which moved predominantly in ships of less than 50,000 tons deadweight. "Bulkers and Tankers Have Same Concerns," in *Fairplay,* April 22, 1993, p. 17.

Chapter 4. Chartering and Tramp Ship Operation

1. A concise but comprehensive survey of the workings of this scheme is available in Hector Gripaios, *Tramp Shipping* (London: Thomas Nelson, 1959), pp. 74-84. See also B. N. Metaxas, *The Economics of Tramp Shipping* (London: Athlone Press, 1971), pp. 229-49, for a wide-ranging critical study of the various stabilization schemes proposed from 1935 to 1963.

2. In 1985, one British bulk carrier operator and three Norwegian operators formed a dry-bulk cargo ship pool which lasted until 1988. ("Norwegian Bulk Pool Restructures," in *Fairplay,* January 21, 1988, p. 8.)

3. The procedure sketched in the text is derived from an untitled information booklet distributed in 1985 by the Baltic International Freight Futures Exchange (BIFFEX). Included in the booklet is a detailed listing of each of the thirteen selected trading routes. The details related to two of the more important routes were set forth, as follows:

From one port, United States Gulf to Antwerp, or Rotterdam, or Amsterdam, lifting 55,000 tons, plus or minus 5 percent, of heavy soya sorghum. Cargo to be loaded and discharged at charterer's expense (FIO). Eleven days allowed for working cargo, Sundays and holidays excepted (SHex). Tendering date, ten days forward from date of freight index; canceling date thirty days forward. Brokerage commissions, 3.75 percent.

From one United States North Pacific port to one port in southern Japan, 52,000 tons, plus or minus 5 percent, of heavy sorghum to be loaded and discharged at charterer's expense (FIO). Eleven days allowed for working cargo, Sundays and holidays excepted (SHex). Tendering date, ten days forward from date of freight index; canceling date thirty days forward. Brokerage commissions 3.75 percent.

4. The approximate specifications of a 52,000-ton deadweight bulker in service in 1992 were: Length overall, 218.85 meters (735.34 feet); length between perpendiculars, 205.25 meters (689.6 feet); beam, 30.5 meters (102.48 feet); draft, 40.3 feet. Propulsion,

10,000 brake horsepower diesel. Gross register tonnage, 29,900; net register tonnage, 20,600; deadweight, 52,000 tons.

Chapter 6. Terminal Management

1. For a detailed analysis of terminal security procedures, see Warren H. Atkins, *Modern Marine Terminal Operations and Management* (Oakland, California: The Port of Oakland, 1983), pp. 184-90 (Hereafter cited as Atkins.)

2. An excellent comparison of the organizations of a container terminal and a break-bulk terminal is offered in Atkins, pp. 24-26.

3. For some time, major passenger ports have been trying to have passenger service exempted from the Jones Act. Under the act, cargo which is carried between two U.S. ports must be carried aboard U.S.-registered vessels. If an exemption were granted, then foreign flag carriers could operate passenger service between Los Angeles and San Francisco for example, or between Miami and New York. The argument that has been put forward by some proponents of the exemption is that people are not cargo, and it is demeaning and inappropriate to call them such.

Chapter 7. Terminal Operations

1. Atkins, pp. 190-94.
2. Ibid., pp. 110-111.

Chapter 9. Procurement of Vessel Stores and Supplies

1. U.S. Department of Commerce, Maritime Administration, *Spare Parts Provisioning for Merchant Ships,* 2 vols. (Washington, D.C.: National Technical Information Service, 1979).

This comprehensive study was prepared for the Maritime Administration by Mystech Associates, Inc., of Mystic, Connecticut, after detailed examination of procurement practices of twenty-two ship operators and twenty-six manufacturers and suppliers of spare parts. It was the most detailed exposition of current procedures in this field available at the time this chapter was written.

2. J. V. White, "How Cost Effective Are Pirate Spares?" *The Motor Ship,* March 1982, pp. 39-42.

The author of this article supports strongly the argument that shipowners are well-advised to purchase replacement and spare parts from the original equipment manufacturer. He provides numerous examples of the expensive mistakes made by ship operators overly concerned with initial purchase price rather than reliability and compatibility with the equipment.

3. For a comprehensive explanation of the duties and responsibilities of the ship's agent, see J. D. Eadie's articles entitled "Ships' Agency," which were published intermittently in *Fairplay* between September 23, 1982 and February 3, 1983. The series later was reprinted and issued under separate cover with the overall title of "Ships' Agency."

Chapter 10. Containerization: The Beginning

1. McLean entered the long-distance trucking business in 1933, driving one truck. Over the next two decades, his transportation company grew into a multimillion dollar operation. Headquarters were maintained in Winston-Salem, North Carolina, the state in which McLean was born.

2. New York *Journal of Commerce,* February 17, 1954; *Marine Engineering,* April 1954, pp. 47-48.

3. On January 21, 1955, McLean announced that he had acquired all the capital stock of Pan-Atlantic, and at the same time had resigned the presidency of the McLean Trucking Company. (*New York Times,* February 13, 1955, Part V, p. 9.) The final separation of Pan-Atlantic from Waterman was accomplished on March 1, 1955. (Ibid., March 3, 1955, p. 55.) McLean sold his stock in the trucking company in September 1955. (Ibid., November 28, 1956, p. 70.)

4. The first tanker acquired was the *Marine Leader,* purchased for $1,375,000 from Marine Navigation Co., of New York, on April 5, 1956. After conversion, she was renamed *Maxton* in honor of the North Carolina city in which McLean was born. (*New York Times,* April 6, 1956, p. 46.)

The *Ideal X* (ex *Potrero Hills*) and the *Almena* (ex *Whittier Hills*) were modified at the Baltimore shipyard of Bethlehem Steel Company, while the *Maxton* and the *Coalinga Hills* were adapted to the new service by Mobile Ship Repair, Inc., of Mobile, Alabama.

5. New York *Journal of Commerce,* August 18, 1955.

6. Quoted in *New York Times,* November 28, 1956, p. 70.

7. Later renamed *Seatrain New Orleans,* this 10-knot vessel was built by Swan, Hunter & Wigham Richardson, of Newcastle, England, and delivered on November 15, 1928. She was 130.15 meters long, 18.89 meters in beam, and had a draft of 7.85 meters. Her deadweight tonnage was 10,500. The single hatchway was 13.72 meters long and 16.15 meters wide. In 1938, the ship was lengthened to 137.97 meters, and her capacity increased to approximately 100 cars from her earlier maximum of 90 to 95.

The *Seatrain New Orleans* was operated in the New Orleans-Havana trade from 1929 until that service was abandoned in 1950. In that year she was sold, transferred to foreign registry, and renamed *Sealevel.*

8. International Cargo Handling Coordination Association, *Journal,* 2, Special Issue (September 1955), pp. 16-49, passim.

9. *New York Times,* May 7, 1955; August 16, 1955.

10. Among the properties sold were a shipyard, a hotel, and an office building in Mobile, Alabama.

11. See *Marine Engineering/Log,* December 1957, pp. 67-69, for a complete description of the *Gateway City,* the first converted C-2 to enter McLean's service.

12. *New York Times,* November 23, 1958.

13. When Sea-Land Service, Inc., placed four diesel-powered and crane-equipped ships in service during 1978, McLean had no connection with that organization. The reason advanced by the owners for installing cranes was that the ships were to serve ports in the Middle East which had no facilities for handling containers. New York *Journal of Commerce,* May 5, 1978, p. 32.

14. For an excellent and comprehensive short history of the development of contain-

erized shipping, see David Greenman, "Twenty-five Years of Container Ships," in *Ships Monthly,* January 1992, pp. 14-18, and February 1992, pp. 28-31.

Chapter 11. The Ramifications of Containerization

1. Cargo Systems International; January, 1993; pp. 40-41. Statistics based on a study of dry cargo container demand, published by UK-based CSR Consultants.

2. James Buckley, "Intermodal Transportation Needs Clear Definition," *Container News,* June, 1988, p. 2.

3. For more information on acceptance and use of EDI see John Crichton, "Kicking the Hard-Copy Habit," *Containerisation International,* June, 1993, pp. 36-40.

4. For more information on this subject see, McKenzie, North, and Smith, *Intermodal Transportation—The Whole Story,* (New York: Simmons-Boardman Books, Inc., 1989), p. 243.

5. As early as 1923, a shipment of 7,500 bales of raw silk worth $8,250,000 was sent from Yokohama to Seattle, and was transshipped into two special trains of fifteen baggage cars each. These trains followed schedules equal to those carrying passengers (*New York Times,* January 7, 1923, p. 1). In 1926, a shipment of ten thousand bales of raw silk, worth eleven million dollars arrived in New York just seventeen days after it was loaded in Yokohama. The steamer used was the *Arabia Maru,* of the Osaka Shoshen Kaisha fleet, which sailed from Japan on December 27, 1925. Two trains consisting of eleven and twelve baggage cars respectively were ready when the ship docked in Seattle, and departed on January 10, 1926, arriving in New York on the evening of January 13 (ibid., January 14, 1926, p. 43). A record was claimed for the transcontinental run when a shipment valued at $5,400,000 was moved from Seattle to New York in seventy-three hours and twenty-five minutes; express passenger trains required ninety-five to one hundred hours for the same trip. The demand for speed had two bases: the raw silk deteriorated rapidly, and interest charges amounted to about $1,000 a day. The "silk express" in 1925 handled 261,853 bales of new raw silk, valued at almost $700 million (ibid., September 26, 1925, Section VIII, p. 14).

6. "It is said that westbound traffic is three to four times heavier than eastbound trade, and that there is 'always' a shortage of containers in Nakhodka." New York *Journal of Commerce,* June 23, 1980, p. 22-A.

7. "Land-Water Bridge Service Is Ruled Legal by the FMC," ibid., August 9, 1978, p. 1.

8. "Tributary Cargo Interpretation of FMC Receives Support," ibid., December 4, 1978, p. 9.

9. "McAllister Doubles Container Capacity," ibid., February 24, 1977.

10. "Sea Container's 'Strider' Vessels," *The Motor Ship,* September 1976, pp. 110-13. This is an excellent article describing these feeder ships, which could carry 330 20-foot containers, and had a deadweight of 6,500 tons.

Chapter 12. The Ocean Bill of Lading

1. Quoted in Daniel A. Tadros, "COGSA Section 4(5)'s 'Fair Opportunity' Requirement," in *Tulane Maritime Law Journal,* (Vol. 17, No 1) Fall, 1992, pp. 17-18. Used by permission.

2. For a detailed, clause-by-clause examination of standardized bills of lading, see Per Gram, *Chartering Documents,* pp. 85-196. A number of standardized bills of lading are included in the appendices of this book.

Chapter 13. How Freight Rates Are Made

1. Gunnar K. Sletmo and Ernest W. Williams, Jr., *Liner Conferences in the Container Age* (New York: Macmillan, 1981), pp. 66-67. (Hereafter cited as Sletmo.)

2. "TWRA May Postpone July 1 Rate Hike," in New York *Journal of Commerce,* June 6, 1985, p. 1-A. "Rate Hikes Cancelled by TWRA," in ibid., September 30, 1985, p. 3.

3. Sletmo, p. 114.

4. Ibid., pp. 185-89; 252-54. The problems inherent in the "freight all kinds" rate are described in these pages.

Chapter 15. Steamship Conferences

1. The comments of the Senate Committee on Commerce, in discussing the need to amend the Shipping Act of 1916, are pertinent:

"Your committee has been constantly aware of the fact that further unilateral attempts by this Government to regulate the details of commercial transactions of shippers and carriers which take place and are documented abroad, are likely to have major deleterious effects and negligible counterbalancing benefits. First, they are likely to create further resentment among our foreign friends and, as a consequence, to cause reactions ranging from passive loss of confidence to active retaliation in foreign ports. In the process, they might well force foreign lines out of conferences, thereby destroying conferences and placing the high-cost American operator, even if subsidized, at a serious if not impossible competitive disadvantage. Second, and perhaps equally serious, to the extent such extraterritorial regulation cannot be as effectively enforced against their competitors, our American lines, we would be working at serious cross purposes with fundamental precepts of national maritime policy." (U.S. Congress, Senate, *Senate Report No. 860,* "Steamship Conferences and Dual Rate Contracts," 87th Cong. 1st sess., August 31, 1961, p. 3.) (Hereafter cited as *Engel Report.*)

2. An excellent short history of the origin of the conference system is contained in Inter-American Maritime Conference, *Report of Delegates of the United States* (Washington, D.C.: Government Printing Office, 1941) pp. 159-63.

3. U.S. Congress, *House of Representatives Report No. 498,* "Providing for the Operation of Steamship Conferences," 87th Cong., 1st sess., June 8, 1961, p. 12. (Hereafter cited as *Bonner Report.*)

4. John A. Hobson, *The Evolution of Modern Capitalism.* Rev. ed. (London: Allen & Unwin, 1926), pp. 175-76.

5. Quoted in American Maritime Council, *Foreign Trade and Shipping* (New York: McGraw-Hill, 1945), pp. 25-26.

6. Ibid., pp. 26-27; Daniel Marx, Jr., *International Shipping Cartels: A Study of Industrial Self-Regulation by Shipping Conferences* (Princeton, N.J.: Princeton University Press, 1953), pp. 50-67. (Hereafter cited as Marx.)

7. *Bonner Report,* p. 5.

8. Sletmo, p. 200.

9. Federal Maritime Board *vs.* Isbrandtsen Co., Inc. (354 U.S. 481, 1958). For a commentary on this case, see Allen R. Ferguson, et al., *The Economic Value of the United States Merchant Marine* (Evanston, Ill.: The Transportation Center at Northwestern University, 1961), pp. 389-96.

The Shipping Board was in existence from 1916 until 1936, when it was superseded by the United States Maritime Commission. In 1950, the regulatory functions which had been performed by the commission were assigned to the newly established Federal Maritime Board. The chairman of the board was also the chairman of the Maritime Commission. President Kennedy proposed, and the Congress approved in 1961, a plan by which the Federal Maritime Commission was set up as an independent agency with sole responsibility for regulating maritime commercial activities.

10. *Engel Report,* pp. 5-6.

11. Pearson, p. 23.

12. *Engel Report,* pp. 7-8.

13. Sletmo, pp. 306-7.

14. "Australian Wool Exporters Continue Rate-cut Efforts," New York *Journal of Commerce,* October 8, 1983, p. 24-B.

15. See Sletmo, pp. 278-86, for a comprehensive critique of the Australian experience.

16. Great Britain, Committee on Inquiry into Shipping (Chairman, The Rt. Hon. the Viscount Rochdale): *Report* (London: Her Majesty's Stationery Office, Cmmd. 4337, 1970), p. 132, par. 468-69, quoted in Sletmo, p. xxxi.

17. Marx, p. 240.

18. Personal interview, L. C. Kendall and Sylvester J. Maddock, vice president, traffic, Seas Shipping Company, 1947. An excellent account of the rate war is contained in Robert Greenhalgh Albion, *Seaports South of Sahara* (New York: Appleton-Century-Crofts, 1959), pp. 120-27.

19. *Congressional Information Bureau,* November 15, 1962.

Chapter 17. Scheduling and Bunkering

1. "Bunker Risk Management," in *Seatrade Week Newsfront,* 25 June–1 July 1993, p. 13.

2. "Efficient Use and Proper Handling Are Vital for Good Bunker Management," in *Lloyd's Ship Manager,* July 1989, pp. 1-11 (Supplement).

Chapter 18. Planning for a New Ship

1. Robert Taggart, ed., *Ship Design and Construction, Written by a Group of Authorities* (New York: The Society of Naval Architects and Marine Engineers, 1980), p. 11.

2. Ibid., p. 8.

3. Drewry Shipping Consultants, Ltd., *Shipping Statistics and Economics* (London: March 1993), p. 33.

4. *Ships Monthly,* April 1993, p. 15.

5. Drewry Shipping Consultants, Ltd., *Shipping Statistics and Economics,* p. 33.

6. V. L. Russo and E. K. Sullivan, "Design of the Mariner Type Ships," in *Transactions of the Society of Naval Architects and Marine Engineers, 1953,* quoted in Taggart, op. cit., p. 53. Quotation used by permission.

7. The *Jervis Bay* was built by Ishikawajima Heavy Industries in Kure, Japan, in 1992 for P & O Containers, Ltd. Of a nominal capacity of 4,038 20-foot equivalent units, she had a speed of 22.5 knots, and was propelled by a Sulzer engine rated at 42,116 brake horsepower. At her service speed, she consumed 117.8 tons of high viscosity fuel oil per day.

8. The *Cape Hatteras* was built in 1992 by Schiffwerft GmbH, of Wismar, Germany. On delivery by the shipyard, the vessel was registered in Cyprus, and assigned to trade on the Madras-Singapore route. She was built to accept all sizes of containers in use in 1993, and was given the technical designation of "multi-measurement containership" (MMC). Special movable guides were installed, intended to accept containers between 20 and 49 feet in length. The ship's capacity was rated at 923 20-foot equivalent units, of which 304 were stowed below deck. Reefer plugs were available for 204 containers. Her 11,964 brake horsepower motor gave her a service speed of 18 knots.

9. "Largest Double Hull Delivered in Japan," in *Pacific Magazine,* April 1993, p. 24.

The *Hyundai Admiral* was built in 1992, and when put into service had a slow-speed twelve-cylinder diesel engine rated at 70,320 brake horsepower. At that time, this was the most powerful diesel ever installed in a ship. (*Seatrade Review,* February 1993.) With a capacity of 4,411 20-foot equivalent units, this ship had a deadweight of 52,233 tons. She was 275 meters (924 feet) long, 37.1 meters (123.5 feet) in the beam, and had a draft of 12.5 meters (42 feet). (" 'Hyundai Admiral', First of Five Containerships from Hyundai and for Hyundai," in *Shipping World & Shipbuilder,* December 1992, pp. 20-21.

10. "First Panamax 'Open Hatch' Container Ship," in *Nautical Magazine,* January 1992, p. 48; *Ships Monthly,* January 1992, p. 8.

11. "Cape Hatteras," in ibid., April 1993, p. 12.

12. "Oost Atlantic Lijn: Containerization's Leading Lady," in *Seatrade Review,* April 1993, p. 63.

Chapter 19. Passenger Cruises

1. *Fairplay,* March 11, 1993.

2. Thornton, *British Shipping,* pp. 208-9. John Malcolm Brinin, *The Sway of the Grand Saloon* (New York: Delacorte Press, 1971), p. 445.

3. "Holiday in the Sun," in *Via Port of New York,* December 1959. At least two ships were built for and operated in year-round cruise service prior to World War I. The Hamburg-America Line introduced the *Prinzessin Victoria Luise* in 1900. She had the sharp hull lines of a yacht, but carried 400 passengers, all of whom slept in brass beds. This handsome vessel was assigned exclusively to cruise service. She was wrecked off Jamaica in December 1906. (William H. Miller, Jr., *The First Great Ocean Liners in Photographs, 1897-1927* (New York: Dover Publications, 1984), p. 42. The *Vectis* was built by the British P & O Line in 1904, and was employed full-time in cruises from England to the Baltic Sea, the Mediterranean, and the Canary Islands. (Thornton, op. cit., p. 209.)

4. *Ships Monthly,* April 1993, pp. 21ff.

5. New York *Journal of Commerce,* October 23, 1973, p. 5.

6. Carnival Cruise Line contracted in January 1992 to build a ship of 95,000 gross registered tons, with delivery set in 1996. The contract price, before subsidy, was reported to be between $400 million and $450 million.

7. "Cruise Ship *Fairsky* Will Be Christened in Los Angeles," in *Los Angeles Times,* May 4, 1984, Part V, p. 1.

8. The specifications of the *Costa Allegra* are: length, 183 meters (615 feet); beam, 25.36 meters (84.5 feet); cruising speed, 22 knots; gross tonnage 30,000; crew and staff, 450. Air-conditioned and stabilizer-equipped.

9. "Carnival's Fantasy Becomes Reality," in *The Motor Ship,* March 1990, p. 27.

10. "Conversation with a Cruise Director," in *San Francisco Examiner and Chronicle,* April 25, 1993, p. T-2.

11. "Cruise Trade Booms in Australia," in New York *Journal of Commerce,* October 11, 1984, p. 14-A.

12. "Outlook Seen Brighter for Cruise Ship Activity," in ibid., August 1, 1974.

13. "Bahama Star Cruises Are Cancelled," in ibid., January 5, 1975, p. 24.

14. "Fuel Crisis Scuttles World Cruise," in *Los Angeles Times,* Jan. 1, 1974, p. 10.

15. "New Buildings Reflect Continued Cruise Sector Confidence," in *The Motor Ship,* September 1991, p. 23.

The major companies were Carnival Cruise Lines, providing 26 percent of the available beds; Royal Caribbean Cruise Line, 15.1 percent; Norwegian Cruise Line, 14.4 percent; and P & O Line, 12 percent.

16. "Off to the Icy Waters of Antarctica," in *Los Angeles Times,* November 25, 1984, Part VII, p. 6. "Northwest Cruises Being Discouraged," in New York *Journal of Commerce,* April 4, 1985, p. 1-B.

17. " 'France' into 'Norway' by Hapag-Lloyd," in *The Motor Ship,* July 1980, p. 87.

18. The sister ships, *Sea Goddess I* and *Sea Goddess II,* were built by Wartsila shipyard, in Finland, and delivered, respectively, in the fall of 1984 and May 1985. They are registered in Norway, and in 1993 were under long-term charter to Cunard. They are 102.38 meters (344 feet) long, 14.28 meters (48 feet) in beam, and draw 4.17 meters (14 feet) of water. Cruising speed is 17.5 knots. The crew numbers 80 persons for the passenger load of 116. "U.S. Firm to Offer Fly-Cruise Service," New York *Journal of Commerce,* March 14, 1981; "The Grandest Tour of All," in *Los Angeles Times,* October 7, 1984, Special Section: Traveling in Style; "The Sumptuous Sea Goddess," in *Travel and Leisure,* February 1985.

19. *Seabourn Pride* and *Seabourn Spirit* were built in 1988 and 1989 at a reported cost of $34 million each. They are 130.65 meters (439 feet) long, 18.75 meters (63 feet) in beam, and have a gross registered tonnage of 10,000. A crew of 140 persons serves a maximum passenger load of 204 travelers.

The Royal Viking Line introduced the *Royal Viking Queen* in 1993 in direct competition with the *Sea Goddess* and *Seabourn* ships. At a reported cost of $377,358 per bed, this 212-passenger cruise ship was the most expensive passenger ship ever built.

20. "With the Wind: Caribbean Sailing on a Clipper Ship," in *San Francisco Examiner and Chronicle,* April 24, 1993, p. T-3.

21. Joseph Wechsberg, "The Logistics of Glut," in *Esquire,* December 1976, p. 191.

22. "Charm is Part of the Job," in *Los Angeles Times,* Part VII, p. 23, June 24, 1984.

23. For a detailed, critical and historical survey of the passenger cruise business, see Brinin, op. cit., pp. 486-504.

Chapter 20. Industrial and Special Carriers

1. John I. Jacobs, PLC, *World Tanker Review, July-December 1992* (London, 1992), p. 12.

2. "Side Loader is Designed to Carry Newsprint Rolls," in *The Motor Ship,* February 1990, p. 27.

3. "World's Largest Cement Carriers from ASEA's Sestao Yard," in ibid., December 1980, pp. 103-4.

4. "A Cold Trade Warms Up," in ibid., February 1990, p. 31.

5. "Fresh Fruit Salad," in *Cargo Systems International,* February 1993, pp. 27-29; "Keeping Pallets under Wraps," in ibid., January 1993, pp. 33-35.

6. "Maintaining Market Equilibrium," in *Lloyd's Ship Manager,* August 1992, p. 67.

7. "Chiquita Benefits from Danish Project Ship," in ibid., November 1991, pp. 61-69; "Reefers," in *Shipping World & Shipbuilder,* October 1992, p.14.

8. " 'Geest St. Lucia'—A Reefer from Danyard," in ibid., April 1993, pp. 33-38.

9. "World's Largest Reefer Can Be Run by Crew of Six," in *The Motor Ship,* September 1990, pp. 38-39.

10. "Dealing with a Full Deck," in *Cargoware International,* February 1993, p. 45.

11. The *Comet* was built at Chester, Pennsylvania, in 1958 as a vehicle carrier. She was 138.3 meters (465 feet) long, 23.3 meters (78 feet) wide, and had a draft of 8 meters (27 feet).

12. "Car Carriers Can Also Cope with Mixed Cargoes," in *The Motor Ship,* June 1992, pp. 63-66.

Chapter 21. Tanker Management

1. The first bulk oil-carriers were the products of the remarkable Norwegian team of shipowner Gustav Conrad Hansen and shipmaster Even Tollefsen, who converted the sailing ships *Jan Mayn* (258 registered tons), *Stadt* (377 registered tons), and *Lindesnaes* (674 registered tons) to carry petroleum in bulk. The conversion was done at Tønsberg in 1877-78. See Ragnar Schjøttelvig, "Norwegian Sailing Tankers," in United States Naval Institute *Proceedings,* February 1958, pp. 106-8. This brief article includes a reproduction of a picture of the *Lindesnaes* and the line drawings of her hull as converted.

2. "Of Shoes and Ships," in *Fairplay,* March 19, 1970, p. 14. A photograph of the *Glückauf* is included in this sketch.

3. The motor-tanker *C. O. Stillman* was launched for the Panama Transport Company at the Bremer-Vulkan yard, Bremen, in 1928. She was 178 meters (598 feet) long overall, 22.86 meters (76.8 feet) in the beam, and had a draft of 10.35 meters (34.8 feet). Her deadweight was 24,200 tons, and her liquid capacity was about 200,000 barrels. The French tanker *Scheherazade* was contemporaneous with the *C. O. Stillman*; she was 167 meters (561 feet) long, and her beam was 21.95 meters (73.6 feet). She was reported to have had a capacity of 200,000 barrels.

4. The T-2 tanker was 159.56 meters (536.1 feet) long, with a deadweight of 16,750 tons on a draft of 9.16 meters (34.78 feet). About 140,000 barrels of gasoline could be carried. At a sustained sea speed of 14.5 knots, the ship consumed 285 barrels of high viscosity fuel oil per day. Because of the shortage of gear-making facilities during World War II all these ships were powered with turbo-electric propulsion units. After the war, the T-2 was used by many commercial operators. A number were enlarged in the late 1950s and early 1960s, and their power plants overhauled to permit them to serve effectively until at least 1981.

5. Between 1946 and 1992, the world's tanker fleet grew from 1,947 ships with an average deadweight of 12,183 tons to 3,176 ships with an average deadweight of 86,352 tons. The increase in deadweight tonnage, by decades, was: 1946, 12,183 tons; 1956, 16,930 tons; 1966, 32,122 tons; 1976, 88,209 tons; 1986, 83,845 tons; 1992, 86,353 tons. (John I. Jacobs, PLC, op. cit., London, 1992), p. 37.

Large tankers on order, as of January 30, 1992, included four ships of 300,000 tons deadweight, four of 290,000 to 295,000 tons deadweight, four of 285,000 tons deadweight, and forty-three of 280,000 tons deadweight. (*Fairplay,* January 30, 1992)

The largest tanker in the world in 1993 was the *Jahre Viking* (ex *Happy Giant,* ex *Seawise Giant*), which was launched in Japan in 1975 but not put into service until 1979. She was 458.45 meters (1,540.4 feet) long, 68.86 meters (231.37 feet) wide, and had a maximum draft of 24.61 meters (82.7 feet). Her deadweight was 564,650 tons. Her 50,000 shaft horsepower steam turbines gave her a cruising speed of 13 knots.

The ship was almost destroyed by Iraqi warplanes during the Gulf War of 1990-91. She underwent extensive repairs at the Keppel shipyard in Singapore. She was too large for the yard's dry dock, and therefore all work was accomplished while the ship was afloat alongside a repair pier. She was owned (1993) by Jorgen Jahre Shipping A/S, of Sandefjord, Norway.

6. John I. Jacobs, PLC, op. cit., pp. 3, 11, 12.

7. Drewry Shipping Consultants, Ltd., *The Tanker Charter Market: Structure, Participants and Trends* (London: June 1992), p. 3.

8. A directory of ship repair facilities published by *The Motor Ship,* September 1992, showed these nations had these dry docks: France, 4; Germany, 3; Greece, 1; Italy, 2; Malta, 1; Portugal, 5; Spain, 2; United Kingdom, 2; Dubai, 3; South Africa, 2; Japan, 14; Malaysia, 1; Singapore, 8; Taiwan, 1; United States, 6. All had the capabilities of servicing super-sized ships.

9. *Seatrade Week,* February 12-18, 1993, p. 3.

10. The *San Juan Pioneer* was built in Japan in 1962, and when she entered service was the largest combination ore-oil carrier in the world. She was 253.2 meters (851 feet) long, 32 meters (107.5 feet) in the beam, and her hull measured 19.8 meters (66.5 feet) deep. Her 22,500 shaft horsepower steam turbines gave her a speed of 16.4 knots. To permit rapid conversion from ore to oil cargoes, three holds were fitted with especially designed oil-tight hatches. (*Fairplay,* October 26, 1962.)

11. "Combined Carriers: In Search for the Right Combination," in *Lloyd's Shipping Economist,* April 1993, p. 16.

12. The four cargo pumps of the *Jahre Viking* had a combined capacity of 22,000 tons per hour.

13. "Double Hull Deliveries Accelerate," in *Marine Log,* May 1993, pp. 37-39.

14. "A. P. Moller Bullish on Market as it Takes Delivery of Tankers," in New York *Journal of Commerce,* May 12, 1993, p. 1-B.

15. Drewry Shipping Consultants, Ltd., *Shipping Statistics and Economics,* March 1993, p. 44.

16. "Sophisticated and Safe," in *Lloyd's Ship Manager,* February 1993, pp. 49-51.

17. Bruce E. Keer, "Liquefied Gas Carriers in Port Areas," in *Seaways,* May 1993, pp. 11-12.

18. *Marine Engineering Review,* May 1993, p. 23.

19. "LNG Carriers Supply Far Eastern Energy Needs," in *The Motor Ship,* July 1992, pp. 49-52.

20. "Today's Parcel Chemical Tankers: A 25-Year Development," in *Stolten* (Vol. IX, No. 3), December 1984, pp. 30-33; "Stolt-Nielsen: Four Generations," in ibid., (Vol. X, No. 1), April 1985, pp. 1-7.

21. Edward Crowley, "The Carriage of Chemicals in Bulk," in *Fairplay,* July 30, 1970, pp. 37-39.

22. "In Search of the Universal Cargo Tank Coating," in *Stolten* (Vol. X, No. 1), April 1985, pp. 18-19.

23. "First of Four for Stolt-Nielsen," in *Fairplay,* January 10, 1991, p. 39; "Specialized Tankers," in *Lloyd's Ship Manager,* December 1991, pp. 37-38; "Favorable Outlook: Improved Fortunes for Chemical Tanker Owners," in *Lloyd's Ship Economist,* June 1992, pp. 6-7.

Chapter 22. The American Shipping Subsidy System

1. "Swedish Shipowners Seek Tax Exemption for Seamen," New York *Journal of Commerce,* October 29, 1981, p. 24-B.

2. United States Department of Commerce, Maritime Administration, *Maritime Subsidies, 1978,* (Washington, D.C.: Government Printing Office, 1978), pp. v, vi, and vii.

3. Lane C. Kendall, "The Purpose of Subsidy," United States Naval Institute *Proceedings,* October 1981, pp. 29-31.

4. For a brief but comprehensive analysis of cargo preference legislation, see Clinton H. Whitehurst, Jr., *The U.S. Merchant Marine: In Search of an Enduring Maritime Policy* (Annapolis, Md.: Naval Institute Press, 1983), pp. 23-24.

5. "Title XI Default Is Biggest Ever," New York *Journal of Commerce,* May 3, 1985, p. 1-A. Guarantees have been made on mortgages and bonds on approximately 6,000 vessels, with an aggregate value of $7.3 billion. Ships, barges, tugs, offshore supply craft, floating oil rigs, as well as river boats have been the beneficiaries of this program. The government charges a fee for the guarantee, and in May 1985 its resources for paying these guarantees amounted to $142 million.

6. The pressures brought to bear on shipowners in international trade were demonstrated dramatically by the Swedish Shipowners Association, which compiled the following estimates. A Swedish ship of 20,000 tons deadweight had running expenses of about $1,440,000 per year, excluding capital costs and fuel. A similar vessel under British registry cost about $1,000,000, whereas a bulk carrier of the same tonnage flying the Liberian flag and paying wages below those set by the International Transport Workers Union would have had expenses of only $630,000.

A further example was cited of a Swedish-flag bulk carrier that cost $530,000 a year more to operate than an identical ship owned by the same Swedish firm but registered in Hong Kong and manned by a non-Swedish crew. "Swedish Shipowners Seek Tax Exemption for Seamen," New York *Journal of Commerce,* October 29, 1981, p. 24-B.

7. United States Department of Commerce, Maritime Administration, *Manual of General Procedures for Determining Operating-Differential Subsidy Rates* (Washington, D.C.: Department of Commerce, 1977), p. 20.

8. For an exhaustive analysis of the 1936 law, see Samuel A. Lawrence, *United States Merchant Shipping Policies and Politics* (Washington, D.C.: Brookings Institution, 1966), especially Chapters 6, 7, and 8. An excellent compilation of data relating to the programs of government aid in 58 nations (including the United States) which have merchant fleets is found in *Maritime Subsidies,* previously mentioned. Particular details, such as the exact amount of money expended in the subsidy program, the names of the companies which have held and those which currently do hold operating-differential subsidy contracts, the numbers and types of ships under construction with subsidy assistance, and the total strength of the subsidized fleet at the end of each fiscal year, are available in the *Annual Report of the Maritime Administration* (Washington, D.C.: Government Printing Office).

Glossary

Agents (Vessel). A company or individual who represents the owner of the vessel in the various ports of call for the vessel. These people are engaged in the routines connected with the arrival, working, and departure of the ship.

Arbitraries. Additional charges that are added to the freight rate to cover unusual circumstances involving the cargo carried.

Ballast. Any weight used to improve the stability of the vessel or to change the draft or trim of the vessel.

Baltic Exchange. Located in London near the Thames river and Tower Bridge, this is the site where brokers, who have been elected individually to membership, meet to work out charters for the principals.

Bareboat Charter. A contract between the owner of a vessel and the charterer, whereby the owner transfers operational control of the vessel to the charterer. Also known as *demise charter.*

Beaufort Scale. A scale of wind speeds ranging from 0, calm to 12, hurricane. The scale was named after Admiral Sir Francis Beaufort, who devised it in 1806.

BIFFEX. Baltic International Freight Futures Exchange.

Bill of Lading. A contract for the carriage of goods by a common carrier.

Black Trades. Crude, residual, and darker oils up to the diesel grade.

Boat Note. See Dock Receipt.

Booking Clerk. A senior member of the outward department who controls the space in a break-bulk cargo ship, allocating that space to individual shippers as they make their requests.

Break-Bulk. Cargo that is moved as individual packages. This type of operation does not unitize the cargo.

Bulker. Term used to describe a ship that carries goods (usually dry cargo) in bulk. A bulk carrier.

Bunching. The overlapping of ship schedules in a fleet operation caused by cumulative delays of the various ships in the fleet.

Bunkering. The act of taking fuel oil aboard a ship.

Cabotage Restrictions. Laws that restrict the carriage of goods between a country's ports to carriers registered in that country.

Cell. The actual space on a containership where a container can be stowed.

CFS. Container Freight Station.

Charter Party. A written agreement setting forth the terms and conditions under which the vessel owner makes a ship available to the shipper.

Checkers. Terminal labor hired by the day to inspect, count, and measure cargo and to insert the appropriate data on the dock receipt.

Class Rates. A rate, or charge, which is assigned to a large number of unrelated commodities that have been studied individually and found to require the same revenue for their transportation.

Classification Society. A non-governmental organization which certifies the ship's seaworthiness. These organizations inspect design drawings and specifications before construction begins, supervise construction to assure that standards are met, and perform periodic surveys to determine continued seaworthiness of the ship. Principal societies are Lloyd's Register (England), American Bureau of Shipping, Det Norske Veritas (Norway), and Bureau Veritas (France).

Clean Trades. The more highly refined, clean oil products, such as gasoline lubricating oil and jet engine fuels. These cargoes often require special care and handling.

COGSA. Carriage of Goods by Sea Act.

Commodity Rates. A rate, or charge, for carrying a designated item such as, for example, granulated sugar in bags.

Common Carrier. A carrier that holds itself out to the public as one which, for a reasonable price, is ready, willing, and able to transport goods for anyone, without discrimination.

Comptroller. Officer responsible for the fiscal control of a company, who is assisted by auditors and financial analysts.

Conference. An association of ocean common carriers operating on the same route.

Conference (Closed). Conferences that restrict membership to that number of carriers which will be sufficient to provide transportation for the proffered cargo.

Conference (Open). Conferences that admit to membership any common carriers prepared to serve the trade routes covered by that conference.

Consignee. The company or person ultimately receiving the cargo at the end of the trip.

Container (Marine). A metal cargo box built to ISO standards which can be loaded aboard ships, on truck chassis, or on rail cars.

Container Rates. A rate, or charge, for carrying a whole container.

Contract Carrier. A carrier that operates as a private carrier hauling the goods of a single owner.

Cribs. Early cargo boxes which were developed from the standard wooden pallet and consisted of a base with lattice sides and a plywood top. The sides were collapsible for easier backhaul.

Cross Trades. Revenue earning trade between two countries, neither of which is the country in which the ship carrying the cargo is registered.

Cubic Cargo. Cargo requiring more than 40 cubic feet for stowage of a weight ton.

Daily Cargo Report. The stevedore's report of cargo work on a ship completed during the preceding twenty-four hours. The report covers these details: number of tons of cargo booked into the ship, tons of cargo actually delivered by shippers during the day, tons loaded, tons still to be loaded, hatches worked, number of men engaged, actual time men were employed, and commodities handled during the day.

Dead Freight. The charge for the difference between the amount of cargo loaded and the amount of cargo booked (usually the ship's capacity), when the amount loaded was short through no fault of the vessel.

Deadweight Cargo. Cargo which stows in less than 40 cubic feet per weight ton.

Deadweight Tonnage. The total weight that a ship can carry: total weight of cargo, fuel, water, stores, and crew.

Deferred Rebate. Money paid by a conference to a shipper after a designated period of time during which the shipper's loyalty to the conference has been demonstrated.

Delivery Book. A book maintained by a marine terminal in which the drayman or other inland carrier signs for the cargo. It shows the date and hour when the ocean carrier released the goods.

Delivery Clerk. A key assistant to the terminal manager, in charge of the office through which pass all papers connected with inbound cargo brought to the terminal by ship for loading onto an inland carrier for delivery to the consignee.

Demise Charter. See Bareboat Charter.

Demurrage. 1. The penalty assessed against the voyage charterer for holding the ship in port beyond the period specified for working cargo. 2. The charge against liner cargo left in the transit shed after free time has expired.

Detention. Nonproductive time spent waiting to work cargo due to any cause beyond the stevedoring contractor's control. This detention time will be billed by the contractor.

Dirty (Oil) Trades. See Black Trades.

Dispatch. A premium payment made for reducing the time a ship must spend in port loading or discharging cargo.

Dock Receipt. A document prepared by the shipper that must accompany the cargo to the terminal. It contains these data: name of shipper and consignee; port of destination; description of the goods, including type(s) of package and weight; and the booking number.

Draft. The depth of the ship below the surface of the water.

Dunnage. The lumber used in stowing cargo aboard ship.

EIR. Equipment Interchange Report.

Exclusive Patronage Contract. A contract used by conferences which commit the shipper to give business only to carriers belonging to that conference.

FAK. Freight All Kinds.

Feeder Vessels. Small, local vessels that transport cargo from outports within the hinterland to larger collecting ports (load centers) where the cargo is transshipped to larger vessels for transportation to distant destinations.

FIOT. Free In and Out and Trimmed. Refers to bulk cargoes loaded, trimmed, and discharged at charterer's expense.

Fixture. Refers to confirmed and signed charter party.

Freeboard. The vertical distance from the water line to the top of the weather deck of a vessel.

Free Time. The number of days after the ship completes discharge during which the consignee may take delivery of his or her goods.

Freight Agent. Generally works under the freight traffic manager, directs the sales staff, and handles departmental administration of the freight traffic department.

Freight Rates. The prices (or rates) charged for the services of water carriers.

Freight Tariffs. See Tariffs.

Freight Traffic Manager. Serves as a deputy to the vice president, traffic, and supervises the freight traffic department; assures that departmental policies are carried out in the most effective manner.

Full and Down. A vessel loaded in such a way that all cubic space is filled and the hull is immersed to the load line.

Gangs. A group of longshoremen assigned to work as a unit.

Gatehouse. The primary entry and exit point of a marine terminal.

Gross Form. A form of a voyage charter in which the owner of the ship pays for every item of expense, including loading, discharging, port fees, and all expenses in connection with the cargo, as well as the operating charges such as crew wages, subsistence, and fuel.

Headhouse. The structure at the land end of a finger pier which houses cargo receiving platforms and terminal management offices.

Hinterland. The territory contributing cargo or passengers to a port.

House Flag. A flag designed by a shipping company which incorporates the company's colors and logo.

Hustler. A yard tractor used to move containers on a container terminal.

Industrial Carrier. The marine transportation link in the process of manufacture or distribution (or both) of the materials used or produced by an industrial organization.

Infrastructure. The foundation upon which growth is dependent; a railroad or highway net supporting a marine terminal; a system of communication linking suppliers and users.

Intermodal Transportation. A systems approach to transportation whereby goods are carried in a continuous through movement between origin and destination using two or more modes of transportation in the most efficient manner.

Inward Freight Department. A department of the traffic department which is responsible for the consignee obtaining his or her cargo without delay and in an orderly manner.

ISO. International Standards Organization.

Jitney. A power unit, or tractor, used on a marine terminal to tow a train of two or more trailers loaded with palletized or loose packages or sacks.

Jobber. A wholesale merchant who buys in very large lots and sells in quantities to retailers and heavy consumers.

Jumbo Boom. Shipboard cargo gear designed to lift heavy items.

Landbridge. An intermodal transportation concept that utilizes a significant landmass to bridge two ocean routes. For example, a cargo movement from Japan to Europe that utilizes water transportation from Japan to the West Coast of the United States, land transportation across the United States, and water transportation again from the East Coast to Europe. This has proven to be a time saving alternative to the all water route.

LASH. Lighter Aboard Ship.

Lay Days. 1. The period of days during which the owner must tender (or deliver) the vessel and make it available to the charterer. 2. The number of days allowed to load and discharge the cargo, as stated in a voyage charter.

LCL. 1. Less than Carload Lot (a railroad term). 2. Less than Container Load (a marine term).

Liner Service. An ocean common carrier service which operates on an established route and has published sailing dates and published tariffs.

LNG. Liquified Natural Gas.

Load Center. Major ports where cargo from outports is collected and consolidated for transshipment. Load centers improve the efficiency of ocean transportation by allowing ships to take advantage of economies of scale.

Load Line. Markings on the side of a ship showing the depth to which it can be loaded safely in various areas of the world and seasons of the year.

Long Ton. Equal to 2,240 pounds.

Longshoremen. Dock laborers who actually perform the loading and discharging of cargo from ships.

Loyalty Contract. See Exclusive Patronage Contract.

Marine Terminal. A transfer point where goods are efficiently exchanged between a vessel and other modes of transportation. Consists of a berth for the vessel, cargo-handling equipment, cargo storage areas, and administrative offices.

Mate's Receipt. See Dock Receipt.

Metric Ton. Equal to 2,204 pounds.

Net Form. A form of voyage charter in which the vessel owner pays all normal ship operating costs, and the charterer is responsible for charges accrued for loading and discharging the cargo as well as for port fees (except those related directly and solely to the crew) exacted against ship and cargo.

Neutral Body. An independent organization whose purpose is to police the obligations of the conference and its members.

Neutral Pools. A shorthand reference to those containers owned by leasing companies which are used for one-way movements and then turned over to an agent. This agent places the containers in central collecting points where they form a pool from which individual units can be drawn to meet the needs of shippers within geographical range of that central point.

OBO. Oil-Bulk-Ore.

Off Hire. That moment when the ship's employment under a charter ceases and all payments under the charter are terminated.

Off Soundings. Refers to a ship in international waters, and derives from the fact that its sounding equipment cannot measure the depth of the water.

On Hire. That moment when the ship officially begins working under a charter and payments due under the charter begin.

Operating Department. A department in a ship operating company that is responsible for all matters concerning ship construction, operations, stevedoring, and labor relations.

O.S. and D. Over, Short, and Damaged Cargo Report.

Outports. Smaller ports on the fixed route. Feeder vessels often transport cargo from the outports to load centers.

Outbound Freight Department The division of the traffic department which books cargo for the ship, processes bills of lading, and prepares manifests of all outbound cargo.

Over-Carried. Refers to cargo that has been carried beyond the port at which it was to be discharged.

Parcels. In vessel operations, "parcels" indicates less than shipload lots.

Permit Clerk. A clerk who instructs shippers of large lots of cargo when to send their consignments to the terminal.

Pier (Finger). A marine terminal that projects into the waterway at an angle to the shore, thereby allowing ships to berth on both sides.

Pile Tag. One or more copies of the dock receipt left with the cargo when it is placed on the terminal. When the cargo is loaded aboard a vessel this tag is given to the chief mate for record keeping and for planning cargo operations.

Pools. See Neutral Pools.

Port Marks. A symbol applied to every box, bag, crate, or other container received for shipment that is destined for the same port. For example, Genoa might be designated by a red circle, while Istanbul might be symbolized by a green square.

Press Up. To fill a tank to its maximum capacity.

Private Carrier. A carrier that transports only the goods of a single person or company.

Purchasing Agent. Person responsible for the procurement of stores and other material to meet all ship needs.

Purser. When carried, this person serves as the shipboard agent of the freight and passenger departments; often deals with manifests and other papers.

Receiving Clerk. A key assistant to the terminal manager. Supervises and records all deliveries to the marine terminal of outbound cargo. Issues the dock receipt to shipper acknowledging carrier's responsibility for custody, and shows actual weight, measurement, and condition of cargo received for loading.

Recoopering. Sewing torn bags, securing loose boards in boxes and crates, and similar minor repair work that is done during cargo operations.

Reefer. Shorthand term for refrigerated ships or cargoes.

RO/RO. Roll On/Roll Off.

Roundsman. In a marine terminal, the foreman in charge of the security guards.

Self-Sustaining. When referring to a ship, indicates that the ship can load and unload with its own gear.

Ship Chandler. Companies or individuals who supply the miscellaneous small lot items needed by a ship.

Short Ton. Equal to 2,000 pounds.

Short Delivered. Refers to cargo which, at delivery, is less than the quantity shown on the manifest. This cargo is often discharged at a port prior to the port of destination.

Slips. In a fleet schedule, the delays of a ship along its route.

Space Chartering. The practice of one shipping company chartering a block of space in another shipping company's ship; usually done by companies within a single conference.

Specialized Carrier. A carrier designed for the express purpose of carrying, usually in shipload lots, a particular type of cargo.

Spotted. Cargo delivered to ship's side at the exact location where it will be loaded aboard.

Stowage Factor. The number of cubic feet required to stow one long ton of a given cargo.

Stripping. The act of unloading goods from a container.

Stuffing. The act of loading cargo into a container.

Surcharge. An additional charge (usually a fixed percentage) added to the freight rate.

Taking Exception. Recording of defects or discrepancies in cargo received. Refers to the phrase in the bill of lading that cargo is accepted for shipment "in apparent good order and condition, except as noted hereon."

Tanker. A ship designed to carry liquid bulk cargo.

Tariff. A detailed listing of freight rates and services provided by a carrier.

Tender. To deliver a vessel to the charterer.

TEU. Twenty-foot Equivalent Unit.

Third Party. Any person not contractually related, but who has some interest in the transaction. For example, a shipbroker brings a shipowner and a charterer together, and facilitates the negotiation of a charter for the vessel.

Through Rates. A single rate charged for shipments originating with one ocean carrier but transferred to connecting carriers at intermediate points.

Time Charter. A contract between the ship owner and the charterer for use of the ship for a specific period of time.

Timekeeper. Clerk at a marine terminal who keeps detailed records of the cm ployment of every laborer hired on an hourly basis.

Topping Off. Refers to the final steps in finishing the loading operations of a tanker.

Traffic Department. A department in a steamship company responsible for dealing with customers using the ship for export or import cargoes.

Tramp Shipping. A shipping service in which carriers contract to haul cargo in shipload lots between ports designated by the charterer.

Transit Shed. A large covered space on a marine terminal used temporarily to store cargo to be loaded on a ship or delivered to the consignee.

Unit Trains. A train consisting of identical cars and a single type of cargo. For example, a coal unit train will have only cars carrying coal, and an intermodal unit train will have only cars carrying containers. Normally, unit trains consist of specialty cars.

Upland Area. An outdoor storage area on a traditional break-bulk marine terminal.

Voyage Charter. A contract of affreightment covering the movement of a shipload of a particular cargo from one designated area to another, at a stipulated rate per ton of cargo loaded.

Warranties. Stipulations made by the owner of the vessel as to the details of a ship's characteristics and performance.

Wharf. A marine terminal whose face lies parallel to the shoreline.

Wharfage Report. An inventory of all cargo on which demurrage is payable because it has been left on the pier beyond the allowed free time.

WNA. Winter North Atlantic. A load line assigned by a classification society to ships not over 100 meters long which trade in the North Atlantic Ocean.

Index

Page numbers in italics indicate photographs.

A

Agents, steamship, 10, 311; cruise ship, 356-57
Alaska Steamship Co., 181
Alexander Committee, 273, 278-79
Allowance list, 150-51
American President Lines, 218
Aquamarine, 341
Arbitraries, 253
Arctic, *31*
Atlantic Container Line, 196-97
Atlantic Lady, 327-28
Augusta Victoria, 332

B

Bahama Star, 339
Ballast bonus, 44, 51-52
Baltic and International Maritime Council (BIMCO), 45, 425 (note); standard charter parties, 46-47
Baltic Exchange, 27; brokers as members, 27
Baltic Freight Index, 63-65
Bareboat charter, defined, 30; warranties, 31-32; charterer's responsibilities under, 37
Belcher Port Everglades-Belcher Barge #102, 379
Benjamin Harrison, 329
Bergeland, 55
Berge Sigval, 381; described, 382; power plant, 386
Berge Stahl, 19
Bilderdyk, 319

Bill of lading, 178, 200, 226-40; for containers, 201; intermodal contract, 201, 204; "good order and condition," 201, 228; history, 227-28; deviation, 231; limitation of liability, 230-32; as contract of carriage, 232-34; as receipt, 234-35; as evidence of ownership, 235-36; negotiable (order) bill, 236-38; stolen (notice of), 237; straight bill, 238; in foreign trade, 238-40
Bill of lading clerk, 79-80
Board of directors, 70
Booking clerk, 78-79; contacts with terminal, 78, 86, 127; and containers, 79; on stevedore contractor terminal, 108
Break-bulk (general cargo) terminal, 102-3
Bridgestone Maru, 388
Brokers, ship, 27-28, 58; membership in Baltic Exchange, 27; specialized, 45; responsibilities, 46; relations with owners, 58-63; commissions, 61, 63
Brush, Graham M., 179
Bulk carrier, *20,* 55; specialized, 19-21, economies of scale, 19, 21; cost comparisons, 22-24; impact on general purpose tramps, 53-54
Bulk Eagle, 22
Bulk product terminal, 103-4
"Bunching," 299
Bunkering, 301-14; bunkering plan, 301-7, 310-11; economics of, 302, 309, 313, 314; evaluation of tentative

plan, 302-3; selection of bunkering ports, 310-11; principles of, 304-7, 308-9; load line zones and requirements, 304-6; reserve supply of fuel, 306, 309; diversion for fuel, 306-7; quality of oil, 307-8; factors influencing plan, 310-11; in liner service, 310, 312; agents, 311; contacts for, 311-12; schedule, 312; tanker, 312; tramp, 313-14

C

Cape Hatteras, 190; 326-27

Cargo checker, *125, 126;* duties of, 86-88, in container terminals, 88; inspection of cargo by, 124; working conditions, 125; "taking exceptions," 126; responsibilities of, 125-27

Cargo liner, *5, 9*

Cargo pallets, 116, 122-23; size of, 123; strapping packages to, 187

Cargo segregations, 127-28

Caronia, 333

Carriage of Goods by Sea Act (COGSA), 228; 230-32; "hook to hook" coverage, 230; applies to common carriers, 230; defines deviation, 231; limits liability of carrier, 231-32; obligations imposed on shipper, 234-35

Car-truck carrier, *372;* described, 372

Castillo de Javier, 364

Centralized one-man control station, *384*

"Charge what the traffic will bear," 247-48

Charta partita, 29

Charter parties, 29-37; voyage, 33-34; time, 34; sample charter, 34-37; bareboat, 37; considerations affecting, 40-43

Chemical-carrying tankers, *362, 363;* history, 391; high risk chemical cargoes, 391-93; ships, 392-93, 395-96; restrictions on certain chemicals, 393; "parcel tankers," 393-94; Marine Pollution Convention (MARPOL), 394, Stolt-Nielsen, 394-95

Chevron Oregon, 382

Chiquita Deutschland, 366

"Closed conferences," 279-82; rationalizing tonnage, 280

Combination tankers, 378; ore/oil and ore/bulk/oil fleet, 378-79

Comet, 371

Commissary superintendent, 85; checking supplies, 85

Common carriers, 4, 228-29; defined, 228; status of, 228-29; liability of, 230-32; under Harter Act, 230-31; under COGSA, 231-32

Computers, in tramp management, 42, 55, 67-68; and stevedore rates, 145; inventories of spare parts, 153-54; in containership terminals, 191

Concessionaires, 350-51

Conferences, 269-88; rationale of, 269-70, 288; Calcutta Conference, 269-71; deferred rebate, 271, 273; exclusive patronage (loyalty) contract, 271-72, 276-78, 280; Royal Commission on Shipping Rings, 271-72; Alexander Committee, 273; Shipping Act of 1916, 274, 276, 278; Shipping Act of 1984, 283; exempted from antitrust law, 274-75; "fighting ship," 273-74; dual rates, 276-77; "open" and "closed" conferences, 279-82; shippers' councils, 280-81; restrictions on monopoly power, 282-83, 288; self-policing neutral bodies, 284-85; freight rate "wars," 285-87; rate reviews, 287

Consortium, 196-97, 288

Construction differential subsidy, 405-11; application for, 406-7; national defense features, 407; computation of subsidy, 408; guaranteed mortgages, 408-9; restrictions on domestic trade, 409; replacement of ships, 410

Container freight station, 79; container yard, 88

Containerization, 171-225; terminal operation, 144; origin of, 171-75, 180-82; economics of, 186-88; international trade, 186; McLean's role in, 192; transatlantic service, 193; consortium, 196-97; space chartering, 197-98, 281; container sizes, 204-5; neutral container pools, 206-8, 220-21, 224; benefits of, 222-25; lessons from 224-25

Container revolution, 172; and stevedore contract rates, 144-45; cost of, 189, 193-94; consortium, 196-97

Containers, 171, 173-75; early use of, 180-82; ownership of, 186; economy of handling, 187-88; computers and, 191; in break-bulk ships, 193; sizes, 204-5, 208, 219-20; 20-foot equivalent unit (TEU), 205; interchange of, 205-6; neutral pools, 206-8, 220-21, 224; "package" defined, 215; leasing *vs* owning, 219-22; varieties of, 222; losses of, 222-23; freight rates for, 246

Containerships, *174, 175, 190;* cost of, 194, gantry cranes on, 183, 185, 189; sea speed of, 184, 188-90, 196; variable costs, 198

Container terminals, *119, 189, 195, 207, 223;* terminal configuration, 106; description, 104-5; stevedore contract for, 144-45; container handling cranes, 185; costs of stuffing and stripping containers, 187

Costa Allegra, 335

Costs, 66-68; of tramp ships, 23-24, 241-43; of containerships, 194; variable, 198; in ship time, 216; and freight rates, 254; cruise ship, 334-36

Crane truck, *97,* described, 115-16

Cruise Lines International Association, 348

Cruises, 332-57; history, 332-34; starting ports of, 332, 334, 336, 340; building ships for, 334; overhead expenses, 336; duration of, 337-38, 340, 347; itinerary, 338, 340, 344, 352; frustrated voyages, 339; shore excursions, 340-41; deluxe cruises, 342-44; sail-powered ships, 345-46; promotion of, 343, 345, 347; cost of ships, 346; fares, 349; shops and bars, 350; concessionaires, 350-51; gambling casinos, 351-52; hotel manager, 351; scheduling principles, 352-53; speed, 353; stores and supplies, 353-54; refueling, 355-56; *France*'s world cruise (1972), 354-55; crew, 356-57; cruise director, 357

"Cycling," 118

D

Daily cargo report, 131

Dead freight, 34

Deferred rebate, 271-73

Delivery clerk, 88; transit shed layout and inventories, 88; responsibilities of, 124

Deluxe cruises, 342-44

Demurrage, in voyage charters, 28, 33; charges against liner cargoes, 88, 130

Depreciation of tramp ships, 26

Dispatch, defined, 28

Ditlev Lauritzen, 369; described, 368-69; employment in tramp trade, 368-69

Double-hull tanker, *382;* described, 382; *Olympic Serenity,* 382; *Chevron Oregon,* 382; *Eleo Maersk,* 382

Dual rate system, 276, 277; declared illegal, 277

E

Ekaputra, 391

Eleo Maersk, 382

Endeavor, 20

Energy Independence, 327

Eric R. Fernstrom, 303

Esso Zurich, 376

Exclusive patronage ("loyalty") contract, 271, 272, 276

Executive vice president, 71

Extra labor, 140-41

F

Fair Isle, 185

Fairland, 193

Feeder service, 215-19; and vessel cost, 216; load centers, 217-18; purpose-built ships, 217-18; in Orient, 218; chartered ships, 218-19

"Fighting ship," 273-74

First order effects, 330

Fixtures, described, 28; published ("open market") quotations, 32-46; unpublicized, 46

Forklift truck, *99, 126;* described 114-15; 180

"Fortune" class cargo ship, *18*

France, converted into cruise ship, renamed *Norway,* 341; world cruise (1972), 354-55

Freight rates, 5-7, 241-61; tramp, 12, 14, 25-26, 42-44, 64; lump sum charter hire, 49; value of commodity, 66; theory, 241-50; line rate-making, 243, factors influencing, 244; competition, 245-46; port equalization rates, 245; "load centers," 247; "charge what the traffic will bear," 247-48; loss-absorbing rates, 247-48, 249, 283; price *vs* quality of service, 249; factors in making, 250-54; space occupied, 251-53; heavy lift, 252-53; insurance, 253; class and commodity rates, 255-56; through rates, 256; freight all kinds, 259; container rates, 259-60; project rates, 260-61; "open" rates, 276; required freight rate, 318

Freight rate "wars," 285-87; Robin Line, 285; Pacific route instability, 285-86; Grace Line/Viking Line, 286-87

Freight traffic manager, 76-77

Fuel oil, 306-11; prices, 306; reserve fuel supply requirements, 306; quality of, 307-8; quality assurance laboratories, 307-8; procurement of, 310-11; contractors with suppliers, 311; spot purchases of, 311

Fuel quality analysis, 307-8; laboratories, 307; International Bunker Industry Association, 307-8

Fushimi Maru, 9

G

Gantry cranes, shipboard, *22, 68, 174;* on containerships, 183-84, 185

Garage ships, 172-73

Garden Green, 54

Gateway City, 174, 175; compared to break-bulk ship, 184-85; operations of, 184, 188, 191; self-sustaining, 189

Geest St. Lucia, 368; described, 367; Geest Line, 366-67

General freight agent, 77-78

Glenmoor, 15

Glückauf, 374

"Good order and condition," 201, 228, 232, 233; exceptions to, 234

Grace Line, 286-87

Grain as cargo, 12, 25-26, 39; types of, 49; oil seeds, 49; in tankers, 39, 54-55; charters for, 49-50, 50-51; loading bulk grain, *56*

Great Viking, chartering of, 59-63

Gross form voyage charter, 33

H

Handimax ship, 13

Hansa Bremen, 366

Harbormaster, 90

Harter Act, 228, 230, 231, 232

"Hatch cover-less ships," 326-28

Heavy lift ships, *370;* described, 369-71

Hellenic Innovator, 324

Highlander, employment of, 27-28

Hotel manager on cruise ships, 351

I

Ice clause, 30-31

Ideal X, 174; first voyage, 171, 177, 182; containers aboard, 219

Inbound freight division, 80

Industrial carrier, 358-61; defined, 359;

purposes, 359; ownership, 359-61;
as special carriers, 373
"Insurance items," 155-56
Integrated tug-barge, *379*
Intermodalism, 199-209; definition, 199;
terminal, 107; inspection of contain-
ers, 201; claim for cargo loss, 202-
3; future of, 208-9
International Bunker Industry Association,
307-8
International Load Line Convention, 304
International Standards Organization, 205,
220
Isbrandtsen Company, 277

J
Jahre Viking, (ex *Seawise Giant*), *387;*
described, 386, 435 (note)
Jervis Bay, 325

L
Lake Charles, 389
Landbridge, 209-15; "silk express,"
210-11, 429 (note); trans-Siberia
link, 212; controversy over, 212-15
Lay days, 32, 33
Lindblad Explorer, 340
Liner service company, 70-91; organization charts, 72, 75, 81, 87; traffic
department, 74-80; operating department, 80-91; compared with tramp
service, 3-10; tramp operation by,
14-15; competition for tramp cargoes, 25-26, 39; costs of, 243;
freight rates, 243; customers, 278
Liner train, 211-12
Liquefied gas carriers, 388-91; methods of
transporting gas, 388; size of ships,
388; liquefied petroleum gas carriers, 388-89; liquefied natural gas
carriers, 389-90; trade routes of,
390; requirements for construction
of, 390; "boil off rate," 391
List of cargo received, 130
Load centers, 217-18
Load lines, 304-6; seasonal zones, 305

Longshoremen, 111-14; gangs, 111, 113,
114; working hours, 111; dock
labor, 111; overtime, 112; unions,
111, 112; efficiency, 132
Loyalty (exclusive patronage) contract,
271, 272, 276, 283
Lump sum charter hire, 49

M
Marine Pollution Convention (MARPOL),
394
Marine superintendent, 82-83; port captain, 83; safety, 83; at drydockings,
84
Mario G. L., 13
Maritime Administration spare parts requirements, 148-49; analysis of
parts procurement practices, 149-
50; restrictions on foreign purchases by subsidized operators,
158, 168
Materials handling, principles of, 98-101;
"cycling," 118; pallets, 122-23;
photos, *97, 99, 100*
McLean, Malcom P., 171-75, 182-83;
devises integrated transportation
system, 172, 176; purchases Pan-
Atlantic Steamship Co., 173; converts tankers, 173-75; purchases
Waterman Steamship Co., 183;
converts dry-cargo ships, 183-84;
ownership of containers, 186; role
in container revolution, 192; size of
containers, 204-5
Megara, 388
Melvin H. Baker, 360
Merchant Marine Act, 1936, 402-5; national policy, 402; required records
of national shipping needs, 403-4;
collaborating with shipowners, 404-
5; construction differential subsidy,
405-11; operating differential subsidy, 411-16; obligations of subsidized operators, 415-16
Methane Pioneer, 388
Moordrecht, employment of, 50-51

N

Naess, Erling, 378
Name-plate data, 150, 152, 164; inventories to obtain, 152, 164
Nedlloyd Asia, 326
Negotiation of charter, 59-63
Neo-bulk terminal, 104
Net form voyage charter, 33
Neutral container pool, 205-8; 220-22, 224
North Emperor, employment of, 51-52
Norway, 342; converted to cruise ship, 341; capacity, 336; shops aboard, 350

O

Olympia, 339
Olympic Serenity, 382
"Open conferences," 279, 282, 283
Operating department, 80-91; chart, 81; vice president, 80-82; operating manager, 82; marine superintendent, 82-83; superintendent engineer, 82-84; commissary division, 85; terminal division, 86-91; chart, 87
Operating differential subsidy, 411-16; application for, 411-12; terms of contract, 412-13; computation of subsidy, 413-14; capital construction fund, 415; obligations imposed on ship operator, 415-16
Operations vice president, 80-82; operating manager, 82
Ore/bulk/oil carrier, 378-79; Erling Naess, 378; *San Juan Pioneer,* 378
Oriental Empress, 339
Otello, 372
Outbound freight division, 78-80; booking clerk, 78; permit clerk, 79; bill of lading clerk, 79-80
Over, short, and damaged cargo report, 90, 131-32
Overtime, 112

P

"Package" defined, 215
Passenger terminal, 105-6

"Pedigree" card, 169
Perishable supplies, 160-62, 165-66; contracts for, 165; passenger ships, 166
Permit clerk, 79
Pier, *101, 119;* described, 120; compared with wharf, 120; double-deck, 121-22
Pile tag, 129
Port marks, 129
Power plant selection, 325-26
President, 70-71
Primary ports, 291
Private carrier, 4, 229-30
Purchasing agent, 81 (chart); 146, 164

Q

Quaker City, 332
Queen Elizabeth 2, 348; power plant, 326; world cruise, 1992, 337; promotion of cruise, 347; in transatlantic shuttle service, 349

R

Receiving clerk, 86; transit shed layout, 86; cargo checkers, 86; functions of, 128-29
Refrigerated ships, *366, 367, 368, 369;* defined, 358-59; described, 365-69
Regina Oldendorff, employment of, 49-50
Reserve fuel supply, 306, 309
Robin Line, 285
Rotterdam, 333
Royal Commission on Shipping Rings, 271-72
Royal Majesty, 337

S

Safety, 94, 96, 98-99; of cargo, 124, 132-34; working conditions, 123-24; reserve fuel supply, 306; tankers, 383; inert gas systems, 383
Sagafjord, 338
San Juan Pioneer, 378
Scandic Wasa, employment of, 44
Scheduling, 289-300; in liner service, 289-92; transit time, 290-91; considera-

tions affecting, 291-93; primary and secondary ports, 291-92; ship speed, 292, 302; containership, 294-95; break-bulk liner service, 295, 298; terminal operation, 296, 298; assumptions in, 297; "bunching" and "slip," 299; tramp ship, 299, 313; tanker, 300, 313; tentative schedule, 302-3; cruise ships, 352-53

Scotspark, employment of, 47-49

"S. D. 14," *19,* described, 18

Seabourn Spirit, 344, 345; described, 343-44

Seafaring personnel, accommodation for, *25;* in tramps, 24-25; cruise ship, 356-57; tanker crews, 385

Sea Goddess I, 342-43

Sea-Land Service, 193, 205, 325

Seatrain, 179, 428 (note); and landbridge, 211

Seawise Giant (renamed *Jahre Viking*), described, 386, 435 (note); *387*

Secondary ports, 291-92

Second order effects, 330

Security force, 92-95; bus service in terminal, 94; cleanliness and maintenance, 94; safety of cargo, 95, 132-34; minimum staff, 134

Self-policing neutral bodies, 284-85

Self-unloading ship, *360;* described, 364-65

Ship chandlers, 162-63

Ship design, 323-31; tramps, 8, 321-22, 328; S. D. 14, *19,* described, 18; shipboard gantry cranes, *22, 68, 174;* effect on stores procurement, 164-65; establishing ship's mission, 315-18; pro-forma cost estimate, 318, 328; preliminary design, 320; advances in vessel design, 320-21; liner service, 322; break-bulk, 323-24; containerships, 325, 326-27; costs of speed, 325; factors influencing, 328-30; computers used in, 328, 330-31

Shipping Act of 1916, 274, 276, 278

Shipping Act of 1984, 276, 280, 283

Ship repair yard, *377*

Ship speed, 17, 18, 23, 292, 302, 321, 325; tankers, 374-75; 381, 391, 396; cruise ships, 352-53

Shore excursions, 340-41

"Silk express," 210-11, 429 (note)

"Slip," 299

Space chartering, 197-98, 281, 288

Specialized carriers, 361-73; defined, 361-62; liquefied gas carriers, 362; newsprint carrier, 363-64; bulk cement carrier, 364; refrigerated ships, 365-69; heavy lift ships, 369-71; car-truck carrier, 371-73

Standards book, 153, 167-68

Star Clipper, 346

Stella Maris, 341

Stevedore, 88-89

Stevedore contract, 135-45; commodity rates, 135; information needed for, 136; contract clauses, 137-40; overtime compensation, 141; rate calculations, 142-43; rates for containers, 144-45; computers, 145

Stevedore contractor terminal, 107-9

Stolt-Helluland, 394-95

Stolt Markland, 395

Stores and supplies, 146-70; policy on spare parts, 147-48; purchasing agent, 81, 146; requisitions, 146, 159-60, 167; spare parts, 146, 148-50; inventories, 147, 152-53, 167; name-plate data, 150, 164; allowance list, 150-51; standards book, 153, 167-68; spare parts control system, 153-54, 164; "insurance items," 155-56; genuine parts, 156-57; zero-based policy, 157; principles of purchasing, 158-59; jobbers, 162; reciprocal buying, 162; ship chandlers, 162-63; tramp ships, 163; effect of ship structure on, 164-65; house-marked items, 165; perishable supplies, 160-61, 165-66;

delivery schedules, 166-67; warehouse, 168-70; purchases by U.S. subsidized operators, 168

Subsidy, 397-416; tramp ship, 57-58; theory and forms of, 397-400; U.S. history of, 400-2; "Fifty-Fifty law," 401; Merchant Marine Act, 1936, 401-16; construction differential subsidy, 405-11; application for, 406; computing construction subsidy, 408; operating differential subsidy, 411-16; application for, 411-12; computing operating subsidy, 413-14; obligations assumed under subsidy, 415-16

Superintendent engineer, 83-84; repairs and drydocking, 84; supervision of fueling, 84-85

T

T-2 tanker, *376;* described, 375

Tankers, *376, 381, 387;* 374-96; history of, 374-75, ownership of, 375-76, 379; management of, 377-80, 384; chartered, 379-80; clean and black trades, 380; double hull, 82; safety, 383; inert gas systems, 383; crude oil washing, 383; management contractors, 385; crew rotation, 385; offshore mooring (LOOP), 386; economy of large, 386; restrictions on large, 386; liquefied gas carriers, 388-91; chemical, 391-96; bunkering of, 312; schedule making for, 313

Terminal division, 87 (chart); organization, 86-91; manager, 86; receiving clerk, 86-88; cargo checkers, 86, 88; delivery clerk, 88; chief stevedore, 88-89; timekeeper, 89-90; harbormaster, 90; security and safety, 90-91

Terminal management, 92-109; cost reduction, 96-97; materials handling principles, 98-101; types of terminals, 102-9; responsibility for safety, 94, 96, 98-99; use of overtime, 112

Terminal operations, 110-34; principles of operation, 110; relations with longshoremen's unions, 111-14; overtime, 112; longshoremen gangs, 113; truck traffic control, 117; wharf *vs* pier, 117; "cycling," 118; double-deck pier, 120-21; pallets, 122-23; safety, 123-24; checkers, 125-27; cargo segregations, 128; transit shed layout, 128; records and reports, 130-32

Time charter, 29-30; restrictions on cargo, 30; ice clause, 30-31; charterer to provide under, 34; sample, 34-37; warranties, 32

Timekeeper, 89, 95-96

Tractor-trailer trains, 116

Traffic department, 74-80; chart, 75; vice president, 74-76; freight traffic manager, 76-77; general freight agent, 77-78; outbound division, 78-80; inbound division, 80

Traffic study, 262-68; examples of, 262-64; purposes of, 262; procedure for, 266-68

Traffic vice president, 74-76

Tramp shipping, *13, 15, 18, 19, 20, 22;* 3-69; defined, 3; compared with liner service, 3-10; purpose of, 11, 12, 21; cargoes, 5, 12; freight (charter) rates, 5-7, 13, 25-26, 28; ownership, 14-15, 53; ships, 8, 13, 17-18; history, 16-19; specialization, 19-21, 53-54; costs, 23-24; crew quarters, *25,* described, 24; Baltic Exchange, 27; ice clause, 30-31; fixtures analyzed, 28, 32; types of charter parties, 29-30; computer in management, 42; owners-brokers relationship, 58-63; setting freight rates, 66-67; subsidy, 57-58

Tramp ships, 8; purpose, 11-12, 21; coaling stations and, 16; size of, 17-19;

specialized, 19-20, 322; costs, 23-24, 66-68; accommodations, 24-25; preferred sizes in 1993, 68-69; refrigerated cargo carriers, 368-69.

Trans Dania, 363

Transit shed, *121;* vehicular traffic in, 96; layout, 118-20, 127; single and double-deck, 120-22; cargo segregations, 127-28; demurrage, 130

Tributary cargo, 213-15

Twenty-foot equivalent unit (TEU), 205

V

Variable costs, 198

Viking Line, 286-87

Voyage charter, defined, 29; net and gross forms, 33; responsibilities under, 33-34; comparison with time charter, 42-43; ship under owner's control, 43-44; gross form cost calculation, 66-67

W

Wakagiku Maru, 370

Wallenius Lines, 371-73; car-truck carrier fleet, 371; ships described, 371-72

Warehouse, 168-70; advantages of, 169; disadvantages of, 169-70

Warranties, 32

Wharf, *9, 93;* described, 120; compared with pier, 120; wide apron, 133

Wharfage report, 131

Wind Spirit, 346

"Working the market," 37-38, 43

World Discoverer, 340

Z

Zero-based spare parts policy, 157

About the Authors

Lane C. Kendall was born in New Orleans, Louisiana. He holds bachelor's and master's degrees from Tulane University and pursued graduate studies at the University of California (Berkeley) and Princeton University. His long and distinguished career in the shipping business began with the Grace Line. As a combat cargo officer in the U.S. Marine Corps, he was responsible for all shipping activities of the Second Marine Division. From 1946 to 1960, he taught at the U.S. Merchant Marine Academy, and in 1950 was appointed head of the department of ship management. In 1960, he accepted the position of commercial shipping advisor to the commander of the Navy's Military Sealift Command. Mr. Kendall has received, among other awards, the Navy's Superior Civilian Service Award and the Naval Institute's Award of Merit. He retired in 1969 and has made his home in California.

James J. Buckley graduated from the California Maritime Academy in 1971 with a bachelor of science degree in nautical science. He began his sailing career as an able seaman aboard a U.S. flag merchant vessel, receiving his master's license in 1976, and has sailed as master for eight years on tramp and liner vessels. Captain Buckley earned first class pilotage for San Francisco Bay, and a master of business administration degree. He has worked ashore for a terminal operations and stevedore company. He joined the California Maritime Academy in 1985, where he is a professor, chairman of the department of Maritime Management, and training captain. He has researched and written about port and terminal management and intermodal transportation. Captain Buckley resides in Vallejo, California, with his wife and two children.

ISBN 0-87033-454-9

54500

9 780870 334542